NEO-TRANSITIONAL ECONOMICS

INTERNATIONAL FINANCE REVIEW

Series Editor: J. Jay Choi

International Finance Review publishes theme-oriented volumes on various issues in international finance, such as international business finance, international investment and capital markets, global risk management, international corporate governance and institution, currency markets, emerging market finance, international economic integration, and related issues in international financial economics.

Volume 9: Institutional Approach to Global Corporate Governance: Business Systems and Beyond, Edited by J. Jay Choi and Sandra Dow, 2008, Emerald Publishing (ISBN: 978-1-84855-320-0)

Volume 10: Credit, Currency, or Derivatives: Instruments of Global Financial Stability or Crisis?, Edited by J. Jay Choi and Michael G. Papaioannou, 2009, Emerald Publishing (ISBN: 978-1-84950-601-4)

Volume 11: International Banking in the New Era: Post-Crisis Challenges and Opportunities, Edited by Suk-Joong Kim and Michael D. McKenzie, 2010, Emerald Publishing (ISBN: 978-1-84950-912-1)

Volume 12: Institutional Investors in Global Capital Markets, Edited by Narjess Boubakri and Jean-Claude Cosset, 2011, Emerald Publishing (ISBN: 978-1-78052-242-5)

Volume 13: Transparency and Governance in a Global World, Edited by J. Jay Choi and Heibatollah Sami, 2012, Emerald Publishing (ISBN: 978-1-78052-764-2)

Volume 14: Global Banking, Financial Markets and Crises, Edited by Bang Nam Jeon and María Pía Olivero, 2013, Emerald Publishing (ISBN: 978-1-78350-170-0)

Volume 15: Emerging Market Firms in the Global Economy, Edited by Chinmay Pattnaik and Vikas Kumar, 2014, Emerald Publishing (ISBN: 978-1-78441-066-7)

INTERNATIONAL FINANCE REVIEW VOLUME 16

NEO-TRANSITIONAL ECONOMICS

EDITED BY

RUSTAM JAMILOV
State Oil Fund of Azerbaijan, Baku, Azerbaijan

YUSAF H. AKBAR
Central European University, Budapest, Hungary

Emerald

United Kingdom – North America – Japan
India – Malaysia – China

Emerald Group Publishing Limited
Howard House, Wagon Lane, Bingley BD16 1WA, UK

First edition 2015

British Library Cataloguing in Publication Data
A catalogue record for this book is available from the British Library

ISBN: 978-1-78441-682-9
ISSN: 1569-3767 (Series)

ACKNOWLEDGMENT (DEDICATION)

To Jamilya: Thank you for all your patience, commitment, and love
– Rustam Jamilov

Disclaimer:

This book was started when Rustam Jamilov was a graduate student at the LSE and completed when he subsequently joined the State Oil Fund of Azerbaijan (SOFAZ). Opinions, either by Rustam Jamilov or another contributing author, which are expressed in this book, do not reflect the views of the State Oil Fund of Azerbaijan or the LSE's Department of Economics. No theoretical or empirical result nor any policy recommendation or advice that are expressed in this book should be viewed as an investment philosophy or policy followed, endorsed, or in any other way acknowledged by SOFAZ.

CONTENTS

PART V: INTERNATIONAL TRADE AND ECONOMIC INTEGRATION

LIST OF CONTRIBUTORS

Yusaf H. Akbar	Central European University, Budapest, Hungary
Alexandr Akimov	Griffith Business School, Griffith University, Southport, Queensland, Australia
Matei Alexianu	London School of Economics, London, UK
Pavol Babos	Slovak Academy of Sciences, Bratislava, Slovak Republic
Rustam Jamilov	State Oil Fund of Azerbaijan, Baku, Azerbaijan
Jakhongir Kakhkharov	Griffith Business School, Griffith University, Southport, Queensland, Australia
Martina Lubyova	Slovak Academy of Sciences, Bratislava, Slovak Republic
Paul Marer	Business School, Central European University, Budapest, Hungary
Rajmund Mirdala	Faculty of Economics, Technical University of Košice, Slovakia
Matthias Nnadi	School of Management, Cranfield University, Bedfordshire, UK
Kamil Omoteso	Coventry Business School, Coventry University, Coventry, UK
Dragiša Otašević	Deutsche Bundesbank, Frankfurt am Main, Germany

Zoltán Pogátsa	University of West Hungary, Sopron, Hungary
György Simon, Jr.	Corvinus University of Budapest, Budapest, Hungary
İbrahim Ünalmış	Central Bank of the Republic of Turkey, Ankara, Turkey
Xuan Vinh Vo	School of Banking, University of Economics, Ho Chi Minh City, Vietnam; CFVG, Ho Chi Minh City, Vietnam
Yi Yu	School of Management, Cranfield University, Bedfordshire, UK

PART I
GENERAL TRANSITION

INTRODUCTION TO NEO-TRANSITIONAL ECONOMICS

Rustam Jamilov and Yusaf H. Akbar

ABSTRACT

This paper introduces the readers to Neo-Transitional Economics – a volume which aspires to reinvigorate scholarly interest in transition economics research. The classical transition storyline is briefly revisited, and new directions for empirical and policy-relevant research that target post-transition economies in the post-crisis paradigm are highlighted.

Keywords: Transition economics; comparative economics; economic systems; new transitional economics; economic development; Global Financial Crisis

JEL classifications: O11; O50; P00; P20; P30; P50

"There is no road map for transition"

(G. Roland)

Neo-Transitional Economics
International Finance Review, Volume 16, 3–19

ISSN: 1569-3767/doi:10.1108/S1569-376720150000016003

THE IMPORTANCE OF TRANSITION STUDIES AND OF THE REGION

By many, the emergence and eventual collapse of the Soviet Union is regarded as one of the most remarkable events in economic history. The term "Transition Economics" emerged in the early 1990s as academics and practitioners around the world confronted an unprecedented natural experiment. New theories and policy manuals were constructed from the ground up, and existing approaches were augmented to reflect the new insights revealed by this very peculiar area of economic governance. The area of transition studies now counts thousands of academics scattered around not only the formerly planned economies but the established universities and think tanks of the Western hemisphere. The topic has amassed many hundreds of major scholarly contributions including books and journal articles, catalyzed the organization of numerous conferences and global symposiums, and revolutionized the way economic professionals perform policy-relevant analysis. In 2013, the Commonwealth of Independent States and the Central and Eastern European countries were responsible for far more than $4 trillion in aggregate output. But above all, perhaps, is that this research stream affects the lives of more than half-a-billion people who reside in the states in transition. The macroeconomic and demographic importance of transition studies, both from a historical perspective, and for nowadays' policy making is not to be underestimated.

FROM TRANSITION ECONOMIES AND TRANSITION ECONOMICS TO NEO-TRANSITIONAL ECONOMICS

It is important to distinguish the more analytical, theoretical concept of transition economics from the regional study of transition economies. The former represents a branch of economic *science* that deals with the structural transformation from a state-planned economy to a market-based capitalistic establishment. The latter is a regional study of *countries* that are going through a period of transition. Transition economics is a normative subject dealing with how an economy should transit to a free market-oriented path based on economic theories and empirics and consensus beliefs of established economic thinkers. Transition economies study is a positive, dynamic narrative of how things are actually unfolding in the country of interest. Usually, of course, scholars are adopting a more trans-disciplinary prism when studying the matter. It is common to monitor the successes and failures of transition (post-communist) economies while lending the normative theories from academia and research. This book is a policy-oriented review of transition economies. This will naturally build upon the traditional and contemporary advances in the science of transitional economics, since policy recommendations and advice must draw from rigorous technical analysis. Our emphasis on the most recent (post-crisis) challenges that transition economies are facing is highlighted in the Volume title with the "Neo" prefix. This way we are attempting to portray a mixture of the two related but distinct disciplines and yet emphasize our interest in the most new/untouched questions.

TRANSITION VERSUS EMERGING ECONOMIES

Another important conceptual clarification should be the transition versus emerging economies distinction. First, for a generic classification of countries we are following the standard EBRD list of transition countries. By "transition" we are referring to those transforming from a communist regime. Obviously, nowadays, countries like Russia and Poland are clearly emerging states with vibrant domestic markets. However, our intention in naming them as "transition states" is not to downgrade their accomplishments or purposefully mis-label them but rather to create a simple reference point for analysis and comparison. An emerging economy (such as Russia) could simultaneously be a transition state since it has transited from a communist society. It does not imply that being a *transition economy* equates being a *state in transition*.

Second, the fundamental message of our book is reflected in its title. Neo-Transitional economics literally means a new approach to the study of transition economies. The conventional wisdom is that the classical transition period as we know it has ended back in 2000. What this book argues for is that even if the old transition problems (political stability, democratization, private sector reform, etc.) are largely the questions of the past, recent experiences with the global financial crisis have revealed a new set of challenges. In other words, our idea is that transition economies (states which originally transformed from Communism), although not in the state of classical transition, are not necessarily "emerging" yet. For example, Kazakhstan or Georgia are free market economies very unlike their communist predecessor. However, it's foolish to place them in the same category of economic development with, say, Brazil or even Russia (the BRICs members), not from the point of view of economic output and country size but in lieu of still inadequate institutional and market designs. Therefore, Georgia and Kazakhstan are transition economies which have completed their transition phase and are now rushing to enter the "emerging market" domain. What challenges lie ahead of them on this path? This is the research question of this volume.

Based on the rationales above, we envisioned that positioning the book as a policy study on transition rather than emerging markets would be more conceptually correct. It narrows the focus down to where it should belong: Central and Eastern European transition economies, the Caucasus, Russia, Central Asia, and select Emerging Asia.

TRANSITION ECONOMICS: THE CLASSICAL STORY

We will not go into great depth with regards to the basic story we all know by now. Due to the exhaustive arms race with the United States, the Soviet Union collapsed under the pressure of its own unrealistic ambition. The collapse has brought upon a considerable, although comparatively short-lived, economic crisis, partially exaggerated in lieu of bad statistics and misrepresentation of output data of the communist times. Transition to a capitalist free market system has begun under massive changes to all forms and levels of governance. But that transition was substantially heterogeneous across different countries. Different approaches were adopted with varying degrees of success, with the heterogeneity spanning across the scale and speed of reform, degree of market-orientation, willingness of political opposition, etc. The classical period of transition is said to have finished by the year 2000. Stabilization has largely succeeded in the new millennium and the originally "transition economies" should be better labeled as "post-transition economies" since they are now much closer to the full-blown emerging country status than the fragile transition states of the early 1990s.

We have learnt an abundance of important lessons during the period of extraordinary scholarly attention towards the classical transition economics stream. Those lessons have found their relevance far beyond the realms of policy rooms in transition states and have caused a considerable rethinking of conventional economic dogmas. We have tried to highlight the most crucial perspectives, which will also be important for our analysis of neo-transitional economics.

- Moderate market orientation. Although not without idiosyncratic heterogeneities, the dominant majority of all transition works have concluded that open-minded market orientation, moderate and cautious policy-making, and rapid and effective execution were the hallmark keys for success during the transition period.
- Nature of reforms meant everything.
  - Timing of reforms: quick versus incremental
  - Force of reforms: radical versus incremental
  - Scale of reforms: structural versus selected
  - Credibility of reforms: arbitrary versus anchored
  - Experience has shown that quick, radical, structural, and anchored credible reforms have been, on average, more influential and ultimately successful.
- Statistics matter. Early 1990s have made us witness a radical unexpected decline in output in practically all transition states. Ex post it has become evident that output statistics have been largely overestimated during the communist era and then forcefully undervalued during the early years of transition for the reason of tax evasion.
- High interest rates and inflation dilemma. Money supply providers have been under heavy pressure to provide liquidity in the early years of transition. As a result, the central banks had to choose between agreement (which caused asset bubbles and inflation) and disagreements, resulting in high interest rates and margins explosion. Central bank independence from political influence is therefore absolutely paramount.
- Direct control of money pricing is detrimental. It has been widely acknowledged that direct control of interest rates on deposit or loans is bad for market-oriented development and growth.
- Minimum required reserve is a universally effective policy tool. Multiple studies have concluded that monetary policy through the manipulation of minimum required bank reserves is the most instrument in transition states. This result is robust to such idiosyncrasies like regional and institutional diversity and initial endowment.
- Hayek was right. Friedrich Von Hayek predicted well in the early stages of the communist project that the concept of central planning is prone to imminent collapse due to the inability of any super-minded central planner (even if assuming that one can be designed) to collect, process, and act upon the enormous flow of information. Free markets are therefore much more preferred for this task.
- Initial conditions count. Much of the heterogeneity in success across different transition states can be attributed to the initial endowment

condition and the state of affairs *prior* to the early 1990s. That includes the basic institutional and legal foundations, resource the endowments, as well as the parameters of the growth design formula.

- Institutions matter but not universally. The role of institutions and their efficiency has been acknowledged in every work on transition economies, however, most recent in-depth looks have argued that the impact of institutions was only marginal with the presence of all-around structural reforms and pragmatic policy playing a bigger general role.
- Crises reveal structural problems. Following the tedious but at-the-end-of-the-day successful transition period of the 1990s, the Asian crisis and the dot com bubble crash of the 2000 had revealed one remaining common underlying problem with many transition states: public financing. In particular, excessive public debts, deficits, and tax system inadequacies had been marked as important remaining deficiencies of the region. In the following years, deficits have been trimmed, public books brought to order, and tax systems considerably enhanced. Now, with the aftermath of the 2008 global financial crisis it is becoming clear that lack of financial, monetary, and capital sophistication have become the new common threat to transition economies' long-term growth ambitions.
- Continuous international focus. The mass privatization natural experiment of the transition phase has shown that, on average, outsider privatization has outperformed other alternatives. In addition, for small open economies that transition states are, exportation and attraction of foreign direct investment becomes quintessential.
- Incentives are important. The dilemma for all countries transitioning from being centrally planned to fundamentally profit-oriented capitalistic societies is the correct design of the incentives mechanism, namely the cost and benefit analysis between private sector profits and political dividends with rent-seeking potential.
- Transition states are more homogeneous. The initial conditions, regional disparities, and institutional differences of the past have largely evaporated now with transition states becoming much more alike. The gap between Central and Eastern European transition bloc and the Former Soviet Union grouping is declining, with certain FSU economies (like Russia, Kazakhstan, and Azerbaijan) arguably in a comparable if not superior state than many European developing countries. Rising homogeneity of the transition cluster can facilitate a new wave of empirical panel research, for example.
- Using country-examples as models for development. Many post-transition states have developed a habit of selecting a model of economic

development and basically "copying" its features and practices. Examples of such models include United Arab Emirates, Singapore, China. While modeling is useful for the provision of some initial benchmarks of quality, local idiosyncrasies and country-specific effects are very important, and getting carried away with reaching a utopian economic model can be dangerous.

NEO-TRANSITIONAL ECONOMICS: NEW CHALLENGES IN A NEW PARADIGM

The new post-crisis paradigm has revealed that financial penetration, macro-prudential stability, monetary efficiency, and fiscal prudence are the cornerstones of a sustainable economic formula. It is only natural to expect these qualities to be substantially imperfect in transition countries. Of course, these important features are often defunct in the *advanced* economies of this world, let alone the transition region with little over 20 years in normal existence. However, the rules of the modern game absolutely mandate that post-transition economies target the new set of structural deficiencies with vigorous seriousness and informed care. The purpose of this book lies precisely in the collection of expert opinion on the types and natures of most contemporary challenges to post-transition states as well as the eventual proposal of comprehensive policy recommendations. What we give below is a general framework of subjects for potential contributions which takes the form of a collection of most crucial, from the point of view of the editors, topics in neo-transitional economics.

Note that such issues as intellectual property rights, pension reform, labor market policies, savings promotion, industrial diversification, monetary transmission empirics, interest rate endogeneity, bank sector competition, regional economic integration – have never been investigated in great depth within the framework of transition studies.

Governance and Social Order

- *Continuous democratization.* Empirical literature universally postulates that democracy and liberty are crucial for long-term growth. Social interaction, youth engagement, and dialogue formation are thus an important caveat of not only market strengthening but nation building as a whole.

- *Political stability, investor confidence, and competition management.* Financial planning in transition countries is subject to uncertainty and macroeconomic volatility, and a little bit of confidence boost derived from some political continuity is thus extremely desired. The transformational, charisma-driven leadership rhetoric of the past must be slowly replaced by pragmatic and analytical management of the modern times. In addition, policymakers must allow more unhindered free-flowing competition in all markets, including those deemed "strategically important." Adoption of state-of-the-art managerial techniques and standards is the prerequisite for successful transition and consecutive build-up of the competitive private sector.
- *Intellectual and private property rights security.* Productivity is the main factor of long-term growth. Productivity, in turn, relies on innovation and idea generation which demand a system of incentives and rewards, namely the property rights assignment system and remuneration of originality. Entrepreneurship and small business development, which greatly rely on business innovation, is still a major concern of the region.
- *Pension reform.* Despite the conventional wisdoms that transition countries are populated by young and vibrant populations, the region is slowly and surely getting older. With outdated public pension mechanism unable to shoulder the increasing financial load, a reform of the private pension system is thus a top region-wide priority. Financing aspects put aside, pension stability is a sensitive social topic that is paramount for domestic social stability.
- *The role of cultural persistence in doing business.* Although an often overlooked aspect of the transition experience, culture and habit-formation are important elements of emotional and intellectual maturity of the regional population. Such harmful mentalities of excess bureaucracy, rent-seeking and corruption, statistical exploitations, cautious towards originality of thought must remain in the communist past and leave the path for a new energetic mindset.

Macroeconomic Policy

- *Sustainable long-run growth path.* Transition economies were able to capitalize on factor-driven growth booms and relative institutional moderation and consistently deliver close to double-digit growth rates over the past decade. However, as the playing field levels down and initial conditions converge into a common regional arena, growth must be driven by comparative advantage and real factors which are sustainable (non-depletable) in the long run.

- *Respecting the budget constraint.* Plethora of research works has concluded that tight budget constraints on the sovereign, enterprise, and micro-market levels are necessary for financial and macro-prudential stability. The same logic applies to resource-exporting states for which the budget constraint is softened by the resource.
- *Maintain low levels of public debt.* Recent empirical literature has demonstrated that growth is significantly negatively correlated with public deficits, suggesting that public finance order plays an important role in macroeconomic stability and growth protection. The lessons from the 2000–2001 crisis support the premise of public debt being severely detrimental for regional growth prospects.
- *Public finance and monetary policy nexus.* Studies have shown that balancing the public books cannot solve all of the problems single-handedly. Likewise, persistently negative fiscal outlooks tighten the hands of the monetary policy-maker. As a result, the two disciplines must be governed with care and scrutiny simultaneously, ensuring the all-around positive institutional engagement.
- *Economic diversification as an important growth factor.* Most recent works have shown that among all the countries which have struggled through the recent global financial crisis, those with a higher degree of industrial diversification and lesser dependency on any particular source of growth generation, have suffered a milder slowdown and have recovered relatively quicker than those less diversified. Extensive research has shown that currency devaluations can act as a powerful tool for industrial diversification in, for example, research-rich states.
- *Labor market policies for a flexible social capital.* Multiple policy research works by reputable organizations have shown that substantial microeconomic and institutional frictions exist in the regional labor markets. Across-sectoral wage disparities, employment inequalities, education-occupation divergence, long-term unemployment, youth unemployment are important economic phenomena which have deeply demographic underlying values.
- *Policies on private saving.* A considerable pool of academics would agree that saving is vital for at least three reasons: buffer against negative external shocks, long-term growth, and investment-saving solvency constraint. How to stimulate the private sector to save more? This mandates capital markets development, financial literacy, improving trust in

the financial ecosystem, incentive mechanisms, amendments to laws and provisions. Multiple successful country examples (e.g., Singapore) exist.

- *Limit the role of remittances.* Empirical research has shown that cash remittances act as a determining factor of aggregate output in many CIS countries. However, remittances are a non-productive and highly volatile source of revenue which produce little or no tax revenue for the authorities. Proper incentive mechanisms must be put into action so as to motivate the population to engage with more stable source of wealth generation.

Monetary Policy

- *Old problems persist ….* Dollarization, monetization, currency substitution, structural excess liquidity are still the common problems in the monetary policy in transition narrative. Dollarization levels have declined but are still present with the US Dollar being complemented by the Euro and Russian Ruble. The same could be said of currency substitution as a considerable percentage of domestic financial operations is regularly completed in foreign rather than domestic currencies. This, in turn, makes it difficult to transit to a fully flexible market-driven exchange rate valuation system. Monetization and lack of non-cash payment systems is a continuous problem. Domestic financial and bank sectors are awash with cash which international organizations deem as excess. Excess liquidity negates monetary policy transmission effects.
- *Deeper financial penetration and broader market evolution.* Financial intermediation should step onto a new level of sophistication, from the simple deposit-credit banking essentials to complex futures trading and derivative strategizing. The main source of financing for the non-institutional private sector must therefore be diversified away from banks to non-bank sources. Some empirical, although unsystematic, attempts have shown that the velocity of money has declined considerably in transition countries after the 2008 Financial Crisis. New channels adopted from the developed Western hemisphere and the fast-rising South-East Asia would facilitate financial mobility. Reliance on the mainstream/formal sources of financing such as the central bank refinancing windows must be enhanced, and informal capital sourcing should be limited. This will redirect the financing traffic to the central banks and exogenize the endogenous policy interest rates.

- *Monetary policy transmission mechanism: still a very black box.* The mainstream interest rate channel of monetary transmission is often ineffective in transition countries. The exchange rate and the bank lending channels are the two most powerful tools in the hands of the central banks, in addition to mandatory reserves manipulations. New research and takes on the asset price channel and the risk pricing channel are in great demand. Bank sector competition improvement and elimination of structural excess liquidity are two of the most often cited methods to increase monetary transmission efficiency.
- *Behavioral aspects not to be underestimated.* With the advent of more sophisticated financing mechanisms, non-material components of the financial ecosystem play an important role. Just as always, success of any structural reform will be tied closely to the credibility of the authorizing institution. Monetary policy perspectives will be constantly anchored against past performances. More educated financial agents will develop more fluent and credible monetary expectations. Policymakers must acknowledge policy persistence and potential hysteresis effects of tax and monetary decisions.

Banking and Finance

- *Capital markets formation: priority number one.* Establishment and/or continuous development of proper capital markets is arguably the single most vital policy target for all transition countries. However, the degree of the initial condition is very heterogeneous across countries at the moment. For some we are talking about further sophistication towards, say, futures trading; others still need a decent secondary market for government bonds. Capital markets can contribute to the solution of half, if not more, of the existent macroeconomic and financial problems persisting in transition economies. Such questions like pension reform, de-monetization, risk dispersion, incentives for private savings, can be solved straightforwardly with a working capital market that doesn't restrict access for individual agents.
- *Macro-prudential analysis and control as safety net.* The continuous sophistication of the financial ecosystem requires institutional mechanisms that prevent excess risk taking, prevent formation of bubbles, and ensure long-run sustainability of the system. This requires, first and foremost, a strict but flexible legal foundation that can cope with the fast-paced financial environment. Second, banks in transition countries

must ensure that they adapt the new Basel III accords within the imposed time frame. Finally, formation of new safety facilities through the arms of the central monetary planner and foreign counterparts is essential for prevention of unexpected liquidity shortages, hysteresis effects, capital withdrawal, and bank flights.

- *Bank-sector competition and consolidation monitoring*. Bank sectors in most transition countries tended to evolve in a non-competitive and consolidated matter. Low bank sector competition has a negative effect on retail money pricing as banks are able to impose monopolistic pricing powers on unaware creditors and charge higher-than needed interest rates. Moreover, composition of the bank sector into few very powerful and many weak banks leaves the system very vulnerable to asymmetric shocks. In addition, crisis resistance becomes a challenging tasks for the non-top institutions which struggle to obtain financing. Exclusion of the smaller banks from elite sources of financing, even including the primary markets for government and related bond sales, often leads the smaller banks cash-strapped while leaving the larger banks awash with excess liquidity. The impact of bank sector consolidation and/or liquidity on monetary policy transmission is predominantly negative, although still inconclusive.
- *Financial literacy and financial education as a building block of the modern society*. Of course, we cannot talk about capital markets and any sort of advanced financial instruments when a big proportion of the population in a typical transition state cannot distinguish primary and secondary markets, bonds and stocks, consumer and producer price index etc. Starting from the very basics of financial knowledge, sufficient for investing in basic financial instruments like long-term bonds, private pension packages, stockholder institutions (Central banks, ministries of finance) must provide an accessible platform for financial literacy improvement via physical and electronic (web) interfaces.

International Exposure

- *New regional economic integration perspectives*. Despite the collapse of the region's superpower in Soviet Union, the region's ambitions for integration are ample as ever. Central and Eastern Europe are on course to fully join the European project; Russia with Kazakhstan and Belarus are contemplating a so-called Euro-Asian union; Turkey is voicing its aspirations for a Turk-zone. Stages of economic integration (trade agreements, customs union, free economic area, common currency zone) must be followed carefully according to theoretical predictions and experiences of the past.

- *Common currency area: theory and fiction.* The recent financial crisis has demonstrated how lack of supplementary institutions can destabilize a once powerful currency union. Under heavy negative financial shocks, with the absence of automatically stabilizing mechanisms such as unified fiscal treasury, monetary unification is a dangerous choice. Plenty of existent natural experiments act as living lessons of what to do and what not to do when designing a common currency area.
- *Exportation – the bread and butter of small open economies.* An innovation-driven formation of national comparative advantages is key for long-term sustainable growth foundation for post-transition countries. Be it agricultural goods, tourism, energy resources, or heavy industry – the ability to design, mass-product, and sell nationally branded goods and services on international markets is a sign of a healthy current account and established commercial supply chains. Countries of the region must realize that apart from the obvious need to integrate and cooperate, competition between so-far predominantly homogeneous states will require development of differentiated and unique products based on the nexus of national/local flavor and international technical standards of safety and quality.
- *Membership in international organizations: pros and cons.* With about 100 countries still not in the member-list of the World Trade Organization (WTO), participation and membership at the established supra-national institutions is still an open question. This relates to a great extent to the classical argument on the pros and cons of globalization. Post-transition countries must realize that global integration is inevitable in the long-run. However, this transition must be smooth and local exporters must be competitive enough so that to withstand the pressure from experienced foreign sellers. The ability to compete both on price and quality is paramount.

SUMMARY

Transition countries are coming of age and are approaching the status of fully-blown developing states. While the main problems highlighted in a classical transition storyline, such as large-scale privatization, institutional formation, private sector establishment, socio-political stabilization, have largely been solved, the recent financial crisis has revealed fresh challenges which demand maximum differentiated attention. Such important contemporary issues as capital markets formation, monetary transmission mechanism, growth sustainability, financial sector sophistication, structural excess liquidity, social welfare reform, and labor market frictions remain to be tackled in a systematic, policy-oriented manner. This volume will attempt to fill the escalating literature gap by offering a comprehensive collection of viewpoints from the established scholars and practitioners of the field. The ultimate goal of this book is to provide a policy toolkit for a successful overcoming of all contemporary challenges that lie ahead in the age of neo-transitional economics. There may had been no road map for transition, but there is certainly a map for neo-transition. And this book is attempting to lay it out.

BIBLIOGRAPHY

Aghion, P., & Blanchard, O. (1998). On privatization methods in Eastern Europe and their implications. *Economics of Transition*, *6*(1), 87–99.

Aghion, P., Blanchard, O., & Burgess, R. (1994). The behaviour of state firms in Eastern Europe pre-privatization. *European Economic Review*, *38*, 1327–1349.

Aslund, A. (1994). Lessons of the first four years of systemic change in Eastern Europe. *Journal of Comparative Economics*, *19*, 22–38.

Aslund, A., Boone, P., & Johnson, S. (1996). How to stabilize: Lessons from post-communist countries. *Brookings Papers on Economic Activity*, *1*, 217–313.

Aslund, A., & Jenish, N. (2007). The Euroasian Growth Paradox. In F. Bourguignon & B. Pleskovic (Eds.), *Beyond Transition*, Annual world bank conference on development economics – regional.

Begg, D. (1997). Monetary policy during transition: Progress and pitfalls in central and Eastern Europe, 1990–6. *Oxford Review of Economic Policy, Special Issue: Economics of Transition in Eastern and Central Europe*, *13*(2), 33–46.

Berghof, E., & Roland, G. (1997). Soft budget constraints and credit crunches in financial transition. *European Economic Review*, *41*(3–5), 807–818.

Berkowitz, D. (1996). On the persistence of rationing following liberalization: A theory for economies in transition. *European Economic Review*, *40*(6), 1259–1280.

Blanchard, O. (1997). *The economics of transition in Eastern Europe*. Oxford: Clarendon Lectures, Oxford University Press.

Bolton, P., & Roland, G. (1992). Privatization in central and Eastern Europe. *Economic Policy*, *15*, 276–309.

Caprio, G., Jr. (1995). The role of financial intermediaries in transitional economies. *Carnegie-Rochester Conference Series on Public Policy*, *42*, 257–302.

Coricelli, F., & Milesi-Ferretti, G.-M. (1993). On the credibility of 'Big Bang' programs: A note on wage claims and soft budget constraints in economies in transition. *European Economic Review*, *37*(2–3), 387–395.

Cottarelli, C., & Szapáry, G. (Eds.). (1998). *Moderate inflation: The experience of transition economies*. Washington: International Monetary Fund and National Bank of Hungary.

De Melo, M., & Denizer, C. (1997). *Monetary policy during transition*. World Bank Policy Research Working Paper No. 1706, the World Bank Group.

Dervis, K., & Condon, T. (1994). Hungary – Partial successes and remaining challenges: The emergence of a 'Gradualist' success story? In O. Blanchard, J. Kenneth, A. Froot, & J. D. Sachs (Eds.), *The transition in Eastern Europe* (pp. 123–149). Chicago, IL: University of Chicago Press.

Durjasz, P., & Kokoszczyński, R. (1998). Financial inflows to Poland 1990–96. *Empirica*, *25*, 217.

Egert, B., Crespo-Cuaresma, J., & Reininger, T. (2007). Interest rate pass-through in central and Eastern Europe: Reborn from ashes merely to pass away? *Journal of Policy Modeling*, *29*, 209–225.

Egert, B., & MacDonald, R. (2009). Monetary transmission mechanism in central and Eastern Europe: Surveying the surveyable. *Journal of Economic Surveys*, *23*(20), 277–327.

Fischer, S., & Gelb, A. (1991). The process of economic transformation. *Journal of Economic Perspectives*, *5*, 91–106.

Frye, T., & Shleifer, A. (1997). The invisible hand and the grabbing hand. *American Economic Review*, *87*, 354–358.

Halpern, L., & Wyplosz, C. (1997). Equilibrium exchange rates in transition economies. *International Monetary Fund Staff Papers*, *44*(4), 430–461.

Hart, O. (1983). The market mechanism as an incentive scheme. *Bell Journal of Economics*, *14*(2), 366–382.

Hart, O., & Moore, J. (1990). Property rights and the nature of the firm. *Journal of Political Economy*, *98*, 1119–1158.

Hart, O., & Moore, J. (1999). *On the design of hierarchies: Coordination versus specialization*. Mimeo, London School of Economics.

Hart, O., Shleifer, A., & Vishny, R. W. (1997). The proper scope of government: Theory and an application to prisons. *Quarterly Journal of Economics*, *112*(4), 1127–1161.

Hayek, F. (1945). The use of knowledge in society. *American Economic Review*, *35*, 519–530.

Hayek, F. A. von. (1935). *Collectivist economic planning*. London: Routledge.

Hellman, J., Jones, G., & Kaufmann, D. (2003). Seize the state, seize the day: State capture and influence in transition economies. *Journal of Comparative Economics*, *31*, 751–773.

Jamilov, R. (2012). Macro-Economic Imbalances and Micro-Market Frictions. Background paper for *Towards Decent Employment through Accelerated Structural Reform in Azerbaijan*, UNDP Policy Paper.

Jamilov, R. (2013a). Capital mobility in the caucasus. *Economic Systems*, *37*(2), 155–170.

Jamilov, R. (2013b). Growth design and monetary policy after the crisis. In R. Mirdala (Ed.), *Financial aspects of the recent trends in the global economy*. Bucharest, Romania: ASERS Publishing.

Jamilov, R. (2013c). Inclusive Prosperity: Towards a Sustained and Secure Society. Background paper for *Demographic Study of Azerbaijan*, UNDP Policy Paper.

Jamilov, R. (2013d). J-curve dynamics and the Marshall Lerner condition: Evidence from Azerbaijan. *Transition Studies Review*, *19*(3), 313–323.

Jamilov, R. (2013e). Under the Damocles sword: The bank lending channel in a transition economy. Paper presented at the 10th Monetary Transmission Mechanism in Transition Countries seminar, Swiss National Bank, Zurich.

Jamilov, R. (2014). Interest Rate Pass-Through and Monetary Policy Asymmetry: A Journey into the Caucasian Black Box. *Journal of Asian Economics* (2014), 31–32, 57–70 (With Balazs Egert); CESifo Working Paper No. 4131; EconomiX Working Paper No. 2013-9; William Davidson Institute Working Paper No. 1041.

Johnson, S., Kaufmann, D., & Shleifer, A. (1998). The unofficial economy in transition. *Brookings Papers on Economic Activity*, *2*, 159–239.

Kornai, J. (1990). *The road to a free economy*. New York, NY: Norton.

Kornai, J. (1998). *From socialism to capitalism*. London: Center for Post-Collectivist Studies.

Kutan, A., & Brada, J. C. (1999). *The evolution of monetary policy in transition economies*. ZEI Working Paper No. B 19-1999.

Maliszewski, W. S. (2002). *Monetary policy in transition: Structural econometric modelling and policy simulations*. Warsaw: Center for Social and Economic Research.

Maskin, E., & Tirole, J. (1999). Unforeseen contingencies and incomplete contracts. *Review of Economic Studies*, *66*(1), 83–114.

Mckinnon, R. (1973). *Money and capital in economic development*. Washington, DC: Brookings Institution.

McKinnon, R. (1991). *The order of economic liberalization*. Baltimore, MD: John Hopkins University Press.

McMillan, J., & Naughton, B. (1992). How to reform a planned economy: Lessons from China. *Oxford Review of Economic Policy*, *8*, 130–143.

Mehrotra, A. (2008). Demand for money in transition: Evidence from China's disinflation. *International Advances in Economic Research*, *14*, 36–47.

Negro, M. D., & Obiols-Homs, F. (2001). Has monetary policy been so bad that it is better to get rid of it? The case of Mexico. *Journal of Money, Credit and Banking*, *33*(2), 404–433.

Perotti, E. (1993). Bank lending in transition economies. *Journal of Banking and Finance*, *17*, 1021–1032.

Perotti, E. (1995). Credible privatization. *American Economic Review*, *85*(4), 847–859.

Perotti, E. (1998). Inertial credit and opportunistic arrears in transition. *European Economic Review*, *42*, 1703–1725.

Perotti, E., & van Oijen, P. (1999). *Privatization, political risk and stock market development*. Center for Economic Policy Research Discussion Paper No. 2243.

Persson, T., Roland, G., & Tabellini, G. (1997). Separation of powers and political accountability. *Quarterly Journal of Economics*, *112*(4), 1163–1202.

Pissarides, F., Singer, M., & Svejnar, J. (1996). *Small and medium size enterprises in transition, evidence from Bulgaria and Russia*. Mimeo, European Bank for Reconstruction and Development, London.

Portes, R. (1991). The path of reform in Central and Eastern Europe: An introduction. *European Economy*, *2*(Special issue), 3–15.

Qian, Y., & Roland, G. (1996). The soft budget constraint in China. *Japan and the World Economy*, *8*(1), 207–223.

Qian, Y., Roland, G., & Xu, C. (1999). Why is China different from Eastern Europe? Perspectives from organization theory. *European Economic Review*, *43*(46), 1085–1094.

Rodrik, D. (1992). Political economy and development policy. *European Economic Review (Papers and Proceedings)*, *36*(2), 329–336.
Roland, G. (1990). Complexity, bounded rationality and equilibrium: The Soviet-type case. *Journal of Comparative Economics*, *14*(3), 401–424.
Roland, G. (1997). Political constraints and the transition experience. In S. Zecchini (Ed.), *Lessons from the economic transition* (pp. 169–188). Dordrecht: Kluwer.
Roland, G. (2000). *Transition and economics*. Cambridge, MA: MIT Press.
Roland, G., & Verdier, T. (1999). Transition and the output fall. *Economics of Transition*, *7*(1), 1–28.
Sachs, J. (1993). *Poland's Jump to the market economy*. Lionel Robbins Lectures. Cambridge, MA: MIT Press.
Sachs, J., & Woo, W. (1992). Structural factors in the economic reforms of China, Eastern Europe, and the former Soviet Union. *Economic Policy*, *9*(18), 101–145.
Schmidt, K., & Schnitzer, M. (1993). Privatization and management incentives in the transition period in Eastern Europe. *Journal of Comparative Economics*, *17*, 264–287.
Shleifer, A., & Treisman, D. (2000). *Without a map*. Cambridge, MA: MIT Press.
Shleifer, A., & Vishny, R. (1994). Politicians and firms. *Quarterly Journal of Economics*, *109*, 995–1025.
Shleifer, A., & Vishny, R. (1997). Corruption. *Quarterly Journal of Economics*, *108*(3), 599–617.
Svejnar, J. (1989). A framework for the economic transformation of Czechoslovakia. *PlanEcon Report*, *5*(52), 1–18.
Szapáry, G., & Jakab, Z. M. (1998). Exchange rate policy in transition economies: The case of Hungary. *Journal of Comparative Economics*, *26*(4), 691–717.
Treisman, D. (1999a). The causes of corruption: A cross-national study. Paper presented at the Fifth Nobel Symposium in Economics: The Economics of Transition, Stockholm.
Woo, W. (1994). The art of reforming centrally planned economies: Comparing China, Poland and Russia. *Journal of Comparative Economics*, *18*(3), 276–308.

NEO-TRANSITIONAL ECONOMIES: THE BROAD CONTEXT

Paul Marer

ABSTRACT

This is an exploratory paper of personal reflections on economic system issues, based on half a century of wide-ranging professional experiences, summarized in the section "Professional Background."

The following broad generalizations are elaborated: (1) For a country's sustained good economic performance, there is no alternative to a predominantly market-driven economy, supported by appropriate institutions. (2) In societies at all levels of development, it is essential to have mutually supporting cooperation between the private sector and the state (section "An Economic System with Universal Features?"). (3) The quarter-century transformation progress of the 29 former centrally planned economies of the USSR and Eastern Europe has been most uneven, as documented in the section "Relationship between Economic and Political System Transformation." (4) Regarding China, it is NOT the country's authoritarian political system but the skillful transformation of its economy into a market-driven one that has been principally responsible for the country's impressive, long-term economic performance (section "China's Economic Growth and Development Model"). The paper concludes by suggesting that the most fundamental

Neo-Transitional Economics
International Finance Review, Volume 16, 21–52

ISSN: 1569-3767/doi:10.1108/S1569-376720150000016001

determinants of a country's long-term economic success are some combination of its geography, institutions, culture, and momentous historical events.

Keywords: Centrally Planned Economies (CPEs); China; Deng Xio Ping; economic system transformation; established market economies (EMEs); transformation depression

INTRODUCTION AND OUTLINE

This is an exploratory paper of personal reflections, based on half a century of professional experience related to economic system issues.

The section "Professional Background" summarizes the author's wide-ranging professional experiences. Much of my professional work has been a dual one: contributing to academic scholarship and trying to put such scholarship into the service of practical and implementable economic policy advice to governments working on economic system change, as well as to international economic organizations promoting and supporting economic system change in various countries.

Economic and political system change is an immensely broad topic; it has relevance to just about all the countries of the globe, irrespective of their size, location, and level of development.

From this large universe, my life work has concentrated on economic system changes in what used to be called the "centrally planned economies" (CPEs), both of the *traditional* command economy types (TCPE) as well as of those CPEs that have been "*modified*" (MCPEs) in various more and less successful attempts to improve their economies' performance. Much of this kind of work by the profession had been concentrated during four decades: from 1950s through the 1980s.

After the nearly simultaneous (1) fall of the Berlin Wall, and the collapse of communism in Central and Eastern Europe and of the Soviet Union itself; and (2) China's dramatic and permanent rejection of such senseless economic system experiments as the Great Leap Forward and the Cultural Revolution (during the 1960s and 1970s), the focus of the professions interested in those countries had turned to the many complex issues of economic and political transformation.

During the approximately two decades that had followed those dramatic events in what used to be called the Communist world – from the early 1990s until the end of the 2000s – a great deal of attention had focused on the tremendously complex issues of economic and political transformation. In almost all cases, the explicit or implicit assumption of scholars and policymakers outside those countries – and many of their counterparts inside those nations, too – used to be that successful transformation by and large meant the approximate replication of the economic and political institutions of (what I prefer to call) the "established market economies" (EMEs). In popular parlance, this was the world of the "West," whose systemic essence was predominantly market-driven economic systems and democratic political arrangements.

Rather suddenly, since the beginning of the current decade, the agendas of scholars and policymakers concerned with economic and political system issues have changed. With the onset of the Great Recession of 2008–2010, from which sustained recovery by much of the West seems to have become an increasingly elusive hope – combined with the continued spectacular economic performance of China for about 35 years – the new system issue seems to have become (to phrase it bluntly): "Is Western-type democracy and the vaunted market economy failing? Is it not China we should look to for finding new and more effective solutions to solving the economic malaise that seems to have permanently infected the capitalist economies and their allegedly democratic political systems?"

It is on these questions that this introductory paper offers personal reflections.

The section "Professional Background" sketches the author's professional experiences. Some readers may react to my annotated biography favorably, "yes, he has had a long, broad-based, and often pretty high-level set of experiences, so his views should be taken seriously." Others may conclude: "aha, now I do see where his prejudices come from, so his views should be discounted."

The section "An Economic System with Universal Features?" reflects on the question: Is there a single economic system with universally applicable features? "Yes," I conclude, and attempt to sketch its dozen key features.

The section "Relationship between Economic and Political System Transformation" offers the author's views on the relationship between economic and political systems; more accurately, on the relationship between economic and political system transformation.

The section "From transition to neo-transition: A progress report" summarizes the large body of literature on the two decades of comparative economic and political system transformation experiences of the 29 countries of the former Soviet Union and the countries of Central, Eastern and Southern Europe during 1990–2010.

The section "China's Economic Growth and Development Model" comments on China's 35-year transformation experience and then discusses whether we should look to China for finding effective solutions to the economic and political malaise that seems to have infected the EMEs.

The section "Key Determining Factors in Sustainable Economic Development for Any Country" concludes with a broad set of observations about the author's understanding on what key factors largely explain the age-old problem of why some countries were/are able to develop in a sustainable way, benefiting a large majority of their people, while other nations have lagged behind, either in terms of economic development or in the sharing of its fruits with a broad swath of their citizenry.

The section is Summary and Conclusions.

PROFESSIONAL BACKGROUND

My Ph.D. thesis (University of Pennsylvania, Wharton School, 1968) examined economic relations between the "centrally planned economies" (CPEs) of Eastern Europe (EE) and the USSR. During the next several decades I taught courses and wrote articles and books on central planning, eventually turning to an examination of various attempts to improve it by modifying certain of its traditional features. I studied "modified centrally planned economies" (MCPEs), such as Yugoslavia from the 1950s until its collapse in 1992. Hungary and Poland were two other MCPEs, different from Yugoslavia and from each other, during the 1970s and 1980s. I was asking this question: Given primarily the political but also the economic/trade constraints imposed on the countries of EE by the Soviet Union, how far can system modifications go to make an MCPE's economic performance sustainably better than that of the Stalinist command economy?

From the 1970s through the early 1990s I served as advisor, co-editor, and contributor to the US Congress, Joint Economic Committee's tri-annual published volumes of expert studies on the economies of Central and EE (1974, 1977, 1980–1981, 1985, 1988–1989, 1994).

In 1981 and again in 1982 the World Bank sent me to China to make a series of presentations to *Deng Xio Ping's* lead economists on economic reforms in Hungary.

In 1982, when first among the CPEs Hungary had applied for IMF membership, I was on the IMF staff in Washington, DC for six months (on leave from Indiana University) to work on the country's accession.

During 1983–1984 I directed a team project for the World Bank on estimating, in an internationally comparable way, the dollar GDPs of the non-market economics of the USSR and the EE countries (Marer, 1985).

In 1985 I was privileged to be a member of a small group of US economists invited to Moscow to discuss the planned economic reforms with one of Gorbachev's chief economic advisors, *Aganbegyan* and his colleagues. The essence of Aganbegyan's planned reforms was administrative decentralization to the regions as well as to the typically giant, monopolistic state-owned enterprises (Aganbegyan, 1988). Every member of the US delegation was of the view that the reforms will disappoint because, in the absence of real markets and real competition, administrative decentralization will result in increased wages and prices, without additional output. As we now know, *Gorbachev's* economic decentralization was one of his three – well-intended but fundamentally misconceived (in terms of achieving their objectives) – reforms that, in combination, principally caused the *timing* of the collapse of the Soviet Union and of communism in Europe.[1]

Early in 1989, with fundamental "winds of change" in the air, I devoted an intensive year putting together and co-managing the work of a distinguished joint Hungarian-international group of experts to come up with a comprehensive economic transformation program for Hungary, my country of birth and research focus at the time. The book-length report of the Hungarian-International Blue Ribbon Commission (BRC) was published (in English and in Hungarian) in April 1990, on the day of Hungary's first post-communist democratic election; its findings and recommendations were widely reported in the Hungarian and international press.[2]

Shortly thereafter, at the behest of the OECD, I organized an international conference of a hundred experts in Paris in November 1990 on the many tasks of transition and co-edited the resulting two-volume of studies (Marer & Zecchini, 1991, 1992).[3]

During 1991 I led a World Bank project on how to adjust the economic statistics of the "historically planned economies" to bring them in line with the standard statistical series published by the World Bank (Marer, Arvay, O'Connor, & Schrenk, 1992).

In 1990 I was appointed by President *George H. W. Bush*, then reappointed four and eight years later by President *Bill Clinton*, to serve on the Board of Directors of the Hungarian-American Enterprise Fund (HAEF), established to supervise the spending of the $78 million the US Congress gave to Hungary to promote private enterprise. My 16-year service on the

HAEF Board – with frequent exchanges with members of a dozen sister boards the US had set up in other countries of EE, Russia, and Central Asia – provided a micro perspective on economic transformation's promises and pitfalls (USAID, 2013b).

In 2000 I relocated to Hungary. Since then I have been serving as professor at the George-Soros – established Business School of Central European University in Budapest, with several leaves for personal reasons and for short teaching assignments elsewhere. I had been observing Hungary's head start and impressively rapid economic and political transformation during the 1990–1999 decade. Since then I have been witnessing the country's trials and tribulations and gradual but continuous falling behind most of the other EE countries – in system transformation as well as in economic performance.

In 2004 and again in 2006, I spent a semester in China, teaching MBAs at the country's top specialized educational institution, the China Europe International Business School (CEIBS) in Shanghai. Its full-time MBA is taught in English. Practically all CEIBS professors – Chinese and Western – had Ph.Ds from leading business schools around the world. With one exception: *Wu Jinglian* was the only faculty member who lectured in Chinese, always of course with an interpreter, since a portion of the student body and the faculty was not Chinese. In one of his lectures I attended, Prof. *Wu* said this:[4] "Around 1979, *Deng Xio Ping* had a meeting with his Council of Economic Advisors [headed by *Wu*] where the leader observed: 'Look at the Chinese around the world: in Taiwan, Singapore, Malaysia, US, Canada, Australia; everywhere they are economically hugely successful. But here in China, we are not. So there is nothing wrong with us, ethnic Chinese; it is our economic system that is at fault. Go and search the world and bring back ideas and practices we can use to improve our economy's performance'." That's when – 25 years after the event – I understood what so baffled me at the time: why on earth would the Chinese be interested in a US Midwest university professor's views on economic reforms in tiny Hungary?[5]

In 2012, I was invited to join four US economists to assess USAID's 20-year effort to assist the transformation of the 29 countries of EE and the former Soviet Union. USAID's contributions to those counties cost US taxpayers $20 billion (with much of it going to US consultants). The study was to assess the more as well as the less favorable results of USAID's activities in the region, and the lessons learned. The comprehensive, well-documented assessment is available on the world wide web (USAID, 2013a). The section "Relationship between Economic and Political System

Transformation" cites from those sections of the report for which I was principally responsible.

AN ECONOMIC SYSTEM WITH UNIVERSAL FEATURES?

Yes, I think there is one: a well-functioning market economy. This simple statement is anything but original. Yet, it is important to restate it emphatically because the many insightful criticisms of "capitalism," as it is experienced by societies around the world, have tempted many to reject the entire market economy concept.

The simple truth, as I see it, is that centuries of search for and experimentation with alternatives to a market-driven economy has found no viable substitutes for it. Even if we acknowledge that there has never been, and perhaps never will be, a perfectly functioning market economy, it is much more fruitful to devote efforts to mitigate such an economy's shortcomings than to continue the certain-to-be-futile search for a better alternative.

How is one to define a well-functioning market economy?

The first time I gave focused thought to this question was after a hugely disappointing meeting of the BRC in Brussels in late 1989. Much of the two-day meeting was spent on the distinguished foreign members of the BRC giving the Hungarians a slew of well-intentioned advice. The Japanese representative suggested that the Hungarians adopt certain Japanese practices, such as industrial policy (close cooperation between government and large businesses, with the government elite sharing "visions" of what would make sense for business to focus on). The Austrian representative was extolling the virtues of his country's syndicalism (close cooperation between government, business, and the unions). The Korean spokesperson was singing the praises of the *cheabols*. The US member of the BRC, an ultra-conservative (in the American use of the term) onetime presidential hopeful repeated, like a mantra: *just get the government out of the way and let the markets make most resource allocation decisions.*

Along with the Hungarians on the BRC, I was frustrated because, at that meeting, no progress had been made on designing a meaningful and implementable transformation program for Hungary. As I put it later: all those brilliant foreign advisors were suggesting a recipe for the frosting the Hungarians should put on their future economic system cake, instead of focusing on what the cake should be and how to bake it. So I spent the next month thinking about the cake: the essential features of a well-functioning market economy. I defined such an economy as one that has been able to sustainably improve the economic well-being of a large majority of its people. All the country examples I found were what I called "established market economies" (EMEs) – the group generally labeled as the developed West. (I prefer the EME term, in part because neither Japan nor Australia and New Zealand are geographically "West.")

For the next meeting of the BRC I came up with the following dozen basic features that were (and still are) by and large shared by the EMEs and several others, with short explanations about what the list implies about the main tasks and directions of system transformation:[6]

1. *The rule of law* must replace rule by authority. This is the touchstone of basic political rights and economic freedoms, the two being inseparable. This means, among others, the protection of private property, the enforcement of private contracts, and business laws that permit enterprises to organize themselves as subsidiaries, joint ventures, joint stock and limited liability companies, without a great deal of arbitrary intervention in their activities by the authorities.
2. *The predominant private ownership of the means of production.* Making the private sector the dominant one in a former CPE should be designed so that the new private owners can effectively exercise the functions of ownership: deciding what business to be in (and out), how to finance it, and appointing and holding accountable those who manage the enterprise. Even state-owned enterprises (SOEs) tend to be more efficient when they function in a competitive, private-sector environment than when they are the dominant economic actors, as they are in a CPE. SOEs are difficult to insulate from political and bureaucratic pressures. Therefore, large-scale privatization is essential. Even though there are really no good ways to accomplish it during the early period of transformation, that unpleasant task must still be done. Ideally, the least bad option should be chosen. For the countries of EE, "selling to the highest bidder," with certain conditions of course, would appear to be the preferred option, in spite of the tremendous difficulties of implementation.
3. *Strong competition.* This is one of the most important features of a well-functioning market system. Effective competition requires sound and predictable rules and regulations in all areas of production and trade. It is the government's responsibility to establish and to enforce antitrust and like laws. Countries with large domestic markets that can

accommodate more than a handful of firms in each sector and can assure strong competition among them can afford to practice limited trade protection without damaging the economy, especially if export-promotion is also pursued. However, countries that are small or medium-sized must be more open to import competition and, increasingly, also to foreign investment.

4. *Sound currency*. Reasonable price stability (ideally, in the low single digits), and the expectation that any price rise that exists or may start will not get out of hand, are essential for motivating firms and households in their capacity as savers, investors, and providers of labor services to take the long view and to focus on real economic activities instead of on hoarding, speculation and other kinds of manipulation to try to protect the value of their assets. High inflation also deprives the price system of its ability to give meaningful signals for resource allocation, so it is a sure road to sustained poor economic performance.
5. *Currency convertibility*, at least for the current account, is essential for enterprises wanting to import, and for foreign investors wishing to repatriate their investment earnings. Convertibility is a way to link the domestic economy with the global market. No meaningful import competition or trade along the lines of comparative advantage is likely to take place without the currency being convertible.
6. *An adequate level of domestic savings*. In the long run, over the span of decades, countries must rely largely on domestic savings to finance an adequate level of domestic investment. Large net borrowing from abroad can assist a country only for a certain time. Excessive, long-term reliance on the inflow of foreign capital can make a country vulnerable to unpredictable global business cycles and trends.
7. *Efficient financial intermediation*. Countries that have reached a certain level of development need a reasonably sophisticated and competitive banking system, largely private, with investors risking their own funds and seeking profits. Savers and investors should also have an array of attractive financial instruments, such as savings accounts, stocks and bonds, and the like. The entire financial system must be subject to prudential regulation and monitoring by the independent (non-political) authorities of the state.
8. *Taxation*. The rate of taxation, direct plus indirect, on business profits and on personal incomes must not be prohibitive, that is, be so high as to act as a disincentive to strong economic effort by investors, entrepreneurs, managers, professionals, and ordinary workers. There is no

precise figure on the threshold level at which taxation begins to seriously inhibit economic effort; that level depends on a country's economic circumstances and culture. But a tax burden that is greater than 50% is certain to be constraining; some believe that the threshold rate is considerably lower. At the same time, taxes must be high enough to finance the many essential activities of the state.

9. *Infrastructure and the environment.* A sound infrastructure (e.g., a well-functioning system of telecommunications, an adequate network of transportation, good schools, hospitals, and housing) is needed both for the sake of business efficiency and as a vital component of the standard of living. In addition, people increasingly want the government to help protect the environment. Businesses and people are generally willing to pay for such benefits through some combination of user charges and taxes.
10. *An appropriate level of welfare expenditures.* In just about every society, people want some degree of employment security and a backup system of minimum income maintenance in case of dismissal, old age, and ill health. The level of welfare expenditures (as % of GDP) is partly a function of a country's level of income (*ceteris paribus*, the higher the income level, the greater the share of GDP that a country can afford to devote to welfare) and partly that of its culture. It is an essential principle of efficient and affordable welfare policy that as large a share of payments as possible be allocated based on need, not citizenship.
11. *Opportunities to seek individual fulfillment.* This means, first and foremost, the political and economic freedom to pursue goals as investors, entrepreneurs, farmers, professionals, and wage earners. In addition, people want to work at a proper, safe, and well-managed workplace; they seek an equitable system of personal compensation and a reasonably fair distribution of income and wealth. And since more and more of the simple jobs are being automated (except in the poorest countries), both future employability and personal fulfillment require broad and affordable opportunities for a good education (for oneself and for one's offspring), as well as opportunities for continuously upgrading of skills and retraining.
12. *A strong but limited and not-too-corrupt government.* (For the sake of simplicity, "authority," "government," and "the state" are used interchangeably, even though they are separate through overlapping institutions.) A government must be strong because it has a large list of essential tasks to perform if the economy is to function well. Consider the items from the above list: a good legal system, including a reliable

and independent judiciary, is a state responsibility. SOEs cannot disappear overnight; even EMEs have SOEs, some countries quite a few, that have to be centrally supervised, if not managed. Creating the conditions and enforcing sufficient competition is certainly a governmental responsibility. Assuring a sound currency and its convertibility are likewise tasks for government bodies. Efficient financial intermediation requires good prudential supervision. Taxation is a quintessential government function. So are decisions concerning the infrastructure (even if building and maintaining it are given to the private sector). Environmental regulations and their enforcement are likewise governmental responsibilities. So is the design and delivery of the welfare system. A not too highly skewed distribution of income and wealth is also a state responsibility.

At the same time, however, the scope of the government must be limited so as not to encroach upon the many activities that the private sector does much better. Limited government means that the share of GDP redistributed by the government should remain well below 50%, perhaps not too far below that watershed in wealthy EMEs, where taxes and welfare spending can be higher. At the same time, the GDP redistributed by the government should remain much below 50% in the emerging economies, such as those of EE, some of which had become, regretfully, "premature welfare states," to use *Janos Kornai's* apt phrase, which undermines their longer-term economic prospects (Kornai, 2008).

Some corruption is inevitable in the state as well as in the private sectors. What is crucial is that corruption be fought by the authorities and not be allowed to become all-pervasive.

* * *

Other than the fact that the above list and brief explanations were crafted in the midst of planning system transformation, there is nothing original about any part of it. Nevertheless it intended – and hopefully had made, and perhaps can still make – several contributions.

First, it refocused discussions in the BRC from the frosting to the cake. And it is probably still not a bad list to start with, or refer to, when fundamental economic system change is undertaken or continues.

Second, the task list is specific enough to offer a general guide on what needs to be done, pointing out basic directions. At the same time, the list is not so specific as to try to squeeze any country into an economic-system straightjacket.

Third, the list shows how many complex and interdependent transformation tasks there are. So many participants in the BRC's sessions argued that *only* by doing this or that single thing (usually what the speaker had specialized in) was *the* key to successful transformation. Even today one reads arguments that this or that aspect, or just a small number of factors, is/are the keys to a country's economic success. Even such a broad and simple general list as I just presented shows the immense complexity and interdependence of the factors that are essential for sustained good economic performance.

Finally, the list reveals that juxtaposing "the state" *versus* "the market" as a general ideological debate on a desirable economic system is a fundamental misconception of how an economy really functions, or should function. Both are essential and interdependent. If both sectors function well, the economic system will be a normal one; if one or both function poorly, the economic system – whatever it is labeled – will not deliver.

While there has never been an EME where all these factors have worked well and in harmony with one another for extended periods, in the economically successful countries most, if not all of the factors listed had worked reasonably well, from the end of World War II until the Great Recession of 2009–2012 (for about two generations), occasionally punctured by internally- or externally generated economic crises.

Oh, but what about China? some may ask. "It does not seem to fit the mold you just presented." I will return to that question in the section "China's Economic Growth and Development Model" of this chapter, after some further reflections.

RELATIONSHIP BETWEEN ECONOMIC AND POLITICAL SYSTEMS TRANSFORMATION

A pluralistic and relatively stable political system provides the most supportive environment for economic development.

I don't use the term "democracy," for several reasons.

One, there is a huge range of "political practices" that can fit under a "democracy" label. Whether one or some other type of democracy is the right one to promote the economic development of this or that country is an open question; the answer is not obvious until the specifics are examined.

Two, *even a truly democratic political system* (like those that prevail in the United States and in most of the countries of the EU) *and an efficient market economy* (even a high-income one), *are not necessarily ideal partners, always*. For example, special interests may be much too powerful so that political decisions are distorted. In other cases, political gridlock can prevent economic policy steps that would clearly be in the national interest to take.

Three, for democracy to have a chance to work well, there must be an informed and reasonably active and responsible electorate. A necessary though not sufficient condition for this is a sizeable middle class. Clearly, such a class is not present in many "transition" and other less-developed economies.

Four, in certain situations, the replacement of an authoritarian regime with a democratic one can trigger major problems, as for example, in Southeast Asia. In the Philippines, Indonesia, Thailand, Burma, Laos, Malaysia, and Vietnam, the Chinese – usually a tiny proportion of the populations of those countries – have long enjoyed overwhelmingly dominant economic positions. Rich and powerful minorities engender resentment, everywhere. When those minorities are ethnically different (or labeled to be so, as the Jews were by the Nazis) that resentment can carry a dangerous charge that can be unleashed by a too quick, unprepared move toward democracy. In extreme cases it can lead to mass killings, as it happened in Indonesia repeatedly, such as during the mid- to late-1990s, with the fall of strongman Suharto, followed by populist democracy.[7]

Thus, in certain not-too-rare circumstances, the Western mantra that free markets and democracy must always be coupled may well be ill-conceived and could even be a recipe for disaster.

The Western assumption that the introduction of democracy everywhere will engender a more liberal and tolerant society is not always true. The opposite can also occur; a case in point is Iraq today. One of my few critical observations of USAID's assistance work in the Balkans, in Central Asia, and in the Middle East is that it has been guided by the unexamined assumption that promoting Western-type democracy is always, self-evidently, the right thing to do.

Absolutely, and by no means, do I wish to suggest or imply that the opposite of democracy, which is dictatorship, is – or can be – the preferred political arrangement. The dangers of dictatorships are immense. Such systems can be devastating, and can result in the deaths of tens of millions of innocent people. Mao Zedong's Great Leap Forward (1958–1961) and his Cultural Revolution (1966–1976) did just that. The mass killings and forced starvation during the Great Leap Forward is little known, certainly so in China, even though it has been persuasively demonstrated that up to 45 million people had died needlessly. This finding is based on the comprehensive, multi-year research by a reputable scholar, based on his access to a large sample of the Communist Party's own local archives in China, recording the events of that period.[8]

If I would have to summarize in one sentence the kind of political system that would serve any society well and would also effectively promote sustained economic development, it would be something like this: *the political system should be accepted by the majority; have strong checks and balances to prevent extreme measures against ordinary citizens, businesses, and NGOs; be largely transparent and truthful on why its leaders make key decisions; and have mechanisms in place to rectify big mistakes.* Yes, such a system might as well be called a democracy, but not all democracies conform to these standards.

FROM TRANSITION TO NEO-TRANSITION: A PROGRESS REPORT

Terminology

In much of the literature, "transition" and "transformation" are used interchangeably; in some cases the countries in that group are labeled "transition economies," in other cases, as "transforming economies," both abbreviated as TREs.

I think that a distinction between these terms is meaningful and important. A "transition economy" denotes a country whose economic and political system destination is known and is supported by the majority, including the elite: that of a predominantly market-driven economy, with a democratic (in a Western sense) political system.

In my interpretation, a "transforming economy" denotes a former CPE where there is no clear social or political consensus on the final economic and political system destination. Most ordinary people probably don't even give a thought to the issue, so it is the ruling elite's views, attitudes, and actions that matter the most. And not what they say (their lip-service in favor of a market economy and democracy is pervasive) but what they do. If, during more than two decades since transition/transformation had begun, little progress has been made toward a market economy and the kind of democracy that deserves that label, then those countries should be labeled "transforming" rather than "transition" countries.

Fig. 1 is a visual summary of how far the 29 countries of EE and the former Soviet Union had come during the first two decades of their post-Communist era with respect to *economic transition or transformation* toward a market economy and toward a democratic form of government.

EE Graduates (n = 11), refer to those countries that no longer receive USAID assistance, that is, have "graduated." A more appropriate term for the purposes of this paper would be: the EE members of EE: the Czech Republic, Estonia, Latvia, Lithuania, Hungary Poland, Slovakia, Slovenia, Bulgaria, Romania, and Croatia.

The Balkans (n = 6): Albania, Bosnia & Herzegovina, Kosovo, Macedonia, Montenegro and Serbia.

Eurasia (n = 7): Russia, Ukraine, Belarus, Moldova, Armenia, Azerbaijan, and Georgia.

CAR = Central Asian Republics (n = 5): Kazakhstan, Kyrgyzstan, Tajikistan, Turkmenistan, and Uzbekistan.

Combining and then averaging many indicators, separately for economic and for political transformation, each country earns two scores. A score of 1 means that the country has made very little progress; a score of 5 that it has been fully transformed: that in terms of its institutions and how they function, the country has become by and large comparable to the functioning democracies and "established market economies" (EMEs) referred to in the section "An Economic System with Universal Features?"

The most striking pattern revealed in Fig. 1 is the high correlation between political and economic transformation. Causation runs both ways. Although the methodologies undergirding the results are solid, judgments are certainly involved in the selection and the weighting of the indicators. It is also difficult to quickly reflect progress or reversals that may occur from time to time. For example, until just a few years ago, Ukraine (after the Orange Revolution in 2004) was certainly more democratic than Russia (as is shown in the figure). Then the country clearly moved backward under the presidency of *Viktor Yanukovich* (2006–2014). Today (2014) Ukraine has once again started to make strides toward moving (with reference to Fig. 1) in a northeasterly direction.

Among the 29 former CPEs plotted in Fig. 1, it is found, not surprisingly, that the *11 EU members from EE* are in the most advanced cluster by themselves.

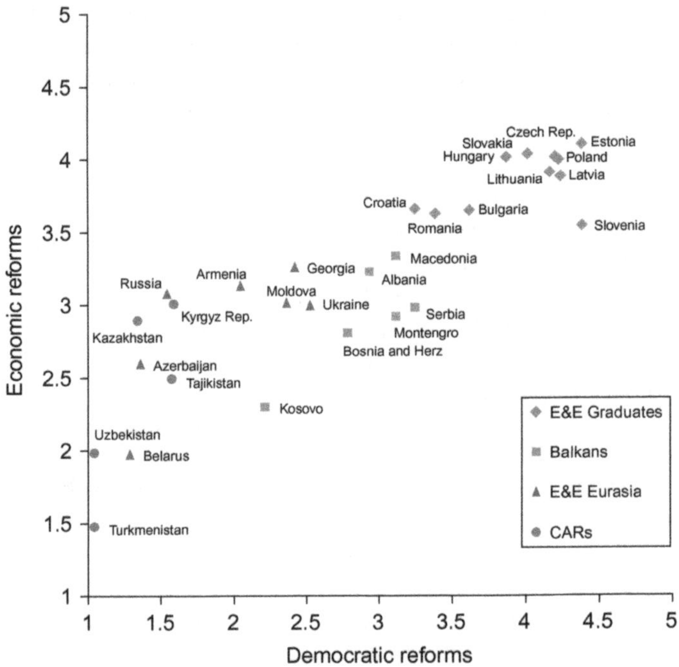

Fig. 1. Economic and Political Transition/Transformation Progress of the 29 Countries of Eastern Europe and the Former Soviet Union as of 2011. *Sources*: Democracy scores: Freedom House, *Nations in Transit 2011* (June 2011), and *Freedom in the World* (2012). Economic scores: EBRD, *Transition Report 2011* (November 2011). The figure was constructed by Ron Sprout for USAID's *Monitoring Country Progress* (MCP) system and published in *Twenty Years* (for full reference, see USAID, 2013a). Details on the MCP system are available via http://www.usaid.gov/where-we-work/europe-and-eurasia/wp/index/index.html.

Several factors account for the transformation lead of the 11 EU members among the 29. In terms of the four sets of factors mentioned in the previous section, the following interpretation are plausible reasons explaining their comparatively good progress:

- *The historical experience* of democratic and market-economy traditions and related institutions and culture (mindset) aspects. Re-establishing those is easier than building them anew, especially in view of the fact that the EE countries had lived under a CPE system for only two generations (about 40 years), whereas the countries of the former Soviet Union (except the Baltic states) for about twice that long.

- *Geography*. Being neighbors of the countries of Western Europe, whose freedoms and living standards the populations of EE countries have long coveted (already well before World War II), the invitation to join the rich and democratic club of the EU, subject to substantial and clearly specified "transition/transformation" conditions, has proved irresistible to these countries. Especially so in light of the clear and substantial economic and political benefits of membership. In this sense, therefore, the geographic location of this group of countries had played a major role in determining the direction and speed of the evolution of their post-CPE systems. In every EE country there was a popular as well as elite consensus that meeting the EU's accession conditions should have the highest priority.

  Paradoxically, once EU membership had been achieved, some of the fundamental, long-term cultural (mindset) characteristics of the people in the various countries have begun to reassert themselves; a case in point is Hungary: its current ruling elite has been turning away from "liberal democracy" and toward a more nationalistic, more state-driven, and increasingly authoritarian mix of economic and political system.

Quite impressive also has been the transformation progress of five of the six countries of the *Balkan group* (the new country of Kosovo, born under extraordinarily difficult circumstances just recently, is the clear laggard). The political and economic transformation of the Balkan countries has lagged behind those of Central EE, owing to the former group's later start and much worse initial conditions. At the same time, they are ahead of every member of the two Eurasian groups.

A key aspect of the Balkan's recent past (since the collapse of Yugoslavia) and future progress is largely a function of their evolving relationship with the EU. The fact that EU membership is not imminent for them, as well as the persistent economic and political problems in the Eurozone, is not helpful in promoting the rapid further transformation of the Balkan countries.

As a group, the *five Central Asian Republics (CARs)* lag behind the most, especially in democratic transition, on which their scores range between 1 and about 1.6. Their long *history* of authoritarian rule has resulted in "path dependence," meaning that it is exceedingly difficult for democracy to take root in such isolated countries, surrounded by other authoritarian states (geography), with little or no experience with civil society, a market economy, the *institutions* that support it, and with the *culture* of responsibility and accountability – institutions and traditions that in the West have taken centuries to evolve. It is somewhat hopeful, however, that all five have made progress in establishing market institutions. For example, the scores of around 3 for Kyrgyztan and Kazakhstan do suggest meaningful progress.

The combined (democratic and market) scores of *the seven Eurasian countries – Russia, Ukraine, Belarus, Moldova and the three nations in the Caucasus* – clearly lag behind those of the European countries (Central Europe, the Baltics, and southeastern Europe). For this group, too, one finds that each has made greater progress in economic than in political transformation, essentially for the same set of reasons as the CARs. A key aspect of their "progress" has been the rapid growth of their private sectors' share in GDP (Fig. 2).

Many Western observers have long equated economic transformation with privatization and have been measuring its progress by the growing share of private ownership and of the private sector's share in GDP. A key message of this paper is that without parallel progress on those other institutional and policy aspects that characterize successful market economies (listed in the section "An Economic System with Universal Features"), the prospects of a country's genuine economic transformation, a prerequisite for its successful long-term development, do not appear to be good.

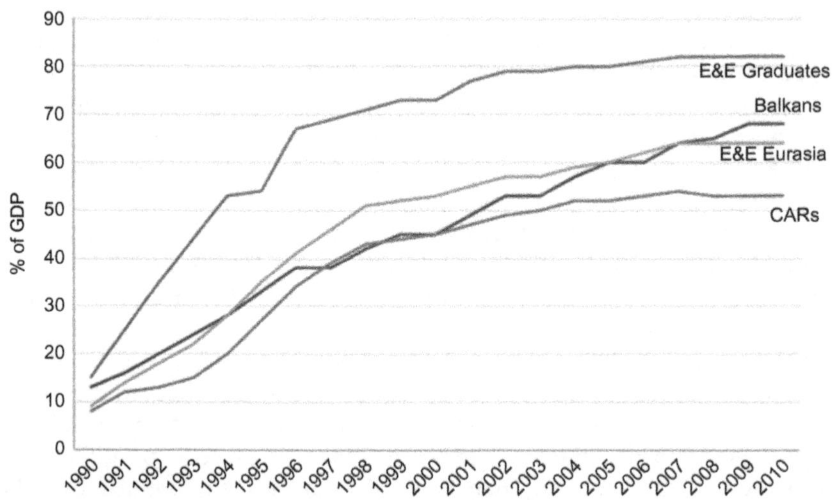

Fig. 2. The Rate of Growth and Share of the Private Sector in GDP in the Four Group of Transition/Transforming Economies, 1990–2010. *Source*: EBRD, *Transition Report* (2011 and earlier editions). The figure was constructed for the USAID by Ron Sprout.

Another common misconception of many observers of the post-CPE countries is that their economic (and, by implication, transformation) success can be and should be measured by their GDP growth rates. Not that growth rates are unimportant. But relying *just* on such an approach would be a mistake. One reason is that linking cause and effect is problematic; another, that there are pitfalls in interpreting properly the indicators that we do have.

A major problem with the use of GDP growth as a measure of performance during the early stages of transformation – lasting up to a decade or even longer in some countries – is that none of the post-CPE economies could avoid experiencing a so-called "transformation depression," that is, GDP declines ranging from 20 percent to 50 percent, or more (Fig. 3).

The most striking fact revealed in Fig. 3 is the length and depth of the so-called "transformation depression" that all the countries had experienced after the collapse of Communism and central planning. Even in the countries of EE – impacted less severely (20–25% decline in real GDP) and for a shorter period (up to five years) than the rest of those in transition – the contraction was about as long and severe as the Great Depression of the 1930s was in the West.[9]

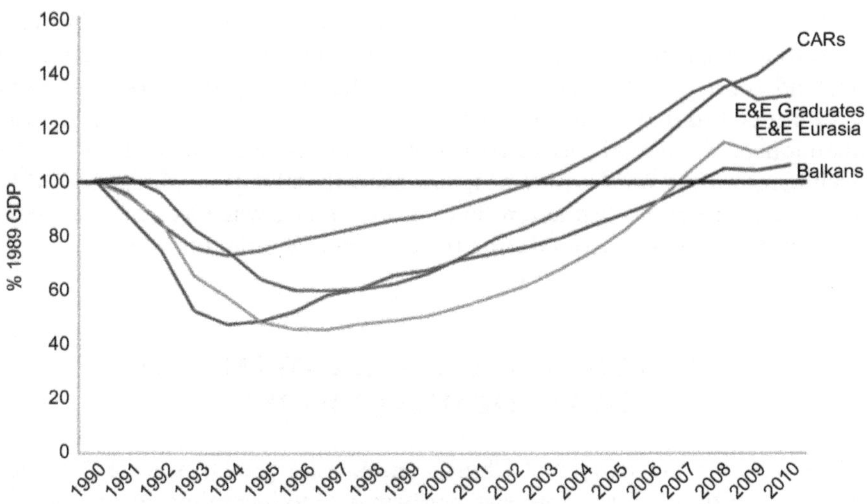

Fig. 3. Real GDP in 2010 as Percent of 1989 GDP in Each of the Four Group of Transition/Transforming Economies. *Source*: EBRD, *Transition Report 2011*. The figure was constructed for USAID by Ron Sprout.

There are very important conceptual, statistical, and interpretation issues concerning the "transformation depression" and the ensuing tempos or recovery.

One, the conditions in which the countries of the region found themselves upon the introduction of real markets were significantly different. I have co-authored a book which documents this and spells out their consequences for transition/transformation for Russia, the Czech Republic, Hungary, and Poland (Ernst, Alexeev, & Marer, 1996). The main differences among the countries were preparation toward adopting a market economy (the MCPEs being way ahead as compared with the TCPEs), the extent of mis-development (itself has many dimensions, such as the shares of the main industries, agriculture and services in GDP), and the degree of macroeconomic imbalance, that is, open and repressed inflation. If the Balkan and Central Asian countries would have been included in the comparison, and historical, cultural, and institutional factors also considered, the divergence in initial conditions among the 29 countries would have been immensely greater.

Be that as it may, "transformation depression" is really a misnomer because the economic plunge was not caused by the systemic transformation per se, but by other factors. Most important among them was the disintegration of economic space in the former Soviet bloc, with terrible medium-term consequences.

At the same time, it should be noted that to the extent that a CPE system produced many goods and some services for which there was no effective demand on a true market basis, the fact that their production had been discontinued and the capacity that had been built to produce them was abandoned, the actual measured GDP decline is overstated. That is, the decline in welfare was considerably less than the plunge in measured GDP. This is an important distinction that is rarely made when assessing the performance of these countries during the early post-Communist period.[10]

CHINA'S ECONOMIC GROWTH AND DEVELOPMENT MODEL

What were/are the sources of China's spectacular growth since 1978? Can we trace the roots of its impressive performance to its authoritarian system? My conclusion is a resounding "no," in support of which I offer the following facts.

The most fundamental source of China's rapid economic growth has been due to the transformation of its economic system from an incredibly messy, poorly functioning CPE into a predominantly market-driven economic system. During the late 1970s and early 1980s, several hundred million peasant households, that were packed into inefficient communes and treated like sardines, were given back their land, under 99-year lease arrangements, in effect reintroducing massive private agriculture, benefiting directly or indirectly about 75% of China's population. Such transformation was/is not possible in the USSR or in EE where collective farms have been mechanized, where the peasants who knew about agriculture had mostly been transferred to cities and to factories over several generations. In China, accompanying the privatization of agriculture, the green light had been given to form so-called township and village enterprises (TVEs) that mushroomed all over and have been operating like true private businesses.

Deng Xiao Ping's slogan in the early 1980s: "to get rich is glorious," has been a symbol of China's capitalist transformation. What better symbolizes China's capitalism than the 2014 listing of Ali Baba, a privately owned conglomerate, on the NY stock exchange, the biggest IPO ever in the world's largest capitalist stock exchange?

A few additional facts: approximately two-third of China GDP originates in sectors that are not controlled by the state.

Only about 15% of China's huge labor force is employed by its central and local government bureaucracies and wholly state-owned enterprises.

China has been the greatest beneficiary of the modern era of globalization, becoming the world's manufacturing center, thanks to opening up its economy widely to FDI, to its immense, disciplined, and until recently inexpensive labor force, and its significantly undervalued exchange rate.

There is no country in the world where market-based competition is greater than in China. Some years back I did a case study of its light-source industry – and found that China had more than 2,000 companies producing light sources and lighting equipment! Intense competition in a more or less free-market setting (in all but in a few high-priority sectors) has been a key driver of China's good economic performance. While several transition economies in EE can boast the same, on a much smaller scale, one cannot imagine that happening in Russia, where entrepreneurship has taken mainly the form of oligarchs grabbing state assets and milking their ventures' monopoly or oligopoly power.

One additional factor that has contributed spectacularly to China's economic success has been the extraordinarily high savings rates, not only of its households but also of its businesses and of the central government itself. This has made possible the world's most massive and longest-lasting investment boom, a key driver of its spectacular economic growth.

China has benefited from the advantages of its backwardness, both in copying technology and in being able to leapfrog to move ahead rapidly, as for example, avoiding investment in landlines, jumping straight to mobile telephone systems.

One unique aspect of China political and economic system is the meritocracy that prevails at the central government level. China has the most awesomely efficient system for selecting cadres for key governmental and economic positions, especially at the central level as well as for running its SOEs. Starting at college level, detailed records are kept of every promising person, each subject to comprehensive annual evaluations. An absolutely necessary but not sufficient condition of career progress is, of course, loyalty to the single party. Once that is given, promotion is based on meritocracy. Take the current leader, *Xi Jinping*: he had run a large enterprise and then an industry and was also the boss of a region with millions of people, so he has been tried and tested in numerous settings.

And let us not forget about the immense costs of China spectacular growth, such as the pollution that has made many of its major cities practically unlivable, as well as increased income and wealth inequality.

Looking back, is it fair to compare China's 8–10% headline annual growth rate for 35 years with the United States' 3% and West Europe's even slower tempo during the same period? No, I don't think it would be fair, partly because China had started from an incredibly low base and, more importantly, because none of the major drivers of China's growth were duplicable anywhere near on a similar scale in the United States and in other EMEs.

Would it be fair to compare China's 8–10% annual growth with India's slower economic progress? Somewhat more fair, yes, than in the case of EMEs, but still not completely fair. In addition to some of the reasons already mentioned, India's historical experiences and the common aspects of its inherited culture would be certain to prevent an imposed, Chinese-type authoritarian system to yield economic growth dividends over time similar to China's. India also differs from China in the immense diversity of its many subcultures.

Can and should India copy China? No. Can India learn from China? Perhaps yes, certain things, such as focusing on getting rid of certain obstacles to a more rapid growth, be they aspects of India's political and legal system, excessive government bureaucracy, and perhaps also certain dysfunctional aspects of its work culture. Of course, all of this is easy to recommend on paper but immensely difficult to get done.

The key point of this discourse is *not* to conclude that for accelerating economic development, an authoritarian political system is clearly superior to democratic one. Yes, trim those aspects of a democratic political system that clearly constrain and stand in the way of development, but don't throw out the baby with the bathwater.

A word about China's economic future: I am convinced that its growth rate for the next 35 years will be only a fraction of what it had been during the past 35 years. China has now reached a major inflection point in its growth trajectory. It has already been slowing down, the official growth target has recently decreased from 10% to 7.5% and will move further down, soon. This is not the place to enumerate all the well-known reasons for its permanent growth slowdown. Suffice it to say that, in the absence of some unforeseen cataclysm in China or around the glove, China can be expected to growth at around 5% per annum during the next several decades. Still impressive, but not as spectacular as up to now, not a growth performance that countries such as India and other emerging economies could not achieve with major reforms.

KEY DETERMINING FACTORS IN SUSTAINABLE ECONOMIC DEVELOPMENT FOR ANY COUNTRY

Let us agree that the list in the section "An Economic System with Universal Features?" correctly identified the common features of successful economies. Let us agree, further, that the political system sketched at the end of that section is a desirable companion to an economic system that strives to create the right kinds of institutions and policies for development. The question then is: How does a society get there? How can the desirable economic and political system features *be implanted or nurtured* in a newly transforming economy, or neo-transition economy, or, for that matter, in any less-developed country that would like to narrow the development gap with EMEs?

This is a most difficult – but also a very important – question to try to answer.

My search for an answer has led me to the literature on economic development. Scholars have long been investigating why certain countries are rich, what roads had they traveled to get there, and why have others remained poor, why their struggles to escape from widespread poverty have been so much less successful than those of others?

Let me sum up my key take-aways from the literature on development, hoping that its insights may help with the "implant" question. That is, whether and how the transforming and neo-transition economies (and others) might be willing and able to create, adopt and maintain their own suitable versions of a society that is moving in the direction of building the "common economic success features," along with a supporting political system with the above-noted characteristics.

There are four sets of factors (perhaps expandable into five or collapsible into three sets) that, in some combination, largely determine which neo-transition economies (and other emerging or not-yet-emerging economies) might be more (or less) willing and able to build and strengthen the economic and political institutions that are most likely to engender long-term economic success. They are: *geography*, *institutions*, *culture*, and *key historical events/experiences*.

A fifth variable could perhaps be added: the ethnic mix of a people who live in a nation state, be they the majority or one of the minority groups there. If a nation has important minorities that are not well assimilated into the dominant culture, that can cause significant problems for the nation's long-term development, as will be illustrated under culture.[11]

Geography

Geography is location + climate + natural resources, that is, endowments that normally cannot be changed.

With respect to location, a critical factor is access to water transportation inland and access to the seas for participation in regional and global commerce. Countries that are landlocked, such as many in sub-Saharan Africa and in Central Asia's Uzbekistan, Kyrgyzstan, Tajikistan, and Afghanistan, have huge development disadvantages.

Climate is obviously important. High-yield agriculture is often a precondition for economic take-off. High productivity agriculture requires rich soil, sunshine, water, and the right topography, none really changeable (with rare exceptions, such as in tiny Israel perhaps).

Another important aspect of climate is ecology, the interaction among organisms and their environment. A tropical country ravaged by disease, with a high mortality rate, and a large number of children per women of child-bearing age (to compensate for high child mortality), has a huge handicap in saving and investing enough in physical and human capital, both essential for long-term economic growth.

These and other geographic factors often shape decisively which countries develop earlier and which ones emerge later, or not at all.

While each country's geophysical conditions are relatively static, what those conditions mean for economic development can change quickly. For example, being mountainous used to be, *ceteris paribus*, an obstacle to development. This has changed with the invention of hydro-power.

Countries with abundant natural resources (for which there is global demand) have an obvious "geography" advantage. The issue for them is whether they use the money earned to finance broad-based development or squander their resources for other purposes. That, in turn, is largely a question of institutions and culture.

Today, access to renewable resources and the ability to adjust to climate change are key links between geography and economic growth.

Geophysical handicaps don't seal a country's fate. Those handicaps can be overcome, provided that institutions and culture are strong and are harnessed for that purpose.[12]

Institutions

Broadly defined, institutions are society's human-made systems: rules and regulations (formal and informal), including norms and common practices that create incentives for human behavior. A country's political, legal, social, and economic systems are its most important institutions.

One problem – notably important in the case of the transforming economies – is that certain institutions may appear to be similar at first glance, even though there may be fundamental differences in how they operate in practice. For example, many "democratic" countries have "one person one vote" rules but dictators widely hated in their own countries often manage to get 99% of the votes cast (*vide*: North Korea). Another example is educational attainment, measured by what percent of the right age group completes primary, secondary, and tertiary schools. However, such institutional facts do not show, for example, whether the curriculum is preparing students to function well in a modern world or mainly inculcates them with the anti-modern doctrines of the Wahabi version of Islam.

According to a highly regarded recent study, the key difference between rich and poor countries is the degree to which their institutions keep a small elite from grabbing most of the power and wealth. In poor countries, the powerful and the rich crush/overwhelm the powerless and the poor.[13]

Culture

For economic development (and thus for our purposes), culture is defined as belief systems that characterize and differentiate the members of one distinct group from *comparable* other groups from *comparable* groups in other countries.

Belief systems include comprehensive ones, such as religions; Confucianism (not a religion); political and economic ideologies; as well as partial ones, so-called "culture dimensions," such as who do you trust and distrust.

For the purpose of linking culture and economic development, the most appropriate groups to focus on are those based on ethnicity and comprehensive belief systems. They may overlap, as in the case of the Chinese and Confucianism.

Max Weber, a German sociologist in the early 20th century, was one of the first to link cultural and religious values to economic development. He argued that the "Protestant ethic" – supported by Reformation's teachings that the pursuit of wealth was a duty – inculcated the virtues needed for economic development. In his view, that was a key reason that the predominantly Protestant countries and regions of Europe tended to be richer than those of the predominantly Catholic parts of Europe. (There are many exceptions of course, as for any broad generalization.)

An even more persuasive example of the importance of culture promoting economic development is the adherence of the Chinese to Confucius-based values, such as hard work, obedience, the importance of education, and long-term thinking. The latter is manifest, for example, in the extraordinarily high rate of savings of Chinese individuals, households, businesses, and the central government; also the high priority and resources the Chinese (Asians generally) tend to devote to their children's education.

In cultures where women have low status and females obtaining a good education is discouraged or prevented, half the population is excluded from being part of the educated workforce, to the detriment, clearly, of economic growth.

These cultural aspects are very important base factors in shaping growth rates and other indicators of economic performance.

It is possible to collapse institutions and culture into a single factor, "culture," on the grounds that it is the fundamental aspects of a group's culture that do shape the kinds of institutions that a given society creates and maintains.

Historical Events and Experiences

Examples abound in which historical events have shaped for a long time a country's economic situation. Two very simple recent examples can illustrate this.

The current borders of the countries in the Middle East were drawn mostly by the colonial powers for their own purposes, not on the basis of what entities (for example, predominantly Shia or Sunni) would mitigate strife within and among the countries and thereby promote their economic development.

France's and its neighbors' fear of an even stronger Germany in the wake of reunification in 1990 gave the decisive push for deeper European integration via the adoption of a common currency. That event initially promoted – but more recently has severely retarded – the economic performance of the eurozone's southern members. With no solution in sight for the eurozone's many problems linked to its common currency, the future of European integration, and thus their members' long-term economic prospects, have come under question.

SUMMARY AND CONCLUSIONS

This has been a highly unconventional essay – more of a personal manifesto on a range of loosely related topics than a focused paper on a particular issue. The editors deserve some of the blame – or credit – for having given the author *carte blanche* for such wide-ranging ruminations.

The section "Introduction and Outline" introduced the topics to be explored briefly in this paper. The section "Professional Background" was the author's extended biographic statement, showing the types of career experiences that have been shaping – for better or for worse – his reasoning and opinions.

The section "An Economic System with Universal Features?" sketched his views on what dozen features that any economy aspiring for long-term economic success (defined there) should try to create. Partitioning those factors into a dozen categories is of course arbitrary. While compressing them into fewer categories would not be advisable due to the loss of essential details, expanding the dozen factors into several dozen or several hundred could make sense, especially when it comes to implementation, although the greater the detail the more it tends to obscure the essential message. One key take-away of that section is that for sustained good economic performance there is no alternative to a predominantly market-driven economy, supported by appropriate, market-oriented institutions. Another important take-away is that the state has a critically important role in making a market-driven economy function well, that the dichotomy between state versus the market is a false one; that mutually supporting cooperation between them is essential for economic success. Another key point made is that labeling and judging political systems, such as democracy versus totalitarianism, is often grossly misleading and is generally unhelpful. Much more preferable is describing and then shaping those essential features of a political system – characterized briefly at the end of that section – that are supportive of a country's long-term economic success.

The section "Relationship between Economic and Political System Transformation" summarizes the economic and political transformation experiences of 29 former CPEs, the countries that by and large used to form the Soviet empire between the end of World War II and the collapse the USSR and of communism there and in EE. Several chapters in this volume focus on individual country and sector transformation details, so this part of the introductory essay is intended as a useful summary, providing context for the more specialized contributions.

The section "From Transition to Neo-Transition: A Progress Report" offers thoughts on the relationship between economic and political systems. Its key take-aways are that it is often misleading to judge the functionality of a country's political system by its label; another, that don't indict the many possible versions of, say, "democracy" or "authoritarianism" by the particular manifestation that either type of system takes in any particular country at any given time. The author defines a "good" political system – good in a sense that it would protect basic rights and support economic development – without resorting to labels.

The section "China's Economic Growth and Development Model" is devoted to the transformation experiences of China, so very different from those of the 29 countries discussed in the section "Relationship between Economic and Political System Transformation." The key message of this section: it is not China's authoritarian political system that has been largely responsible for the country's impressive economic growth during the past

35 years; rather it is the masterful transformation of its terrible political and economic dictatorship into an impressively well-functioning market economy. While one may doubt whether such a successful economic system transformation could have taken place under instant political "democracy" at transformation's early stages, the emphasis should be on China gradually becoming a capitalist economy, not that China has remained politically totalitarian. I would add, further, that it would not be fair to say that if China had India's messy democracy it would not have been nearly as successful. While this statement is almost certainly true, there are many other real and hypothetical political systems that could be called "democratic" without the dysfunctional aspects of India's or the USA's or other countries' de facto "democratic" systems. Key points: don't judge a political system by its label and don't assume that a change in political system in any direction would be sufficient to fundamentally alter a country's long-term economic performance.

The section "Key Determining Factors in Sustainable Economic Development for Any Country" asks: if it is not the political system, what then are the *fundamental* determinants of a country's long-term economic success. The proposed answer: geography, institutions, culture, and key historical events.

NOTES

1. *Gorbachev's* second reform was his abrogating the Brezhnev Doctrine. The doctrine was announced by Soviet leader *Leonid Brezhnev* after Soviet and allied troops interfered militarily in Czechoslovakia in 1968 to stop the "Prague Spring" reform movement. After the invasion, Brezhnev stated that if a country within the Soviet bloc would try to pursue policies independent of Moscow, any such deviation would be stopped by the Red Army, if necessary. I had the good fortune of being an invited participant in the April 1987 US-USSR roundtable on "East Europe in Soviet-American Relations" in Alexandria, Virginia, at which *Gorbachev's* high-ranking representative, Academician *Oleg Bogomolov*, announced, on behalf of his boss, that the USSR pledges never again to interfere militarily in EE because he considers that pledge essential for a sustained improvement of Soviet-American relations. Lasting *detente* with the United States, in turn, was a precondition for *Gorbachev* being allowed by his Politburo colleagues to reduce military expenditures, a key pillar of his *prestroika* initiative to restructure the Soviet economy. *Zbigniew Brzezinski*, National Security Advisor to US President Carter, responded publicly at the conference that, in his view, *Gorbachev* will not be able to keep this pledge because if it became credibly known that the Red Army would not be used to underprop the Communist regimes in EE, that would promote independence movements not only in EE but also among the many nationalities in the Soviet

Union itself, which *Gorbachev* would have to stop, most probably with the Red Army. However, *Gorbachev* kept his pledge, even allowed the reunification of the two Germanies, thereby promoting precisely those forces of empire disintegration that *Brzezinski* had warned about in 1987.

The third "reform" that *Gorbachev* implemented was fundamental weakening the authority of the conservative, change-resistant, Soviet Communist Party bureaucracy in order to get the *nomenklatura* out of the way of his *perestroika* and *glasnost* ("openness") initiatives. Making the Party bureaucrats uncertain about whether and how they can exercise authority helped to dissolve the very glue that kept the Soviet empire together. Thus, *Gorbachev's* three simultaneous reform initiatives: administrative decentralization of the economy, abrogating the Brezhnev doctrine, and reducing the power of the Party bureaucracy were the fundamental causes of the *timing* of the Soviet Union's and of European communism's collapse during 1989–1991.

2. *Hungary in Transformation to Freedom and Prosperity: Economic Program Proposals of the Joint Hungarian-International Blue Ribbon Commission* (Indianapolis, IN: Hudson Institute, 1990). A good summary of the BRC's recommendations can be found in "A Recipe for a Free-Market Hungary," *The Wall Street Journal*, April 6, 1990.

3. A summary of the conference and of the two volumes is available in my "The Transition to a Market Economy in Central and Eastern Europe," *The OECD Observer*, April/May 1991.

4. His lecture on China's economic reforms, delivered at CEIBS on September 22, 2004.

5. Wu Jinglian discusses that period of China's economic reforms efforts and its economists' interest in reforms elsewhere, including in Hungary, in his major work, available in English (2005).

6. Paul Marer, "Models of Successful Market Economies" in the above cited Marer and Zecchini (1991). I am freely using some of this chapter's text without quotation marks.

7. A rich and compelling book on this topic is Chua (2002).

8. Dikotter (2010). An excerpt: "State retribution for tiny thefts, such as stealing a potato, even by a child, would include being tied up and thrown into a pond; parents were forced to bury their children alive or were doused in excrement and urine, others were set alight, or had a nose or ear cut off. One record shows how a man was branded with hot metal. People were forced to work naked in the middle of winter; 80 percent of all the villagers in one region of a quarter of a million Chinese were banned from the official canteen because they were too old or ill to be effective workers, so were deliberately starved to death." The Great Leap forward ranks, alongside the gulags in the Soviet Union and the Holocaust by Nazi Germany and his allies, as one of the three greatest, man-made mass extinction events of the 20th century. A video summary of the book by its author documents and illustrate the story; worth the time needed to view it: https://www.youtube.com/watch?v=DqFBa9ePWpo

9. The depression's length and depth for the EE group is slightly overstated here by the inclusion of Croatia, whose economy had suffered additional damage during the post-1989 Balkan wars.

10. Anders Aslund is one of the few economists who does call attention to this: (2001).

11. Assimilation is not the same as integration. A group that retains its own identity, culture and customs for generations without adopting the identify, culture, and customs of the host society can be well-integrated but not really assimilated. Examples are the Orthodox Jewish and the Quaker communities in the United States and the Shia versus Sunni Moslem communities in Iraq and elsewhere.

12. For an excellent exposition of the importance of geography for development, see McCord and Sachs (2013).

13. A well-reasoned and documented argument that institutions matter a great deal for economic development is Robinson and Acemoglu (2013).

ACKNOWLEDGEMENT

The author thanks Rustam Jamilov for constructive suggestions on an earlier draft.

REFERENCES

Aganbegyan, A. (1988). The economic challenge of Perestroika *(trans. Pauline M. Tiffin)*. Bloomington, IN: Indiana University Press.

Aslund, A. (2001). *The myth of output collapse after communism*. Washington, DC: Carnegie Endowment for International Peace.

Chua, A. (2002). *World on fire*. New York, NY: Anchor.

Dikotter, F. (2010). *Mao's great famine: The story of China's most devastating Catastrophe*. New York, NY: Walker and Co.

Ernst, M., Alexeev, M., & Marer, P. (1996). *Transforming the core: Restructuring industrial enterprises in Russia and Central Europe*. Oxford: Westview Press.

Jamilov, R., & Akbar, Y. (2015). Introduction to neo-transitional economics. In Jamilov, R., & Akbar, Y. (Eds.), Neo-transitional *economics* (Vol. 16). International Finance Review. Bingley, UK: Emerald Group Publishing Limited.

Jinglian, W. (2005). *Understanding and interpreting Chinese economic reforms*. Mason, OH: Thomson Southwest.

Kornai, J. (2008). *From socialism to capitalism*. Budapest: CEU Press.

Marer, P. (1985). *Dollar GDPs of the U.S.S.R. and the countries of Eastern Europe*. Baltimore, MD: Johns Hopkins University Press.

Marer, P., Arvay, J., O'Connor, J., & Schrenk, M. (1992, May). *Historically planned economies: A guide to the data*. Washington, DC: The World Bank.

Marer, P., & Zecchini, S. (Eds.). (1991). *The transition to a market economy: The broad issues* (Vol. 1). Paris: OECD.

Marer, P., & Zecchini, S. (Eds.). (1992). *The transition to a market economy: Special issues* (Vol. 2). Paris: OECD.

McCord, G., & Sachs, J. (2013, October). *Development, structure and transformation: Some evidence on comparative economic growth*. NBER Working Paper No. 19512. Retrieved from http://www.nber.org/papers/w19512. Retrieved December 5, 2014.

Robinson, J. A., & Acemoglu, D. (2013). *Why nations fail: The origins of power. Prosperity and poverty*. Boston, MA: Crown Business.

USAID. (2013a, July). *Twenty years of USAID economic growth assistance in Europe and Eurasia*. Washington, DC: USAID. Retrieved from http://www.usaid.gov/sites/default/files/documents/1863/EE_20_Year__Review.pdf

USAID. (2013b, September). *The enterprise funds in Europe and Eurasia: Successes and lessons learned*. Washington, DC: USAID.

DEVELOPMENT AND TRANSITION IN SERBIA: ECONOMIC ASPECTS

György Simon, Jr.

ABSTRACT

The study deals with key questions of Serbia's economic development, including the regularities of transforming self-managed socialism to a standard capitalist system. It is based on the concept of endogenous growth and the general theory of market transition. In the empirical part of investigation, the main directions of economic development and transition in Serbia are analysed. Crucial issues of economic policy are also considered with a particular emphasis on the latest phase of transition. Concerning the problems of economic efficiency, an attempt is made to quantify the various types of technical progress and determine their contribution to its overall rate. The macroeconomic role of external factors is quantitatively shown through a globalisation effect related to inflows of FDI. The author believes that the Serbian economy, despite all its problems and difficulties, in principle has the potential necessary for finding adequate answers to the challenges of 'neo-transition'. Of these challenges, he regards as most serious Serbia's ability to comply with the standards of accession to the European Union, which, among others, requires closer regional cooperation.

Keywords: Economic development and market transition; globalisation; integration; Serbia

Neo-Transitional Economics
International Finance Review, Volume 16, 53–96

ISSN: 1569-3767/doi:10.1108/S1569-376720150000016004

INTRODUCTION

The economic aspects of development and transition in Serbia, a country of key importance in the Balkans and a potential future member of the European Union (EU), have some peculiarities which in many respects places it apart from other European nations. A proper analysis of these characteristics requires an investigation of regularities standing behind them in a *longer perspective*, which can contribute to a *clearer vision of the problems and challenges of the current neo-transitional phase* of Serbia's economic development. It is this subject to which the present research is devoted.

In the *specialist literature*, Palairet (2001) analysed the protracted secular decline in the Serbian economy between 1978 and 2000, which antedated the ascendancy of *Slobodan Milošević*[1] but intensified thereafter. Hafner (2002) emphasised that problems originating from the collapse of the Yugoslav state had generated disproportions and insufficient linkage of Serbia's socio-economic development to worldwide trends. In the opinion of Mrdaković Cvetković (2006), the Serbian economy should attract additional sources for its development from abroad and enhance its domestic accumulation by way of stimulating savings. Stefanović (2008) viewed *foreign direct investment* (FDI) as an essential incentive for development and transition. He pointed out that Serbia's economy in the new millennium faced an acute problem of lacking capital, which necessitated a more active attraction of FDI. Cerović and Nojković (2009) investigated the relationship between economic growth and transition. Their empirical results showed a significant impact of initial conditions on economic performance and the outcome of the transition process. Mićić (2009) drew attention to the need for a new industrial policy in view of raising the competitiveness of Serbia's industry in domestic and foreign markets. Uvalić (2010) examined 20 years of economic transition in Serbia. She evaluated in great detail the post-2000 achievements and failures of the radically new course in transition taken after the downfall of the Milošević regime, including macroeconomic performance, institutional reforms, integration with the EU and the impact of the recent global economic and financial crisis. Estrin and Uvalić (2013) revealed the main differences in the volume and structure of FDI in the Western Balkans[2] as compared to Central and Eastern Europe. Using a gravity model of transition economies for the period 1990–2011, they have found that even when the size of economy, distance, institutional quality and prospects of EU membership are taken into account, Western Balkan countries receive less FDI.

The following *theoretical considerations* will provide a framework for our analysis. First, the concepts of economic development and transition and the main characteristics of the stages of transition will be defined. Then the basic version of an endogenous growth model will be presented, which explains economic development, too. The *main directions of development and transition* in the Serbian economy will be analysed with a special attention to the so-called *neo-transitional phase*. Concerning *economic efficiency*, an attempt will be made to quantify components of technical progress and determine their contribution. Finally, before conclusion, the *external factors* of economic growth will be considered by revealing a *globalisation effect* and Serbia's role in regional cooperation.

ECONOMIC DEVELOPMENT AND TECHNICAL PROGRESS

Economic development implies *qualitative* improvements in the use of production factors and structural change. In practice, it is closely related to *economic growth*, usually considered as a *quantitative* change. Moreover, these two concepts are actually *inseparable* from each other, as all countries and social systems are always in the process of development, in which even small quantitative changes of population or wealth can lead to major systemic qualitative changes.

Kaldor (1957, p. 599) has contended that 'the prime mover in the process of economic growth is the readiness to absorb technical change combined with the willingness to invest capital in business ventures'. He developed the concept of *technical progress function* to explain the growth rate of *labour productivity as a measure of technical progress*. Simon Sr. (2008) generalised Kaldor's concept by a more differential treatment of the effect of capital intensity and by an explicit consideration of the role of *education* and *research and development* (R&D). He viewed economic growth as an interaction of labour, physical and human capital and time, which results in the emergence of output. He distinguished reproductive and creative labour. In this context, R&D is the specialised and learning by doing is the non-specialised form of creative labour. Considering the factors of production, Simon Sr.'s *endogenous growth model* can map *three* fundamental *types of technical progress*, and thus economic growth and development, based on *immobile, mobile and creative effects*. These effects reflect learning by doing, the equipment of workers with physical capital and the joint result of education and R&D, respectively. *The first two components operate at the place of application and the third one at the place of creation of new technology.* The variables of the basic version of the *Simon model*, first called so by Ligeti (2002, p. 134), with the exception of M meaning working years, can be found in the appendix and are a function of time. The time index (t) is put out in the case of retarded effects. In the formulas, a capital letter denotes a function and a small letter a parameter, except the variable t.

The endogenous growth model in point can be written down as follows:

$$Y = g\mathrm{M}\exp[F_{\mathrm{K}}(G_{\mathrm{I}} + G_{\mathrm{M}} + G_{\mathrm{KR}})] \tag{1}$$

where the parameter g is the output produced without fixed capital during a working year that approximately corresponds to an economy's initial level of productivity. Among the components in parentheses, G_{I} is a function concerning the immobile, G_{M} the mobile and G_{KR} the creative technical progress.

In formulas:

$$G_{\mathrm{I}} = 1 - \exp\{-g_{\mathrm{I}}F_{\mathrm{K}} - g_{\mathrm{Z}}F_{\mathrm{Z}}\};$$
$$G_{\mathrm{M}} = g_{\mathrm{M}}F_{\mathrm{K}}\exp(-g_{\mathrm{KM}}F_{\mathrm{K}} - g_{\mathrm{ZM}}F_{\mathrm{Z}});$$
$$G_{\mathrm{KR}} = G_{\mathrm{H}}G_{\mathrm{R}}G_{\mathrm{T}},$$

where $G_{\mathrm{H}} = g_{\mathrm{H}}F_{\mathrm{H}}\exp(-g_{\mathrm{KM}}F_{\mathrm{K}})$, $G_{\mathrm{R}} = 1 + g_{\mathrm{R}}F_{\mathrm{R}}^2$ and $G_{\mathrm{T}} = \exp(g_{\mathrm{T}}\Delta t)$, where $\Delta t = t - 1950$.

The *intensity functions* are $F_{\mathrm{K}} = \ln(1 + n_{\mathrm{K}}K/L)$ (capital intensity function); $F_{\mathrm{H}} = \ln(1 + n_{\mathrm{H}}H/L)$ (education function); $F_{\mathrm{R}} = \ln(1 + n_{\mathrm{R}}R_{t-2}/L)$ (research intensity function); and $F_{\mathrm{Z}} = \ln(1 + n_{\mathrm{Z}}\,Z/L)$ (arable land intensity function).

The normalising coefficients are $n_{\mathrm{K}} = 1/385$, $n_{\mathrm{H}} = 1$, $n_{\mathrm{R}} = 1$ and $n_{\mathrm{Z}} = 1$, where the parameter n_{K} refers to the 2000 dollar prices. In the case of *manufacturing*, the components related to land are not taken into consideration.

In the Simon model, the elasticity of output by labour is unity, whereas that by the other factors is jointly zero. Therefore, that model is *homogeneous of degree one, similarly to the neoclassical production function* (see Solow, 1956). As the parameters of the Simon model were determined on the basis of a worldwide investigation of 131 countries (Table 1), a *world model* is at issue supposed to be applicable to any country (see Simon Sr., 2005). Therefore, it will be expedient to apply this model here to the Serbian economy.

Table 1. Parameters of the Basic Simon Model.

No.	Denotation	Estimated Value	*t* Statistics
1	g	522	22.46
2	g_{I}	0.0781	22.45
3	g_{M}	0.319	22.42
4	g_{H}	0.273	22.29
5	g_{R}	278	17.44
6	g_{T}	0.0065	20.28
7	g_{Z}	0.082	20.95
8	g_{KM}	0.34	−22.52
9	g_{ZM}	0.30	−19.14

Source: Simon Sr. (2008, p. 20).

Like in the Solow model, the *returns to factors of technical progress* in the basic Simon model can be written down additively by a logarithmic conversion of both sides of relation (1). The difference is that in our case, the returns to factors of technical progress, except labour, are considered:

$$\Delta \ln\left(Y/g\mathrm{M}\right) = \Delta F_{\mathrm{K}} G_{\mathrm{I}} + \Delta F_{\mathrm{K}} G_{\mathrm{M}} + \Delta F_{\mathrm{K}} G_{\mathrm{KR}} + \Delta \varepsilon \qquad (1')$$

where ε is the estimation error.

The *mechanism of technical progress* outlined by Simon Sr. (2008) suggests that the *specific marginal product of physical capital, with other factors unchanged, will tend not to zero, but to capital productivity* if the quantity of capital is increased beyond all limits. But such an increase is possible only in a *long historical perspective* when today's economy gradually transforms into *automated social production* in which essentially only the *immobile effect* will be operative.

As seen from Table 2, the determination of the Simon model fits the actual productivity values of Serbia, and the standard errors are also acceptable. The cumulative results are better than the annual ones, that is the estimation errors do not cumulate but decrease in time. This is a general feature of the fit of the Simon model, describing in essence the process of economic development. For Serbia, the lower determination for annual results, especially concerning manufacturing, may primarily reflect data problems, which will be discussed below.

Table 2. Fit of the Simon Model for Serbia, 1961–2012 (Dependent Variable: Y/M).

Sphere	Number of Observations	R^2		Standard Error (%)	
		Annual	Cumulative	Annual	Cumulative
Manufacturing and non-manufacturing	572	0.582	0.993	4.5	0.9
Manufacturing	260	0.517	0.991	5.1	0.8
Non-manufacturing	312	0.646	0.994	3.9	0.9
National economy					
Aggregated	312	0.618	0.995	4.4	0.9
Disaggregated	312	0.690	0.998	2.3	0.2

Source: Calculated from the appendix. This also concerns the following tables if not otherwise indicated.
Note: Here R^2 is the uncorrected coefficient of determination, considering that the parameters of the model were not estimated specially for Serbia.

THE CONCEPT AND THEORETICAL FOUNDATIONS OF ECONOMIC TRANSITION

Transition usually implies changing the institutional system of a country, that is the group of institutions and related mechanisms providing a framework for the behaviour of individuals and their interaction. *Economic transition* encompasses the abandonment of a state-guided centrally planned or self-managed market socialist system and construction of the standard capitalist system dominated by not public (social) but private ownership and characterised by a market coordination of the economy instead of a bureaucratic one (see Balcerowicz, 1995; Kornai, 1993).

Economic policy can accelerate or decelerate transition. Its set of tools may, on the one hand, mobilise domestic resources and, on the other, help use opportunities stemming from an economy's openness. The former instruments embrace investment, employment, structural, educational, and science policies; the latter include primarily trade policy and policies related to foreign loans and FDI.

The *complex indices* based on general macro indicators and characterising the success of an economic policy are such that their *negative or zero values are favourable, whereas the positive ones are unfavourable.* The most important are the following indices:

1. The *misery index* is the sum of the rates of inflation and unemployment.
2. The *index of unpopularity* equals the rate of inflation minus three times the growth rate of real gross domestic product (GDP).
3. The *index of disequilibrium* is derived as the budget deficit plus the current account balance (both in percentage of GDP) (Veress, 1997, pp. 239–240).

The transition from socialism to capitalism is a peculiar mix of revolution and evolution. It is a trial-and-error process retaining or liquidating old institutions and accepting or rejecting new ones. The firmer are the foundations of capitalism; the better will be the system's performance in the middle and longer distance (Kornai, 2007, pp. 77–78).

The *starting point* of transition is usually 1989, the year the Berlin Wall fell and many countries in Eastern Europe changed their regimes. Most of them had centrally planned economies under an administrative command system. The only exception was Yugoslavia where full-fledged worker-managed market socialism took root (Rosser & Rosser, 2004, p. 75).

The purpose of the *first*, early regime-changing *phase* of transition is to create fundamental conditions indispensable for a functioning market economy. These are economic stabilisation, price and trade liberalisation, institutional reform with a wide-range deregulation, including the reorganisation of the financial system and a transformation of property rights in the framework of privatisation, the so-called *SLIP tasks*, accompanied by the replacement of the command with market mechanisms in decision making and a liberalisation of the political system. These measures result in the end of *transformational recession* and a switch over to a *sustainable growth* path. Concerning economic policy, a country's membership in the *Organisation for Economic Cooperation and Development* (OECD) is a good indicator of a market maturity in a western sense (see Csaba & Hámori, 2004, pp. 341–359).

In the course of transition, it was not easy to stabilise the economy, as the sudden freeing of prices from central control often led to inflationary outbursts. In most countries, there was a sharp decline in total output, while unemployment was rising. It was still harder to establish a framework for the open and stable functioning of markets, including the banking, financial and accounting systems, a proper competition policy, laws of corporate governance and bankruptcy, opening to trade and investment and foreign currency convertibility. Regarding privatisation, the continuance of state subsidies, known as the *soft budget constraint*,[3] may be more important than the actual pattern of ownership, with countries subsidising firms to avoid increasing unemployment. In many countries, the decay of former social safety nets, accompanied by income inequalities and soaring poverty rates, represented formidable challenges. In many countries, the failure to establish a well-functioning new set of institutional arrangements forced much economic activity underground, with a relationship between income inequality and the size of the underground economy apparently emerging. Moreover, the break-up of the old order in Eastern Europe have seriously aggravated problems of crime and corruption. All that revealed a poor quality of government and a not far advanced level of democracy, especially in the Balkans (Rosser & Rosser, 2004, pp. 75–76).

By the *second phase* of transition, the SLIP tasks should have been accomplished. The institutions of financial intermediation or at least the commercial banks must be well-operative. Now the decision makers are to transform the energy sector, infrastructure, pension system and public health, where deregulation is not enough and complete privatisation is either impossible or not really expedient. When the first phase has come to an end, the question is not the share but the efficiency of the private sector, not the adjustment of inflation and interest rate but the maintenance of their steadily low level. Instead of liberalisation, the reshaping of institutions is put on the agenda. Thus, *sustainability becomes the success indicator of solving second-generation tasks.* Here the methods of trial and error, public debate, and organisation and keeping together of a *reform coalition* are determinant. Now effectiveness and expediency instead of radical measures become the measure of new systemic solutions. Whereas the first phase has aimed mainly at the elimination of distortions, the second is to *create conditions for sustainable development*. By reaching the pre-crisis level, development policy tasks have not yet been solved. Moreover, it is the moment when it turns out that thereafter the conditions of development must be brought into being, including improvements in R&D, education and public security (see Csaba & Hámori, 2004, pp. 361–378).

The author agrees with János Kornai that transition can be considered completed if a country is no longer a one-party state, most of its enterprises are privately owned and the market is the dominant force in decision making. Thus, we can state that transition has actually come to an end in the new post-communist Member States of the EU (Kornai, 2007, pp. 115–117). But it continues in less advanced countries like Serbia.

MAIN DIRECTIONS OF ECONOMIC DEVELOPMENT IN SERBIA

It is difficult to investigate Serbia's economic development with the generally used analytical tools and methods. The main reasons are the specific conditions of Yugoslav socialism and later a decade-long war economy, exacerbated by international isolation, to which the low quality of statistics, especially for the 1990s, must be added (cf. Palairet, 2001, pp. 904–905). Moreover, in the case of Serbia, one can speak of a '*triple transition*' involving political changes, economic reforms, and state- and nation-building (Panagiotou, 2012, p. 39; Sasse, 2005, p. 10).

Between 1961 and 2012, the economy of Serbia grew at a slower rate than the economies of the European Union and the United States. Prior to transition, Serbia's economic growth exceeded that of the EU and U.S., but this achievement was annulled by catastrophic developments during the last decade of the 20th century. Although the growth of Serbian economy was outstandingly rapid through the end of the 1970s, it showed signs of stagnation which turned into the Yugoslav crisis of the 1980s followed by a transformational recession in the 1990s. The acceleration of transition at the turn of millennium resulted in an internationally remarkable rate of GDP growth, comparable to the country's economic results before transition (see Table 3).

Serbia's transition to a market economy since 1989 has been a *contradictory process with repeated setbacks*. It has been not just protracted but also of a different quality than in other Eastern European countries, *gathering a decisive impetus only after the downfall of the Milošević regime* in October 2000. For Serbia, the developments of the 1990s could not be repeated due to dramatic external changes and substantial internal differences, mainly the conservation of Yugoslav heritage in economic activities and, not least, in popular mentality (cf. Uvalić, 2010).

How did the main indicators of *living standard* and *competitiveness* change in Serbia over the investigated period?

Overall, Serbia's GDP per inhabitant and per person employed considerably declined in comparison with the relevant indicators of the EU-15 and U.S., as the general trend of *economic divergence* prevailed. However, between 1960 and 1980, Serbia managed to come closer to the EU and U.S. levels in terms of living standard, and there was even some convergence with the United States regarding productivity. The trend of convergence with the EU and U.S. re-emerged with respect to both indicators

Table 3. Average Annual Change Rate of GDP *in Serbia, the European Union and United States* (at Comparable Prices of 2000, %).

Country, Group	1961–2012	1961–1989	1990–2012	1961–1970	1971–1980	1981–1989	1990–2000	2001–2012
Serbia	1.63	4.26	−1.59	6.01	5.88	0.60	−6.80	3.45
EU-15	2.80	3.54	1.88	4.99	3.16	2.38	2.73	1.10
United States	3.07	3.60	2.39	4.19	3.19	3.41	3.14	1.71

Note. Figures for Serbia here and below exclude Kosovo.
Calculated from: Statistički godišnjak Srbije, Sistem nacionalnih računa Republike Srbije, RZS, Beograd; Statistički godišnjak Jugoslavije/Srbije i Crne Gore, (Savezni) zavod za statistiku, Beograd; National Accounts Statistics, UN, New York; Statistical Abstract of the United States, U.S. Department of Commerce, Bureau of the Census, Washington, D.C., various volumes; U.S. Department of Commerce, Bureau of Economic Analysis; EBRD, Selected Economic Indicators Database; Eurostat, New Cronos Database; *Heston*, Summers & *Aten* (2006); *Bolt* and *van Zanden* (2013).

Table 4. Serbia's GDP per Inhabitant and per Person Employed (in U.S. Dollars of 2000, at PPP*).

Year	GDP per Inhabitant			GDP per Person Employed		
	Serbia (USD)	In percentage of		Serbia (USD)	In percentage of	
		EU-15	United States		EU-15	United States
1960	2,260	26.2	16.1	9,040	46.2	24.4
1970	3,760	29.1	20.2	12,210	39.2	26.2
1980	6,190	36.7	26.9	14,770	36.0	28.7
1989	6,380	31.3	22.3	13,260	27.4	22.4
2000	3,090	12.3	8.8	7,500	13.3	10.4
2012	4,910	18.1	12.7	15,650	25.8	18.5

Source: see Table 3, as well as Yearbook of Labour Statistics, ILO, Geneva, various volumes.
Note: USD 1 = RSD 17.13 and PPS 0.92.

only under the conditions of accelerated transition after the turn of millennium (see Table 4). At the same time, as noted by Teokarević (2011, p. 61), the present standard of living in Serbia is for many people not very different from the war economy of the 1990s.

TRANSITION AND 'NEO-TRANSITION'

When Serbia stepped in a higher phase of socio-economic development in the early 1990s, it turned out that the old economic policies and management methods were incapable of ensuring better achievements or at least maintaining the continuity of foregoing results. The increasing economic and political problems and internal contradictions demonstrated the weaknesses of the Yugoslav model of socialist self-management. Later the protracted transition, incomplete market institutions and the inadequate content of economic policy became the determinant group of factors which still condition the weak competitiveness of Serbian economy (Božić Miljković, 2012, pp. 68–69).

It should be noted that *transition in Serbia has gone through several economic policy cycles* since 1989.

1. Initially, the Serbian leadership countered the radical measures of the federal government headed by *Ante Marković* with a more modest and slower reform policy than in the other former Yugoslav republics. After the disintegration of the former Yugoslavia, Serbia together with Montenegro formed the *Federal Republic of Yugoslavia* (FRY) on 27 April 1992. Milošević's authoritarian nationalist regime involved a rejection of the liberal project, yet maintained a façade of democracy, mixing elements of state socialism, self-management and capitalism. The *suspension and then actual annulment of transition during the 1990s* determined the domination of inefficient social and public ownership, whereas the lack of financial and fiscal discipline led to widespread corruption. The state became an all-powerful arbitrator in a *militarised economy* with selective tax benefits for certain subsidised branches and privileged taxpayers. *Between 1991 and 2000, foreign exchange deposits of the population were frozen. Nominal market institutions did not function* and laws were often unconstitutionally replaced by government decrees. Instead of liberalisation, the government generally took measures aimed to maintain a *rigorous administrative control* (Mijatović, 2005; Pavlaković, 2005). Serbia's economy, which had never recovered from the political crises of the late 1980s, suffered severely from *sanctions* imposed by the United Nations during the wars of Yugoslav succession in 1991–1995 and by the UN and EU during the Kosovo conflict in 1998–2001, not to mention the separate restrictions introduced by the United States (see Đorđević & Lopandić, 2001).
   1.1 The sanctions severely stifled the economy, contributing to shortages of food, goods and fossil fuels. They created conditions for the emergence of a strong criminal element with close ties to the regime. Thus, paramilitary units emerged which cooperated with the regular army (Šešelj's Chetniks, Arkan's Tigers). War and

international sanctions turned weapon smuggling and sanction busting into big business, creating an entire class of wealthy individuals engaged in criminal activities with links to the political, military and economic leaderships. Rampant corruption spread through all facets of society, and the drastic decline in the standard of living, accompanied by economic instability, continued into the post-Milošević era (Pavlaković, 2005, p. 22).

1.2 Yugoslavia was the first country in Eastern Europe to establish diplomatic relations with the European Communities (EC) in October 1968. Two trade agreements were concluded in March 1970 and June 1973, respectively, to make possible the entry of a higher proportion of Yugoslav exports into Western European markets. Yugoslavia signed a *Trade and Cooperation Agreement* (TCA) *with the EC* in April 1980 which took effect three years later and embraced a wide range of issues relating to trade, economic, financial, and scientific and technological cooperation. Simultaneously, a separate agreement was concluded with the European Coal and Steel Community. However, the Yugoslav conflict induced Brussels to abrogate these agreements in November 1991 (Lopandić, 2007, pp. 72–73; Simon Jr., 1997, pp. 14–16, 2001, p. 219). From 1996, the FRY enjoyed a partial preferential treatment for its agricultural and textile exports to the European Union's internal market. Following the normalisation of Yugoslav-Macedonian relations, the EU in its declaration of 9 April 1996 recognised the FRY as one of the successor states of former Yugoslavia and in 1997 for a short time repeatedly put into effect the commercial part of the TCA (Réti, 1998, p. 59; Simon Jr., 1997, p. 17, 2003, p. 118).

1.3 Air strikes by NATO in March-June 1999 destroyed a significant portion of Serbian transport infrastructure and industrial facilities. The subsequent *de facto* loss of the mineral-rich province of Kosovo, along with an embargo on petroleum imports, further aggravated Serbia's difficulties somewhat softened only by humanitarian aid, though at the same time it brought about the cessation of huge budgetary outflows that Kosovo had received since the socialist era. After the democratic changes of 2000, international aid began to flow into the country on a larger scale and sanctions were lifted (see Jelić, 2006; Kovačević & Trifunović, 2009).

2. The *reform programme* announced in October 2000 envisaged a growth of production and employment and a rise in living standard and economic efficiency, as well as a gradual integration with the European

Union (Lazarević & Basara, 2003, p. 65). Within the *Stabilisation and Association Process* (SAP), Serbia (together with Montenegro) became a potential candidate country for EU membership in November 2000. It was also decided that the country would benefit from the EU's autonomous trade preferences.

2.1 *Macroeconomic stabilisation* begun by the government of *Zoran Đinđić* in January 2001 and accomplished by the middle of the decade was based on a tight fiscal policy supported by conditional external financing and a debt rescheduling by international banks. Đinđić and his successors pursued a mix of liberal and social-democratic reform policies with the *European Union as the external mover of transition*. Under the impact of successive agreements with the *International Monetary Fund* (IMF), Serbia's budget became more transparent and comprehensive. As quasi-fiscal deficits were eradicated, the rate of *corporate income tax* was eventually cut to 10% (Bisić, 2005, pp. 143–144).

2.2 On 4 February 2003, the FRY was transformed into the *State Union of Serbia and Montenegro*. After Đinđić's assassination on 12 March 2003, his successor, *Zoran Živković*, shifted the centre of gravity in economic policy towards harmonisation with Montenegro and partially abandoned trade liberalisation. Yet, Belgrade's potential candidate status was confirmed by the EU at the Thessaloniki Summit held in June 2003. Simultaneously, instead of autonomous, extraordinary preferences were introduced by Brussels in the field of trade support.

2.3 *Vojislav Koštunica's* government, which came to power in March 2004, introduced an EU-conform value-added tax (VAT) in January 2005. This was enhanced by the beginning of negotiations for concluding a *Stabilisation and Association Agreement* (SAA) with the EU in October 2005. However, the negotiations were temporarily suspended between May 2006 and June 2007 because of problems concerning Belgrade's cooperation with the International Criminal Tribunal for the former Yugoslavia.

2.4 Fiscal policy was subsequently loosened, as frequent elections encouraged governments to grant generous public-sector wage increases. The dissolution of the State Union came when the Republic of Serbia proclaimed its *independence* on 5 June 2006 following the secession of Montenegro. On 29 April 2008, Serbia's SAA with the EU was officially signed in Luxembourg together with the accompanying *Interim Agreement* (IA). The government of

Miodrag (Mirko) *Cvetković*, formed in July 2008, had to deal with the consequences of the global economic and financial crisis by means of a package aimed at stimulating production, exports and investment and supported by stand-by arrangements with the IMF. On 9 September 2008, the National Assembly of Serbia ratified the SAA and on October 16 the Serbian government unilaterally decided to begin with the implementation of the trade part of IA from 1 January 2009. On 1 March 2012, the European Council granted Serbia official candidate status for EU membership. On 27 July 2012, the government of *Ivica Dačić* took office. On 1 September 2013, the SAA entered into force following its ratification by all EU member states. This opened the way for the start of membership negotiations on 21 January 2014. The parliamentary elections of 16 March 2014 resulted in the formation of a new government majority headed by *Aleksandar Vučić*, which confirmed Serbia's European orientation (see e.g. Alinčić et al., 2008; Lopandić, 2007; Mijatović, 2005; Panagiotou, 2012; Wikipedia, 2014a).

As regards *progress in transition*, the *European Bank for Reconstruction and Development* (EBRD) assesses it through a set of special indicators. These have been used to track developments since 1989. The measurement scale for the transition indicators ranges from 1 to 4+, where 1 represents little or no change from a socialist planned economy and 4+ represents the standards of a developed capitalist market economy. As seen from Table 5, Serbia's overall indicator of transition has come significantly closer to the latter standards since the beginning of that process and especially after 2008 by which year *the key mechanisms of market economy in Serbia had already been formed.*

Table 5. Transition Indicators of Serbia.

Indicator	1989	2000	2008	2009	2010	2011	2012
Large-scale privatisation	1.0	1.0	2.7	2.7	2.7	2.7	2.7
Small-scale privatisation	3.0	3.0	3.7	3.7	3.7	3.7	3.7
Enterprise restructuring	1.0	1.0	2.3	2.3	2.3	2.3	2.3
Price liberalisation	2.7	2.3	4.0	4.0	4.0	4.0	4.0
Trade and foreign exchange system	2.0	1.0	3.7	4.0	4.0	4.0	4.0
Competition policy	1.0	1.0	2.0	2.0	2.3	2.3	2.3
Total	1.8	1.6	3.1	3.1	3.2	3.2	3.2

Source: EBRD, Transition Indicators Database.

Accelerated reforms made the now full-fledged market institutions, including a modernised tax system, totally operable. The majority of socially owned and public enterprises were privatised and restructured. The reform of financial sector not only yielded positive results in price and currency stabilisation, but also increased savings and foreign exchange reserves. The abolition of export quotas and reduction of customs tariffs liberalised the trade regime. A certain progress was achieved in the development of small- and medium-sized enterprises (SMEs), in social protection and insurance, and in reforming education, health care, the civil service and pension system. *Currently, the privatisation of large enterprises and transformation of the non-bank financial institutions are under way, with measures taken to improve competitiveness in the energy sector and infrastructure.*

Despite a substantial progress in privatisation (see e.g. Kontić, 2007; Stošić, 2006), Serbia's *enterprise structure* is still quite complicated comprising: (1) newly formed private enterprises; (2) fully privatised socially owned enterprises; (3) partly privatised 'mixed' enterprises, having private and socially owned capital; (4) holding companies formed on the basis of consolidation, mergers and organisational transformation; (5) socially owned enterprises that did not go for transformation; (6) socially owned enterprises financed by means of soft loans from the government's development funds and partly or largely state-owned on the basis of their debt; (7) state-owned enterprises, most of which emerged during the 1990s (Kovačević, 2003, p. 75).

Vujačić and Vujačić (2011) point out that in the course of *privatisation*, inadequate attention was paid to the need for institutional coherence, which led to results that were not in accord with the goals set out. Stančić, Todorović, and Čupić (2012) note that the ownership concentration in Serbian corporations is very high. Dominant shareholders tend to appoint weak boards, which can lead to serious conflicts between dominant and minority shareholders. *In the absence of strong boards, policy makers in Serbia should develop better legal and institutional mechanisms for protecting minority shareholders.*

A typical example of a privatised Serbian enterprise is *Fiat Automobiles Serbia*, the former *Zastava Automobiles*. This firm based in the city of Kragujevac has produced Italian *Fiat*-based automobiles since 1955. During the 1990s, its production became unstable because of supply problems, while trade sanctions imposed on Yugoslavia made exports impossible. Zastava subsidiaries in the UK and U.S. were forced to cease trading. Moreover, in 1999 NATO bombed the factory in Kragujevac because

Zastava Arms was a major supplier to the Yugoslav Army. In October 2000, after sanctions against the FRY were lifted, car export resumed. In October 2005, an agreement with Fiat was reached for production of the *Fiat Punto* by Zastava under the trademark of *Zastava 10*. In March 2007, Zastava 10 had an 11% share in the Serbian car market. Zastava automobiles were sold in Serbia, Montenegro, Croatia, Macedonia, Greece, Bulgaria, Lebanon, Libya, Syria, Tunisia, Poland, and Egypt (where Zastava cars are produced under the brand of the state-owned *Nasr* car company). On 28 July 2008, Fiat signed a letter of intent to acquire Zastava's Kragujevac plant, investing EUR 700 million in return for a 67% stake in the company then owned by the Serbian state and an additional EUR 100 million of investment from the Serbian government. This was later revised to EUR 300 million. The last Zastava branded car rolled out of the factory on 21 November 2008. After that day, the only car in production remained Zastava 10 which changed name to Punto (see Wikipedia, 2014b).

Erdős (2006, p. 110) emphasises that catching-up is impossible without accelerating technological development and requires an increase in R&D spending. The difference between fast and slowly developing economies mostly arises from the fact that the former sooner adopt or introduce in production the new technologies which are partly the result of their own R&D. As industry, first of all manufacturing, today is still to a significant extent the main field of technological development, it is mostly here that goods embodying modern technology must be produced. Therefore, economic policy aimed to accelerate technological development also appears as a part of industrial policy.

The key component of human capital is embodied in the R&D and innovative activity which has a particular significance for socio-economic development as its main factor and mover. As seen from Table 6, Serbia's R&D expenditure in relation to GDP declined by about three-fifths in the period between 2000 and 2008, but by 2012 surpassed the initial level. Although Serbia's indicator on the whole exceeded the level of Bulgaria, Romania and Macedonia, it lagged behind that of Croatia, Slovenia and even Montenegro, not to speak of the average of the EU-27. Serbia does not have far-reaching ambitions in this respect, as it planned to attain by 2012 only the European Union's expenditure level of the preceding decade. For that purpose, the Serbian government intended to mobilise not only domestic assets, but also the loans received from the EU and the World Bank (RZR, 2009, p. 136). However, the global crisis that broke out in 2008 prevented the attainment of that objective.

Table 6. Gross Expenditure on Research and Development in Percentage of GDP.

Country, Group	2000	2001	2002	2003	2004	2005	2006	2007	2008	2009	2010	2011	2012
Bulgaria	0.51	0.46	0.48	0.48	0.49	0.46	0.46	0.45	0.47	0.53	0.60	0.57	0.64
Croatia	1.08	0.94	0.95	0.98	1.05	0.87	0.76	0.81	0.90	0.85	0.75	0.76	0.75
Macedonia	0.44	0.32	0.26	0.23	0.25	0.25	0.21	0.18	0.23	0.20	0.19	n.a.	n.a.
Montenegro	0.85	0.75	0.74	0.80	1.02	0.92	1.24	1.15	1.21	1.12	0.68	0.41	n.a.
Romania	0.37	0.39	0.38	0.39	0.39	0.41	0.45	0.53	0.58	0.47	0.46	0.50	*0.42*
Serbia	*0.93*	*0.54*	*0.51*	*0.56*	*0.32*	*0.43*	*0.48*	*0.50*	*0.38*	*0.92*	*0.79*	*0.77*	*0.96*
Slovenia	1.39	1.50	1.47	1.27	1.40	1.44	1.56	1.45	1.66	1.85	2.10	2.47	2.80
EU-27	1.86	1.86	1.87	1.86	1.83	1.82	1.85	1.85	1.91	2.01	2.01	2.05	2.06

Source: Izveštaj o razvoju Srbije, RZR, Beograd, various volumes; Eurostat, New Cronos Database; OECD, Main Science and Technology Indicators Database; UNESCO Institute for Statistics, Montréal Data Centre.

ECONOMIC POLICY ISSUES

The degree of success of Serbia's transitional *economic policy* can be indicated by the *calculated macro indices* mentioned above. As seen from Table 7, the total index, calculated for the post-Dayton[4] period (1996–2013), markedly improved in 1997, mainly due to a very rapid economic growth and significant decreases in inflation and current account deficit. Then it rose sharply under the impact of the Kosovo crisis in 1998–1999. The present phase of market reforms initially further worsened the total index, but an improvement began after 2001. This was interrupted in 2008 but resumed a year later. The indicator in point deteriorated again in 2011 and 2012 but somewhat improved in 2013. Its most favourable value was attained in 2004 as a result of outstanding growth and a marked improvement in economic equilibrium. In that year, inflation decreased and the general government balance became positive. The subsequent deficit remained under 3% up to 2009, but later became higher. In 2012, the authorities implemented a range of tax increases, lowered the indexation of wages and pensions and adopted a medium-term fiscal strategy (IMF, 2013, p. 45). IMF arrangements have helped improve policy implementation but progress has been undone between programs, especially during political transitions related to government changes (Ibid. 75).

What characterised the *dynamics of* Serbia's *gross domestic product* after 1989?

Table 7. Calculated Macro Indices of Serbia between 1990 and 2013 (Average of Annual Values, %).

Year	Inflation: Consumer Price Index *a*	Rate of Unemployment *b*	Misery Index *c* (*a* + *b*)	Real GDP *d*	Unpopularity Index *e* (*a*−3*d*)	General Government	Current Account	Disequilibrium Index *h* −(*f* + 2*g*)	Total *c* + *e* + *h*
						Balance in percentage of GDP			
						f	*g*		
1990	578.2	10.9	589.1	−7.9	601.9	n.a.	n.a.	n.a.	n.a.
1991	122.3	12.1	134.4	−11.6	157.1	n.a.	n.a.	n.a.	n.a.
1992	8924	13.5	8937.5	−27.9	9007.7	n.a.	n.a.	n.a.	n.a.
1993	216[a]	14.2	216[a]	−30.8	216[a]	n.a.	n.a.	n.a.	n.a.
1994	3.3	14.3	17.6	2.5	−10.8	−2.8	n.a.	n.a.	n.a.
1995	78.6	13.4	92.0	6.1	60.3	−5.4	n.a.	n.a.	n.a.
1996	94.3	12.2	106.5	7.8	70.9	−4.8	−9.6	24.0	201.4
1997	18.3	12.3	30.6	10.1	−12.0	−9.5	−6.5	22.5	41.1
1998	30.0	12.8	42.8	1.9	24.3	−6.8	−4.2	15.2	82.3
1999	41.1	13.3	54.4	−18.0	95.1	−10.4	−4.4	19.2	168.7
2000	70.0	12.1	82.1	5.2	54.4	−1.0	−2.4	5.8	142.3
2001	91.8	12.2	104.0	5.6	75.0	−6.2	2.4	−1.4	177.6
2002	19.5	13.3	32.8	3.9	7.8	−8.3	−4.1	16.5	57.1
2003	11.7	14.6	26.3	2.4	4.5	−1.1	−7.5	16.1	46.9
2004	10.1	18.5	28.6	8.3	−14.8	0.9	−13.4	−25.9	−12.1
2005	16.5	20.8	37.3	5.6	−0.3	0.9	−8.4	−15.9	21.1
2006	12.7	20.8	33.5	5.2	−2.9	−2.6	−9.8	22.2	52.8
2007	6.5	18.1	24.6	6.9	−14.0	−2.4	−13.7	29.8	40.4
2008	11.7	13.6	25.3	5.5	−4.8	−2.0	−21.6	45.2	65.7
2009	7.7	16.1	23.8	−3.1	17.0	−3.7	−7.1	17.9	58.7
2010	6.2	19.2	25.4	1.6	1.4	−3.6	−7.2	18.0	44.8
2011	11.0	23.0	34.0	1.6	6.2	−4.9	−9.1	23.1	63.3
2012	7.8	23.9	31.7	−1.5	12.3	−6.5	−10.7	27.9	71.9
2013	7.8	23.6	31.4	2.4	0.6	−4.8	−7.0	18.8	50.8

[a]In thousand billions of index points.

Calculated from: Statistički godišnjak Srbije; Bilten javnih finansija, Ministarstvo finansija, Beograd, Yearbook of Labour Statistics, various volumes; EBRD, Selected Economic Indicators Database; Eurostat, New Cronos Database; IMF, World Economic Outlook Database; WIIW database incorporating national statistics.

Because of the Yugoslav conflict and the ensuing embargo, a very sharp *transformational recession* occurred in the Serbian economy between 1990 and 1993. At the nadir of this downturn, in 1993, Serbia's GDP was slightly over two-fifths (41%) of its 1989 level. After rising to 53% in 1998, it fell back to 44% in 1999 as a consequence of NATO bombings. The recent global crisis led in Serbia to a macroeconomic decline of over 3% in 2009. As a result of resumed growth, the country's GDP in 2013 stood at 71% of its 1989 value. All this indicates that *the Serbian economy is still far away from the end of the reconstruction period* (see Table 7).

In Serbia's economy, *agriculture dominated by individual producers still plays an important role*. The long transformational crisis has brought about *structural changes* in favour of branches with simpler technologies and lower import content such as agriculture, food industry and generation of electric energy. The agricultural sector has shifted from livestock to crop production and from commercial to subsistence provision. Industry similarly has regressed from the high-technology production of consumer durables to the making of single-use commodities. The structural shifts extended also into the run-down of infrastructure and towards the attrition of human capital (Palairet, 2001, p. 917). The *partial deindustrialisation* which took place in the former communist states of the Balkans after 1989 was aggravated in the case of Serbia by the wars and sanctions of the 1990s. Their negative consequences were felt even later, as the share of *manufacturing*, which traditionally dominates Serbian industry, declined between 2000 and 2012 from 23.3 to 16.7% of total gross value added and from 23.7 to 17.1% of total employment (calculated from: RZS database). Deindustrialisation, which almost became the symbol of Serbian transition, has not yet been replaced by an opposite trend, as Serbia's manufacturing production in 2012 still made up less than two-fifths of its 1989 level (see the appendix).

Mass unemployment, which had already existed before transition, was primarily related to the *crisis of large-scale industry* built under socialism when many manufacturing sites were selected to provide job opportunities for political constituencies rather than for inherent advantages in the production process. That problem was exacerbated by a *massive influx of refugees* starting with the outbreak of the Yugoslav conflict from the Serb-populated areas of Croatia, Bosnia and Herzegovina and later Kosovo. High unemployment in Serbia has also been a consequence of slow job creation, which can be attributed mostly to a poor business environment and in particular to strong regulations on protection of employment. Overall, more attention has been paid to the preservation of existing jobs than to creation of new opportunities for employment. In addition, job creation is also slowed down by relatively high unit labour costs, mostly a result of the pressure on wages by insiders, that is workers in socially owned enterprises or privatised companies (Popović, 2005, pp. 51, 62–63).

But the most unfavourable development has been the *hyperinflation*[5] which occurred in the early 1990s and was one of the highest in world history. A short-term stabilisation effort was made during July-September 1992, based on a deceleration of money supply growth and a mild form of price control. However, inflation accelerated again in the first months of 1993 and 'exploded' in July reaching rates of several thousand per cent per month. Finally, in January 1994 the federal government carried out a successful anti-inflationary and economic *recovery programme* based on strict measures of monetary and fiscal policies. The currency and prices were stabilised, official exchange reserves sharply increased, and there was a remarkable recovery of public finances (see Avramović, 1995) though later *galloping inflation* returned.

After the *October changes of 2000*, the new authorities temporarily succeeded in curbing the inflation, primarily due to a price liberalisation initiated by the outgoing regime. But high public spending crowded out both domestic investment and exports, thus making the accomplished results unsustainable. Financial sanctions were also lifted after the victory of democratic forces, which generated an additional positive effect on economic activity and the population's personal incomes. However, the failure to impose hard budget constraints and successfully carry out institutional reforms led to a new rise in aggregate demand, unemployment and balance-of-payments deficit. The *policy of encouraging domestic demand* had helped to mitigate the consequences of price liberalisation for the poorest segments of the population, but in time it turned into a 'reform trap', which practically blocked further change for a while (Popović, 2005, p. 33, p. 35, pp. 49–50). High inflation, coupled with a constant devaluation of the dinar, has hit the population very hard with the result that around 700,000 people are estimated to be currently living under the poverty line (Teokarević, 2011, p. 61).

ECONOMIC GROWTH AND EFFICIENCY

Let us now see the *main characteristics of Serbia's economic growth* in the investigated period of 1961–2012 (Table 8).

Table 8. Main Characteristics of Serbia's Economic Growth.

Year	National Economy			Manufacturing		
	Y	*Y/M*	*K/Y*	*Y*	*Y/M*	*K/Y*
1960	15.03	9.043	1.850	1.12	2.188	2.518
1989	50.37	13.255	3.613	6.84	6.140	2.905
2000	23.21	7.502	4.160	2.61	3.561	4.276
2012	34.87	15.651	3.014	2.62	6.895	6.107
Period	Average annual change (%)					
1961–2012	1.63	0.95	1.01	1.75	2.22	1.76
1961–1989	4.26	1.33	2.33	6.44	3.62	0.49
1990–2012	−1.59	0.73	−0.79	−4.09	0.51	3.28
1990–2000	−6.80	−5.04	1.29	−8.39	−4.83	3.58
2001–2012	3.45	6.32	−2.65	0.03	5.66	3.01

Note: *Y* and *K* are in billion dollars of 2000; *Y/M* is in thousand dollars per working year.

1. The rate of macroeconomic growth in Serbia after the turn of millennium, viz. in 2001–2012, was not much lower than under socialism between 1961 and 1989. Considering the whole investigated period, the Serbian economy was characterised by a *predominantly intensive growth*, over half of which was ensured by the rise in productivity.
2. The rise in *productivity* in the transition period was slower than in the socialist era.
3. The *capital-output ratio* (*K/Y*) showed in most cases a diminishing trend at a macro level, while it was increasing in manufacturing industry. As a consequence of general *capital deepening*, capital productivity (*Y/K*) in 2012 reached only three-fifths of the 1960 level in the total economy and two-fifths in manufacturing.
4. The capital-output ratio is twice higher in manufacturing than in the national economy, that is capital productivity is about half of the latter.
5. Productivity in manufacturing is still far from catching up with the macroeconomic average. In this respect, one should bear in mind that at a manufacturing level, Serbia's renewed growth was substantially slower than in the economy as a whole. The sluggish recovery in manufacturing was connected with the fact that the majority of industrial enterprises had long lost their markets. In addition, the accumulated losses, redundancy and low capacity utilisation rates made business operation even more difficult (Bukvić & Kovačević, 2008, p. 61).

What was the *role of individual factors in* the Serbian economy's *technical progress*?

This question can be answered with the help of the general model described above. Here Serbia's data from the appendix were put in relation (1′) so as to determine the factors of technical progress.

What conclusions can be drawn from the obtained results shown in Table 9?

1. The actual performance of Serbian manufacturing was on the whole significantly lower than its performance according to the model. However, the macroeconomic results were much better in the given respect.
2. The performance of manufacturing deviated much more from the model calculations than the performance of total economy.
3. Regarding the rate of technical progress, Serbia's economy managed on the whole to achieve better results in the socialist era than during transition.
4. It was the immobile factor related to learning by doing that had the largest share in the total economy's technical progress followed by the mobile and creative factors, reflecting the equipment of workers with physical capital and the combined effect of education and R&D, respectively.
5. The manufacturing production was primarily determined by the mobile component of technical progress. Here the immobile component held the second and the creative component the third place.

Table 9. Returns to Factors of Technical Progress in Serbia.

Period	Annual Average in Per cent					In Percentage of $\Delta\ln(Y/gM)$			
	$\Delta\ln(Y/gM)$	$\Delta F_K G_I$	$\Delta F_K G_M$	$\Delta F_K G_{KR}$	$\Delta\varepsilon$	$\Delta F_K G_I$	$\Delta F_K G_M$	$\Delta F_K G_{KR}$	$\Delta\varepsilon$
National economy[a]									
1961–2012	1.055	0.504	0.345	0.227	−0.021	47.8	32.7	21.5	−2.0
1961–1989	1.317	0.632	0.435	0.253	−0.003	48.0	33.0	19.2	−0.2
1990–2012	0.724	0.345	0.236	0.174	−0.031	47.6	32.6	24.1	−4.3
2001–2012	6.130	2.832	1.919	1.526	−0.147	46.2	31.3	24.9	−2.4
Manufacturing									
1961–2012	2.207	0.790	1.024	0.640	−0.247	35.8	46.4	29.0	−11.2
1961–1989	3.559	1.185	1.676	0.964	−0.266	33.3	47.1	27.1	−7.5
1990–2012	0.504	0.197	0.229	0.158	−0.080	39.1	45.5	31.3	−15.9
2001–2012	5.507	2.142	2.363	1.636	−0.634	38.9	42.9	29.7	−11.5

[a]Calculated from aggregated data.

6. After the turn of millennium, the creative factor came nearer to the second place in the total economy, while the share of mobile factor was declining in manufacturing.

How did the *elasticity of output by growth factors* change in Serbia over the investigated period? Data in Table 10 allow us to draw the following conclusions.

1. The *elasticity by fixed capital* rose to the end of the socialist era in the national economy and to the end of study period in manufacturing. At the macro level, it substantially declined between 1989 and 2000 and did not reach the 1989 level by 2012.
2. The *weight of education* used to be higher in manufacturing than in the economy as a whole. It constantly rose between 1960 and 2000, but fell back after the turn of millennium.
3. The *elasticity by researchers* was continuously increasing. In this respect, manufacturing also surpassed the macroeconomic average.
4. The role of the *time factor* rose in importance as the time of the creative economic activity in the general model made it possible to achieve increasing results.
5. The *elasticity by arable land* declined under socialism, but later began to rise, presumably under the impact of post-socialist deindustrialisation.
6. The situation of *workers in production* is fundamentally determined by the joint elasticity of output by factors L and M, the indicator $L + M$. If it is positive, it will pay off for the working collectives or entrepreneurs to draw new workers into production. If it is negative, the reduction of personnel will be more advantageous.[6] In Serbia, the indicator at issue was continuously declining, but remained positive both at the macro and industrial levels to the end of the investigated period. This means that the Serbian economy, despite all its crisis phenomena, in principle possesses the practical conditions necessary for the solution or at least mitigation of the acute problem of unemployment through creation of new jobs.

What changes happened to the *returns to* key *growth factors*?

As seen from Table 11, the *returns to* the gross volume of *fixed capital* in manufacturing were, as a rule, below the macroeconomic average. These returns were usually declining. The only increase in this respect occurred at the macro level during the acceleration of transition. The *returns to education* increased significantly in the course of the first two decades of the investigated period. After 1989, however, they suffered a setback, especially

Table 10. Elasticity of Output by Growth Factors in the Serbian Economy.

Factor	National Economy[a]						Manufacturing					
	1960	1970	1980	1989	2000	2012	1960	1970	1980	1989	2000	2012
K	0.416	0.468	0.494	0.509	0.494	0.499	0.355	0.414	0.436	0.442	0.453	0.540
H	0.196	0.204	0.217	0.230	0.256	0.241	0.232	0.233	0.240	0.250	0.280	0.267
R	0.0056	0.0125	0.0202	0.0286	0.0484	0.0557	0.0095	0.0189	0.0294	0.0411	0.0623	0.112
Δt	0.00353	0.00381	0.00424	0.00465	0.00555	0.00578	0.00365	0.00414	0.00472	0.00517	0.00590	0.00756
Z	0.013	0.011	0.008	0.007	0.009	0.010	–	–	–	–	–	–
L	−0.634	−0.699	−0.743	−0.779	−0.813	−0.811	−0.600	−0.670	−0.710	−0.738	−0.801	−0.927
$L + M$	0.366	0.301	0.257	0.221	0.187	0.189	0.400	0.330	0.290	0.262	0.199	0.073

Note: $\Delta t = g_T F_K G_{KR}$.

[a]Calculated from disaggregated two-sector data (manufacturing and non-manufacturing).

Table 11. Returns to Fundamental Growth Factors in the Serbian Economy.[a]

Factor	Unit of Measurement	Sphere	1960	1970	1980	1989	2000	2012
K	Dollar/dollar %	National economy	22.5	18.4	16.6	14.1	11.9	16.6
		Manufacturing	14.1	13.9	15.5	15.2	10.6	8.8
H	Dollar/schooling year	National economy	357	429	456	387	217	409
		Manufacturing	102	152	200	195	113	200
R	Thousand dollars/person	National economy	0.018	0.050	0.105	0.121	0.097	0.154
		Manufacturing	0.005	0.015	0.038	0.052	0.043	0.101

[a]In dollars of year 2000.

at the macro level, which lasted until the turn of millennium. The subsequent acceleration of market reforms resulted in an improvement of relevant performance. The *returns to research and development* were relatively low, particularly in manufacturing, and their increase was also interrupted by the extraordinary circumstances of the 1990s.

INVESTMENT, EXTERNAL CONDITIONS AND THE GLOBALISATION EFFECT

An efficient economic growth must be fuelled by investment with an economic policy encouraging that investment increases faster than output (cf. Erdős, 2006, p. 26). Serbia's GDP grew on average by 1.6%, whereas fixed investments declined by 0.7% per annum over the investigated period of 1961–2012 (calculated from the Appendix). Before transition, in 1961–1989, the growth rate of GDP and investment in Serbia accounted for 4.3 and 2.5%, respectively, which does not attest to an investment-led growth either. *A protracted socio-economic crisis led to a drastic decline in investment activity after 1989.* By 2000, the real value of fixed investments fell back to less than a fifth of their 1989 level. More than a decade total investment was lower than depreciation, that is the consumption of fixed assets. Modest investment activity, weak corporate governance and hidden unemployment restrained productivity, the low level of which caused low incomes and corporate insolvency (Simon Jr., 2003, pp. 110–111).

The October changes of 2000 brought about a recovery in investment activity. In 2001–2012, investments in Serbia increased by 4.6% per annum in contrast to a 3.5% GDP growth which thus became clearly investment-driven. Nevertheless, by 2012 just over a third of the 1989 level of investment was achieved (see the appendix).

The *National Investment Plan* (NIP), accepted by the government in September 2006 and aimed fundamentally at infrastructural investments was regarded as an important instrument of promoting the country's European integration (Novák, 2007, pp. 115–117; Popović, 2005, p. 71). However, despite the NIP and other documents adopted by the government, Serbia does not seem to have any effective anti-crisis strategy. The same is true for such pressing issues as reducing the overgrown public sector, or the elimination of excessive regulations that prevent rather than support the development of private business, or the fight against corruption. Among the main reasons why effective, systematic and long-term solutions to such pressing issues have not been found, one can cite the survival of vested interests of wealthy and influential oligarchs, incompetence and poor coordination within the government (Teokarević, 2011, pp. 61–62).

In the *external economic sphere*, Serbia from the early 1990s had an official and a free market *exchange rate*. The former served to make the elite rich, while the latter was used in everyday transactions. The *unified exchange rate introduced in October 2000* was used as a *nominal anchor* for curbing inflation. It involved a strong real appreciation of the dinar against the dollar, which suited importers, and continued under the regime of *managed float after a 'small speculative shock' in November 2002*. The *return to the nominal anchor from 2005* led to a slight depreciation, but in 2006 the dinar became more expensive again, having substantially weakened only under the impact of the global crisis after 2008 (see EBRD, Selected Economic Indicators Database). Actually, *the dinar has always been overvalued.* Exporters have been discouraged by the privileged position of importers. The tight monetary and budget policy pursued under the pressure of IMF, which found expression in cutting subsidies, streamlining public administration and ensuring a balanced budget, contributed to the strengthening of macroeconomic stability. However, it also reduced private consumption, narrowed borrowing and investment opportunities. *The strong dinar caused a catastrophic deficit of current account balance*, unfavourably touching the sustainability of rapid growth. Today the stability of the dinar is still under threat, as Serbia has one of the highest inflation rates in Europe (Mijatović, 2005, pp. 20–21; Popović, 2005, p. 54, pp. 56–57, pp. 81–82, p. 87; Novák, 2007, p. 119; Teokarević, 2011, p. 61).

Serbia is a closed economy by regional standards, with a stable ratio of goods exports to GDP of about 20% over 2006–2012. The degree of Serbia's economic openness has temporarily been further reduced by the recent economic crisis. The share of merchandise exports in Serbia's GDP is usually only half of the share of merchandise imports, which is conditioned by a relatively low coverage of imports by exports (see Table 12).

Since the achievement of independence, more than half of Serbia's foreign trade has fallen upon the European Union. Of the other partners, the Newly Independent States, that is the former Soviet Union except the Baltic States, have a particularly significant share in Serbia's imports (see Table 13).

Serbia has comparative advantages for primary goods and products of lower phases of processing. This caused it serious difficulties in the neo-transitional period. The bulk of commodity flows determining the profile of

Table 12. Share of Foreign Trade in Serbia's GDP (at Current Prices, %).

Year	Exports of Goods (1)	Imports of Goods (2)	Degree of Openness (1 + 2)	Coverage of Imports by Exports, %
2006	21.4	44.9	66.3	47.7
2007	23.2	47.4	70.6	49.0
2008	15.8	43.8	59.6	36.0
2009	14.1	35.9	50.0	39.4
2010	25.2	44.5	69.7	56.6
2011	25.6	43.6	69.2	58.8
2012	27.9	45.4	73.3	61.4

Calculated from: Eurostat, New Cronos Database.

Table 13. Serbia's Foreign Trade by Main Partners.

Year	In Percentage of Exports				In Percentage of Imports			
	EU-27	NIS	U.S.	Others	EU-27	NIS	U.S.	Others
2006	58.2	7.2	1.1	33.5	54.4	19.6	1.8	24.2
2007	58.1	6.8	1.0	34.1	55.1	17.1	2.0	25.8
2008	48.5	6.3	0.5	44.7	51.4	19.2	2.1	27.3
2009	46.7	6.9	0.9	45.5	52.9	15.6	2.5	29.0
2010	58.7	8.3	0.7	32.3	54.8	15.6	1.9	27.7
2011	59.0	9.4	0.7	30.9	53.5	17.0	1.8	27.7
2012	59.2	10.2	0.9	29.7	55.5	15.5	2.1	26.9

Calculated from: See the preceding table.

exports have not changed substantially since the 1990s. These are, above all, food items, agricultural raw materials, basic metals, chemicals, textiles and clothing; that is mainly products of decreasing importance in international trade. The structure of imports, though less unfavourable than that of exports, also points to a weak economic performance (Nikolić, 2006: 306).

The high degree of *dependence on fuel imports* (see Table 14) explains the willingness of Serbian government to maintain close ties with Russian suppliers of crude oil and natural gas and its keen interest in Moscow's pipeline projects such as the South stream. The latter project has caused frictions not only in relations with the European Commission which promotes alternative projects excluding Russia. Although machinery and vehicles is a very significant commodity group, it has a more pronounced role in imports than exports, which attests to a considerable economic and technological lag. This determines *low* international *competitiveness* of Serbian products, which ranks below their regional peers.[7]

Serbia's external debt is relatively high by international standards. Moreover, its total debt stock has almost doubled since the proclamation of independence. The relative weight of long-term debt increased from 88.3% in 2006 to 89.7% in 2012. The share of non-guaranteed private long-term loans rose from 49.3 to 50.0%, respectively, which attested to an unfavourable debt structure. At the same time, the share of short-term debt declined from 11.3 to 3.0%, which was a positive development. *The recent financial crisis led to an increasing use of IMF credit.* The latter's contribution to total debt stock jumped from 0.4% in 2006 to 6.8% in 2009 and

Table 14. Commodity Structure of Serbia's Foreign Trade.

Year	In Percentage of Exports							In Percentage of Imports						
	1	2	3	4	5	6	7	1	2	3	4	5	6	7
2006	18.4	4.8	3.5	10.1	11.0	52.0	0.2	6.1	5.1	19.8	14.2	25.6	29.1	0.1
2007	17.9	5.9	2.6	10.5	12.7	49.9	0.5	5.4	3.9	17.2	14.0	28.7	30.8	0.0
2008	16.0	5.5	3.4	10.1	17.4	46.7	0.9	5.6	4.2	20.4	13.8	27.1	28.9	0.0
2009	22.1	5.2	4.8	8.0	15.2	43.1	1.6	7.2	3.8	16.1	17.0	26.6	29.2	0.1
2010	21.1	6.5	5.3	9.0	14.5	42.1	1.5	6.9	4.5	20.1	15.6	23.5	29.3	0.1
2011	20.9	7.6	4.2	8.6	15.0	42.7	1.0	6.9	4.5	20.9	15.6	23.6	28.3	0.2
2012	21.1	6.9	3.5	8.1	22.4	37.1	0.9	6.8	3.5	17.6	16.5	23.5	32.0	0.1

Note. 1 = food and drink, 2 = raw materials, 3 = energy carriers, 4 = chemicals, 5 = machinery and vehicles, 6 = other manufactured goods, 7 = other.
Calculated from: RZS database.

7.3% in 2012. Although overall interest payments by Serbia remained relatively low, the total debt stock after 2008 exceeded 80% of gross national income (GNI), while total debt service used to be higher than the relevant 25% critical level (see Table 15).

On 6 July 2010, an *Agreement on Macro Financial Assistance* (MFA) to Serbia in the amount of EUR 200 million was signed. This was conditional upon Serbia maintaining a disbursing programme within the IMF as the key facility to help the government in addressing the country's external financial needs. The MFA funds would become available upon a satisfactory fulfilment by the Serbian authorities of a set of requirements mainly related to reforms aiming at establishing a more transparent, coherent and responsible public finance management system (Panagiotou, 2012: 136).

Donor conferences held in December 2000, June 2001 and November 2003 provided *humanitarian assistance* and loans on favourable terms (Pobulić, 2006, p. 287). In 1999–2008, the country received USD 5.8 billion dollars (EUR 4.9 billion) of official aid, three-fifths of which consisted of grants (53.9% was development and 6.1% humanitarian assistance) and two-fifths of concessional loans. This made up on average 2.8% of GDP. The most important donor was the European Union, whose principal programme commitments within the SAP accounted for EUR 1.7 billion, or 0.8% of Serbian GDP, over the period at issue (calculated from: *Izveštaj o međunarodnoj pomoći Republici Srbiji, Ministarstvo finansija, Beograd*, various volumes). The EU *Instrument for Pre-Accession Assistance* allocated about EUR 1.2 billion to Serbia for the period 2007–2012 (Panagiotou, 2012, p. 136). *A considerable part of these foreign assets was transferred to imports*. Yet, they became an additional stimulus for domestic production and strengthened the purchasing power of population. Their formidable volume mitigated the negative socio-economic consequences of the events of the 1990s and fostered further economic growth (Mijatović, 2005, pp. 28–29; Kovačević & Trifunović, 2009, p. 67). However, their *long-term growth effect* was *negligible*.

In Serbia, because of low domestic savings, *foreign capital is an important source of financing not only fixed investments but also consumption*. The most important data on direct investments regarding Serbia are contained in Table 16. They show that the Serbian economy between 1980 and 2012 was characterised by net capital imports, the extent of which was increasing over time, whereas on average about a fifth of total FDI inflows went to manufacturing (see the appendix). It should be noted that a drastic decline in FDI after 2006, along with high foreign trade, current account and budget deficits, forced the government to keep borrowing which seriously

Table 15. External Debt of Serbia, 2006–2012.

Year	Total Debt Stock	Long-Term Debt	Of which: Public and publicly guaranteed loans	Of which: IBRD	Of which: Non-guaranteed private loans	Use of IMF Credit	Short-Term Debt	Total Debt Stock	Interest Payments on External Debt	Total Debt Service as % of Exports[a] and Primary Income
	USD million							In percentage of GNI		
2006	19,886	17,560	7,752	2,127	9,808	85	2,241	69.0	2.1	n.a.
2007	26,212	23,873	8,469	2,326	15,404	90	2,249	68.7	2.4	25.7
2008	30,493	26,719	8,399	2,276	18,320	87	3,687	65.7	2.7	30.0
2009	33,814	27,915	8,839	1,783	19,076	2,299	3,600	85.5	2.6	37.0
2010	32,935	27,417	9,505	1,818	17,912	2,720	2,798	91.2	2.4	30.9
2011	31,724	27,779	11,339	1,859	16,440	2,783	1,162	75.1	2.3	31.5
2012	34,438	30,904	13,696	1,915	17,208	2,517	1,017	94.8	2.8	36.7

Source: The World Bank, World Development Indicators Database.
[a]Goods and services.

Table 16. Serbia's FDI Inflows and Outflows in Percentage of GDP and Fixed Assets.

Year	Cumulative Foreign Direct Investment in U.S. Dollar Prices of 2000					
	In percentage of GDP			In percentage of fixed assets		
	Inflow (1)	Outflow (2)	Balance (1−2)	Inflow (1)	Outflow (2)	Balance (1−2)
1980	0.04	–	0.04	0.01	–	0.01
1989	0.16	–	0.16	0.05	–	0.05
2000	6.66	0.01	6.55	1.60	0.002	1.598
2012	63.69	4.89	58.80	21.13	1.62	19.51

Note. FDI data in current prices were deflated with the U.S. investment price index taken from the Bureau of Economic Analysis, U.S. Department of Commerce.

aggravated the problem of external indebtedness (Teokarević, 2011, p. 61). On the other hand, significant capital exports from Serbia appeared only starting in 2000 when the lifting of sanctions allowed Belgrade to become again a full-fledged participant of international economic relations.

Foreign investors usually choose Serbia as a destination country of their business mindful of a number of circumstances. They consider (1) Serbia's strategic geographical location half-way between Western Europe and the Middle East, (2) attractive investment incentives based on a competitive tax regime, (3) the multilingual and highly skilled workforce, (4) customs free access to 15% of the world market, and (5) low overhead costs (cf. Invest in Serbia, 2014).

A serious problem is that since 2000, most FDI has entered the sector of non-tradable goods. That has had negative effects on Serbia's economy from the viewpoint of development, since the country needs FDI above all in the sector of tradable goods, as they encourage productivity and technical progress. Thus, *attracting more FDI inflows to the tradable sector would undoubtedly raise Serbia's export potential.* Foreign investors in Serbia have so far been primarily interested in profiting from the privatisation of former socially and state-owned companies. The benefits that Serbia has had from the inflow of FDI since 2000 relate, among others, to significant transfer of technology, enhancement of competition on the local market, the training of employees (see Filiopvić et al., 2012).

In our days, *globalisation* has a manifold and increasing effect on the development of almost all countries. Therefore we can speak of a *globalisation effect* in the case of Serbia, too. Concerning the mechanism of economic growth, the most important is the effect of capital imports, which is

Table 17. FDI and Globalisation Effect in Serbia, 1980–2012 (Dependent Variable: $Y - Y_{est}$).

Sphere	$\hat{h}$	se ($\hat{h}$)	R^2	*t* statistics
National economy	0.00612	0.0168	0.998	3.06
Manufacturing	0.00351	0.0620	0.982	2.90

essentially double: quantitative and qualitative. The quantitative effect is connected with the fact that capital imports increase the stock of physical capital if they are higher than the burden of interest and profit repatriation. The qualitative effect means first of all an *improvement in efficiency*.

For the purpose of investigating the globalisation effect in the Serbian economy, the following model of linear regression will be applied:

$$Y - Y_{est} = \hat{h}K_G + \varepsilon \tag{2}$$

Here Y and Y_{est} are the actual and estimated values of Serbia's GDP and MVA in real terms considering the share of FDI in fixed assets, K_G is the globalising capital (the cumulative real stock of FDI in the national economy and manufacturing) and ε is a residual. The initial data of regression analysis are shown in the appendix.

It is visible that *manufacturing industry had an important contribution to the production of the rather weak globalisation effect in Serbia*. What is the role of globalising capital in it? On the basis of relation (2), the main indicators summarised in Table 17 were obtained using here the ordinary least squares method. It can be stated that there is a *very close correlation* between the FDI stock flowed in Serbia (K_G) and the achieved productivity surpluses ($Y - Y_{est}$), especially at a macro level. At the same time, the estimated value of regression coefficient ($\hat{h}$) is significant and the standard error is also acceptable both in the national economy and manufacturing.

SERBIA AND REGIONAL COOPERATION IN SOUTH-EAST EUROPE[8]

The *process of* contemporary South-East European *regional cooperation* was originally *initiated* by the meeting of foreign ministers of Albania,

Bulgaria, Greece, Romania, Turkey and Yugoslavia in Belgrade on 24–26 February 1988. At a second meeting held in Tirana on 24–25 October 1990, the Balkan foreign ministers declared their belief in democracy and expressed commitment to European integration. However, the break-up of former Yugoslavia and ensuing wars interrupted this cooperation.

Following the end of Bosnian War, France launched the *Process of Stability and Good-Neighbourliness in South-East Europe*. The FRY took part in the *Royaumont* meeting of 13 December 1995, which established a Balkan round table within the Pact for Stability in Europe under the aegis of the EU Common Foreign and Security Policy. In February 1996 the *Royaumont Process* was *converted into an EU initiative* to encourage regional projects aimed at close cooperation and confidence building among its participants in areas like media, exchanges of academicians, customs cooperation and interaction between local authorities. Yugoslavia (Serbia and Montenegro) together with Albania, Bosnia and Herzegovina, Bulgaria, Greece, Romania and Turkey signed on 7 July 1996 the *Sofia Declaration*, which was to enhance good-neighbourly relations, develop economic cooperation, humanitarian, social and cultural contacts, and combat organised crime, illicit drug and arms trafficking and terrorism. The FRY was invited to the founding session of the *South-East European Cooperative Initiative* (SECI) held in Geneva on 5–6 December 1996 under the auspices of the United States and the United Nations Economic Commission for Europe, but a political crisis in Serbia induced the U.S. administration to cancel the invitation. Only after the regime change in Belgrade would Yugoslavia be admitted to that forum on 6 December 2000. The *SECI projects* were to improve frontier traffic, develop important international roads, create a regional grid of pipelines and electric power, support SMEs and promote foreign direct investment.

On 10 June 1999, the Royaumont Process was superseded by the *Stability Pact for South Eastern Europe* (SP/SEE) concluded in Köln on the European Commission's initiative. Yugoslavia signed it on 26 October 2000. This pact seated in Brussels was to mobilise non-governmental organisations' assets for development projects covering democracy and human rights, the economy and security policy. The EU and U.S. were coordinators of various initiatives, of which the *Szeged Process* facilitated Serbia's democratisation from October 1999.

On 20 May 2000, the *Adriatic-Ionian Initiative* was launched as a forum for dialogue and cooperation, joined by the FRY on 24 November. It is aimed at resolving international crises through mutual cooperation among various peoples with special regard for economic and technical assistance, trade, environmental protection, culture, education and tourism, and combating all forms of crime.

On 25 November 2000, the FRY became a member of the *Central European Initiative* (CEI), whose original purpose was to help transition countries in Europe to integrate with the EU and achieve a higher level of socio-economic development. The former Yugoslavia had already participated in the work of this forum from 1989 to 1992. Since the EU enlargement in May 2004, the CEI has focused its attention on the Balkans.

In February 2001 the FRY was admitted to full membership in the *South-East European Cooperation Process* (SEECP), initiated by the Sofia Declaration, and on 27 May 2002 became one of the founders of the *Danube Cooperation Process*.

On 1 January 2006, Serbia and Montenegro joined the *Central European Free Trade Association* (CEFTA). A new CEFTA agreement covering the extra-EU Balkan countries and superseding the earlier bilateral trade agreements was signed in Bucharest on 19 December 2006. It was ratified by Serbia on 24 September 2007 and established a *free trade area* by 31 December 2010.

Meanwhile, at the Zagreb summit of the SEECP in May 2007, the transition from the stability pact to a regionally owned cooperation framework began. It was largely completed on 27 February 2008, when a *Regional Cooperation Council* (RCC) was established with Serbian participation, operating under the guidance of the SEECP, as a successor of the SP/SEE. The RCC, whose secretariat in Sarajevo provides simultaneous services for the SEECP, promotes the cooperation and integration of the Balkan countries in order to reinvigorate economic and social development to the benefit of the region's peoples. Within this framework, the activities of SECI, which continue under the aegis of the RCC, are now exclusively concentrated on the coordination of member states' efforts to fight cross-border crime.

CONCLUSION

The *Yugoslav self-management system* made it possible for *some elements of market relations* to have already emerged, especially with the economic reforms of the 1960s. Although market institutions were formally established in Serbia after 1989, the process of transition came to a halt when the Milošević regime practically cancelled the reform measures of the

Marković government. The delay in market reforms, coupled with wars and sanctions, led to a relatively weak business environment, reduced attractiveness to foreign investors and therefore constrained job creation. Only since the regime change in October 2000, has the reform process gathered renewed impetus, due to a *combination of liberal and social-democratic policies pursued in a manner similar to many other transition countries.*

In this investigation, we set out from the consideration that *economic growth is primarily determined by the mechanism of technical progress.* Our empirical results allow us to draw the following *final conclusions.*

1. The Serbian economy's catch-up *development* had a predominantly *intensive character* over the period 1961–2012. The results obtained with the Simon model can be summarised as follows.
   1.1. The overall *rate of technical progress* used to be about twice as fast in manufacturing as in the total economy.
   1.2. At a *macro level*, the most important factor of technical progress was its immobile component, followed by the mobile and creative components.
   1.3. Technical progress in *manufacturing* was largely determined by the mobile factor. Here the immobile factor held the second place and the creative one came third.
2. The inflow of *FDI showed a higher production effect after 2000*, which can be explained by an increased interest of foreign investors in the Balkan market. However, the *globalisation effect* of capital imports remained rather *weak*, whereas the *overvalued dinar* seriously restricted the export expansion of Serbian producers up to the outbreak of the recent global crisis.
3. *The European Union an external determinant has been the primary mover of transition in Serbia since 2000, with the desired EU membership as the mainspring of that process. The first phase of transition* establishing macroeconomic stability and market institutions *had already been finished by 2008.* But despite improved credibility and business, investment and competitive environment, *Serbia is still far away from a real market economy.* An essentially *big bang approach* to the economy *conducted as a gradualist programme* determined the fact that after the October changes of 2000, the new window of reform opportunity had not been used in the best way. Since then significant progress in transition had been made, but many necessary reforms were still incomplete when the recent crisis erupted. As a result, substantial unfinished

structural reforms remained, with *more progress needed in* such essential areas as *privatisation, enterprise restructuring and competition policy*.

4. Prior to the recent crisis, the Serbian economy's *growth performance* based largely on capital inflows supporting a boom in domestic demand was associated with *rising vulnerabilities*, in particular a higher share of non-tradable products and deteriorating external position. Economic growth suffered a setback with the onset of the global crisis slowing down the pace of convergence. As a result, *Serbia's income gap remains larger in comparison with more advanced regional economies*.
5. *Today only a small number of new companies enter the Serbian market* characterised by large budgetary transfers, considerable subventions, all-encompassing state intervention, high business risk and a still very profitable rent seeking.
6. Despite Serbia's increasing integration into global markets, *structural bottlenecks continue to undermine competitiveness and constrain growth potential*. They include a difficult business environment, inflexible labour markets as well as a still large and inefficient sector of socially and state-owned enterprises. These bottlenecks are connected in part with the country's *late start in the transition towards a market economy*. Therefore, tackling *these challenges*, which are *in many respects common across the Western Balkans*, is possible through comprehensive *structural reforms* which would be essential to achieve a more sustainable economic growth. This should improve competitiveness, leading to a *more durable export-oriented growth model*.
7. Structural *employment losses* since 2008 have partly been attributed to lay-offs related to the pre-crisis privatisation and restructuring, as former socially owned enterprises had contractual obligations to refrain from lay-offs for three years following privatisation. As *privatisation peaked in 2005–2006*, the lay-offs coincided with the onset of the recent crisis in 2008–2009. *Losses incurred by non-private companies heavily burden domestic savings, contribute to external disequilibrium and significantly weaken the competitiveness of the corporate sector*.
8. The Serbian government has recently recognised the importance of *structural adjustment policies* in its medium-term fiscal strategy. It has realised that the removal of structural bottlenecks requires the implementation of such *key reforms* as *improving the business environment* through a multi-pronged approach to support a dynamic private sector based on measures in the areas of competition policy, tax administration, property rights and legislation governing real estate; and *raising*

the cost competitiveness of Serbian economy with a focus on removing disincentives for job creation and making the wage bargaining and employment procedures more flexible, while maintaining adequate social protection.

9. Serbia needs *further reforms of structural character* in education, health care and the pension system. In addition, the relatively low level of R&D expenditure should be raised to improve economic efficiency and accelerate technical progress.
10. Expanding the low export base to anchor sustainable growth and external liquidity will crucially depend on improving competitiveness. In this respect, the *most serious challenges facing Serbia are related to the country's ability to comply with the standards and requirements posed by the process of EU accession*, which, among others, requires *closer regional cooperation.*

NOTES

1. Slobodan Milošević was president of Serbia in 1991–1997 and president of Yugoslavia in 1997–2000. *Gy.S.*
2. The region of the Western Balkans includes Albania, Bosnia and Herzegovina, Croatia, Macedonia, Montenegro, Serbia and Kosovo. *Gy.S.*
3. A soft budget constraint means that a loss-making enterprise can rely on immediate subsidies from the state budget and thus becomes less perceptible to relative price changes. See Kornai (1993, p. 168).
4. The Dayton Agreements were a U.S.-brokered peace accord ending the Bosnian War which broke out in April 1992. They were initialled in Dayton, Ohio, on 21 November and officially signed in Paris on 14 December 1995 by the presidents of Serbia Slobodan Milošević, Croatia Franjo Tuđman and Bosnia and Herzegovina Alija Izetbegović. *Gy.S.*
5. The *hyperinflation* in Serbia was a result of *three factors* (cf. Avramović, 1995). First, there was enormous demand for foreign exchange in the face of reduced supply. Second, the credit and monetary policies pursued were accommodating to cost and price increases. Third, the state budget financed the estimated minimum public expenditure, irrespective of whether real revenue was available.
6. The negative return to factor *L* originates from the fact that if solely the number of persons employed increases, there will be a decrease in intensities in the returns derived from that increase (Simon Sr., 2008, p. 14).
7. The World Economic Forum's *Global Competitiveness Index*, based on a comprehensive assessment of countries' competitiveness, ranks Serbia 95th out of 144 countries in 2012–2013. Serbia has scored lower than the regional average in each area considered. In particular, Serbia's competitiveness appears to be hindered by its macroeconomic environment, business sophistication, goods market efficiency, higher education and training, and institutions. Perception of corruption could also

be holding back Serbia's attractiveness to international investors (see IMF, 2013, p. 35).

8. Based on: Simon Jr. (2011, pp. 13–14).

REFERENCES

Alinčić, M. E., Crobrnja, M., Denić Jovanović, M., Miljković, V. D. J., Orlović, S., Savić, N., ... Višković, J. (2008). *Integration perspectives and synergic effects of European transformation in the countries targeted by EU enlargement and neighborhood policies: Serbia*. Budapest: Center for EU Enlargement Studies (CENS), Central European University.

Avramović, D. (1995). Reconstruction of the Monetary System and Economic Recovery of Yugoslavia, 1994: Analytical Framework, Results and Problems, WIIW Research Reports, 216, The Vienna Institute for International Economic Studies.

Balcerowicz, L. (1995). *Socialism, capitalism, transformation*. Budapest: Central European University Press.

Bisić, M. (2005). Public finance policies. In. B. Begović & B.Mijatović (Eds.), *Four years of transition in Serbia* (pp. 117–185). Belgrade: Center for Liberal Democratic Studies.

Božić Miljković, I. (2012). Konkurentnost balkanskih zemalja u spoljnoj trgovini u uslovima globalizacije. *Međunarodni Problemi*, *64*(1), 67–81.

Bukvić, R., & Kovačević, I. (2008). Serbian manufacturing industry. *Survey – Republic of Serbia*, *49*(3), 61–82.

Cerović, B., & Nojković, A. (2009). Transition and growth: What was taught and what happened. *Economic Annals*, *54*(183), 7–31.

Csaba, L., & Hámori, B. (2004). Posztszocialista rendszerek és előzményeik. In B. Zoltán & K. Szabó (Eds.), *Gazdasági rendszerek, országok, intézmények: Bevezetés az összehasonlító gazdaságtanba* (pp. 243–392). Budapest: Aula.

Đorđević, B., & Lopandić, D. (2001). Introduction of sanctions against the FR of Yugoslavia and their lifting, 1991–2001. *Yugoslav Survey*, *42*(3), 25–40.

Erdős, T. (2006). *Növekedési potenciál és gazdaságpolitika*. Budapest: Akadémiai Kiadó.

Estrin, S., & Uvalić, M. (2013). Foreign direct investment into transition economies: Are the Balkans different? Europe in Question Series Discussion Paper No. 64, London School of Economics and Political Science.

Filiopvić, D., Golić, R., Joksimović, M., Milinčić, M., Stojković, S., Šabić, D., ... Vujadino, S. (2012). The impact of FDI on the transitional economy in Serbia – Changes and challenges. *Acta Polytechnica Hungarica*, *9*(3), 65–84.

Hafner, P. (2002). Održivi razvoj i privreda Srbije. *Ekonomske Teme*, *40*(4), 49–56.

IMF. (2013). Republic of Serbia: Selected Issues Paper, IMF Country Report No. 13/207, International Monetary Fund, Washington, DC.

Invest in Serbia. (2014). On the Spot: Business & Investing in Serbia. Retrieved from http://www.investinserbia.biz. Accessed on February 19, 2014.

Jelić, M. (2006). International aid to Serbia, 2000–2005. *Survey – Serbia & Montenegro*, *47*(1), 83–94.

Kaldor, N. (1957). A model of economic growth. *The Economic Journal*, *47*(268), 591–624.

Kontić, L. (2007). Privatizacija. In M. Đurković (Ed.), *Srbija 2000–2006: Država, društvo, privreda* (pp. 149–170). Beograd: Institut za evropske studije.

Kornai, J. (1993). *A szocialista rendszer: Kritikai politikai gazdaságtan*. Budapest: Heti Világgazdaság Kiadói Rt.

Kornai, J. (2007). *Szocializmus, kapitalizmus, demokrácia és rendszerváltás*. Budapest: Akadémiai Kiadó.

Kovačević, I. (2003). Privatisation in Serbia, 1989–2003. *Survey – Serbia & Montenegro, 44*(4), 69–90.

Kovačević, I., & Trifunović, M. (2009). European Union aid to Serbia. *Survey – Republic of Serbia, 50*(2), 61–84.

Lazarević, G., & Basara, M. (2003). Reforms in Serbia. *Survey – Serbia & Montenegro, 44*(1), 61–82.

Ligeti, Z. (2002). *Gazdasági növekedés és felzárkózás*. Ph.D. thesis, BKÁE, Budapest.

Lopandić, D. (2007). *Reforma Evropske unije, Zapadni Balkan i Srbija*. Beograd: Zakasnela integracija, Institut ekonomskih nauka.

Mijatović, B. (2005). General overview of transition. In B. Begović, & B. Mijatović (Eds.), *Four years of transition in Serbia* (pp. 9–32). Belgrade: Center for Liberal Democratic Studies.

Mićić, V. (2009). Srbija i industrijska politika EU. *Industrija, 37*(1), 121–129.

Mrdaković Cvetković, R. (2006). Privredni razvoj i priliv inostranih sredstava u zemlje u tranziciji. *Ekonomski anali, 51*(171), 75–89.

Nikolić, G. (2006). Ekonomski odnosi sa inostranstvom u postmiloševićevskom periodu. In S. Mihailović (Ed.), *Pet godina tranzicije u Srbiji* (pp. 300–320). Beograd: Socijaldemokratski klub i Fondacija Friedrich Ebert.

Novák, T. (2007). Szerbia Montenegró nélkül – ördögi körben? In N. Tamás & T. Szemlér (Eds.), *Európa peremén: Új tagok és szomszédok* (pp. 115–129). Budapest: MTA VKI.

Palairet, M. (2001). The economic consequences of Slobodan Milošević. *Europe – Asia Studies, 53*(6), 903–919.

Panagiotou, R. (2012). *The economies of the Western Balkans: Transition, growth, and EU Accession*, Reports 70. Centre of Planning and Economic Research, Athens.

Pavlaković, V. (2005). Serbia transformed? Political dynamics in the milošević era and after. In S. P. Ramet & V. Pavlaković (Eds.), *Serbia since 1989: Politics and society under Milošević and after* (pp. 13–54.). London: University of Washington Press.

Pobulić, S. (2006). Peti oktobar i pravci socijalno-ekonomskog razvoja. In S. Mihailović (Ed.), *Pet godina tranzicije u Srbiji* (pp. 286–299). Beograd: Socijaldemokratski klub i Fondacija Friedrich Ebert.

Popović, D. (2005). Economic activity and macroeconomic policies in transition. In B. Begović & B. Mijatović (Eds.), *Four years of transition in Serbia* (pp. 33–116). Belgrade: Center for Liberal Democratic Studies.

Rosser, J. B., Jr., & Rosser, M. V. (2004). *Comparative economics in a transforming world economy*. Cambridge, MA: MIT Press.

RZR. (2009). *Izveštaj o razvoju Srbije*. Beograd: Republički zavod za razvoj.

Réti, T. (1998). A balkáni gazdaságok: Elzárkózás vagy felzárkózás? *Külgazdaság, 42*(3), 53–72.

Sasse, G. (2005). Lost in transition: When is transition over? *Development and Transition, 1*(6), 10–11.

Simon, G., Jr. (1997). Az európai integráció és a Balkán. Magyar Külügyi Intézet, Budapest.

Simon, G., Jr. (2003). Ekonomska tranzicija u Jugoslaviji – jedno viđenje spolja. *Međunarodni problemi*, *55*(1), 104–128.
Simon, G., Sr. (2005). Növekedéselmélet – világmodell – gazdaságfejlesztési stratégia. *Külgazdaság*, *49*(3), 31–51.
Simon, G., Sr. (2008). Basic questions of economic growth mechanism. *Economic Annals*, *53*(176), 7–37.
Simon, G., Jr. (2011). *Characteristic Features of Political Transition in Serbia*. Retrieved from Social Science Research Network, Working Paper Series, Rochester, New York. http://ssrn.com/abstract=1923126
Solow, R. M. (1956). A contribution to the theory of economic growth. *Quarterly Journal of Economics*, *70*(1), 65–94.
Stančić, P., Todorović, M., & Čupić, M. (2012). Value-based management and corporate governance: A study of Serbian corporations. *Economic Annals*, *57*(193), 93–112.
Stefanović, M. (2008). Uticaj stranih direktnih investicija na razvoj nacionalne ekonomije. *Ekonomske teme*, *46*(2), 131–145.
Stošić, I. (2006). Rezultati, perspektive i prepreke upravljanja promenama u procesu privatizacije preduzeća u Srbiji. In B. Drašković (Ed.), *Stanje i perspektive privrede Srbije* (pp. 97–106). Beograd: Institut ekonomskih nauka i Beogradska bankarska akademija.
Teokarević, J. (2011). Ten years of post-Milošević transition in Serbia: Problems and prospects. In J. Rupnik (Ed.), *The Western Balkans and the EU: The hour of Europe*. Chaillot Paper No. 126. (pp. 59–78). Paris: European Union Institute for Security Studies.
Uvalić, M. (2010). *Serbia's transition: Towards a better future*. Basingstoke: Palgrave Macmillan.
Veress, J. (Ed.). (1997). *Bevezetés a gazdaságpolitikába*. Budapest: Aula.
Vujačić, I., & Vujačić, J. P. (2011). Privatization in Serbia – Results and institutional failures. *Economic Annals*, *56*(191), 89–105.
Wikipedia. (2014a). *Accession of Serbia to the European Union*. Retrieved from http://en.wikipedia.org/wiki/Accession_of_Serbia_to_the_European_Union. Accessed on February 20, 2014.
Wikipedia. (2014b). *Fiat Automobili Srbija*. Retrieved from http://en.wikipedia.org/wiki/Accession_of_Serbia_to_the_European_Union. Accessed on February 20, 2014.

APPENDIX

Variables

Y = gross domestic product/value added in billions of 2000 U.S. dollars, at purchasing power parity (PPP);
N = mid-year population (in millions);
K = average annual gross fixed capital (in the national economy including dwellings) in billions of 2000 U.S. dollars, at PPP;
L = average annual number of persons employed (in millions);
R_{t-2} = full-time equivalent number of scientists and engineers engaged in R&D (considering a two-year lag, in thousands);
H/L = number of schooling years per capita (for population aged 15 and over);
Z = arable land (in million hectares);
I = investment (gross fixed capital formation) in billions of 2000 U.S. dollars, at PPP.

Note

All data for Serbia refer to the present territory of the republic excluding Kosovo. The relevant mid-year fixed asset values were calculated, as the averages of corresponding year-end values, from data provided by the Federal Statistical Office of Yugoslavia (SZS) and, for the years after 2001, from the annual financial statements of enterprises. Current values were converted to real ones with the help of the investment price index. The conversion to U.S. dollars was made on the basis of PPP values of investments.

DATA SOURCES

Bolt, J., & van Zanden, J. L. (2013). *The first update of the maddison project. Re-Estimating Growth Before 1820*. Maddison Project Working Paper WP-4, Groningen and Utrecht. Detailed data downloaded from: http://www.ggdc.net/maddison/maddison-project/data/mpd_2013-01.xlsx

EBRD, Selected Economic Indicators Database.

Eurostat, New Cronos Database.

Heston, A., Summers, R., & Aten, B. (2006). *Penn World Table 6.2*. Center for International Comparisons of Production, Income and Prices at the University of Pennsylvania (CICUP), Philadelphia.

Izveštaj o razvoju Srbije, RZR, Beograd.
National Accounts Statistics, UN, New York.
RZS database.
Statistički godišnjak Jugoslavije/Srbije i Crne Gore, (Savezni) zavod za statistiku, Beograd.
Statistički godišnjak Srbije, Sistem nacionalnih računa Republike Srbije, RZS, Beograd.
WIIW database incorporating national statistics.
Yearbook of Labour Statistics, ILO, Geneva.

FURTHER READING

Barro, R. J., & Lee, J.-W. (2010). *A new data set of educational attainment in the world.* NBER Working Paper No. 15902. National Bureau of Economic Research, Cambridge, MA. Detailed data downloaded from: http://www.barrolee.com
FAO Production Yearbook, Rome.
National Bank of Serbia – Annual financial statements of enterprises.
RZS. (2008). Dva veka razvoja Srbije – Statistički pregled, Beograd.
Serbian Chamber of Commerce.
SZS. (1989). Jugoslavija 1918–1988. Statistički godišnjak, Beograd.
UNCTADstat Database.

Table A1. Serbia's Main Macroeconomic and Manufacturing Indicators.

Year	Y	N	K	I	L	R_{t-2}	H/L	Z	Y	K	L	R_{t-2}
	National economy								Manufacturing			
1960	15.03	6.639	27.80	2.42	1.662	4.794	4.97	3.88	1.12	2.82	0.512	2.201
1961	15.57	6.689	30.25	2.89	1.831	4.943	5.03	3.88	1.19	3.14	0.522	2.269
1962	16.42	6.740	34.28	2.92	1.868	5.096	5.09	3.86	1.25	3.59	0.529	2.339
1963	18.40	6.788	38.54	2.91	1.887	5.254	5.15	3.86	1.46	4.04	0.551	2.412
1964	20.35	6.833	41.96	3.22	2.013	5.417	5.21	3.84	1.75	4.48	0.611	2.487
1965	20.75	6.876	45.67	3.02	2.049	5.585	5.27	3.84	1.89	4.89	0.630	2.564
1966	22.53	6.928	49.69	3.41	2.018	5.758	5.37	3.82	1.94	5.29	0.621	2.643
1967	22.88	6.967	53.68	3.49	2.020	5.937	5.48	3.83	1.93	5.75	0.615	2.725
1968	23.27	7.008	57.52	3.78	2.040	6.234	5.58	3.82	2.00	6.19	0.601	2.861
1969	26.18	7.123	62.64	3.99	2.130	6.456	5.69	3.83	2.22	6.69	0.627	2.963
1970	26.95	7.165	68.53	4.38	2.207	6.686	5.80	3.82	2.44	7.29	0.647	3.069
1971	29.41	7.212	74.80	4.42	2.309	6.900	5.93	3.82	2.73	7.99	0.677	3.167
1972	30.69	7.252	81.28	4.28	2.394	6.934	6.07	3.81	2.96	8.63	0.706	3.183
1973	32.28	7.284	87.49	4.20	2.440	7.013	6.20	3.81	3.18	9.21	0.727	3.129
1974	34.97	7.326	93.94	4.54	2.549	7.351	6.34	3.80	3.57	9.87	0.756	3.374
1975	35.92	7.369	100.3	4.93	2.667	7.341	6.49	3.80	3.77	10.57	0.792	3.370
1976	37.78	7.419	107.5	5.81	2.758	7.721	6.59	3.79	3.92	11.36	0.812	3.544
1977	40.81	7.463	115.1	6.55	2.872	7.711	6.70	3.78	4.33	12.14	0.837	3.539
1978	42.88	7.504	123.5	7.14	3.012	7.433	6.81	3.77	4.75	13.06	0.867	3.412

Table A1. (*Continued*)

Year	Y	N	K	I	L	R_{t-2}	H/L	Z	Y	K	L	R_{t-2}
	National economy								Manufacturing			
1979	46.48	7.542	133.1	7.60	3.148	8.083	6.92	3.76	5.18	14.26	0.904	3.710
1980	47.71	7.709	141.7	6.87	3.231	9.199	7.03	3.75	5.48	15.41	0.934	4.222
1981	48.53	7.736	148.2	6.31	3.319	8.514	7.14	3.76	5.78	16.21	0.953	3.908
1982	49.58	7.764	154.1	6.18	3.383	8.907	7.25	3.75	5.80	16.86	0.985	4.088
1983	48.36	7.788	159.6	5.53	3.436	9.443	7.37	3.73	5.88	17.44	1.012	4.334
1984	49.04	7.814	163.5	5.12	3.503	9.489	7.48	3.72	6.27	17.82	1.029	4.355
1985	48.96	7.835	166.5	5.00	3.588	10.244	7.60	3.72	6.39	18.15	1.064	4.702
1986	50.77	7.854	170.0	4.22	3.687	10.501	7.67	3.72	6.60	18.55	1.097	4.820
1987	50.03	7.868	173.1	5.22	3.773	11.227	7.74	3.71	6.66	18.90	1.107	5.153
1988	49.43	7.884	177.3	4.42	3.803	10.917	7.81	3.71	6.73	19.38	1.105	5.011
1989	50.37	7.894	182.0	4.95	3.800	11.872	7.88	3.70	6.84	19.87	1.114	5.446
1990	46.39	7.898	186.1	4.02	3.720	12.716	7.95	3.69	6.01	20.18	1.056	5.197
1991	41.01	7.824	190.5	3.42	3.674	12.683	8.05	3.69	4.84	20.59	0.994	4.960
1992	29.57	7.818	193.8	2.39	3.567	11.870	8.15	3.69	3.50	20.94	0.936	4.733
1993	20.46	7.812	190.8	1.49	3.461	10.721	8.26	3.69	2.38	20.85	0.909	4.245
1994	20.97	7.805	183.5	1.31	3.399	10.944	8.36	3.70	2.41	20.51	0.912	4.067
1995	22.25	7.797	174.2	1.26	3.299	11.031	8.47	3.70	2.53	21.59	0.895	4.113
1996	23.99	7.785	155.6	1.19	3.273	11.481	8.54	3.68	2.77	20.95	0.878	3.751
1997	26.41	7.769	118.5	1.20	3.137	12.113	8.62	3.67	3.19	16.28	0.840	3.960
1998	26.91	7.568	100.4	1.17	3.139	11.994	8.70	3.66	3.27	12.35	0.812	4.190
1999	22.07	7.540	85.77	0.865	3.103	12.093	8.77	3.66	2.28	10.28	0.826	4.108
2000	23.21	7.516	96.55	0.980	3.094	11.577	8.85	3.67	2.61	11.16	0.733	3.758
2001	24.51	7.503	102.3	0.940	3.106	12.163	8.89	3.67	2.72	14.20	0.704	3.949
2002	25.47	7.515	102.1	0.932	3.000	11.969	8.92	3.67	2.70	13.69	0.645	3.848
2003	26.08	7.533	101.8	0.961	2.919	10.071	8.96	3.64	2.57	12.48	0.597	3.826
2004	28.25	7.463	101.7	1.23	2.931	10.855	8.99	3.64	2.82	12.39	0.551	3.804
2005	29.83	7.441	102.0	1.29	2.733	11.353	9.03	3.63	2.80	12.95	0.497	3.782
2006	31.38	7.412	102.5	1.49	2.631	11.637	9.06	3.62	2.96	13.62	0.519	3.761
2007	33.54	7.382	103.3	1.66	2.656	11.551	9.08	3.60	3.11	14.53	0.522	3.739
2008	35.39	7.350	104.5	1.80	2.822	12.079	9.11	3.60	3.14	16.02	0.484	3.910
2009	34.29	7.321	105.9	1.43	2.616	10.580	9.13	3.60	2.64	16.05	0.451	3.500
2010	34.84	7.291	106.6	1.36	2.397	11.534	9.16	3.59	2.66	16.01	0.406	3.141
2011	35.40	7.234	105.8	1.47	2.253	12.006	9.19	3.60	2.65	15.95	0.387	2.872
2012	34.87	7.199	105.1	1.68	2.228	12.637	9.22	3.60	2.62	16.00	0.380	2.894

PPP conversion rates. USD 1 = RSD 17.13 for GDP, 32.84 for MVA and 49.85 for fixed assets and investment. (In 2000, gross value added of all industries amounted to USD 21.28 billion at the PPP for GDP.)

Table A2. Serbia: Foreign Direct Investment.

Year	FDI Flows in Million Current Dollars			U.S. Investment Price Index 2000 = 100[a]
	Inflows, total	*Of which*: Into manufacturing	Outflows, total	
1980	12	3	–	66.44
1981	7	2	–	73.66
1982	0	0	–	78.65
1983	9	2	–	78.97
1984	−4	−1	–	80.24
1985	8	2	–	81.49
1986	−14	−3	–	83.74
1987	4	1	–	86.15
1988	11	3	–	88.99
1989	5	1	–	91.87
1990	34	8	–	93.86
1991	60	15	–	95.30
1992	126	31	–	95.27
1993	96	23	–	96.55
1994	63	15	–	97.97
1995	45	11	–	99.33
1996	0	0	–	99.26
1997	740	85	–	99.23
1998	113	14	–	98.52
1999	112	14	–	98.75
2000	50	7	2	100
2001	165	38	12	101.24
2002	475	105	20	101.99
2003	1,365	287	−10	103.58
2004	966	204	−6	107.19
2005	1,609	320	59	111.41
2006	4,350	792	85	115.35
2007	3,462	488	938	116.66
2008	3,492	493	319	117.57
2009	2,364	333	67	115.60
2010	1,813	255	235	113.81
2011	3,258	460	191	120.20
2012	650	92	75	121.94

[a]U.S. Department of Commerce, Bureau of Economic Analysis.

PART II
INSTITUTIONS AND GOVERNANCE

REGULATORY EVOLUTION, MULTINATIONAL FIRMS, AND NEO-TRANSITION ECONOMIES

Yusaf H. Akbar

ABSTRACT

While the liberalization of economies within the transition paradigm is viewed to take place primarily on a macroeconomic (primary) level, this paper switches emphasis to the secondary and tertiary level of post-transition. While macroeconomic reforms may provide the playing field, secondary reforms level the playing field and tertiary reforms develop the capabilities necessary for firms and individuals within firms to compete in the landscape of liberalized economies. It is necessary to examine the transformations on three levels. First, the development of public policy and institutions aimed at regulating certain industries or firms. Second, the explicit market strategies of firms operating in the industries that shape market structure and inform public policy. Third, the nonmarket strategies of firms aimed at influencing the form and substance of public policy. Drawing on research in three related areas: institutional voids (IVs), the role of market and nonmarket strategies of firms, respectively, this paper examines the current state of transition in CEE/FSU countries. The main conclusions of the paper are first, transition and

Neo-Transitional Economics
International Finance Review, Volume 16, 99–119

ISSN: 1569-3767/doi:10.1108/S1569-376720150000016005

post-transition has been and continues to be profoundly impacted by the liberalizing influences of multinational firms. Second, this causation from the strategies and tactics of multinational firms to the extent of transition also helps to explain the degree of modernization of economies in a given transition economy. Third, it is important to distinguish between local and foreign firms on the transition process. Foreign firms are more likely to pursue liberalization agendas when it strengthens their competitive advantage over local firms. Conversely, local firms – especially those who rely on the capacity to navigate institutional voids – may be opposed to liberalization, as liberalization would threaten their sources of competitive advantage.

Keywords: Liberalization; competitive advantage; nonmarket strategy; multinational firms

The liberalization of economies within the transition paradigm is viewed to take place on three levels: macroeconomic (primary), industry level (secondary), and enterprise level (tertiary). While this edited volume focuses mainly on macroeconomic changes and policy developments in the post-transition economies of Central and East Europe and the former Soviet Union (CEE/FSU), the following paper switches emphasis to the secondary and tertiary level of post-transition.

If macroeconomic transformation and institutional development provide the bedrock of support for the emergence of functioning markets, secondary and tertiary reforms reinforce those foundations on a day-to-day basis to facilitate a functioning market economy. Moreover, secondary and especially tertiary reforms exert a profound influence on individual behaviors that may provide longer lasting support for functioning market economies as the transformation of individual or industries practices feed through to the broader economy (Feinberg & Meurs, 2008; Shinkle & Kriauciunas, 2012). Put another way, while macroeconomic reforms may provide the playing field, secondary reforms level the playing field and tertiary reforms develop the capabilities necessary for firms and individuals within firms to compete in the landscape of liberalized economies. A clear analogy here would be two of the three Copenhagen Criteria used by the EU to assess the eligibility of a candidate country to join the EU (Council of the European Union, 1993).

An important way in which we can assess the degree of transition is the notion of economic diversification. Economic diversification is the capacity for an economy to produce a diverse range of goods and services across multiple industries. Diversification can take varying forms including within sectors with the production of new products and services; increased international trade from existing sectors; and the development of entirely new sectors for a country's economy (Wiig & Kolstad, 2012). There are numerous advantages that are a result of diversified economies: reduced exposure to industry specific shocks; higher growth from more diversified income streams from international trade (Frankel & Romer, 1999); more effective allocation of factor endowments; and greater potential for participation in economic integration internationally through increased trade and inward foreign direct investment (FDI) (United Nations, 2011). There is also evidence that suggests that economic diversification is related to the entrepreneurial dynamism of an economy. As Hare (2012) succinctly puts it: "[G]rowth occurs most successfully in economies with high business start-up and closure rates (in other words, most new firms fail, often quite rapidly), with a few new firms growing to become the success stories of the future."

Economic diversification can also exert profound influence on societal and political forces too. An economy dominated by a narrow group of industries may find political power being concentrated in the hands of relatively few people. Economic policy may then become captured by the vested interests of a narrow set of firms and individuals distributing income from a broader portion of the public toward the well organized group through various forms of sectoral protection or privilege (Olson, 1965). On a societal level, economies with higher diversification levels may benefit from more sophistication and diversity of cultural and economic choices given the broader range of industries in an economy.

In this paper, it is argued that in order to better understand the nature of transition in CEE/FSU, it is necessary to examine the transformations that occur below the macroeconomic radar which typically occur through three related processes. First, the development of public policy and institutions aimed at regulating certain industries or firms. Second, the explicit market strategies of firms operating in the industries that shape market structure and inform public policy. Third, the nonmarket strategies of firms aimed at influencing the form and substance of public policy.

This paper examines these three factors in more detail. The post-transition paradigm is thus placed within the context of institutional features of markets and the strategic aspects of firms' behavior in promoting or hindering the development of market institutions associated with transition.

Drawing on research on three related areas, institutional voids (IVs), and the role of market and nonmarket strategies of firms, respectively, the paper examines the current state of transition in CEE/FSU countries. The main conclusion of the paper is three fold. First, transition and post-transition has been and continues to be profoundly impacted by the liberalizing influences of multinational firms. Second, this causation from the strategies and tactics of multinational firms to the extent of transition also helps to explain the degree of modernization of economies in a given transition economy. Third, it is important to analytically distinguish between the impact of local and foreign firms on the transition process. Foreign firms are more likely to pursue liberalization agendas (directly and indirectly) when it strengthens their competitive advantage over local firms. Conversely, local firms – especially those who rely on the capacity to navigate institutional voids – may be opposed to liberalization, as liberalization would threaten their very sources of competitive advantage.

The paper is organized as follows. The section "Institutional Voids Matter ..." draws upon the literature on Institutional Voids describing the state of transition and post-transition economies in this context. It outlines the ways in which different IVs hinder transition processes. It also reproduces previous research (Akbar & Kisilowski, 2015) that examines the extent of modernization of CEE/FSU economies.

The next two sections explore the conceptual relationships between the market strategies (the section "Market Strategies, Institutions, and Transition") and the nonmarket strategies (the section "Nonmarket Strategies, Institutions, and Transition") of firms on the one hand and the degree of transition of CEE/FSU countries on the other. Leveraging two strategy literatures – the first related to the Resource Based View (RBV) of strategy and the second on nonmarket strategies of firms, this section proposes conceptual avenues for understanding how firms impact on secondary and tertiary aspects of transition.

The section "Nonmarket Strategies, Institutions and Transition" provides empirical evidence for the conceptual relationships building on the work of Akbar (2003) and Akbar and Kisilowski (2015). The main findings are as follows. First, the market strategies of multinational firms play a clear role in facilitating regulatory convergence toward international best practices because such convergence directly favors the sources of competitive advantage of the multinational firms. The process through which this occurs has direct and indirect elements. First, the arrival of best practice changes the tactics of firms in the host economy. In order to compete with the multinational firms, local competitors need to raise their game to international levels. As competitive practices converge toward international best practice, the resistance to transition and liberalization reduces among local firms. Second, the nonmarket strategies of multinational firms are aimed at promulgating laws and regulations that favor their sources of competitive advantage. These firms use numerous tactics to achieve these goals that are examined in more detail in this section. The section "Conclusions and Implications for Understanding the Transition Paradigm" provides conclusions and offers thoughts for future research and on policy implications.

INSTITUTIONAL VOIDS MATTER ...

One of the most striking aspects of transition and post-transition and perhaps the best explanation for transition outcomes has been the incomplete and uneven nature of institutional development across the region. In the early days of the transition process in CEE/FSU, the debate over "shock therapy" and "gradualism" (Balcerowicz, 1994; Fischer, 1993; Healey, 1991; Kornai, 1995; Roarry, 1992; Rybczynski, 1991; Sachs, 1993) appears with hindsight to have been a false dichotomy predicated on an assumption about the importance of the redundancy of states and the capacity for markets to replace centrally planned economic structures. A generation on from the changes in 1989, it is now clear that neither the view that the preservation of some aspects of pre-existing institutions from the state socialist system would be useful for market economy functioning (gradualism) nor the view that markets would spontaneously develop in response to liberalization (shock therapy) appear to be valid. By 2002, the European Bank for Reconstruction and Development (EBRD) reported that by 2001, most post-Communist countries had not returned to their 1989 levels of economic output (Fidrmuc, 2003). Moreover the same organization reported that by 2006, most households reported that they worse off than under communism. Even more revealing was that there appeared to be no clear correlation between the degree of market liberalization and economic output levels. EBRD (2007) reported that two countries who pursued very different pathways after 1991 appeared to have made progress. One country pursued a broad policy of liberalization (Poland) while the other has resisted liberalization (Belarus). Poland was at 169 percent of its 1989 level, while Belarus was at 146 percent in 2007. The average of CEE countries in the process of joining the EU at the time was 151 percent of 1989 levels. Perhaps most revealing was that Azerbaijan (160), Mongolia (153), Turkmenistan (204), and Uzbekistan (150) also posted rapid growth rates in the 2000s largely off the back of natural resource exports. Perversely, in the latter countries, liberalization of natural resource exports merely served to entrench the wealth of post-Communist elites rather than leading to the creation of a middle class. Absent an enlightened autocrat in many of the FSU countries, elites continued to plunder the wealth of these societies through a complex web of opaque relationships between state-owned firms and private conglomerates moving wealth overseas into offshore investment funds and bank accounts. An instructive case in point was the election in 2014 of Petro Poroschenko, one of Ukraine's wealthiest men, to replace the equally wealthy Viktor Yanukovich. Both of these "oligarchs" rose to power through the development of interwoven relationships between state-owned enterprises, privatization programs, and cheap state financing.

If inequality and income distribution are considered, some interesting results emerge. Izyumov and Claxon (2009) considered three different types of post 1989 capitalism in CEE/FSU countries: "democratic capitalism" which consist of Czech Republic, Estonia, Hungary, Latvia, Lithuania, Poland, Slovak Republic, Slovenia; "autocratic capitalism" which are made up of Kazakhstan, Kyrgyz Republic, Tajikistan, Turkmenistan, Uzbekistan; and "clan capitalism" countries such as Armenia, Azerbaijan, Georgia, Moldova, Russia, Ukraine and much of the former Yugoslavia, Bulgaria, and Romania (Izyumov & Claxon, 2009, p. 2). They found inequality was the lowest in countries belong to the "democratic capitalist" with both "autocratic" and "clan" capitalisms producing greater inequality. The implication of this study is clear: the nature of democratic institutions and processes plays a key role in explaining the nature and performance of transition.

By 2008, less than 20 years after the changes, the open and liberalized economies of CEE/FSU suffered massive output contractions caused by the financial sector meltdown that began with the US subprime mortgage collapse. Arguably, many of the gains from transition were wiped out by this meltdown. Ironically, authoritarian countries with large mineral wealth weathered the recession more effectively than open, liberal democratic societies. Across the EBRD countries of CEE/FSU, 29 percent of households saw a drop in their wages and one in five families experienced a job loss (EBRD, 2012).

Reflecting Two Decades after Transition Begun ...

What emerges from the analysis above is that the degree and success of transition appears less to do with the spontaneous creation of markets through liberalization or the reform of pre-existing institutions, as it is do with the formation of new economic, political, and social institutions that support new market structures and industries. This is an important implication for the understanding of policies designed to achieve levels of economic convergence between developed and transition economies. First, transition is not a purely technocratic process with objective outcomes. Rather it is a process of contestation and the management of competing interests with inevitable debates and pressures for redistribution of the gains from liberalization with the pressing need for inclusion of private sector and civil society organizations. Second, the relative power of different actors within a transition economy influences institutional development profoundly and economic and political pluralism is far from guaranteed by a process of liberalization *per se*. Third, the role of MNEs in the process of institutional development is a potentially dissonant one. While the arrival of FDI may cause tensions and trade-offs regarding income distribution within societies, their role as suppliers of best practice at the secondary and tertiary level of transition may play a fundamental role in "upgrading" business practices and eliminate IVs.

More on Institutional Voids

Khanna and Palepu (2010) and Steenkamp (2005) built on the concept of Institutional Voids (IVs) first developed by Khanna and Palepu (1997) and Arnold and Quelch (1998). IVs relate to the lack of developed and functional intermediaries, regulatory frameworks, and contract enforcement in an economy. By their nature, IVs are most relevant at the industry and enterprise level of an economy. They can distort market transactions, raise the cost of doing business, and moderate the value of competitive resources (Akbar, Bortoluzzi, & Tracogna, 2014). They also create differential sources of competitive advantage and disadvantage for firms. For example, local firms that are accustomed to the underdeveloped institutional context of markets may develop more effective tactics for coping with IVs whereas foreign firms may be less capable to execute these tactics either because of a lack of knowledge required to carry out these tactics or because of legitimacy challenges to such nonmarket strategies from headquarters or their home country or host country populations.

Moreover, the persistence of IVs slowdown the process of transformation implied by the nature of transition itself and arguably hinders the economic modernization of the societies of CEE/FSU. Inefficient or opaque business practices, corruption, and nepotism may endure because public and private institutions that are typically associated with rooting out and mitigating the effects of such practices may not be sufficiently developed to cope with them.

The macroeconomic impact of IVs on transition is also clear in two ways. First, relative to developed economies, the informal economy will play a larger role in the wealth creation of the country making it much more difficult for governments to raise revenue for the financing of government activity – leading to higher deficits, lower growth, and cost of borrowing (Peev & Mueller, 2012). Second, both anecdotal examples and more systematic research suggest that countries with higher levels of corruption and nepotism face greater levels of income inequality creating social and political tensions in the country (Andres & Ramlogan-Dobson, 2011; Ashiku, 2011; Dobson & Ramlogan-Dobson, 2012).

What are the specific kinds of IVs that relate to current state of transition in CEE/FSU? Khanna and Palepu's (2005) taxonomy of IVs can be useful in this regard. They identify several domains where IVs are important: political and social systems, openness, product markets, labor markets, and capital markets. For the purposes of parsimony and in the context of institutional development, political and social systems and openness appear to be crucial. For example, an economy open to FDI does not *per se* guarantee institutional development such as the case of Ukraine. On the other hand, institutional development can occur without countries being the most open to FDI such as Slovenia. In Table 1, the findings of a study by Akbar and Kisilowski (2015) are reported.

The authors develop a Political-Economic Modernization Spectrum to describe variations in institutional development across CEE/FSU countries. They placed the CEE/FSU countries in four groups – respectively, with low, medium–low, medium–high, and high levels of political-economic modernization. Table 1 shows the membership of each group. The index was a composite based on the European Bank for Reconstruction and Development (EBRD) Transition Indicators as well as on the Democracy Index developed by Freedom House. Political-economic modernization is closely linked to an EECA's relationship with the EU, as all highly modernized countries are full members of the EU. Furthermore, none of the

Table 1. Political-Economic Modernization Spectrum of CEE/FSU Countries.

	Low Modernization (0–50)	Medium–Low Modernization (51–62)	Medium–High Modernization (63–75)	High Modernization (76–100)
Country	Chechnya[a]	Kosovo (53)	Georgia (65)	Slovenia (79)
	Dagestan[a]	Russia (55)	Serbia (65)	Hungary (79)
	Tatarstan[a]	Kyrgyz Republic (57)	Montenegro (66)	Slovak Republic (82)
	Turkmenistan (28)	Bosnia and Herzegovina (59)	Albania (67)	Lithuania (83)
	Belarus (35)	Ukraine (61)	Macedonia (68)	Latvia (84)
	Uzbekistan (35)	Armenia (61)	Romania (73)	Poland (84)
	Azerbaijan (46)	Moldova (61)	Croatia (74)	Estonia (86)
	Tajikistan (49)		Bulgaria (75)	Czech Republic[b]
	Kazakhstan (49)			

Source: Akbar and Kisilowski (2015).
Notes: Numbers in brackets are weighted averages of means of 2013 EBRD Transition Indicators, expressed in percentage terms (weight of 2) and the 2013 Freedom House Democracy Indices, expressed in percentage terms (weight of 1).
EBRD data is available at http://tr.ebrd.com/tr13/en/
Freedom House data is available at http://www.freedomhouse.org/report-types/nations-transit
[a]Autonomous Republic within the Russian Federation. No EBRD or Freedom House figures available for them separately, so we base our categorization of these republics on Bruno, Bytchkova, and Estrin (2011).
[b]Czech Republic has "graduated" from EBRD transition programs and thus transition indicators are not compiled for the country. The country was considered "consolidated democracy" by the Freedom House.

countries that are rated low on modernization possess formal associational agreements with the EU. At best, they participate in the rather loose EU Neighborhood Policy. What can be concluded from their mapping of CEE/FSU countries is that the EU process of integration that goes well beyond "negative integration" (Balassa, 1961), that is, the opening and the de-regulation of economies is more likely to lead to higher levels of modernization. There is of course a certain circularity in the fact that countries that have already committed to domestic institution building are more likely to be able to join the EU. Nevertheless, there is a qualitative difference in the conditions for joining the EU compared to a more broad and nebulous concept of liberalization. In particular, while advocates for market liberalization assume the emergence of democratic institutions to support markets, the EU accession process explicitly requires it.

The classification in Table 1 is in line with that of other scholars who have studied heterogeneity of the region (Izyumov & Claxon, 2009).

Comparing Table 1 to their classification, there is considerable overlap with "autocratic capitalism" countries being "Low Modernization" countries in Table 1 (with the exception of Kyrgyz Republic (medium–low)); "clan capitalism" being closely aligned to "medium–low" (with the exception of Azerbaijan and Georgia) and "democratic capitalism" encompassing all of the "High Modernization" countries in Table 1.

Similarly regarding political transition, Table 1 is analogous to Hodgson (2006), who used the Polity IV Democracy Index first developed by Monty Marshall and Ted Gurr of the University of Maryland for selected countries in Central and East Europe. Based on a score of 10 (full democracy) to 0 (full anocracy), the countries that scored 8–10 in the Polity IV index used in the study, all are placed in "High Modernization" in Table 1; fully anocratic or partially anocratic countries fall into "low- or medium-low modernization" of Table 1 as well.

In summing up, transition and post-transition cannot be simply characterized as a dichotomy between shock therapy and gradualism. Rather the extent of transition and various elements of the outcomes of transition are contingent on institutional development, notably those institutions that have democratic goals as their primary focus.

MARKET STRATEGIES, INSTITUTIONS, AND TRANSITION

The explicit activities of firms impact the nature of economic modernization itself. This can happen in both conventional, direct ways such as active legislative influence and regulatory capture. It can also occur through the execution of market strategy. Akbar (2003) examined how the execution of strategies based on EU regulatory standards aided the implementation of EU legislation in candidate countries in the process of joining the EU. In addition to the injection of new capital and technology, the study also found that foreign firms that had invested in industries such as telecommunications, banking, and electricity had brought with them best practices based around EU benchmarks and this enabled policymakers to drive through new industry standards compliant with EU requirements facing little resistance from industry actors.

The indirect impact of strategy execution by MNEs occurs because governments of the countries receiving FDI have committed themselves to a process of regulatory convergence toward "higher" standards. The latter commitment is of course a form of transition and the most important historical precedent for such a process was the decade long EU accession process for 11 EU member states from CEE/FSU (EU-11).[1] In engaging themselves in the process of adopting and effectively implementing the *acquis communautaire* of the EU, the EU-11 governments agreed to undertake the most comprehensive exercise in economic and political transition across the CEE/FSU region and without question the most extensive attempt at liberal institution building in the history of many of these countries. The process of transition is so impressive that four of the EU-11 will have adopted the Euro as their currency by 2015 (Estonia, Latvia, Lithuania, and Slovakia).

Another key element in this project of regulatory convergence has been the widespread arrival of inward-FDI into the EU-11 as illustrated in Table 2 below. The advantages and disadvantages of FDI have been widely discussed ((Borensztein, De Gregorio, & Lee, 1998; Durham, 2004 (on the impact on macroeconomic growth); Costa & de Queiroz, 2002; Lall, 1997 (industry and technology level spillovers); and Miskun and Tomscik (2002) and Kosova (2004) on crowding out impacts of inward-FDI)). Much of the discussion surrounds the direct and spillover benefits of inward-FDI to the economy and technological development of the recipient countries. While the evidence on direct benefits such as job creation; increases in productivity and improved consumer choice is not in doubt, the spillover

Table 2. Inward FDI Flows as a Percentage of GDP (1989–2012) – Selected EU Member States.

Country	1990–1995	1996–2001	2002–2007	2008–2012
Bulgaria	2.4	14.4	50.8	78.6
Czech Republic	7.5	26.4	51.6	60.8
Croatia	1.3	10.3	40.3	53.3
Estonia	5.8	35.5	74.2	81.3
Hungary	12.1	43.4	61.6	69.7
Latvia	4.9	23.1	33.1	42.6
Lithuania	2.2	15.7	31.5	34.0
Poland	2.3	14.5	32.3	41.2
Romania	0.8	12.6	27.4	39.9
Slovakia	2.9	20.1	62.9	57.1
Slovenia	7.6	12.0	22.6	30.8
EU-average	11.5	22.0	37.3	43.3

Source: Calculations based on World Bank Data.

benefits such as technology transfer, infrastructure development and improved fiscal positions of governments remains in question (UNCTAD, 2005).

One of the key conditions for spillover benefits to be maximized is the absorptive capacity of a recipient country. Absorptive capacity refers to the ability of a country to diffuse knowledge, technology, and best practice it has absorbed from the initial FDI activity into the broader economy. Factors that promote such absorption include integration of local supply chains with the inward FDI activity and active collaboration between educational institutions and the MNE subsidiaries set up through inward-FDI. The more embedded the MNE subsidiary is with the local economy, the greater the possibility for spillover benefits to accrue to the host economy (Fu, 2008; Khordagui & Saleh, 2013).

Regulatory convergence can be considered a spillover benefit of inward-FDI. In much the same way as technology transfer requires absorptive capacity, regulatory adoption also requires a corresponding capacity in the state. Before examining the factors that promote such adoption, it is first necessary to outline the process by which inward-FDI stimulates regulatory convergence.

Competitive Advantage, Best Practice, and Regulatory Convergence

The literature on business strategy from an RBV perspective (Anand & Delios, 2002; Barney, 1991; Helfat & Peteref, 2009; Kogut & Zander, 1993) suggests that the possession of valuable resources and capabilities that are rare and difficult to imitate places a firm at a potential competitive advantage vis-à-vis its rivals. Moreover, the RBV approach is complementary to the positioning view of strategy that suggests that success is achieved by the appropriate leverage of these resources and capabilities in a distinctive way (Porter, 1985). From a global strategy perspective, MNEs are at a competitive advantage in host economies because they possess "monopolistic" advantages (Calvet, 1981; Dunning, 1988) such as brands, technologies, and organizational forms that are superior to their host competitors. The general strategy literature on distinctiveness and the "monopolistic" advantages approach are clearly corollaries and they lead to the same conclusion: MNEs outcompete local firms where they can most effectively leverage their distinctive resources and capabilities and position themselves in a unique or differentiated way in host markets.

Yet as Khanna and Palepu (2005) suggest, the context under which MNEs can best leverage their distinctive resources and capabilities plays an important and determining role in the success of their strategies. In particular, IVs may undermine the effective leverage of or even eliminate the value of the fundamentally distinctive nature of those resources and capabilities possessed by the MNE. By way of example, where there is an absence of effective intellectual property protection and associated institutions such as court enforcement, an MNE's brand or technology may be easier to copy thus eroding a source of competitive advantage. Another example could be the absence of an effective intermediary such as a functioning payments system that could prevent the distribution of an MNE's services in the local market. In short, where IVs are widespread, the fundamental advantage of being an MNE could be undermined.

The MNE is thus presented with a challenge: in the absence of functioning institutions to protect and support their sources of competitive advantage, how should they compete with local firms? One solution from the literature on global strategy is to internalize as many transactions as possible within the corporate space thus minimizing external leakage into the local market. Traditionally, the MNE will perform greater value added activities in their developed contexts either at home or in other developed markets.

Yet eventually, the MNE, especially one whose strategy is to serve the local market, will need to open up its processes at which point it becomes vulnerable to copying (both legal and illegal) and the challenges of strategy execution in the face of IVs. It is here that the MNE may turn to the leverage of higher standards and superior resources as a means of competitive protection. For example, investing in branding and advertising that communicates the superiority of their products and services. Even if an MNE has invested in a host country to produce for re-export, they can leverage their superior HR strategies to attract the best local talent by offering higher wages, valuable training opportunities, and superior career pathways relative to local firms. Both market-serving and resource-seeking MNEs could also use more advanced equipment, plant and technology relative to local firms enabling them to offer higher quality products and services.

All three of these instances of MNE strategic execution activities lead to two outcomes – one direct and the other indirect. First, if local firms wish to compete with the MNEs, they must devise strategies that can cope with the leveraging of superior resources, capabilities, and positioning possessed by MNEs. Inevitably, they face a choice between competing on the basis of low-cost, lower pricing or they can try and raise their game and assume a differentiated position. The latter implies the creation or acquisition of new and viable resources and acquisitions that they can use to defend their market positions.

Either way, there is an indirect effect and is central to the argument presented here. The competitive interaction between MNEs and local firms raises informal industry standards. As the informal industry standards rise, governments can adopt legislation to institutionalize these standards. If the MNEs are operating on the basis of EU standards, then emerging national legislation can be more effectively harmonized with EU standards enabling accession countries to meet the requirements of membership. Since some local firms will also be seeking to compete on equivalent or superior standards to those used by MNEs and so their resistance to new laws enshrining EU standards will be limited to those firms that try to compete on the basis of older, national standards. In short, the competitive interaction between MNE and host firms on the basis of standards promotes transition toward to higher standards derived from advanced economies.

Akbar (2003) examined this phenomenon in the context of three sectors in CEE: banking, energy, and telecoms. The study discovered that FDI facilitated the introduction of EU legislation related to competition, health and safety, and technical standards across these sectors. Both regulators and senior management from both foreign and local firms in these industries confirmed these developments in the study. The following section takes a different view of the role of MNEs in transition economies – the explicit corporate political strategies pursued by firms and how that impacts regulatory convergence.

NONMARKET STRATEGIES, INSTITUTIONS, AND TRANSITION

In examining the nature of nonmarket strategies of firms operating in the CEE/FSU region, Akbar and Kisilowski (2015) have examined the degree of economic modernization in CEE/FSU countries. They demonstrated an empirical causation between the degree of economic modernization and the evolution of nonmarket strategies toward proactive, low risk strategies. This causation is intuitive. Institutional development that underpins economic modernization typically raises transparency in public institutions and reduces the potential for corruption. The enforcement of laws also reduces threats such as intimidation and extortion. This allows firms to modify their nonmarket strategies. Table 3 illustrates the causation.

For the purposes of this paper, an examination of explicit political corporate strategies is therefore also necessary. Akbar and Kisilowski (2015) examined the nature of direct influence of firms in the institutional development process in the CEE region. They examined three kinds of firms active in the region: MNEs, state-influenced enterprises (SIEs), and independent local enterprises (ILEs). Each of these firms had different goals when it came to institutional development. Moreover, these goals varied as a function of the level of pre-existing institutional development that the firms faced. In broad terms, in low levels of pre-existing institutional development, MNEs would either pursue initiatives aimed at liberalization (to lever open a closed market) or if they were granted a monopoly by an authoritarian government, they would pursue defensive initiatives aimed at maintaining the status quo. By contrast, SIEs would undertake defensive strategies in low levels of institutional development aiming at protecting their state sheltered position against the threat of competition from MNEs and ILEs, respectively. The ILEs' approaches to low levels of institutional development are more difficult to generalize. The size of ILEs matters in this context especially as regards their influence with governments. Larger ILEs who are well connected with governments will behave more like SIEs in low institutional development environments. Smaller, less influential

Table 3. Types of Nonmarket Strategies in CEE/FSU Countries.

Type of Initiative	Conducive Level of Modernization	Strategic Posture Represented	Associated Level of Nonmarket Risk	Most Frequent Users
Violence	Low	Proactive	High	SIEs/ILEs
Bribery solicitation	Generally low	Proactive	High	SIEs/ILEs
Bribery extortion	Low	Reactive	Medium–high	ILEs
Litigation	Generally low	Reactive	Medium–low	MNEs
Involving international actors (e.g., IOs)	Low High	Reactive Proactive	Low	MNEs
Nepotism	Generally high	Proactive	Medium-high	SIEs
Grants and tenders	High	Proactive	Low	MNEs/SIEs/ILEs
Corporatism and protectionism	High	Proactive	Low	MNEs/SIEs/ILEs

Source: Akbar and Kisilowski (2015).

ILEs will tend to navigate their nonmarket strategies below the political radar.

As countries become more institutionally developed, there is a convergence of political strategies pursued by all three firm types. This convergence is toward lower risk but proactive initiatives around leveraging influence over strong institutions. Such tactics would include active participation in privatization tenders and public–private initiatives; corporatist lobby activity and in the case of MNEs, managing a multi-level political game with home and host governments as well as international organizations. Arguably, the net result of this convergence is that MNEs and smaller, less influential ILEs will gain influence and are more likely to pursue liberalization agendas since they both gain through liberalization. As discussed in the section "Competitive Advantage, Best Practice, and Regulatory Convergence" above, MNEs actively pursue institutionalization agendas to leverage their sources of competitive advantage and ILEs benefit from institutionalization because it typically increases transparency through clearer, more predictable rules and processes thereby requiring less of a reliance on opaque, potentially corrupt means of influence peddling.

Arguably, there is circularity to the conventional transition paradigm when analyzed in this context. Transition is argued to increase transparency, improve the allocation of economic resources, and their efficiency of use. It is also expected to bring democratic reforms based on pluralist, liberal institutions. It is also expected to promote the economic interests of MNEs where they cannot secure a monopoly position through exclusive agreement with a host government. Thus the actions of MNEs are argued to be central to the achievement of transition. From a prescriptive point of view and assuming that the conventional transition paradigm is indeed beneficial, countries that have made relatively less progress on transition should encourage the entry of MNEs into their economies.

However, governments in countries that lag in transition face conflicting pressures from SIEs and influential ILEs who will resist liberalization. It becomes even more complicated when the SIEs are controlled by close connections of the ruling governments. For example, the Uzbek economy has been described as "a coterie of movers and shakers close to President Islam Karimov" (Lillis, 2012). Mehriban Pashayeva, the wife of the President of Azerbaijan, controls virtually all of the luxury retail branding rights in the country (Akbar & Kisilowski, 2015). Without the arrival of MNEs, liberalization and institutional development is likely to remain limited since SIEs and many ILEs have little to gain from institutional development. The arrival of MNEs threatens the position of dominant local actors who will invest political and social capital in slowing the transition process. Thus the fundamental following questions remain: how does this confrontation of interests become resolved? How do the governments in transition economies decide which interests to support? Are there other actors such as international organizations and foreign governments that actively pressurize countries to liberalize?

There is a literature drawing on both developing and developed contexts on all these questions. For example Manzetti (1994) documents how coalitions formed to drive distribution of the gains from privatization in Argentina in a far from ideal way as advocated by efficiency arguments. Priebjrivat and Rondinelli (1994) address privatization in Thailand. They find that economic and political crises, the IMF and World Bank aggressively push governments in developing to countries to force through privatization of state-owned enterprises in the context of broader structural adjustment programs and as a condition of borrowing for economic development. Naturally MNEs benefit from these outside pressures as being purveyors of expertise and political influence within International Organizations.

Parker (1999) has also considered the history of privatization within the EU. Aside from discussion of efficiency benefits of privatization, he also demonstrates that there are significant distributional consequences of privatization that imply that governments cannot and do not solely focus on efficiency arguments for privatization but also consider the interests of "insider" coalitions at state-owned firms as well as the political implications of wealth redistribution toward foreign capital. This study is prescient in the light of current debates in Hungary concerning "re-nationalization" and taxation of foreign investors (Balogh, 2013; De Cleerq, 2014; Eddy, 2013).

CONCLUSIONS AND IMPLICATIONS FOR UNDERSTANDING THE TRANSITION PARADIGM

Without question, the economic "high ground" of macroeconomic transformation is a core feature of the transition process that reached its 25 year anniversary in 2014. Yet this paper has sought to develop a more granular understanding of the transition paradigm by examining meso- and micro-level transformations in the countries of Central and East Europe and Central Asia. It was argued that in order to understand the nature of transition, it was important to examine complementary transformations that occur below the macroeconomic radar and which have typically taken place through three connected sources. First, the evolution of public policy and institutions designed to shape the regulatory contours of certain industries or firms. Second, the impacts of market strategies of firms operating in the industries that shape market structure and thereby inform public policy. Third, the nonmarket strategies of firms aimed at explicitly influencing both the shape and elements of public policy.

If macroeconomic liberalization has opened the door to foreign investment, it has been the actual investment and the conduct of the companies making these investments and the response of local competitors that have also had a profound impact on the transition process itself. There is clearly a need for analysis of conflicting interests within a country when trying to understand how transition has proceeded. These conflicts occur through interactions between local and foreign firms in a market and nonmarket context. In the market context, this paper examined how it is a fundamental source of competitive advantage for MNEs to use higher standards to compete with local firms. These standards are often those that are compliant with EU regulations providing an indirect source of transformation, forcing prevailing industry practices toward EU standards and leading to faster regulatory convergence between "lower" local standards to "higher" EU ones. Local firms can try and slowdown the introduction of these standards; adopt the new standards; or exit the industry.

The second mechanism that produces conflict between local and foreign firms is through the exercise of nonmarket strategies. Here, the paper looks at three categories of firms drawing on the work of Akbar and Kisilowski (2015): multinational enterprises, state-influenced enterprises (SIEs), and independent local enterprises (ILEs). Both SIEs and ILEs fear the arrival of MNEs due to the apparent superior capabilities and resources possessed by the latter. However, whereas SIEs face challenges of their dominant position from the arrival of MNEs, ILEs face fundamental challenges to their survival due to difficulties they face in competing with MNEs.

This paper has explored how the transition process is profoundly impacted by industry and enterprise level conduct and actions. An understanding of these processes is a vital complement to the macroeconomic tradition of transition studies and should be the focus of ongoing scholarship in the area of transition research. One area that this paper has not directly engaged in but is nevertheless worthy of discussion is the distributional consequences of transition and the extent to which the original goals of transition: the creation of functioning markets; the increasing diversification of the economic base of these countries; the embedding of transparent and democratic, pluralist economic institutions has been achieved.

NOTE

1. The EU-11 in chronological order of accession are: 2004 – Czech Republic, Estonia, Hungary, Latvia, Lithuania, Poland, Slovakia, Slovenia; 2007 – Bulgaria, Romania; 2013 – Croatia.

REFERENCES

Akbar, Y. (2003). *The multinational enterprise, EU enlargement and Central Europe: The effects of regulatory convergence*. London: Palgrave.

Akbar, Y., Bortoluzzi, G., & Tracogna, A. (2014). Beyond entry mode – SME escalation in emerging markets: A conceptual framework. *Journal International Business and Entrepreneurship Development*, *7*(4), 326–340.

Akbar, Y., & Kisilowski, M. (2015). Nonmarket strategy in Central Asia and Eastern Europe. In T. Lawton & T. Rajwani (Eds.), *Routledge companion to nonmarket strategy*. London: Routledge.

Anand, J., & Delios, A. (2002). Absolute and relative resources as determinants of international acquisitions. *Strategic Management Journal*, *23*(2), 119–134.

Andres, A. R., & Ramlogan-Dobson, C. (2011). Is corruption really bad for inequality? Evidence from Latin America. *Journal of Development Studies*, *47*(7), 959–976.

Arnold, D. J., & Quelch, J. A. (1998). New strategies in emerging markets. *Sloan Management Review*, *38*(3), 7–20.

Ashiku, M. (2011). Political transition, corruption in new democracies. *International Journal of Business Management & Economic Research*, *2*(3), 238–249.

Balassa, B. (1961). Towards a theory of economic integration. *Kyklos*, *14*(1), 1–17.

Balcerowicz, L. (1994). Understanding postcommunist transitions. *Journal of Democracy*, *4*(5), 75–89.

Balogh, E. (2013). Nationalization Hungarian style. *Hungarian Spectrum*, June 27.

Barney, J. (1991). Firm resources and sustained competitive advantage. *Journal of Management*, *17*(1), 99–120.

Borensztein, E., De Gregorio, J., & Lee, J.-W. (1998). How does foreign direct investment affect economic growth? *Journal of International Economics*, *45*(1), 115–135.

Bruno, R. L., Bytchkova, M., & Estrin, S. (2011). *Institutions and entry: A cross-regional analysis in Russia*. Institute for the Study of Labor.

Calvet, A. L. (1981). A synthesis of foreign direct investment theories and theories of the multinational firm. *Journal of International Business Studies*, (Spring-Summer), 43–60.

Costa, I., & de Queiroz, S. R. (2002). Foreign direct investment and technological capabilities in Brazilian industries. *Research Policy*, *31*, 1431–1443.

Council of the European Union. (1993). *Presidency conclusions*. Copenhagen European Council, 7.A.iii. Retrieved from http://www.europarl.europa.eu/enlargement/ec/pdf/cop_en.pdf

De Cleerq, G. (2014). Insight: Europe's utilities squeezed by creeping nationalization. *Reuter's Newswire Sunday*, January 19.

Dobson, S., & Ramlogan-Dobson, C. (2012). Inequality, corruption and the informal sector. *Economics Letters*, *115*(1), 104–107.

Dunning, J. H. (1998). An overview of relations with national governments. *New Political Economy*, *3*(2), 280.

Durham, J. B. (2004). Absorptive capacity and the effects of foreign direct investment and equity foreign portfolio investment on economic growth. *European Economic Review*, *48*(2), 285–306.

EBRD. (2007). *Transition report*. London: EBRD.

EBRD. (2012). *Transition report*. London: EBRD.

Eddy, K. (2013). Hungary: Re-nationalisation speeds up. Beyond BRICS. *Financial Times*, March 28.

Feinberg, R., & Meurs, M. (2008). Market reform and infrastructure development in transition economies. *Review of Development Economics*, *12*(2), 237–247.

Fidrmuc, J. (2003). Economic reform, democracy and growth during post-communist transition. *European Journal of Political Economy*, *19*, 585.

Fischer, S. (1993). Socialist economy reforms: The lessons of the first three years. *American Economic Review*, *2*(8), 390–395.

Frankel, J. A., & Romer, D. H. (1999). Does trade cause growth? *American Economic Review*, *89*(3), 379–399.

Fu, X. (2008). Foreign direct investment, absorptive capacity and regional innovation capabilities in China. *Oxford Development Studies*, *36*(1), 89–110.

Hare, P. (2012). Institutions and the diversification of economies in transition. In R. Vos & M. Koparanova (Eds.), *Globalization and economic diversification: Policy challenges for economies in transition*. London: Bloomsbury Academic.

Healey, N. (1991). Prospects for economic reform in the USSR. *Economic and Political Weekly*, *26*(41), 23–46.

Helfat, C., & Peteraf, M. (2009). Understanding dynamic capabilities: Progress along a developmental path. *Strategic Organization*, *7*(1), 91–102.

Hodgson, G. (2006). Institutions, recessions and recovery in the transitional economies. *Journal of Economic Issues*, *15*(4), 875–894.

Izyumov, A., & Claxon, T. (2009). Models of capitalism and income distribution in transition economies: A comparative perspective. *Journal of Economic Issues*, M.E. Sharpe, Inc., 43(3), 733–758.

Khanna, T., & Palepu, K. (2010). *Winning in emerging markets: A road map for strategy and execution*. Cambridge: HBR Press.

Khanna, T., Palepu, K., & Sinha, J. (2005). Strategies that fit emerging markets. *Harvard Business Review*, *83*(6), 63–76.

Khanna, T., & Palepu, K. G. (1997). Why focused strategies may be wrong for emerging markets. *Harvard Business Review*, *75*(4), 41–51.

Khordagui, N., & Saleh, G. (2013). FDI and absorptive capacity in emerging economies. *Topics in Middle Eastern and African Economies*, *15*(1), 141–172.

Kogut, B., & Zander, I. (1993). Knowledge of the firm and the evolutionary theory of the multinational corporation. *Journal of International Business Studies*, *24*, 625–645.

Kornai, J. (1995). *Highways and byways: Studies on reform and postcommunist transition*. Cambridge, MA: The MIT Press.

Kosova, R. (2004). *Do foreign firms crowd out domestic firms? The evidence from the Czech Republic*. Unpublished Ph.D. dissertation, University of Michigan Business School.

Lall, S. (1997). Investment, technology and international competitiveness. In J. H. Dunning & K. A. Hamdani (Eds.), *The new globalism and developing countries*. Tokyo: UNU Press.

Lillis, J. (2012). *Uzbekistan: Tashkent's sticky fingers spoiling foreign investors' appetites*. Retrieved from http://www.eurasianet.org/node/65735

Manzetti, L. (1994). The politics of privatization and deregulation in Latin America. *The Quarterly Review of Economics and Finance*, *34*(Special Issue), 43–76.

Miskun, J., & Tomscik, V. (2002). Does foreign direct investment crowd in or crowd out domestic investment? *Eastern European Economics*, *40*(2), 38–56.

Olson, M. (1965). *The logic of collective action: Public goods and the theory of groups*. Cambridge, MA: Harvard University Press.

Parker, D. (1999). Privatization in the European Union: A critical assessment of its development, rationale and consequences. *Economic and Industrial Democracy*, *20*(1), 9–38.

Peev, E., & Mueller, D. (2012). Democracy, economic freedom and growth in transition economies. *Kyklos*, *3*(65), 371–407.

Porter, M. (1985). *The competitive advantage of nations*. New York, NY: Free Press.

Priebjrivat, V., & Rondinelli, D. A. (1994). Privatizing Thailand's telecommunications industry: A case study of politics and international business. *Business and the Contemporary World*, *6*(1), 70–83.

Roarry, M. (1992). Economic reform in Eastern Europe and the Soviet Union. *European Research*, *3*(Pt. 1), 1–41.

Rybczynski, T. M. (1991). The sequencing of reform. *Oxford Review of Economic Policy*, *7*(4), 1–9.

Sachs, J. (1993). *Poland's jump to the market economy*. Cambridge, MA: MIT Press.

Shinkle, G. A., & Kriauciunas, A. P. (2012). The impact of current and founding institutions on strength of competitive aspirations in transition economies. *Strategic Management Journal*, *33*(4), 448–458.

Steenkamp, J. B. E. M. (2005). Moving out of the U.S. silo: A call to arms for conducting international marketing research. *Journal of Marketing*, *69*, 6–8.

UNCTAD. (2005). *World investment report*. Geneva: United Nations.

United Nations Conference on Trade and Development (UNCTAD). (2011). World Investment Report, United Nations, Geneva.

Wiig, A., & Kolstad, I. (2012). If diversification is good, why don't countries diversify more? The political economy of diversification in resource-rich countries. *Energy Policy*, *40*(1), 196–203.

THE NEO-TRANSITIONAL PARADOX: RESTRICTIVE CAPITAL REGULATIONS, AUTHORITARIAN STATE AND LIMITED WELFARE TYPE OF CAPITALISM EXAMINED IN INTERNATIONAL CONTEXT

Martina Lubyova and Pavol Babos

ABSTRACT

In this paper we show that the neo-transitional economies are less neoliberal than could be expected given their 25-years long transition towards building market environment, supporting entrepreneurship and restoring capitalism in general. According to factor analysis results based on a cross-sectional sample of 134 countries during the period of 2010–2012 we find that the neo-transitional economies are characterised by relatively restrictive trade and capital regulations, average level of labour protection and low activity of state in terms of tax-based redistribution and social cohesion support. We briefly review several theoretical frameworks, such as the World System Theory, Commodity Chain and

Neo-Transitional Economics
International Finance Review, Volume 16, 121–147

ISSN: 1569-3767/doi:10.1108/S1569-376720150000016006

Global Capital theory, and Varieties of Capitalism framework, and point towards their limitations in explaining these transitional outcomes. We conclude that these frameworks are not capable of providing the explanations mainly because of their limited or no concern for labour and capital, and their interactions with the national institutions. We conclude that the history of industrialisation and path dependence provides a more plausible framework for explaining the neo-transitional outcomes. Furthermore, the consideration of the 'resource curse' and authoritarian regimes in many CIS countries can explain their neglect for tax-based redistribution and the high degree of government interventions in trade and capital regulations.

Keywords: Economic integration; international economic order; varieties of capitalism

JEL classifications: F66; P5

INTRODUCTION

Several proponents and scholars of modern political economy claim that following the death of the Washington consensus (Deepak, 2012; Estevadeordal & Taylor, 2008; Maxwell, 2005) the neoliberalisation has also been sliding back from its best. The discussion of the neoliberalism's failure is voluminous and rich. Some argue that the neoliberal project failed because the neoliberal policies were not able to secure at least the same level of economic growth as did the Keynesian policies (e.g. Harvey, 2006). Others argue that the neoliberal ideology has suffered a blow because Western states lost their hegemony in the global economy (Birch & Mykhnenko, 2010; Wong, 2009). Finally, the financial crisis that started in 2007 provided a considerable amount of ammunition to deny and condemn the idea inherent to neoliberalism – that free markets will be the most efficient mechanisms to allocate resources and drive the economic progress.

Although there is certainly a lot of substance to the arguments reviewed above, neoliberalist project influenced the transitional economies of post-communist states rather heavily. The neoliberal approach was handy for achieving the main goals of the economic transition – restoration of private property and creation of the free market economy. Neoliberalist approach to economic development and growth became so prominent that it became the base for international institutions' recommendation and policies.

The World Bank (WB), the International Monetary Fund (IMF) and the World Trade Organisation (WTO) were among the most known proponents of trade liberalisation, deregulation and monetisation. The economic reforms in the post-socialist states of Europe and Central Asia were, more often than not, consulted and advised by international institutions such as the IMF and the WB. Governments had to liberalise the markets of goods and services, liberalise trade, deregulate prices. Many states were dependent on the foreign direct investments to innovate or at least maintain the technological level of their industries. In an attempt to attract investors, governments lowered taxes, provided tax holidays, adjusted labour codes and much more. Those countries that aspired to a membership to various international organisations (be it the European Union [EU], Organisation for Economic Cooperation and Development [OECD] or WTO) had to further adjust their legislation. Thus, there is no surprise that the post-socialist states restarted their economies in a more or less neoliberal way after the collapse of communism.

However, the mantra of deregulation, privatisation and liberalisation has not been pursued so evidently recently. On the contrary, the global financial crisis facilitated processes and policies that went quite the opposite direction. Several post-socialist countries witnessed nationalisation or buy-back of the previously privatised companies, governments seized the pension funds and regulation, specifically on the labour markets, became heavier. Therefore it is understandable that one might claim neoliberalism to be retreating.

In this paper we map the effects of transition in the post-socialist region and argue that few countries are open to neoliberal ideas and practices. We show that, on average, the post-socialist states are less open to neoliberalism than Western industrialised countries in many respects. Additionally, we argue that within the former Soviet bloc the countries with economies based on export of oil, gas and minerals are even less prone to neoliberal approaches to trade and capital restrictions than other post-socialist states.

The next section starts with conceptualising our approach to neoliberalism and its link to transitional economies. Subsequently we present empirical data to support our main claim. The section 'Theoretical Frameworks for Explaining the Neo-Transitional Outcomes' starts with an argument that in order to understand the lower openness of the post-socialist states to neoliberalism, we need to include the labour and its relation to capital into the analysis. Then we proceed to explain the main differences between the labour-capital relations in Western Europe on the one hand and the post-socialist states on the other hand. Finally, we conclude that the most plausible theoretical framework for explaining our empirical findings is represented by *the history of industrialisation and path dependence. Within the CIS region the theory needs to be enriched by the consideration of the 'resource curse' that enables resource-rich countries to neglect the tax-based redistribution and to build authoritarian societies beyond the level that should be acceptable in the 21st century.*

NEO-TRANSITIONAL ECONOMIES AT A GLANCE: RESTRICTIVE CAPITAL AND TRADE REGULATIONS, LIMITED DEGREE OF TAX REDISTRIBUTION AND LOW SOCIAL COHESION SUPPORT

Post-communist societies and economies have been in the state of transition for almost a quarter of century now. Most of that time, the economic transition has been driven by the neoliberal way of thinking. Therefore, we need to explain our understanding of neoliberalism, especially from the point of view which affects post-communist, transitional economies.

Traditional political economic approach to neoliberalism is based on the claim that a free market is the most effective way to organise human activities and that the micro gains and spill-over effects will also lead to more equality and less social disparities. However, the neoliberalism is not a pure economic concept. The neoliberal turn was supposed to change social relations as a whole by the means of market expansions. Government retrenchment, in turn, created pressure on individuals to become more responsible for their health, education and their well-being in general.

Our approach to this issue and to studying neo-transitional positions of the post-socialist countries is different. We depart from the above-mentioned political economic concept of neoliberalism and acknowledge the market mechanisms to be at the core of the concept. However, we do not aim to measure the neoliberalism itself. We build on the concept's terms and look to what extent the transitional processes affected the social relations and economic policies of the transitional economies. Since the free market and little government intervention are the flagships of neoliberalism, we work under the following assumptions: the more the government is open to neoliberalism, the less it will regulate the financial markets and capital flows. Additionally, the more the government is open to neoliberalism, the less it will intervene in the market economy in order to redistribute and correct its failures.

In our previous research (Lubyova & Babos, 2014; Lubyova & Vojtkova, 2014) we performed, among others, a factor analysis to see whether there is empirical evidence supporting our thesis of three latent dimensions as described above. We tested more than 10 different indicators and groups of variables and we found that they are strongly correlated into blocks that represent certain underlying factors. Speaking in the terms of the VoC framework, the groupings of variables obtained through factor analysis are taken as proxies for the functioning of various institutional aspects of socio-economic systems, such as capital markets, labour markets, social cohesion, education systems, goods market and so on.

We build our empirical analysis on selected indicators capturing the degree of government interventions and regulations, notably the indexes of economic freedom compiled by The Heritage Foundation and other relevant characteristics (see Appendix A for the description of indicators). We use the factor analysis technique to group these indicators into composite factors that represent the main institutional blocks of the national economies. Our empirical analysis of 54 countries in Lubyova and Babos (2014) and 134 countries in Lubyova and Vojtkova (2014) revealed the existence of three such distinct institutional blocks: *trade and capital market, labour market, and government interventions in terms of tax-based redistribution and social cohesion.*

VoC works, such as, for example, Knell and Srholec (2007) use factor analysis to assess the prevailing type of institutional coordination. We use factor analysis in an analogical way to capture the degree of global openness (or lack of government interventions and regulations). In line with the neoliberal global agenda, we assume that less intervention by the national governments in terms of trade and capital regulations attracts global entrepreneurship. Likewise, less labour protection and higher skills of labour force and less active governments in terms of taxation and redistribution are attractive for global capital and thus increase the global openness of the countries (see Box 1 for a more detailed description of variables and their links to the global openness).

Based on groups of highest factor loadings, we construct global openness indices for three principal factors for each country similar to the construction of a coordination index in the previous literature (notably Knell & Srholec, 2007). Variables are normalised and factor scoring coefficients are used as weights. In this way, we were able to construct indexes that measure the degree of government intervention and regulation in trade and capital markets, and labour markets. We denote these indexes as *Capital Restrictions Index and Labour Market Protection Index, respectively.*

Box 1. Analysis of the Degree of Global Openness and Non-Interventionism of Governments in Capital and Labour Markets Tax-Based Redistribution.

In our empirical analysis based on cross-sectional data for 54 countries in Lubyova and Babos (2014) and for 134 countries in Lubyova and Vojtkova (2014) we apply factor analysis to selected indicators of non-interventionism of the government during 2010–2012, notably the indexes of economic freedom compiled by The Heritage Foundation and other relevant characteristics. We use the factor analysis technique used in the varieties of capitalism literature to group the various indicators into composite factors that represent the main institutional blocks of the national economies. The factor analysis grouped our variables into the following three factors: trade and capital market regulations, labour market regulations, and government interventions in terms of tax collection and redistribution of resources.

Firstly, there was a *labour factor* which indicates the state's activities and interventions in the labour markets. This factor included indicators such as minimum wage, regulatory burden, hire and fire practices, the skill level of the labour force and so on. The factor analysis proved that these variables are closely correlated and constitute a relatively homogeneous picture about the labour market regulatory framework. Secondly, trade and capital market indicators were, similarly as the labour market ones, found to correlate with each other and to form the second distinctive factor – the *trade and capital factor* – that includes characteristics such as the financial institutions independence, investment freedom, price stability, tariff and trade quotas, and others. This factor represents the second regulatory framework of a country's institutional setup. To put it simply, this factor tells us to what extent the state regulates the choices of investors or provides the capital a relatively free environment. Thirdly, the factor that we called *social cohesion factor* was based on variables measuring redistribution, tax rates, indebtedness and fiscal policy. In general, the third factor aims at correcting the negative consequences of the market economy.

We use the technique based on factor analysis to capture the degree of global openness (or lack of government interventions and regulations) as follows: (i) an increasing degree of monetary, trade, investment, and financial freedom implies more global openness in the trade and capital market segment; (ii) in the labour market segment, global openness is assumed to increase with the index of labour freedom, higher mean years of schooling of the adult population, and higher share of long-term unemployment[2] (openness is also assumed to increase with the ease of shareholder suits index, taking into consideration the perspective of employees as potential shareholders; the ease of shareholder suits index measures the strength of minority shareholder protections against directors' misuse of corporate assets for personal gain); (iii) for the government interventions segment, we assume more global openness with a decreasing degree of national regulations (captured by a decreasing fiscal freedom index), as well as decreasing degree of national government interventions (captured by government spending relative to GDP and by maximum tax rates on income and corporate income). In this way the indicators can be used as proxies for the non-interventionism of the government or the openness of the national economies to the global deployment of production factors (capital and labour).

Variables are normalised and factor scoring coefficients are used as weights. Based on groups of highest factor loadings, we construct global openness sub-indices for three principal factors for each country, as well as an overall global openness index as a weighted average of the three sub-indices.

For a full list of countries included in the analysis and the corresponding indices values see Appendix B.

The higher are the values of these indexes, the lower is the degree of government interventions and regulations and the more opened these markets are for global entrepreneurship. Similarly, for the third institutional block we constructed a *Government Intervention Index* that increases with the degree of government interventions in terms of tax redistribution and public expenditures. Finally, we constructed a composite *Global Openness Index* from the three sub-indices as a weighted average using equal weights. As we assume that the global openness increases with decreasing degree of government interventions, the Global Openness Index can be used as a proxy for the overall degree of openness of the national economies to global capital or entrepreneurship in general.

It should be no surprise that the three regulatory frameworks relate to each other, which allows researchers and analysts to construct and compare the overall regulatory framework of the transitional economies. The resulting values of indices plot an image of several clusters of countries with different profiles. We review the clusters shortly here, since we believe it is an important stepping stone to a better understanding of the transitional economies in the post-socialist region.[1]

Fig. 1 presents the Global Openness Index on a map of Europe and Central Asia. The map clearly shows that the global openness decreases as we move from Western Europe eastward: Central Eastern European members of the European Union are less open than their Western counterparts and more open than the post-socialist non-members. Central Asian countries and Russia belong to the least open countries. *In our view, this decreasing gradient of global openness (or increasing gradient of restrictions and interventionism by the governments) from West towards East tells the transition story*. In what follows, we look at the three sub-indices to identify different types of 'capitalism' that occurred in the neo-transitional economies and to compare them with the Western countries. We also try to explain our results by grouping the countries into several clusters with common background.

In Figs. 2 and 3 we present the values of all the above-mentioned indexes for individual countries. Fig. 2 plots the Capital Restriction Index against the Government Intervention Index. Western countries are clustered in the upper right corner of the chart with the highest degree of government

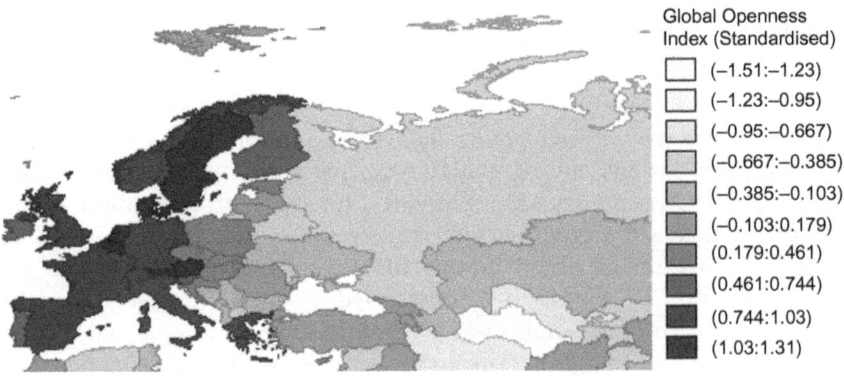

Fig. 1. Global Openness Index Map of Europe and Central Asia. *Source*: Authors' processing of the GOI values calculated in Lubyova and Vojtková (2014). *Notes*: Darker shades represents higher GOI value. In other words, the lighter shades on the map show countries with lower global openness. See Appendix A for the list of country codes and values of indices.

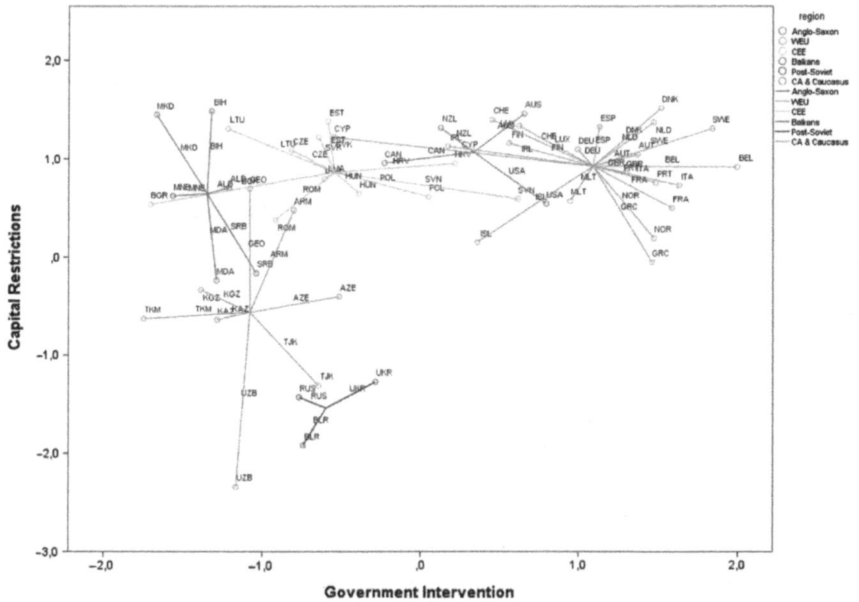

Fig. 2. Clusters of Countries According to the Government Interventions in Terms of Social Cohesion and Capital Regulations. *Source*: Authors based on values of indices calculated in Lubyova and Vojtkova (2014). *Note*: See Appendix A for the list of country codes and values of indices.

interventions in redistribution and social cohesion and the lowest degree of the capital restrictions (i.e. highest trade and capital freedom). In a sense, this position can be understood as a liberal stance to let in the global capital, combined with a strong interventionist position to protect the vulnerable citizens through tax-based redistribution and fiscal measures. The group of post-socialist European countries regulate capital to a similar extent, but intervene to a lesser degree to support the social cohesion. The CIS countries, as the figure shows, constitute the group of states least open to capital and at the same time the least degree of interventions aimed at supporting social cohesion. *The position of the neo-transitional countries thus can be understood as least liberal towards deployment of global capital and entrepreneurship and at the same time most passive in terms of tax-based redistribution and fiscal measures aimed at supporting social cohesion.*

Fig. 3 shows another noteworthy picture: countries that are less open in terms of the global index have their labour force more protected.[2] The

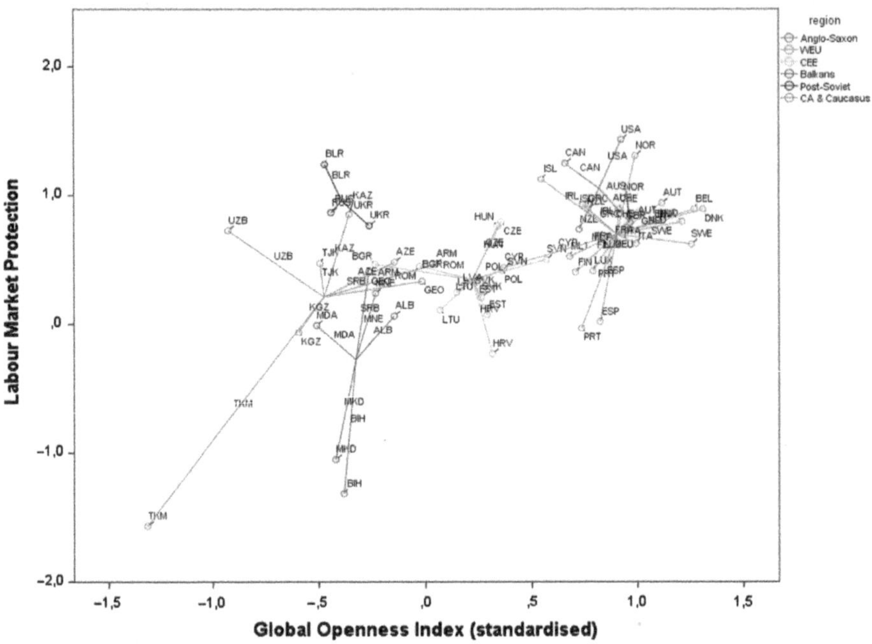

Fig. 3. Clusters of Countries According to the Global Openness and Labour Regulations. *Source*: Authors based on values of indices calculated in Lubyova and Vojtkova (2014). *Note*: See Appendix A for the list of country codes and values of indices.

countries with higher degree of global openness are naturally attractive for global capital. These countries intervene less in labour market regulations in order to protect their citizens – individual workers. In terms of our results, the Western countries have relatively more opened labour markets (and highest values of the overall Global Openness Index). The neo-transitional countries have less opened labour markets, although one has to note that the degree of labour market openness varies largely across the latter group and it is high on average. While Turkmenistan is the country with the least opened labour market in terms of our methodology, other countries, such as Russia and Kazakhstan surpass the level of many Western countries in this regard.

Naturally, a question arises what has led to the institutional setup of the transitional economies as depicted in Figs. 2 and 3, in particular when we consider that the pressure of neoliberalism in the post-socialist countries was rather strong. One would expect the region to become more open to investors, lift the restrictions of capital markets and emulate the labour market institutions of the West. The explanation of why the position of the neo-transitional economies to global investors has developed against these expectations may be rather complex. In the following part of this paper we point to the direction where the answers can be found.

THEORETICAL FRAMEWORKS FOR EXPLAINING THE NEO-TRANSITIONAL OUTCOMES

In this section we search for theoretical frameworks that could explain the results of our comparative analysis as described by the above-mentioned neo-transitional outcomes. Given that the transitional economies have been developing in a globalising competitive environment, we start by discussing the potential of global frameworks, such as the world systems theory (WST) and Commodity Chains and Global Capital (GCC) framework. However, as these influential theories do not take into consideration the labour-capital interactions, we turn towards a more comprehensive Varieties of Capitalism (VoC) framework. Finally, we conclude that focusing on Industrialisation and Path Dependence arguments provides the best framework for explaining our regional clusters.

World System Theory

The three clusters of countries depicted in our figures (i.e. Western countries, Central and Eastern European EU members, and Central and Eastern European non-EU countries plus Balkans) might conspicuously resemble three categories of the World System Theory (Wallerstein, 1974, 1989). The World System Theory (WTS) constructs a framework that studies capitalism and changes in the global capitalist world in long-term perspective. Practitioners of the WTS work with three elements of the system. There is the core zone with high value-added production and the periphery with low technological level and low-skilled labour force. The former exploits the latter in order to gather the economic surplus and transfer it back to the core economies. In addition, there are also semi-peripheries, which are literally in between the two extreme types. WTS approach allows for mobility, both upward and downward, of countries among the different zones. It is tempting to claim that the multinational companies outsource their production from core countries (Western countries) to periphery countries (CIS a non-EU Central and Eastern Europe) so that they can use the comparative advantage of their own technological superiority and the local cheap labour. The position of Central Eastern European countries could then be explained as semi-peripheral.

However, the problem with the WTS is that the theory cannot explain why certain countries choose to adopt policies and measures that welcome capital while other states choose to regulate more. The WTS is also incapable of grasping the differences in the extent to which individual states intervene in the economy and redistribute resources. The problem here is that the WTS's understanding of capitalism is overly focused on the production and firms while it completely overlooks the social relations and historical developments of capitalist societies (Selwyn, 2012; King & Wood, 1999). In particular, the interactions of labour and capital with each other and with other factors of production go unnoticed in the WTS framework. Therefore, the WTS cannot explain the difference in openness to neoliberalism across countries, although it allows for mobility of countries across zones.

Commodity Chains and Global Capital

A more empirical approach to study global capitalism and development was introduced by Gereffi and Korzeniewicz (1994). In their 'Commodity Chains and global Capital' (known also as GCC) the authors departed from the WTS theory and shifted towards the firm-level analysis. They highlight that it is among firms' abilities and competencies to govern the whole sectors of national economies. By means of international trade firms can also push for change of standards or legislative changes. Firms' activities thus might have positive effects on the whole economy by making pressure for technological change, capital-labour relations and the whole economic development of a country. This theory certainly has merit. Several Central European countries witnessed a similar process in the 2000s. Foreign investors, large multinational companies moved to Central Europe and brought technological progress with them. They also made pressure for a change of many policies, or at least they were able to negotiate an opt-out from others. In line with the GCC argument we can say the foreign capital has shifted Central European economies to more innovative and effective production by introducing new methods of production and new sources of supply.

Both the WST and the GCC theories have a lot to say about the capitalist development in the post-socialist Europe. However, we argue, in line with Selwyn (2012) that an important element is missing there. Neither of the two approaches takes into consideration the social relations, especially the capital-labour relations and their interactions with other elements of the system. The national economy is to the same extent a political entity as it is an economic one. The class conflict between labour and capital is, in our opinion, disentangleable from the development of (not only) transitional economies. Selwyn labels the capital-labour relations as 'organic co-determinant of capitalist development' (2012, p. 210).

Varieties of Capitalism

Finally, the Varieties of Capitalism theory (VoC; Hall & Soskice, 2001) represent an influential approach to studying capitalism from a global perspective. VoC's primary concern is national economy and more specifically the coordination of its actors. National economies develop specific institutional setting which drives firms, banks, educational institutions and other involved actors to coordinate their activities in a certain way. By specialising and coordinating in a distinct way from each other there is comparative advantage with different ways of specialisation and innovation paths in different countries.

Practitioners of the VoC approach have empirically studied the post-socialist countries and the volume of published results is relatively rich (Babos & Klimplová, 2013; Drahokoupil & Myant, 2011; Lane & Myant, 2007; Feldmann, 2006; Nölke & Vliegenthart, 2009, and many others). However, there is no consensus on what kind of capitalism has evolved in the post-socialist Europe and some scholars even question whether the VoC theory is applicable to the post-communist states (a good introduction to this debate can be found in Bluhm, 2010).

The issue is that the VoC theory studies capitalist institutions. The founding fathers of the theory argued that the VoC application should be limited only to developed economies (Hall & Gingerich, 2009; Hall & Soskice, 2001). For instance, Hall and Soskice excluded Mexico from their analysis arguing that although the country is OECD member, it still is 'a developing nation' (2001, p. 21). In this regard it is questionable to what extent the VoC analysis can be performed, for example, on countries of Central Asia, Caucasus region or Belarus. Despite the discussion, several attempts have been made. Lane and Myant studied the post-soviet republics and concluded that most of them are hybrid state-market uncoordinated capitalisms, while some of them have not developed a capitalist system yet (Uzbekistan, Belarus, Turkmenistan) and are likely to remain statist economies, on the other hand.

Admittedly, the VoC approach sheds light on the capitalist (and some non-capitalist post-soviet) regimes of the post-socialist world. And VoC has definitely done a great job bringing the labour back in to the analysis. However, even those who apply the VoC approach to describe the regimes of the Eastern Europe and Central Asia fall short of explaining, why has the given specific configuration of mutual social and economic relationships developed in one country and not in the other. At the beginning of the paper we set the aim to go beyond the description of the transitional economies' status quo. We would like to point to direction which might bring us some explanations of how did the differences between the post-socialist countries emerged and persisted even after 25 years of transition that started with rather high neoliberal influence. In order to do so, or at least to make the first step it is necessary to look at the mutual societal relationship between the three actors: capital, labour and government. Two countries with the same leading sectors, same production specialisation and being in the same WST zone might still have a rather different degree of openness to global investors and capital, if they have different configuration of the capital-labour-government relations. This is the reason why studying the mutual relationships of *all the three* factors might prove helpful in understanding the results of the transition in the post-socialist world. This is also the added value of the analysis in this paper.

Industrialisation and Path Dependence: Bringing the Labour Back in

In this part of the paper we argue that the openness of countries to neoliberalism is conditioned by the way societies industrialised and modernised in the past. In order to explain our argument the best, we need to briefly review the different processes of modernisation in Europe, Russia and Central Asia.

Many people, scholars including, may ask why the Eastern Central Europe or Central Asia have not been economically developing to the same level and at the same pace as the West. On the other hand, others claim that such a question is not phrased properly and we should ask why is it the West developing in its specific way (Brenner, 1991; Chirot, 1991; Gellner, 1988; Suda & Musil, 2000). In other words, we should not be so much curious specifically about the backwardness of the post-socialist countries, since they are (or at least most of them are) 'like the rest of the world, slow to change and progress' (Chirot, 1991, p. 4).

If we accept this line of thinking (and we do so in this paper), we need to ask which factors contributed to the West's special position. Gellner has studied the transitions of agrarian societies to industrial (or modern) states. In his book he brought several conditions which, if present at the same time, should give rise to successful modern societies as was the case of England or the Netherlands. In Box 2 we review some of the most important conditions and compare the main differences between the West and the East.

Although Gellner continues with several more requirements for the West's specific development path (which could be synonymously understood also as reasons for East's backwardness) it is sufficient for our argument to review our remote historical sociological comparison as it is in the Box 2. *The central message is that while the West has started with processes of industrialisation, modernisation and urbanisation already in 16th century, the empires that covered today's post-socialist states remained heavily agrarian societies for centuries longer*. As Musil argues, this had consequences in the political sphere as well. Mainly it was evident in different participation of society in decision making process, in the articulation of interests and the structure and orientation of political parties (2000, p. 176).

Different historical development in Europe also meant different nature of the class conflict and the role of state in it. In the West middle classes learned how to defend their interest and the labour gained structural and political power. However, in the East the middle class was almost non-existent and the peasants never gained any power. Although, it must be noted, that agrarian parties were dominant forces in the interwar period in some countries, they never truly defended the interests of their constituencies (Musil, 2000).

The position of labour in the East has not improved after the Communist regimes were installed (whether before or after the World War II, depending on the region). Communist regime faced very weak to zero middle classes, very low level of urbanisation and industrialisation. The state took a dominant position in almost all processes of economy and imposed modernisation from above. What has naturally developed in the West for centuries has been forced in the East in decades. Musil points out that many scholars agree that there were many similarities between feudalism and communism. 'Labour relations in the latter are often characterizes as a new serfdom' (2000, p. 191).

Box 2. Main Conditions of Transition from Agrarian to Industrial Societies According to Gellner.

One of the most important conditions is the *separation of church from state*. Looking back couple of centuries, only in the West the historians can speak of the separation of state powers from the church. There were basically three empires in the region that could be now labelled as post-socialist countries: the Austro-Hungarian, the Russian and the Ottoman. In all three of the empires the power was shared between aristocracy, army and clerics. As Musil points out, the requirement that the states exercised power with restrain 'would be difficult to claim' (Musil, 2000, p. 173).

Another point Gellner has made is that the *peasants should be free and aristocracy permeable*. Regarding the farmers, situation across Europe was, again, rather different in times of modern states emergence. While the northwester parts of Europe witnessed relatively free farmers, the working class of Eastern agrarian societies was firmly bound to Aristocracy. This bond was strong to such an extent that landlords often decided about private matters and lives of peasants. The difference in upward mobility between the Western and Eastern openness of aristocracy was also notable (Musil, 2000).

Expanding the 'bribery fund,' as Gellner calls it (1988, p. 160), was another pre-requisite to fast growing Western societies. As the author explains, the emerging production-oriented class of capitalists needed to bribe the old rulers so that they refrain from attempts to stop the process societal change. On the other hand, the industrialisation was also coupled with urbanisation and the new class of urban poor emerged. Gellner argues that this people needed to be bribed as well in order to keep the social order. This is also a beginning of the social programmes that later developed into what we know as modern welfare. However, in the Eastern part of Europe, the bribery fund was not expanding. Musil explains that one of the reasons is the unavailability of resources. Ruling elites had to maintain strong armies and for this reason they bribed aristocracy by 'giving it a free hand in exploiting the peasants' (2000, p. 174), which in turn lead to 'the creation of a dependent and powerless peasant mass. … This situation, understandably, was a formidable barrier to the development of capitalism in agriculture' (*ibid.*).

We will not explain all the key concepts of the communist regimes and its economic logic (e.g. abolition of private ownership, central planning). However, the key to understanding of the labour's position in the system is that the communist economic system was a command system. This means that no sphere of economy (or society for that matter) was autonomous or independent. So despite the growing number of people working in the industrial sphere of economy and living in cities the labour class was gaining neither structural nor political power. Instead of trade unions or other organisation of labour it was the state which protected the labour and exploited it at the same time.

Jones and Grupp (1987) highlighted that the even the modernisation processes within the Soviet Union were not homogeneous. As authors point out, modernisation started firstly in the European, northern and western part of the Soviet Union and only later proceeded to southern regions. After the collapse of communist regime labour thus remained weak, without any structural or associational power and incapable of articulating its political interests. In addition to this, the moderator and supervisor of the class conflict, the state, left labour unprotected and unprepared for the globalisation and neoliberalism that was knocking at its door at the time.

This Section reviews the structural differences of the economic development since the early times of the capitalism formation. We have shown that the class conflict had different nature, and many times also different actors as we move from England to Azerbaijan or Russia. The historical development has set certain structural legacies and limits to the relations among capital, labour and state. We argue that, after the collapse of the communist regime, labour and government as important actors in the post-socialist states were not able to accommodate capital, globalisation and neoliberalism as smoothly as their Western counterparts.

The 'Resource Curse' and Authoritarian States in the CIS

As we showed in the beginning of this paper, there are two clusters of post-socialist countries with different degree of openness to neoliberalism. A closer look indicates that among countries with the least government intervention score and the lowest capital regulation here are countries reliant on natural resources. Russia, as well as several Central Asian countries and the Caucasus countries are rich in oil and/or minerals and their economies are rather dependent on exporting the natural resources. It is possible that the natural resources richness contributes to lesser openness to neoliberalism in the post-socialist region. Researchers mainly in the political science and economics have for several years discussed a thesis of the 'resource curse' or the 'oil curse' (Luong & Weinthal, 2010; Oskarsson & Ottosen, 2010; Ross, 2001). The argument is that natural resources hinder democratisation because it provides government with enough financial resources to 'care' for business elites as well as voters. Oil and gas money thus relieves pressure for accountability.

It is neither our intention nor the role to investigate the oil curse in detail in this paper. However, we argue that the availability of natural resources might shape the social relations and mainly capital-labour conflict in the CIS countries. If a government enjoys high revenues from oil exports then the pressure for tax-based redistribution is lower, as many public projects can be paid out of the oil and gas receipts. In such a situation the government can finance its social system from the oil revenues and does not have to manage different types of arrangements between employers and workers (or unemployed). Having satisfactorily high oil revenues also allows states to avoid pressures for modernising economy and supporting other sectors. On the other hand, the post-socialist countries without rich natural resources have to moderate the labour-capital conflict in different way: by providing the type of structure and institutions which leads to economic development reliant on and driven by the capital. Therefore, we argue, there is higher pressure to organise and institutionalise the class conflict for states without natural resources. We depict the share of export of resource in total export in Fig. 4.

Another factor that can contribute to the explanation of our results is the existence of authoritarian state regimes in many CIS countries. While we are not able to disentangle explicitly the relationship among resource abundance, authoritarian state and the degree of government restrictiveness or openness in this paper, we hypothesise that the former two factors tend to reinforce each other (as resource richness makes countries less prone to the pressure of international financial institutions and more capable to run their economies in an isolated mode).

We argue that the combination of resource richness and authoritarian state regimes increases the likelihood and the severity of the restrictions on trade and capital. According to our comparative analysis results (Fig. 2), the capital restrictions are the lowest in Georgia, Armenia and Kyrgyzstan – the countries that are not abundant with natural resources and need to attract foreign capital by providing relatively more liberal and open environment. At the same time, these countries have less authoritarian regimes, which is documented by the frequency (and existence of)

Fig. 4. Share of Fuel Exports in GDP. *Source*: Authors' processing of the World Bank's World Development Indicators. *Notes*: Darker colour symbolises higher share of fuel exports in the country's GDP. White areas denote countries where data is unavailable. The fuel export is measured as SITC Section 3 (Petroleum oils, natural gas and other fuels) according to the UN Comtrade categorisation.

general elections or changes of governments. On the other hand, the resource-rich countries such as Azerbaijan, Turkmenistan, Kazakhstan, Russia and in particular Uzbekistan are characterised by rather restrictive regulations at trade and capital markets. The latter group of countries includes also Tajikistan and Belarus that are less rich in natural resources, but belong to the more authoritarian regimes.

CONCLUSIONS

In this paper we illustrated that the neo-transitional economies are less neoliberal than could be expected given their 25-years long transition towards building market environment, supporting entrepreneurship, and restoring capitalism in general. According to factor analysis results based on a cross-sectional sample of 134 countries during the period of 2010–2012 we find that the neo-transitional economies are characterised by relatively restrictive trade and capital regulations, varying level of labour protection, and low activity of state in terms of tax-based redistribution and social cohesion support.

It is not our aim to underestimate or dispute the importance and contribution of many theories we reviewed above. Varieties of Capitalism,

Global Commodity Chain, World System Theory, and Schumpeterian approach all develop the political economic research and provide useful explanations to many problems. In this paper we made an attempt to build on the foundations of these theories to explain the neo-transitional outcomes by bringing back into picture labour, capital, and their interactions with the national institutions. We do so because we believe it is of utmost importance to study the mutual relationships of state, capital and labour in order to understand the situation of post-socialist region 25 years after transition to market economy. Omitting the labour and capital from any capitalist analysis causes shortcomings understanding of the key issues. On particular, labour is one of the two parties of the traditional class conflict. The development of the class conflict and its nature in different countries shaped the way economic institutions evolved, the way capital accumulation and movement is regulated and the extent to which states manage or intervene in economy. Modern welfare policies, redistribution, labour market policies and protection, all of these are descendants of the institutions formed and created as the by-product of class conflict in the process of industrialisation and modernisation. Since history and political science teach us that once established, institutions change very slowly and it might takes even decades or centuries. Research in the field of institutional economy should thus not forget about the origins of capitalist institutions – the class conflict.

Therefore, while we acknowledge the contribution of global theoretical frameworks such as the VOC, GCC, and WST to modelling and explaining the world economic development, we highlighted the complexity of today's world and stressed the importance of including the societal relations into political economy research and understanding the variety of neo-transitional outcomes. We conclude that the history of industrialisation and path dependence provides a more plausible framework for explaining the neo-transitional outcomes. Furthermore, the consideration of the 'resource curse' and authoritarian regimes in many CIS countries can explain their neglect for tax-based redistribution and the high degree of government interventions in trade and capital regulations.

NOTES

1. For full results, indices and rankings see Lubyova and Babos (2014), Lubyova and Vojtkova (2014).

2. Given that the Global Openness Index is an average of the three sub-indices, the variability of the sub-indices translates into the variability of the Global Index. The scatter plot at Fig. 2 should not be interpreted in terms of causal relationship; rather, it helps us to depict the values of particular indices and the resulting clusters of countries.

ACKNOWLEDGEMENTS

This work was supported by the Centre of Excellence 'CESTA' of the Slovak Academy of Sciences (Contract No. III/2/2011) and by the project VEGA 'Štrukturálna adaptácia malej otvorenej ekonomiky' (2/0058/10).

REFERENCES

Babos, P., & Klimplová, L. (2013). Uncoordinated lands: The Czech Republic and Slovakia in a view of the varieties of capitalism. *Contemporary European Studies*, *8*(2), 71–98.

Birch, K., & Mykhnenko, V. (2010). *The rise and fall of neoliberalism. The collapse of an economic order?* London: Zed Books.

Bluhm, K. (2010). Theories of capitalism put to test: Introduction to a debate on central and Eastern Europe. *Historical Social Research*, *35*(2), 197–218.

Brenner, R. (1991). Economic backwardness in Eastern Europe in light of developments in the west. In D. Chirot (Ed.), *The origins of backwardness in Eastern Europe: Economics and politics from the middle ages until the early twentieth century* (pp. 15–52). Berkeley, CA: University of California Press.

Chirot, D. (1991). *The origins of backwardness in Eastern Europe: Economics and politics from the middle ages until the early twentieth century*. Berkeley, CA: University of California Press.

Deepak, L. (2012). Is the Washington consensus dead? *Cato Journal*, *32*(3), 493–512. Retrieved from http://papers.ssrn.com/sol3/papers.cfm?abstract_id=2240348##. Accessed on August 12, 2014.

Drahokoupil, J., & Myant, M. (2011). *Transition economies: Political economy in Russia, Eastern Europe, and Central Asia*. Hoboken, NJ: Wiley.

Estevadeordal, A., & Taylor, A. M. (2008). *Is the Washington consensus dead? Growth, openness, and the great liberalization, 1970s–2000s*. NBER Working Paper No. 14264. Retrieved from http://www.nber.org/papers/w14264. Accessed on August 12, 2014.

Feldmann, M. (2006). Emerging varieties of capitalism in transition countries: Industrial relations and wage bargaining in Estonia and Slovenia. *Comparative Political Studies*, *39*(7), 829–854.

Gellner, E. (1988). *Plough, sword and book*. Chicago, IL: University of Chicago Press.

Gereffi, G., & Korzeniewicz, M. (1994). *Commodity chains and global capitalism*. Westport, CT: Praeger.

Hall, P. A., & Gingerich, D. W. (2009). Varieties of capitalism and institutional complementarities in the political economy: An empirical analysis. *British Journal of Political Science*, *39*(3), 449–482.

Hall, P. A., & Soskice, D. W. (2001). *Varieties of capitalism: The institutional foundation of comparative advantage* (p. 557). New York, NY: Oxford University Press.

Harvey, D. (2006). Neoliberalism as creative destruction. *Annals of the American Academy of Political and Social Science*, *610*, 22–44.

Jones, E., & Grupp, F. W. (1987). *Modernization, value change and fertility in the Soviet Union*. Cambridge, Cambridge University Press.

King, D., & Wood, S. (1999). The political economy of neoliberalism: Britain and the United States in the 1980s. In H. Kitschelt, P. Lange, G. Marks, & J. Stephens (Eds.), *Continuity and change in contemporary capitalism* (pp. 371–397). Cambridge: Cambridge University Press.

Knell, M., & Srholec, M. (2007). Diverging pathways in Central and Eastern Europe. In D. Lane & M. Myant (Eds.), *Varieties of capitalism in post-communist countries* (pp. 40–62). New York, NY: Palgrave Macmillan.

Lane, D., & Myant, M. (2007). *Varieties of capitalism in post-communist countries*. New York, NY: Palgrave Macmillan.

Lubyova, M., & Babos, P. (2014). Different labour markets within the varieties of capitalism in Central and Eastern Europe. *The Journal of Comparative Economic Studies*, *9*(1), 69–88.

Lubyova, M., & Vojtkova, M. (2014). Analysis of the degree of the attractiveness of national economies for Foreign investors in the new globalized environment. *Ekonomicky Casopis [Journal of Economics]*, *62*(6), 557–578.

Luong, P. J., & Weinthal, E. (2010). *Oil is not a curse: Ownership structure and institutions in Soviet successor states*. Cambridge: Cambridge University Press.

Maxwell, S. (2005). *The Washington consensus is dead! Long live the meta-narrative!* London: Overseas Development Institute, Working Paper 243. Retrieved from http://www.odi.org/sites/odi.org.uk/files/odi-assets/publications-opinion-files/2476.pdf. Accessed on August 12, 2014.

Musil, J. (2000). The burden of the past. In Z. Suda & J. Musil (Eds.), *The meaning of liberalism: East and West* (pp. 167–196). Budapest: Central European University Press.

Nölke, A., & Vliegenthart, A. (2009). Enlarging the varieties of capitalism: The emergence of dependent market economies in East Central Europe. *World Politics*, *61*(4), 670–702.

Oskarsson, S., & Ottosen, E. (2010). Does oil still hinder democracy? *The Journal of Development Studies*, *46*(6), 1067–1083.

Ross, M. L. (2001). Does oil hinder democracy? *World Politics*, *53*, 325–361.

Selwyn, b. (2012). Beyond firm-centrism: Re-integrating labour and capitalism in to global commodity chain analysis. *Journal of Economic Geography*, *12*(1), 205–226.

Suda, Z., & Musil, J. (2000). *The meaning of liberalism: East and West*. Budapest: Central European University Press.

Wallerstein, I. (1974). *The modern world-system 1: Capitalist agriculture and the origins of the European world-economy in the sixteenth century*. New York, NY: Academic Press, Inc.

Wallerstein, I. (1989). *The modern world-system, II: Mercantilism and the consolidation of the capitalist world-economy, 1730s–1840s*. San Diego, CA: Academic Press.

Wong, L. (2009). The crisis: A return to political economy? *Critical Perspectives on International Business*, *5*, 56–77.

APPENDIX A

Table A1. Sources of Statistical Data and Definitions of Variables.

Variable	Source	Source	Factor Analysis Results
	Database	Institution	Principal factor with highest loadings
Monetary Freedom	Index of Economic Freedom Database 2012	The Heritage Foundation	Capital regulations
Trade Freedom	Index of Economic Freedom Database 2012	The Heritage Foundation	Capital regulations
Investment Freedom	Index of Economic Freedom Database 2012	The Heritage Foundation	Capital regulations
Financial Freedom	Index of Economic Freedom Database 2012	The Heritage Foundation	Capital regulations
Gov't Expenditure % of GDP	Index of Economic Freedom Database 2012	The Heritage Foundation	Government interventions
Fiscal Freedom	Index of Economic Freedom Database 2012	The Heritage Foundation	Government interventions
Income Tax Rate (%)	Index of Economic Freedom Database 2012	The Heritage Foundation	Government interventions
Corporate Tax Rate (%)	Index of Economic Freedom Database 2012	The Heritage Foundation	Government interventions
Labour Freedom	Index of Economic Freedom Database 2012	The Heritage Foundation	Labour regulations
Protecting Investors – Ease of shareholder suits index (0–10)	Doing Business Indicators 2010	World Bank	Labour regulations
Mean years schooling (adults)	Human Development Index database 2011	UNDP	Labour regulations
Long-term unemployment (% of total unemployment)	Human Development Index database 2011	UNDP	Labour regulations

Details and definitions of variables can be found at:
The Heritage Foundation Index of Economic Freedom Database, 2012.
http://www.heritage.org/
UNDP Human Development Index Database, 2011.
http://hdrstats.undp.org/en/tables/
World Bank Doing Business Indicators, 2010.
http://www.doingbusiness.org/data/exploretopics/protecting-investors

APPENDIX B

Table B1. List of Countries, Country Codes and the Values of the Openness Indices.

Code	Country	Capital Restrictions	Government Interventions	Labour Protection	Global Openness
LBR	Liberia	−0.25538	−0.06704	−4.21936	−1.51393
TKM	Turkmenistan	−0.62977	−1.74775	−1.5676	−1.31504
NPL	Nepal	−0.73355	−0.29194	−2.44396	−1.15649
MDV	Maldives	−1.06285	−1.9095	−0.28509	−1.08581
HTI	Haiti	−0.21626	−0.09846	−2.10355	−0.80609
YEM	Yemen	−0.52042	−0.03761	−1.67896	−0.74566
SYR	Syrian Arab Republic	−1.5616	−0.0342	−0.2275	−0.60777
KGZ	Kyrgyzstan	−0.3342	−1.38633	−0.06382	−0.59478
MDA	Moldova	−0.23611	−1.28808	−0.01026	−0.51148
KHM	Cambodia	−0.1033	−0.60481	−0.82156	−0.50989
DZA	Algeria	−0.86983	−0.23349	−0.23985	−0.44772
IDN	Indonesia	−0.70849	−0.05765	−0.43634	−0.40082
GHA	Ghana	−0.52506	−0.14954	−0.32732	−0.33397
MNG	Mongolia	−0.05366	−0.82704	−0.07767	−0.31946
DOM	Dominican Republic	−0.18986	−0.32328	−0.27642	−0.26318
UZB	Uzbekistan	−2.34087	−1.16796	0.724838	−0.928
SAU	Saudi Arabia	−0.61918	−2.22586	0.733747	−0.70376
BHS	Bahamas	−0.64608	−2.06531	0.737557	−0.65794
KWT	Kuwait	−0.21971	−2.28194	0.735959	−0.58856
TJK	Tajikistan	−1.30999	−0.64577	0.470252	−0.49517
BLR	Belarus	−1.91589	−0.74435	1.237945	−0.4741
RUS	Russian Federation	−1.42697	−0.76929	0.863684	−0.44419
BOL	Bolivia	−0.9704	−0.49632	0.148413	−0.43944
QAT	Qatar	−0.03758	−2.22216	1.096052	−0.38789
KAZ	Kazakhstan	−0.64019	−1.28537	0.847875	−0.35923
SRB	Serbia	−0.16225	−1.03928	0.405331	−0.2654
UKR	Ukraine	−1.2716	−0.2831	0.761992	−0.26423
AZE	Azerbaijan	−0.40238	−0.51504	0.47955	−0.14596
CRI	Costa Rica	−0.02544	−0.08301	0.244473	0.045341
URY	Uruguay	−0.2449	−0.07918	0.549926	0.075282
TTO	Trinidad and Tobago	−0.31623	−0.32276	0.914451	0.091822
BTN	Bhutan	−1.83169	0.193578	−0.1286	−0.58891
MRT	Mauritania	−0.17446	0.313551	−1.71201	−0.52431
LAO	Laos	−1.5808	0.535225	−0.42793	−0.49117
PAK	Pakistan	−1.40854	0.439753	−0.4945	−0.48776

Table B1. (*Continued*)

Code	Country	Capital Restrictions	Government Interventions	Labour Protection	Global Openness
BGD	Bangladesh	−1.88615	1.008895	−0.40048	−0.42591
GNQ	Equatorial Guinea	−1.12452	0.570733	−0.60457	−0.38612
CAF	Central African Republic	−0.92846	1.260745	−1.31842	−0.32871
VNM	Vietnam	−1.06297	0.303152	−0.12793	−0.29592
TUN	Tunis	−0.96203	0.463566	−0.272	−0.25682
ZMB	Zambia	−0.68728	0.621498	−0.6133	−0.22636
HND	Honduras	−0.13114	0.012332	−0.48744	−0.20208
PNG	Papua New Guinea	−0.82634	0.689724	−0.35431	−0.16364
GTM	Guatemala	−0.02219	0.23042	−0.61166	−0.13448
GAB	Gabon	−0.52368	0.620277	−0.46761	−0.12367
PHL	Philippines	−0.40508	0.352076	−0.11512	−0.05604
NIC	Nicaragua	−0.18421	0.462757	−0.28733	−0.00293
GUY	Guyana	−0.98228	1.336747	−0.19624	0.052741
MAF	St. Vincent a Grenadines	−0.07549	0.622643	−0.08088	0.155423
IRN	Iran	−2.83988	0.192753	0.295561	−0.78385
VEN	Venezuela	−3.50136	0.849404	1.061541	−0.53014
IND	India	−1.65675	0.590749	0.025383	−0.34687
ECU	Ecuador	−1.5189	0.280348	0.316474	−0.30736
SYC	Seychelles	−2.27602	0.636572	1.20638	−0.14436
SUR	Surinam	−1.18659	0.891253	0.082858	−0.07083
CHN	China	−1.1198	0.728315	0.185187	−0.06876
ARG	Argentina	−1.90953	1.108025	1.005118	0.067872
THA	Thailand	−0.64106	0.436536	0.551977	0.115816
MEX	Mexico	−0.12043	0.217825	0.347835	0.148409
BRA	Brazil	−0.39294	0.754268	0.215355	0.192229
BRB	Barbados	−0.31738	0.762876	0.83312	0.426206
GRC	Greece	−0.04889	1.461744	0.888354	0.76707
BFA	Burkina Faso	1.366856	−0.16344	−4.12884	−0.97514
DJI	Djibouti	0.827898	−0.0541	−2.68462	−0.63694
PRY	Paraguay	0.660769	−1.66459	−0.5783	−0.52738
MKD	Macedonia	1.449828	−1.66713	−1.04943	−0.42224
BIH	Bosnia and Herzegovina	1.485501	−1.31988	−1.31617	−0.38352
JOR	Jordan	0.77833	−1.11328	−0.19286	−0.17594
SLV	Salvador	0.787635	−0.2444	−0.27171	0.090509
CHL	Chile	1.287669	−0.12476	−0.08515	0.359253
OMN	Oman	0.179982	−2.07754	0.053326	−0.61474
ARE	United Arab Emirates	0.135419	−2.36117	1.005758	−0.40667
BHR	Bahrain	0.772773	−2.43809	0.748399	−0.30564

Table B1. *(Continued)*

Code	Country	Capital Restrictions	Government Interventions	Labour Protection	Global Openness
BGR	Bulgaria	0.535626	−1.70457	0.461797	−0.23571
MNE	Montenegro	0.623079	−1.56475	0.238703	−0.23432
ALB	Albania	0.703959	−1.20966	0.06374	−0.14732
ROM	Romania	0.378418	−0.91686	0.448199	−0.03008
GEO	Georgia	0.695199	−1.08113	0.331896	−0.01801
BLZ	Belize	0.00037	−0.107	0.061818	−0.01494
MUS	Mauritius	1.053522	−1.06325	0.085271	0.025179
ARM	Armenia	0.474154	−0.80115	0.465335	0.046113
LTU	Lithuania	1.307234	−1.21688	0.109201	0.066517
PAN	Panama	0.247528	−0.11829	0.184003	0.104412
MYS	Malaysia	0.00345	−0.23044	0.565851	0.112955
BWA	Botswana	0.267859	−0.27573	0.379179	0.123768
LVA	Latvia	0.797351	−0.60636	0.246889	0.145961
SVK	Slovakia	1.221984	−0.64447	0.209834	0.262451
EST	Estonia	1.380612	−0.5874	0.073479	0.288898
HUN	Hungary	0.645303	−0.38973	0.760073	0.338547
CZE	Czech Republic	1.088943	−0.814	0.790761	0.355234
CYP	Cyprus	1.220164	−0.55073	0.437262	0.368899
SGP	Singapore	1.153004	−0.73	1.029601	0.484202
CAN	Canada	0.958215	−0.2271	1.246084	0.659067
KEN	Kenya	0.329001	0.202282	−1.78472	−0.41781
SEN	Senegal	0.600199	0.873918	−2.62606	−0.38398
LSO	Lesotho	0.025176	0.801425	−1.90831	−0.36057
SWZ	Swaziland	0.075398	0.342776	−1.35533	−0.31239
MLI	Mali	0.228327	1.257516	−2.26071	−0.25829
CPV	Cape Verde	0.206726	0.518315	−0.9904	−0.08845
DMA	Dominica	0.332813	0.674376	−0.81171	0.065159
MAR	Morocco	0.135976	0.999934	−0.9171	0.072938
ZAF	South Africa	0.060721	0.542896	−0.38051	0.074368
TUR	Turkey	0.20741	0.151148	−0.12645	0.07737
COL	Columbia	0.2144	0.345536	−0.18695	0.124331
LCA	St. Lucia	0.515364	0.339633	−0.47317	0.127275
PER	Peru	0.889446	0.023786	−0.26746	0.215257
HRV	Croatia	0.953846	0.219261	−0.23143	0.313891
PRT	Portugal	0.759304	1.485436	−0.03468	0.736686
POL	Poland	0.612709	0.047947	0.416581	0.359079
JAM	Jamaica	0.01179	0.844736	0.589719	0.482081
KOR	Korea	0.3397	0.461669	0.760606	0.520658
ISL	Iceland	0.151767	0.363246	1.123127	0.546047
SVN	Slovenia	0.591853	0.617088	0.498928	0.56929
MLT	Malta	0.573628	0.948305	0.522841	0.681591
FIN	Finland	1.160068	0.562767	0.401964	0.708266
NZL	New Zealand	1.315171	0.128337	0.732011	0.725173

Table B1. (*Continued*)

Code	Country	Capital Restrictions	Government Interventions	Labour Protection	Global Openness
IRL	Ireland	1.128961	0.175763	0.923407	0.74271
LUX	Luxembourg	1.334932	0.625859	0.411879	0.79089
ESP	Spain	1.324136	1.130743	0.014736	0.823205
ISR	Israel	0.78631	0.955255	0.937443	0.893003
FRA	France	0.499781	1.586204	0.634244	0.906743
CHE	Switzerland	1.397242	0.45566	0.884711	0.912538
USA	The United States	0.543329	0.798742	1.430544	0.924205
DEU	Germany	1.097835	0.995405	0.749933	0.947725
AUS	Australia	1.459664	0.658302	0.783828	0.967265
NOR	Norway	0.193446	1.474193	1.305584	0.991074
ITA	Italy	0.733107	1.63058	0.623141	0.995609
GBR	Great Britain	0.860517	1.298017	0.864787	1.007774
AUT	Austria	1.045182	1.369994	0.936025	1.117067
NLD	The Netherlands	1.372224	1.472543	0.792858	1.212542
JAP	Japan	0.578441	1.667766	1.438973	1.228393
SWE	Sweden	1.308713	1.840017	0.619254	1.255995
BEL	Belgium	0.918298	1.99675	0.889936	1.268328
DNK	Denmark	1.515292	1.518817	0.890965	1.308358

Source: Lubyova and Vojtkova (2014).

THE ROLE OF CORPORATE GOVERNANCE IN A TRANSITIONAL ECONOMY

Xuan Vinh Vo

ABSTRACT

Vietnam started significant transition policy since 1986 with the introduction of extensive policy of Doi Moi process. The transition from a centrally planned economy toward market-oriented economy has brought some significant results; however Vietnam has until recently stood out as a success story among the transitional economies from a developmental perspective. This requires further investigation of other factors relating to the viability assumption of neoclassical economics. This paper aims to investigate the relationship between corporate governance and firm value in Vietnam, a small and open neo-transitional economy. The result suggests a positive relationship of board size and the value of a firm, but it is not significant. The result also shows a lack of significant negative relationship of other two independent corporate governance variables (shareholder concentration and CEO duality) and the value of a firm. However, to some extent, too high shareholder concentration and CEO duality tend to have negative impacts to the firm value. Other control variables such as price-to-book value ratio and return on total assets

Neo-Transitional Economics
International Finance Review, Volume 16, 149–165

ISSN: 1569-3767/doi:10.1108/S1569-376720150000016007

have significant and positive impacts on the value of a firm, while the market capitalization has a negative relationship with the value of a firm.

Keywords: Corporate governance; firm value; shareholder concentration; CEO duality; board size; Tobin's *Q*

JEL classifications: G00; G30; G32; G34

INTRODUCTION

The increasing economic difficulties faced by the centrally planned economies from the early 1980s had further strengthened the neo-liberal perspective on development in many Eastern Europe and East Asia countries. Central to the neo-liberal approach for transition have been the reduction in centralized direction of the economy and direct state involvement in business firms. The phenomenon of transitional economies in Eastern Europe and East Asia during the 1990s sparked a debate about ideal transition paths from centrally planned to a market economy.

Lin (2005) states that many transition policies, based on the existing neoclassical economic theories, failed in Eastern Europe, the former Soviet Union, and East Asia including China and Vietnam due to the implicit viability assumption of neoclassical economics. Under the viability assumption, neoclassical-based reform policies focus on issues related to property rights, corporate governance, government interventions, and other issues that may obstruct a firm's normal management. Therefore, in order to achieve the intended goals of the reform, those issues of these firms' viability problems need to be resolved in neo-transitional economies.

In this paper, we focus on the issue of corporate governance in neo-transitional economies, using Vietnam, a small and open economy as a case study. We argue that firm corporate governance is an important issue to be addressed for a firm to earn a socially acceptable profit in an open, competitive market under the normal management. We analyze the corporate governance issue in the context of its impacts on firm value.

The efficient operation and functioning of capital markets significantly depends on the quality, timely, reliability, and transparency of information disseminated to the markets. One of the blames for most of the corporate failure scandals in the 21st century is poor corporate governance (Jiang, Kim, & Zhou, 2011). Good corporate governance is an important factor in enhancing the value of a firm (Rashid & Islam, 2008).

Much work have been done employing data from both developed and developing markets to investigate the relationship between corporate governance and the value of a firm (Denis & McConnell, 2003; Gompers, Ishii, & Metrick, 2003; Kang & Shivdasani, 1995). However, there is not many published research concerning this issue in Vietnamese setting. This work aims to provide an investigation of the relationship between corporate governance and firm value in Vietnam – one of the emerging markets in the world and still in the early stage of its development. The primary contribution of this paper to the literature is to enrich the literature on this nexus.

The current research employs data of 271 listed firms in Ho Chi Minh Stock Exchange in the year 2012. This paper uses the model developed by Rashid and Islam (2008) to investigate the relationship between corporate governance and the value of a firm in Vietnam stock market.

The role of majority shareholders (concentrated shareholding) is important in examining the value of a firm. There is mixed evidence in terms of whether majority shareholders improve the performance in order to add value to firms. Studies conducted by Pinkowitz, Stulz, and Williamson (2003) and the World Bank (2003) argue that large shareholders are mostly involved in tunneling and suppressing the rights of minority shareholders. On the contrary, Shleifer and Vishny (1986) and Kaplan and Minton (1994) suggest that blockholders play a constructive role in improving the value of a firm in developing markets as they inject the provisions of corporate governance into a firm making it more democratic.

Grossman and Hart (1982) identified that majority shareholders also solve the free rider problem. Free rider problems arise when some of the shareholder do not pay the monitoring cost and acquire benefits from the cost paid by others. Franks and Mayer (1997) and Yafeh and Yosha (1995) support the same views and confirm that majority shareholders discipline the board by removing the underperforming directors and by preventing the managers from over spending the free cash flow. These measures protect the rights of the shareholders and improve the value of a firm.

Board size is also an important aspect for value creation in a firm. There are diverging views about the performance of a firm and its board size. The first view suggests that a larger board is associated with the negative performance of a firm as it creates an agency cost and it is hard for a larger board to make a unanimous conclusion as suggested by Yermack (1996) and Eisenberg, Sundgren, and Wells (1998). Jensen (1993) also suggests that it is difficult for the CEO to control the board when the board size is greater than seven or eight members. The bigger board is involved in passive monitoring and board members do not perform at an optimal level to improve value of the shareholders. On the contrary, Pfeffer (1972) and Zahra and Pearce (1989) presented different views about the board size and firm performance. They suggested that a bigger board is good for a firm because the higher number of directors make the jury more competent and skilled. A bigger board brings higher management skills and makes it easier for the board to make strategic decisions that result in improving the value of a firm.

Similarly, a CEO can easily manipulate a smaller board and can compromise the efficiency and independence of a board. In contrast, larger boards are more independent and efficient, as the CEO cannot manipulate it. Kyereboah-Coleman and Biekpe (2005) also find a positive relationship between the board size and the value of firm in developing markets. Some researchers in the literature of corporate governance have diverging views from the above-mentioned schools of thought. Hart (1995) argues the advantages of bigger board size such as increased management skills are offset by the disadvantages such as lack of coordination and poor decision making by the CEO. Similarly, Claessens, Djankov, and Pohl (1997) found no relationship between the board size and performance of a firm in the developed financial markets.

The role of the CEO and the chairman is important in improving the value of a firm. A single person holding both roles (CEO duality) has an important bearing on the value of a firm and there are two schools of thought in this regard. Fama and Jensen (1983) supported agency theory and suggested that a single person holding the positions of CEO and chairman cannot monitor the organization well. In addition, a person being head of the board and operations is not a healthy sign keeping in mind the principles of corporate governance. They further suggest the agency problem increases when a single person holds both these important roles. The shareholders also bear higher monitoring costs in the absence of the chairman in a firm. The second school of thought about the CEO duality is called stewardship theory. The supporters of this theory are Stoeberl and Sherony (1985), Alexander, Halpern, and Fennell (1993) and Brickley, Coles, and Jarrell (1997). They suggest that CEO duality leads to a higher performance as it provides strength to the organization. The CEO cannot plan and make the decisions beneficial for the shareholders in the case of contention between the CEO and Chairman. The dual leadership firm may lack proper direction affecting the shareholders wealth in a negative manner. Bhagat and Jefferis (2002) argue that the interests of shareholders and the CEO can be aligned with each other obliging the CEO to work for the benefit of shareholders and to create value for them. This type of benefit to shareholders is wasted in the case of the firms having a non-dual structure of leadership. The third school of thought about the relationship between the value of a firm and CEO duality suggests the lack of a significant relationship between the two. Chaganti, Mahajan, and Sharma (1985) and Daily and Dalton (1992, 1993) find no relationship between the firms' performance and CEO duality.

The remainder of the paper is outlined as follows. The section "Data and Research Method" describes the model, data, and analysis methodology. The section "Regression Results and Discussion of Results" presents the results and discussion of the results while the final section concludes the paper.

DATA AND RESEARCH METHOD

Rashid and Islam (2008) develop a multi-factor model for the developing financial market in investigating the relationship between corporate governance and firm value. The following function represents the model for the valuation of the companies in developing financial markets.

$$Tobin's\ Q = f(Log(Size),\ Ac,\ Duality,\ Pb,\ RoA,\ Log(Mc))$$

where Tobin's Q is a proxy for the value of a company; Logsize is the natural logarithm of board size; Shareholder concentration; Ac is Agency cost; Duality is Chairman and Chief Executive Officer duality; Pb is price-to-book value ratio; RoA is return on total assets; and Log(Mc) is logarithm of market capitalization (Table 1).

Tobin's Q serves as a proxy for company performance in a financial market. A value of Tobin's Q greater than one shows that a company creates value for its shareholders. On the contrary, a value of the variable lower than one shows that the firm does not perform well. A well-performing firm is likely to add value to the shareholders. Tobin's Q is used as a dependent variable in the studies about the corporate governance and firm value relationship by Agrawal and Knoeber (1996), Claessens et al. (1997), Loderer and Peyer (2002) and Beiner and Schmid (2005) in both developing and developed markets.

Different researchers in the literature calculate the proxy for Tobin's Q in different ways. For example, Capulong, Edwards, Webb, and Zhuang

Table 1. Variable Definition.

Variables	Proxied by	Symbol	Expected Sign
Dependent variable			
Firm value Tobin's *Q*	(Mkt Cap + TA − Sh *F*)/TA	TQ	
Independent variables			
Return on total assets	Return generated by the assets of a firm	RoA	+ (Positive)
Size	Number of directors in the board	Logsize	+ (Positive)
Duality	Dummy variable: can take values of 0 and 1	Duality	− (Negative)
Agency cost (concentrated ownership)	Majority ownership in a firm	Ac	− (Negative)
Market capitalization	Market capitalization of a firm	LogMc	+ (Positive)
Price-to-book value ratio	Price-to-book value ratio of a firm	Pb	+ (Positive)

Notes: Mkt Cap: Market capitalization; TA: Total assets; Sh F: Shareholders fund.

(2000) use the ratio between market value of equity and debt to the replacement cost of assets as the proxy for Tobin's *Q* in the developing market. On the contrary, Klapper and Love (2002) calculate Tobin's *Q* by taking the ratio of market value of equity and total assets with total assets of a firm. In our current study, we follow the calculation method of Rashid and Islam (2008). The proxy for Tobin's *Q* is calculated by first adding market capitalization and total assets, and then subtracting shareholders' funds. The final value is obtained by dividing the numerator by total assets.

The control variables in our study are return on total assets, price-to-book value ratio, and the market capitalization. These three control variables are widely used and expected to have significant impact on the relationship of corporate governance and value of a firm. Yildrim (2000), Kyereboah-Coleman and Biekpe (2005), and Beiner and Schmid (2005) have used return on total assets in their study for developing and developed financial markets. Leal and Carvalhal-da-Silva (2005) have used price-to-book value ratio in the studies of corporate governance. Black (2001) and Black, Love, and Rachinsky (2006) used market capitalization in studies conducted on the firms in a developing market.

Data

We use the cross sectional data of 271 companies listed in Ho Chi Minh Stock Exchange (HOSE) in the year 2012. Both primary and secondary methods of data collection were used, where the information required was obtained from different websites of stock exchanges, securities companies, and listed companies. Data regarding the internal corporate governance mechanism such as Chairman and CEO duality, board size, and shareholder concentration in a firm are hand collected from the company profiles, annual reports, CG reports of listed companies published on their own company websites and the filed record of the stock exchange.

Shareholder concentration of a firm was computed as the sum of the shareholding percentage of its all large shareholders who have the shareholding ratio from 5% upward. Current Vietnam legal frameworks define large shareholders of a firm are those hold from 5% or above the stocks of a firm.

The data regarding the financial variables such as return on total assets, price-to-book value ratio, and market capitalization were also obtained from Ho Chi Minh city stock exchange and was cross-checked against the companies' financial statements and balance sheets. Finally, we calculated the Tobin's *Q* by first adding market capitalization and total assets of a firm, and then subtracting its shareholders funds. The final value was obtained by dividing the numerator by total assets. The data used to calculating Tobin's *Q* were obtained from Ho Chi Minh city stock exchange and cross-checked with the companies' financial statements and balance sheets (Table 2).

Ownership Concentration (Agency Cost)

The minimum value of ownership concentration (agency cost) for firms listed in HOSE in 2012 is 0 and the maximum value is 0.9267. The mean

Table 2. Summary Statistics.

	AC	Duality	LogMc	Logsize	Pb	RoA	TQ
Mean	0.5331	0.3506	13.2495	1.7278	1.3264	0.0766	1.1525
Median	0.5578	0.0000	13.0372	1.6094	1.1833	0.0600	1.0675
Maximum	0.9267	1.0000	17.5762	2.3979	3.8093	0.5500	3.5555
Minimum	0.0000	0.0000	10.6549	1.0986	0.3874	−0.2370	0.1124
Std. Dev.	0.2040	0.4780	1.3628	0.1976	0.6286	0.0855	0.5993
Observations	271	271	271	271	271	271	271

Notes: AC = Shareholder concentration; Duality = Chairman and Chief Executive Officer duality; LogMc = logarithm of market capitalization; Logsize = logarithm of board size; Pb = price-to-book value ratio; RoA = return on total assets; TQ = Tobin *Q* value.

for ownership concentration (agency cost) in HOSE is 0.5331, much higher than 0.3461 of Malaysia market and 0.2280 of Australia market (Rashid & Islam, 2008).

On an average, the firms of Vietnam stock market which is still developing have a higher shareholder concentration (agency cost) compared to the firms in more developed markets, possibly due to some reasons figured out by IFC (2010) as follows: Firstly, many state-owned enterprises have been equitized and converted into joint stock companies, but the State still remains a majority interest of 51% or even more. Second, many private companies in Vietnam started out as small private companies owned either by a single controlling shareholder, members of a family, or a small group of shareholders. Although many companies have expanded significantly, the controlling shareholders have not changed.

Board Size

The minimum value for board size for firms listed in Ho Chi Minh City stock exchange is 3 and the maximum value is 11 (Table 3). The mean for board size for firms is 5.75. This compares to a minimum value for board size of firms of Malaysia of 5 and maximum of 12. The mean for board size for firms of Malaysia market is 8.05 and that of Australia is 7.08 (Rashid & Islam, 2008). Through comparison, we can see that average board size for firms of Vietnam market is smaller than those of other markets like Malaysia or Australia.

Chairman and Chief Executive Officer Duality

CEO duality is a dummy variable whose value is 1 when a person plays both the roles of CEO and chairman, and is 0 when the roles are separated.

Table 3. Statistics of Board Size.

	Board Size	Logsize
Mean	5.7454	1.7278
Median	5.0000	1.6094
Maximum	11.0000	2.3979
Minimum	3.0000	1.0986
Std. Dev.	1.2464	0.1976
Observations	271	271

Among 271 listed companies in Ho Chi Minh City Stock Exchange in 2012, there are 95 companies whose chairman and CEO is the same person (around 35.8% of the whole sample). In many Vietnamese companies, there is still little separation of ownership and control. Most controlling shareholders also act as Chief Executive Officer (CEO) and also sit on the Board of Directors as Chairman. Failure to separate ownership and management would result in weak accountability, abusive related party transactions, and poor information disclosure.

Return on Total Assets

The minimum value for return on total assets for firms listed in Ho Chi Minh Stock Exchange in 2012 is −0.237 and the maximum value is 0.55. The mean for return on total assets is 0.0766, bigger than 0.048 of Malaysia market but smaller than 0.088 of Australia market (Rashid & Islam, 2008).

The minimum value for return on total assets for firms of Malaysia market is −0.586 and the maximum value is 0.5499. This compares with the minimum value for return on total assets for firms of Australia market equal to −0.3543 and maximum value 0.8567. The mean for return on total assets is 0.0766, bigger than 0.048 of Malaysia market but smaller than 0.088 of Australia (Rashid & Islam, 2008).

After comparison, we can see that the mean, maximum, and minimum values of return on total assets of firms of Australia market (more developed market with better corporate governance practices) are higher than those of firms in Malaysia and Vietnam stock markets, which are still developing and emerging.

Price-to-Book Value Ratio

The minimum value for price-to-book value ratio for firm listed in Ho Chi Minh stock exchange in 2012 is 0.3874 and the maximum value is 3.8093. The mean for price-to-book value ratio is 1.3264. This compares with a minimum value of price-to-book value ratio in firms of Malaysia market equal to 0.29 and of Australia market equal to 0.27. The maximum value of Malaysia market is 8.32 and of Australia market is 36.90. The mean for price-to-book value for firms of Malaysia market is 0.29 and the mean value of Australia market is 0.27 (Rashid & Islam, 2008). The descriptive statistics show that the Australia market (more developed market) is willing to pay higher benefits to companies operating in a market where market participants follow better corporate governance practices than developing markets like Vietnam stock exchange.

Market Capitalization

The minimum value for market capitalization for firm listed in Ho Chi Minh City stock exchange in 2012 is 42,400 and the maximum value is 42,977,072. The mean for market capitalization is 2,113,753 (Table 4).

Tobin's Q

The minimum value for Tobin's *Q* for firms listed in Ho Chi Minh City stock exchange in 2012 is 0.1124 and the maximum value is 3.5555. The mean for Tobin's *Q* is 1.03.

The minimum value for Tobin's *Q* for firms of Malaysia market is 0.37 and of Australia market is 0.40. The maximum value for Tobin's *Q* for firms of Malaysia market is 3.96 and of Australia market is 21.03. The mean for Tobin's *Q* value of Malaysia market is 1.81 and that of Australia market is 1.1525.

The comparison of Tobin's *Q* values between different market shows that firms of the more developed market create higher value for their shareholders.

Correlations

Table 5 presents Pearson correlation coefficients between the firm value measured by Tobin's *Q* and other independent and controlled variables. As

Table 4. Statistics of Market Capitalization.

	LogMc	MKT_CAP
Mean	13.2495	2,113,753
Median	13.0372	459,200
Maximum	17.5762	42,977,072
Minimum	10.6549	42,400
Std. Dev.	1.3628	5,994,233
Observations	271	271

Table 5. Correlation Matrix.

	AC	Duality	LogMc	Logsize	Pb	RoA	TQ
AC	1.0000						
Duality	−0.1103	1.0000					
LogMc	0.1517	−0.0700	1.0000				
Logsize	−0.1210	0.0116	0.2990	1.0000			
Pb	0.1572	−0.0211	0.5550	0.0812	1.0000		
RoA	0.0057	0.0014	0.2920	−0.0226	0.4314	1.0000	
TQ	0.0414	−0.0026	0.2291	−0.0172	0.5600	0.6479	1.0000

Notes: AC = Shareholder concentration; Duality = Chairman and Chief Executive Officer duality; LogMc = logarithm of market capitalization; Logsize = logarithm of board size; Pb = price-to-book value ratio; RoA = return on total assets; TQ = Tobin *Q* value.

shown in Table 5, all controlled variables including RoA, Pb, and LogMc have positive relationships with Tobin's *Q* while CG variables such as Duality and Logsize have negative relationships with Tobin's *Q*. The AC variable representing shareholder concentration has a positive relationship with Tobin's *Q*.

REGRESSION RESULTS AND DISCUSSION OF RESULTS

The value for the *R*-squared in Table 6 is 0.533465 which endorses that 53.35% of the variation in the dependent variable (Tobin's *Q*) is explained by the independent and control variables of the model. The 46.65% variation in the dependent variable remained unexplained by the independent and control variable. With the Prob (*F*-statistic) value of zero, it is possible to infer that the model has the validity.

Board size has a positive relationship with Tobin's *Q* (Proxy of the firm value) with the coefficient value of 0.020232; however, the relationship is insignificant. Somehow, the empirical result show some slight similarity with the viewpoint of Pfeffer (1972) and Zahra and Pearce (1989) when they suggested that a bigger board is good for a firm because the higher number of directors make the board more competent and skilled. A bigger board brings higher management skills and makes it easier for the board to make strategic decisions that result in improving the value of a firm. Given the background of many Vietnamese companies started out as private family shareholding or state-owned companies, a bigger board will bring more expertise and experience to the strategic decision making of the

Table 6. Multiple Regression Result.

Variable	Coefficient	Std. Error	t-Statistic	Prob.
C	1.239487	0.311239	3.982428	0.0001
RoA	3.57213	0.330125	10.82054	0
Logsize	0.020232	0.137109	0.147559	0.8828
Duality	−0.007464	0.053141	−0.14046	0.8884
AC	−0.013342	0.128409	−0.103904	0.9173
LogMc	−0.070019	0.023719	−2.951978	0.0034
Pb	0.408555	0.051597	7.918223	0
R-squared	0.533465			
Adjusted R-squared	0.522862			
F-statistic	50.31235			
Prob (F-statistic)	0			

Notes: AC = Shareholder concentration; Duality = Chairman and Chief Executive Officer duality; LogMc = logarithm of market capitalization; Logsize = logarithm of board size; Pb = price-to-book value ratio; RoA = return on total assets; TQ = Tobin Q value.

companies. However, the relationship between the board size and the firm value of our current study with the sample of 271 companies listed in Ho Chi Minh stock exchange in 2012 is not significant.

As expected, the result shows the negative relationship between the CEO duality and the value of a firm with the coefficient of −0.007464. Given the fact that 95 companies among 271 listed companies in Ho Chi Minh City Stock Exchange in 2012 has one person hold both positions of chairman and CEO, companies' managements should consider the separation of ownership and control to enhance accountability, transparency and information disclosure, which in turns increase the value of the firm for shareholders and related parties. Similar to the case of board side, the result of our current study shows a lack of significant relationship between CEO duality and the value of a firm, which supports the third school of thought about the relationship between the value of a firm and CEO duality. Chaganti et al. (1985) and Daily and Dalton (1992, 1993) find no relationship between the firms' performance and CEO duality. We pointed out in the theoretical background that the value of a firm is not only associated with market value, but the social value and corporate image which takes time to reflect to the market value of a firm. We still suggest that companies should apply the best corporate governance practices to enhance the company image and create the value for stakeholders in the long run.

Regarding the relationship between concentration and value, the coefficient value of shareholder concentration (agency cost) is −0.013342, which suggests a negative relationship with the firm value. The studies conducted by Pinkowitz et al. (2003) and the World Bank (2003) argued that large shareholders are mostly involved in tunneling and suppressing the rights of minority shareholders. The mean for ownership concentration (agency cost) in HOSE is 0.5331, much higher than that of Malaysia market (at 0.3461) and that of Australia market, which is at 0.2280 (Rashid & Islam, 2008). In such background, the regulators should enhance the legal and CG framework to facilitate equal treatment among company shareholders and limit negative impacts caused by large block shareholders as recently shown scandals in Vietnam financial industry.

The result shows that all three control variables (return on total asset, price-to-book value ratio, and market capitalization) have significant relationship with the value of a firm (Tobin's *Q*). Return on total assets and price-to-book value ratio affects the value of a firm positively, with the coefficient value of 3.57213 and 0.408555, respectively. On the contrary, the market capitalization has a negative relationship with the value of a firm, with the coefficient value of −0.070019.

Incremental Regressions

To further test the importance of each independent corporate governance variables in affecting the dependent variable (Tobin's *Q*) in the model, we conducted the incremental regressions by removing the individual independent corporate governance variables from the model and capturing the effect of *R*-squared.

The result shown in Table 7 reveals that the effects on the value of *R*-squared after removal of each individual corporate governance variable are so small and the removal of each corporate governance variable does not have much impact on the portion of the dependent variable (Tobin's *Q*) explained by the independent variables of the model.

Table 7. Results of Incremental Regression Removing Corporate Governance Variables.

R-squared (the whole model)	0.533465	+/−
R-squared (after the removal of board size)	0.533427	−0.000038
R-squared (after the removal of CEO duality)	0.533430	−0.000035
R-squared (after the removal of shareholder concentration)	0.533446	−0.000019

CONCLUSION

The paper focuses on the role of corporate governance in a small and open transitional country of Vietnam from the firm level viewpoint. In particular, the paper aims to investigate the relationship between corporate governance and firm value on a sample of firms listed on Ho Chi Minh City stock exchange. We used the model developed by Rashid and Islam (2008) to investigate the relationship between corporate governance and the value of a firm in Vietnam stock market. Even though it is not statistically significant, the results suggest a positive relationship between board size and the value of a firm. The results also show a lack of significant negative relationship of other two independent corporate governance variables (shareholder concentration and CEO duality) and the value of a firm; however, based on their negative coefficients, we can learn that to some extent, too high shareholder concentration and CEO duality have negative impacts on the firm value.

Adopting best corporate governance practices is to create long-term and sustainable growth and benefits for the company and its stakeholders, but Vietnamese companies currently just stop at the level of compliance with regulatory and mandatory regulations. To put it another way, they just tend to do what they have to do as laws require, rather than embrace long term and international standards. Applying good corporate governance practices does not necessarily bring in the financial value increase in the immediate future, but companies can enjoy other non-financial benefits such as reputation and investors' trust. Board of Directors should set out long-term vision and strategic directions with strong commitment of applying good corporate practices and being ready to go beyond legal requirements. Considering those backgrounds, we can understand why the empirical result of the study does not support a significant relationship between corporate governance and the value of a firm in Vietnam stock market.

We also learn from the paper that control variables such as price-to-book value ratio and return on total assets significantly and positively affect the value of a firm, while the market capitalization has a negative relationship with the value of a firm. The finding of negative and significant relationship between market capitalization and the value of a firm is opposite to the theoretical background and inconsistent with the previous research conducted by Rashid and Islam (2008) in Malaysia and Australia market. Such difference can result from special characteristics of Vietnam stock market, which is still developing. Stock prices in Vietnam market do not necessarily reflect accurately the intrinsic value of the company, but they are based on the supply-demand relationship, which easily leads to inflated or manipulated pricing. Furthermore, some listed companies have grown too fast that the company size is becoming so big and far beyond the controlling and managing capacity of their current Managements. Therefore, bigger companies are not always associated with higher efficiency and better performance.

ACKNOWLEDGMENTS

The author wishes to thank the Editors, Rustam Jamilov and Yusaf H. Akbar for many helpful comments and suggestions that greatly enhance the brevity and quality of the paper. Any remaining errors are my own responsibility.

REFERENCES

Agrawal, A., & Knoeber, C. (1996). Firm performance and mechanisms to control agency problems between managers and shareholders. *Journal of Financial and Quantitative Analysis*, *31*, 377–397.

Alexander, J., Halpern, M., & Fennell, M. (1993). Leadership instability in hospitals: The influence of board-CEO relations and organization growth and decline. *Administrative Science Quarterly*, *38*, 74–99.

Beiner, S., & Schmid, M. (2005). *Agency conflicts, corporate governance, and corporate diversification evidence from Switzerland.* Retrieved from http://papers.ssrn.com/sol3/papers.cfm?abstract_id=666264#PaperDownload

Bhagat, S., & Jefferis, R. (2002). *The econometrics of corporate governance studies*. Cambridge, MA: MIT Press.

Black, B. (2001). Does corporate governance matter? A crude test using Russian data. *University of Pennsylvania Law Review*, *149*(2), 2131–2150.

Black, B., Love, I., & Rachinsky, A. (2006). Corporate governance indices and firms' market values: Time series evidence from Russia. *Emerging Markets Review*, *7*, 361–379.

Brickley, J., Coles, J., & Jarrell, G. (1997). Leadership structure: Separating the CEO and chairman of the board. *Journal of Corporate Finance*, *3*, 189–220.

Capulong, V., Edwards, D., Webb, D., & Zhuang, J. (2000). *Corporate governance and finance in East Asia: A study of Indonesia, Republic of Korea, Malaysia, Philippines, and Thailand* (Vol. 1). Manila: Asian Development Bank.

Chaganti, R., Mahajan, V., & Sharma, S. (1985). Corporate board size, composition and corporate failures in retailing industry. *Journal of Management Studies*, *22*, 400–416.

Claessens, S., Djankov, S., & Pohl, G. (1997). *Ownership and corporate governance: Evidence from the Czech Republic*. World Bank Policy Research Working Paper No. 1737. Washington, DC.

Daily, C., & Dalton, D. (1992). The relationship between governance structure and corporate performance in entrepreneurial firms. *Journal of Business Venturing*, *7*, 375–386.

Daily, C., & Dalton, D. (1993). Board of directors leadership and structure: Control and performance implications. *Entrepreneurship: Theory and Practice*, *17*, 65–81.

Denis, D. K., & McConnell, J. J. (2003). International corporate governance. *The Journal of Financial and Quantitative Analysis*, *38*(1), 1–36.

Eisenberg, T., Sundgren, S., & Wells, M. (1998). Larger board size and decreasing firm value in small firms. *Journal of Financial Economics*, *48*, 35–54.

Fama, E., & Jensen, M. (1983). Separation of ownership and control. *Journal of Law and Economics*, *26*, 301–325.

Franks, J., & Mayer, C. (1997). Ownership and control. *Journal of Applied Corporate Finance*, *9*, 30–45.

Gompers, P., Ishii, J., & Metrick, A. (2003). Corporate governance and equity prices. *The Quarterly Journal of Economics*, *118*(1), 107–156.

Grossman, S., & Hart, O. (Eds.). (1982). *Corporate financial structure and managerial incentives*: Chicago, IL: University of Chicago Press.

Hart, O. (1995). Corporate Governance: Some theory and implications. *The Economic Journal*, *105*(430), 678–689.

IFC. (2010). *Corporate governance manual* (2nd ed.). Washington, DC: IFC.

Jensen, M. (1993). The modern industrial revolution, exit, and the failure of internal control systems. *Journal of Finance*, *48*, 831–880.

Jiang, C. X., Kim, J.-C., & Zhou, D. (2011). Liquidity, analysts, and institutional ownership. *International Review of Financial Analysis*, *20*(5), 335–344.

Kang, J.-K., & Shivdasani, A. (1995). Firm performance, corporate governance, and top executive turnover in Japan. *Journal of Financial Economics*, *38*(1), 29–58.

Kaplan, S., & Minton, B. (1994). Appointments of outsiders to Japanese boards: Determinants and implications for managers. *Journal of Financial Economics*, *36*, 225–258.

Klapper, L., & Love, I. (2002). *Corporate governance, investor protection and performance in emerging markets*. Working Paper No. 2818. World Bank, Washington, DC.

Kyereboah-Coleman, A., & Biekpe, N. (2005). *The relationship between board size board composition, ceo duality, and firm performance: Experience from Ghana*. Working Paper. University of Stellenbosch Business School, Cape Town.

Leal, R., & Carvalhal-da-Silva, A. (2005). *Corporate governance and value in Brazil (and in Chile)*. Working Paper. Inter-American Development Bank, Research Network, Washington, DC.

Lin, J. Y. (2005). Viability, economic transition and reflection on neoclassical economics. *Kyklos*, *58*(2), 239–264.

Loderer, C., & Peyer, U. (2002). Board overlap, seat accumulation and share prices. *European Financial Management*, *8*(2), 165–192.

Pfeffer, J. (1972). Size, composition, and function of hospital boards of directors. *Administrative Science Quarterly*, *18*, 349–364.

Pinkowitz, L., Stulz, R., & Williamson, R. (2003). *Why do firms in countries with poor protection of investor rights hold more cash*. Cambridge, MA: National Bureau of Economic Research.

Rashid, K., & Islam, S. M. N. (2008). *Corporate governance and firm value: Econometric modelling and analysis of emerging and developed financial markets* (Vol. 23, 1st ed.). International Business and Management. Bingley, UK: Emerald Group Publishing Limited.

Shleifer, A., & Vishny, R. (1986). Large shareholders and corporate control. *Journal of Political Economy, 94*, 461–488.

Stoeberl, P., & Sherony, B. (Eds.). (1985). *Board efficiency and effectiveness*. New York, NY: McGraw Hill.

World Bank. (2003). *Corporate governance: An issue of global concern*. Washington, DC: World Bank.

Yafeh, Y., & Yosha, O. (1995). *Large shareholders and banks: Who monitors and how?* Israel: Tel Aviv University.

Yermack, D. (1996). Higher market valuation of companies with a small board of directors. *Journal of Financial Economics, 40*, 185–211.

Yildrim, C. (2000). *Ownership structure, corporate governance and access to foreign capital: Evidence from Turkish firms*. Tilburg: Cent ER Tilburg University.

Zahra, S., & Pearce, J. (1989). Boards of directors and corporate financial performance: A review and integrative model. *Journal of Management Studies, 15*, 291–334.

POST-SOVIET TRANSITION: THE IMPACT OF RUSSIAN INFLUENCE ON INSTITUTIONS

Matei Alexianu

ABSTRACT

The post-Soviet space, consisting of the countries of the former USSR and the Warsaw Pact, is a good testing ground for the dynamics of growth. Motivated by the mixed evidence on economic convergence in the region, this paper explores why countries have performed differently, focusing on institutional strength and its determinants. It proposes the hypothesis that, in the region, Russian influence plays a negative role in institutional development, both through opaque business practices that come with it, and through the isolation from European Union influence it entails. The paper uses recent panel data to test this hypothesis, concluding that there is some evidence supporting a negative effect of Russian influence on post-Soviet states' institutions, but that more rigorous analysis is needed to confirm this link.

Keywords: Political economy; institutions; Commonwealth of Independent States (CIS); post-Soviet space; economic convergence

Neo-Transitional Economics
International Finance Review, Volume 16, 167–189

ISSN: 1569-3767/doi:10.1108/S1569-376720150000016008

INTRODUCTION

The fall of the Soviet Union was a seminal event in the history of the 20th century. For economists, the post-Soviet region, defined here as the independent countries that emerged from the Soviet Union as well as the former Soviet satellites including Yugoslavia, provides a fertile testing ground for the dynamics of growth and transition. The early 1990s saw the birth of numerous new independent states as well as the collapse of the Warsaw Pact and, with it, Soviet hegemony in Central and Eastern Europe (CEE). The convergence hypothesis predicts that, given certain conditions, countries will converge in incomes and/or growth rates. If anything, the fall of the Soviet Union should have sped up this process, yet evidence for convergence in the post-Soviet world remains weak. Persistent differences in income levels across the region naturally lead to questions about the sources of these discrepancies. This paper makes a first step in explaining slow convergence in CEE and central Asia by focusing on the sources of institutional strength, a commonly cited source of economic growth, and proposing a new explanatory variable for institutions – Russian influence. Russia, although no longer a global superpower, remains a regional hegemon and plays an important role in the political economy of its neighbours. The essay argues that when it comes to institutions, this role is largely negative. It uses macroeconomic panel data to build on existing studies and demonstrate the potential significance of Russian influence on post-Soviet institutions.

The paper proceeds as follows. The second section expands on the motivation for the study and examines convergence in the post-Soviet region, concluding that the evidence for this phenomenon is very mixed. The third section reviews the literature on institutions and growth and provides the theoretical link between the motivation and the empirical study that follows. The fourth section explores potential sources of institutional strength and is followed by a discussion of the model and data used. Then the results of the empirical analysis are presented and the essay concludes with a discussion of issues and topics for further research.

CONVERGENCE IN THE POST-SOVIET SPACE

Neoclassical growth theory, with its now famous Solow-Swan model, predicts convergence across economies, assuming a shared steady-state.

Within the post-Soviet world, changes in the political economy of the region should work to reinforce this predicted convergence. In the European part of this area, the European Union has been a strong force for economic integration. Through its conditionality strategy, the organization has pushed for significant political and economic reforms, including macroeconomic stabilization, price liberalization, and privatization in candidate countries prior to accession. EU enlargement appears to have been a success for these countries – Rapacki and Prochniak (2009) find a significant positive impact of EU enlargement on growth in the 10 CEE countries. At the same time, within the established EU member states, there has been an increased drive to liberalize capital and labour markets as well as the birth of a monetary union. Furthermore, EU policies aimed at reducing regional income disparities and improving competitiveness obviously benefit EU states once they have joined (Borsi & Metiu, 2013). All of this further reinforces the prediction of convergence among member and candidate states of the EU.

Even outside Europe, where EU membership is clearly not an option, price liberalization, privatization, and overall transition to a decentralized economy should reinforce convergence within the neoclassical paradigm. Most relevantly for the Solow model's predictions, the post-Soviet space has seen an increase in migration and human capital exchange as it has opened up to world markets (Libman & Vinokurov, 2012a).

Although recent developments coupled with the neoclassical model suggest some sort of narrowing of the 'economic gap' between countries in the post-Soviet space and Western Europe, it is important to distinguish between the various concepts of convergence that are commonly used. The neoclassical growth model predicts convergence in growth rates across economies assuming costless technology transfer, and in levels if countries have identical aggregate production functions. Beta-converge is the concept that, due to diminishing marginal returns and assuming similar savings rates, poorer countries will grow faster than richer ones. Thus, we would expect a negative correlation between initial income level and the growth rate that follows. In contrast, sigma-convergence is the idea that the dispersion (standard deviation) in incomes or growth rates across countries falls over time. Another important distinction is between unconditional convergence (convergence to the same steady state level or rate) and conditional convergence (convergence to a country's own steady state). The latter concept allows the determinants of steady state – initial technology, depreciation, population and technology growth rates, saving and depreciation rates – to differ across economies (Islam, 2003, pp. 313–315). These distinctions are important for understanding the empirical results on convergence in the post-Soviet region.

Overall, the evidence on post-Soviet convergence is mixed. A simple graph (Fig. 1) shows a negative relationship between initial GDP and the average yearly growth rate in the post-Soviet region in the period 1995–2012, which is a rough indication of beta convergence.

Meanwhile, Fig. 2 provides a visual representation of sigma convergence in the region. The distance between each point and the 45-degree line is the growth rate of each country during this period. Aside from the noteworthy growth experienced by these countries, the graph also indicates that overall dispersion in incomes has decreased (from around 6.5 to 9.5 in 1995 to around 7.5 to 10 in 2012). Yet the graph demonstrates that a large dispersion remains in the post-Soviet world more than two decades after the fall of the Soviet Union.

Rigorous studies confirm the mixed results of this rough analysis. In the Commonwealth of Independent States (CIS), a regional organization made up of the former Soviet republics, Libman and Vinokurov (2012b, p. 78) reject sigma convergence in levels, but find it in rates in the first half of the

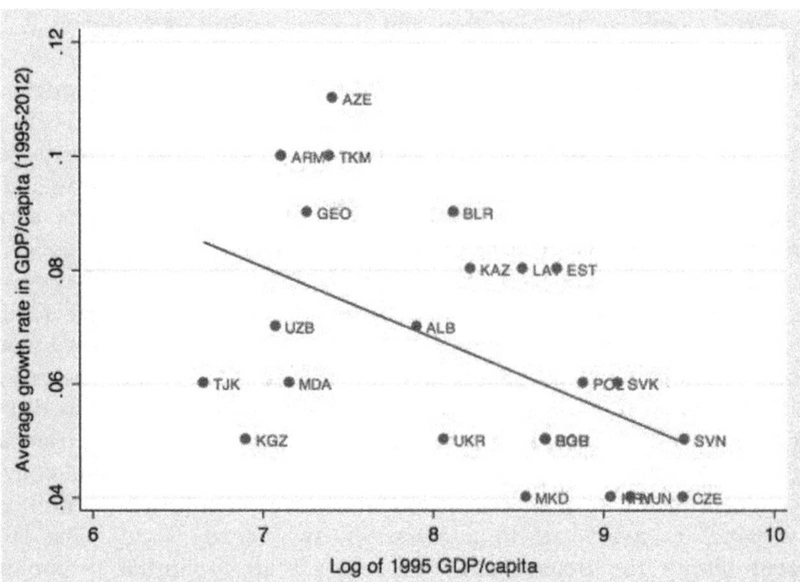

Fig. 1. Beta Convergence.

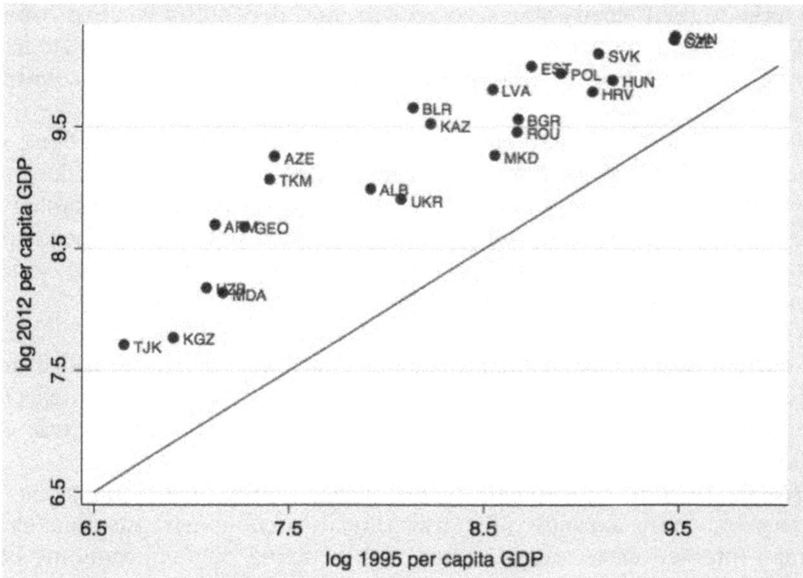

Fig. 2. Sigma Convergence.

2000s. In Europe, Borsi and Metiu (2013) find no conditional sigma convergence in incomes, even though they apply Phillips and Sul's non-linear factor model that allows for heterogeneous technological progress and transitionally divergent time paths. However, they do find evidence for the existence of convergence clubs, in other words, convergence to multiple steady-state equilibria. The convergence club hypothesis, developed by Durlauf and Johnson (1995) and Galor (1996) questions the uniqueness of steady states and develops the concept of attribute-sharing clubs. The characteristics of these clubs underlie the fundamental question that motivates this paper.

INSTITUTIONS AND GROWTH

The determinants of the growth rate in the countries of the post-Soviet region are of primary interest from a development perspective. The fundamental question is about why countries' steady state levels are where they are because, after all, the neoclassical growth model predicts that countries converge to their steady-states, so growth rates depend on where a country is starting from, and where its steady state is. Since starting points are fixed, it is more interesting to examine endpoints – the position of countries' steady states.

Using panel data, Barro (1998) finds significant effects of schooling, life expectancy, fertility, government consumption, rule of law, inflation, and the terms of trade, on growth rates. He argues that these variables are determinants of the steady state, or target y*. So, as this and other papers show, institutions are an important determinant of growth and in fact, some authors have argued that they are its fundamental cause.

Glaeser, La Porta, Lopez-de-Silanes, and Shleifer (2004, p. 272) admit the current dominance of the institutions hypothesis (hereafter called institutionalism) saying, 'recent work … has reached close to an intellectual consensus that the political institutions of limited government cause economic growth'.

North (1990, p. 3), who defines institutions as 'the rules of the game in a society or, more formally, the humanly devised constraints that shape human interaction' is often credited with bringing political economy back to the fore in the study of growth. He argues that institutions are 'the underlying determinant of the long-run performance of economies' (in Aron, 2000, p. 99). Later, Hall and Jones (1999) find that differences in what they call social infrastructure (i.e., institutions and policies that determine the economic environment in a country) drive large variations in productivity and human and physical capital across countries and, in turn, large differences in incomes. Acemoglu, Johnson, and Robinson (2001) further develop this point, using colonial settler mortality rates as an instrumental variable for institutional quality to show that institutional strength has a large effect on incomes per capita. Building on this work along with Frankel and Romer's (1999) gravity model (discussed later), Rodrik, Subramanian, and Trebbi (2004) test between the important fundamental causes of growth – geography, trade integration, and institutions – and find that institutional quality 'trumps' the others. Other authors have taken a micro-level approach – Besley (1995) uses local panel data and finds a positive relationship between property rights and income in rural Ghana. However, this positive causal relationship has not gone undisputed; Glaeser et al. (2004) turn the argument on its head and assert that growth in incomes and human capital actually causes institutional development.

This paper, motivated by the phenomenon of continued income disparities and apparently different steady states, focuses on institutional strength and its role. It takes as given the 'consensus' institutionalist view and looks for the determinants of institutional strength itself. Although this institutionalist starting point provides the link between the paper's motivation and its empirical study, even if that perspective turned out to be wrong, the results set out here would still be of independent interest. Despite their policy conclusions, Glaeser et al. (2004, p. 298) concede 'the merits of … constraints on government as essential human values in their own right'. In other words, institutional strength is an interesting and worthwhile dependent variable on its own.

In the post-Soviet space, the topic of this paper, there is persistently large variation in institutional strength across countries. Fig. 3 illustrates this, using an index measuring the rule of law in 2000 and 2012. This compiled index seems to be the most relevant measure of institutions for economic development, as discussed below.

The question that emerges from this diagram relates to the sources of variation in institutional strength. This is the subject of the rest of the paper, which in addition to the standard drivers, proposes a new variable – Russian influence.

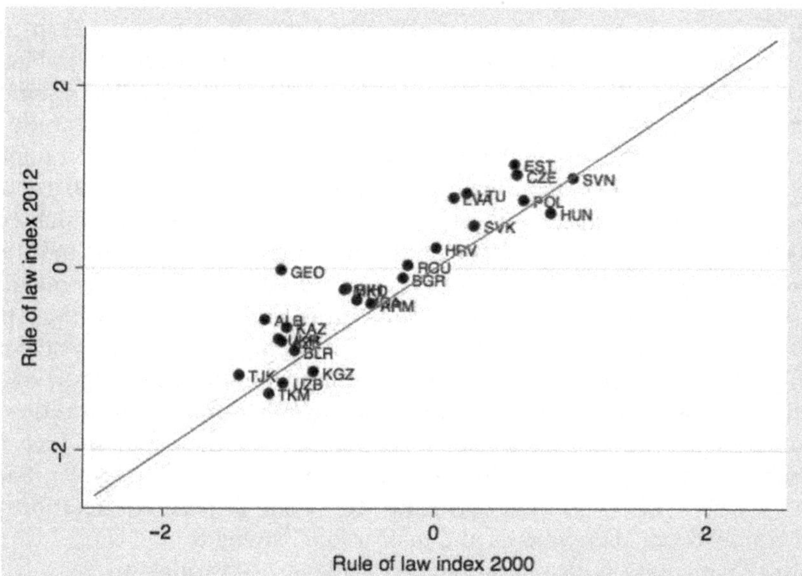

Fig. 3. Institutional Variation.

DETERMINANTS OF INSTITUTIONAL STRENGTH

The question of the sources of institutional strength is less widely discussed in the literature than the impact of institutions on growth. Nevertheless, this paper follows the lead of Islam and Montenegro, henceforth IM (2002), Alonso and Garcimartin (2009), and Siba (2008), three studies of the components of institutional development. The papers propose several explanatory variables, which are now discussed in turn.

International openness is proposed as an important determinant of institutional strength through several channels. First, openness encourages a more competitive domestic environment, which reduces harmful rent seeking. Second, a more competitive environment also favours settings with better institutions and thus incentivizes reform. Third, increased openness allows agents to learn from the good practices of foreign countries with which they interact. Finally, increasing the number of trading partners leads to more uncertainty and thus a demand for better institutions to manage the additional risk (IM, 2002, p. 4).

Islam and Montenegro (2002, pp. 2–3) also include time since independence as an explanatory variable. Building strong institutions takes time, so 'older' countries have a head start in the process. In the post-Soviet context, one would expect the newly independent states to have weaker institutions on average than older European states, such as the Czech Republic.

Several geographic variables are proposed in the literature. For example, Siba (2008, p. 14) includes area as an explanatory variable. Area could be relevant because the larger the country, the harder it should be to impose effective institutions on remote areas, especially if a country's infrastructure is poor. Another classic variable is distance from the equator, which controls for a country's disease and climate characteristics. Given the nature of post-Soviet geography, this is not expected to be relevant, but is included anyway for robustness. Additionally, natural resources are an important explanatory variable included by both Alonso and Garcimartin, and Siba. A high level of resources provides substantial rent-seeking opportunities in the economy, which work against strong institutions. In addition, a resource-rich state can substitute rents for tax revenues and so face less demand for transparency (Alonso & Garcimartin, 2009, pp. 8–9). Sachs and Warner (1997) provide evidence for such a negative relationship between resource endowments and institutional strength.

GDP per capita is also an important explanatory variable to be included in a model explaining institutional strength. There are two major channels present – higher income leads to higher demand for good institutions, and richer countries can afford better institutions (IM, 2002, p. 9). As discussed in the institutions and growth literature, there is almost certainly reverse causality present in this relationship, since good institutions also lead to higher incomes. This problem is discussed in more detail in the empirical section.

Two political variables are also included in the literature – checks and balances, and press freedom. On the one hand, balance between branches of government constrains political change and thus adds stability to the national environment. Additionally, constrained decision makers may be more likely to emphasize economic performance over political gain, and so build up institutional structures. On the other hand, too many constraints can lead to crippling inflexibility and may hamper institutional effectiveness. Meanwhile, press freedom is relevant because free information flow allows individuals to check each other's and governments' activities, and so should lead to better institutions (IM, 2002, p. 6). These variables are likely to be endogenous, since stronger institutions also constrain political actors, for example. Nevertheless, they are used in the empirical tests as robustness checks.

A number of variables are not included in the analysis here because data on them is not readily available for the countries and time period in question. These are inequality, the source of the legal system, and ethnolinguistic fractionalization. However, as will be discussed below, assuming these variables remain fixed over time, the panel structure of the data will take care of those fixed effects. Where the data is time variant (for example, in the case of inequality), in theory a strong instrumental variable will eliminate the omitted variable bias.

In addition to these explanatory variables, a new one is proposed that is specific to the post-Soviet space. This region has an important local hegemon, the Russian Federation, and recent events in Ukraine have shown that it plays an important role in the political economy of the area. Prior to 1989, the Soviet Union was a crucial player in the sample countries' institutional development because they were either part of it in the case of the CIS, the Baltics, and Georgia, or in its sphere of influence as part of the Warsaw Pact. Even now, Russia aims to maintain a sphere of influence for economic and political reasons. For example, one author comments that 'its discourse and policies demonstrate a resolve to maintain a "zone of privileged interest" in the Baltic region and post-communist Europe, often irrespective of the wishes of the countries concerned' (Grigas, 2012, p. 2). In central Asia and Belarus, its influence is even stronger through the CIS, which it dominates, and the recent Eurasian

Economic Community customs union. This union, formed in 2010 and championed by Russian president Vladimir Putin, currently contains Russia, Kazakhstan, and Belarus, with Armenia, Kyrgyzstan, and Tajikistan also planning to join.

Although regional integration may be beneficial for the countries participating in the process, this paper hypothesizes that on balance, Russian influence negatively affects institutions in the post-Soviet sphere. Two mechanisms are proposed – first, perpetuation of weak institutions via relations with Russian businesses and second, Russian-imposed isolation from the beneficial effects of association with the European Union.

Evidence suggests that Russian businesses operating abroad thrive on and perpetuate corruption and lack of transparency, preferring to enter countries that have weaker institutions. Grigas (2012, p. 11) claims that Russian firms attract business and political leaders in other countries with 'bribes, financial incentives and the appeal of a Russian business culture that is network-driven rather market-driven, and is marked by opaqueness, corruption and efforts to influence the conduct of political institutions and the political process in general'. All of this leads to the expectation that countries that are under stronger Russian influence, which is intimately related to business connections, should have weaker institutions.

Additionally, recent events in Ukraine have highlighted the fact that Russia tries to keep countries sealed off from Western influence in general, and EU influence in particular, for strategic reasons. A major example of this is the Eurasian customs union mentioned above, which has been strongly promoted by Russia as a substitute for, rather than a complement to, EU ties. The underlying tension between the two sides has been evident in the Ukrainian crisis, in which the protests that brought down the president were fuelled by his refusal, under Russian pressure, to sign an EU association agreement. This forced isolation from the EU prevents the countries in question from benefiting from EU-driven reforms.

The benefits for the EU's eastern neighbours from interacting with it have been the subject of a number of papers. Dragneva and Wolczuk (2012, p. 9) argue that 'the EU's approach projects the internal "European order", combining norms and values related to democracy, human rights and the rule of law, as well as the economic model of governance, to the countries concerned'. Meanwhile, Belke, Bordon, Melnykovska, and Schweickert (2009, p. 8) find a significant positive impact on institutional reform of cooperation with both the EU and NATO in the CIS, arguing that they can serve as a 'catalyst for institutional convergence' though they admit it is not a 'main driver'. Within Europe proper, Epstein and Sedelmeier (2008) note that conditionality prior to the 2004 and 2007 enlargements is widely cited as having improved institutional outcomes in the acceding countries, moving them towards Western European levels. Furthermore, contrary to the underlying incentive-based view, reform and compliance have continued post-accession despite the decline in material benefits linked to institutional improvements. In theory, then, countries under strong Russian influence and cut off from this factor are expected to have worse institutional outcomes on average.

MODELLING INSTITUTIONAL STRENGTH

This section discusses the data and model used to estimate the effects of Russian influence on institutions in the post-Soviet region. This paper uses panel data on 25 countries from 2000 to 2012. The regions included are Central and Eastern Europe, Central Asia, Albania, Bosnia and Herzegovina, Croatia, FYR Macedonia, and Slovenia and those members of Yugoslavia that were independent in 2000. Ideally, one would use data since the fall of the Soviet Union in 1991, but many of the statistics from the period 1992–1999 for this part of the world are unavailable. The dependent variable is a rule of law measure from the Worldwide Governance Indicators (WGI) compiled by Kaufmann, Kraay, and Mastruzzi (2010). The advantage of this index is that it aggregates many survey assessments and thus deals with some of the most egregious measurement issues. The rule of law seems to be the institutional dimension most relevant for growth since it captures the predictability and fairness of the economic and social environment in a country. Kaufmann et al. (2010, p. 4) describe the variable as measuring the quality of contract enforcement, property rights, police, courts, and the likelihood of crime and violence. Siba (2008, p. 10) focuses on this index, arguing that it 'captures the very essence of institutions'. The variable is scaled from −2.5 to +2.5, with a higher score representing stronger institutions.

Russian influence, the explanatory variable of interest, is not directly observable, so a proxy is used in its place – trade share with Russia. Intuitively, the argument is that the larger the share of imports and/or exports between a country and Russia, the more that country depends on Russia (either as a market for its own goods or as a source of imports) and is under its influence. This is plausible – to give a crude example, during the recent Ukraine crisis, Hungary, whose largest trade partner outside the EU is Russia, has been vocally opposed to economic sanctions on Moscow (Szakacs, 2014). This suggests that Russia may exert substantial (potentially indirect) influence on Hungary in part through trade dependence. Causation is not required for a proxy, however, so the intuitive argument for correlation is sufficient here. A potential problem with this proxy variable is that it may also capture the effect of regional integration. This is an issue that is discussed later, when alternatives are also proposed. In the empirical study, two measures of trade share are used: first, an average of import and export shares with Russia as a proportion of trade with the world and second, a simple export share measure, both obtained from the UN Comtrade and World Bank Direction of Trade Statistics. The average measure is the more intuitive proxy, but the export measure becomes useful when instrumental variables are introduced.

Several controls are also included in the model, as discussed in the previous section. Trade openness is measured as the amount of imports and exports as a percentage of total GDP, using World Bank data. Time since independence, area, distance from the equator, and GDP are all straightforward and standard measures in the model. 'Natural resources' is captured by total natural resource rents as a percentage of GDP, as measured by the World Bank. 'Checks and balances' uses the checks index in the World Bank Database of Political Institutions (Beck, Clarke, Groff, Keefer, & Walsh, 2001), a measure that is scaled from 0 to 18, with a higher score meaning more checks on government. Finally, 'press freedom' uses Freedom House data, scaled from 0 to 100, with lower scores signifying a freer press.

The datasets used are largely complete for the period under study, but in rare cases a few observations are missing. In these cases, the data is imputed as the mean of the other years for the country in question. This approach has potentially serious implications since it artificially reduces standard errors, but in this case, the variables are very stable over time. For example, a few values are imputed in the checks index, which has very low variation within a country over time, whereas for the trade share data, which is much more variable, this was fortunately not necessary. In a more rigorous analysis, regression imputation would be used for the missing data, but given the small number of changes needed, no significant differences in results would be expected.

The underlying model used in this paper is:

$$Ruleoflaw_{it} = \theta_t + \beta_1 \times russia_{it} + X_{it}\gamma + \alpha_i + u_{it}$$

where X is the vector of controls, θ is the year effect, α is the unobserved fixed effect, and *russia* is the proxy for Russian influence (either *AveRussia* or *exports*).

IDENTIFICATION STRATEGY

This section discusses the identification strategy used to isolate the causal effect of Russian influence on post-Soviet states' institutional strength. The panel structure of the data allows for estimation of a fixed effects model, which is very useful for cross-country analysis. Endogeneity concerns arising from omitted or unobservable fixed effects are addressed by exploiting this panel component. The paper assumes that the unobservable variables are likely to be correlated with the error term and uses the first difference (FD) estimator. The FD estimator is preferred to its counterpart, fixed effects (FE) estimation because it requires a weaker exogeneity assumption than FE, namely that the error term must be uncorrelated with regressors this period and one period in the past and future, rather than regressors in all periods, which is the requirement for FE estimation.

Nevertheless, concern remains about potential endogeneity of the included time-varying regressors, especially the influence proxy and GDP per capita. Income is an obvious culprit due to the reverse causality issue discussed earlier – better institutions also lead to higher growth, according to the institutionalist hypothesis. Insofar as the influence proxy – the explanatory variable of principal interest – is correlated with income, the FD estimator for it will also be inconsistent. A classic solution to this problem is an instrumental variable (IV) regression.

This paper proposes four instrumental variables for these two potentially endogenous terms. The first two instruments, for the trade share variable, are based on geographical characteristics. Frankel and Romer (1999) propose geography-based instruments to predict bilateral trade shares and ultimately estimate the impact of trade on growth. In this model, two simple variables are used – a dummy variable for whether the country borders Russia, and a variable that measures the logarithm of the distance between the country's capital and Moscow. The two main criteria – exogeneity and relevance – for good instruments are very likely satisfied for these variables. They are plausibly relevant, since distance and a common border matter for trade between states, and exogenous, as a common border and distance between capitals are likely to affect a country's institutions only via the bilateral trade share (and ultimately, influence). Yet although these appear to be good instruments, geographical characteristics are time invariant and therefore can only be used in cross-sectional (pooled OLS) estimation. Since exploiting the panel data structure is an important identifying strategy, finding a time variant instrument for trade share is important.

The real exchange rate between the local currency and the Russian rouble is used as an instrument for this reason. Standard trade theory predicts that as a country's currency depreciates, its exports will increase, so this instrument should be relevant. It is calculated by hand by multiplying the ratio of the official exchange rates (in LCU per US$ as recorded by the World Bank) by the ratio of CPIs in the country of interest and Russia. The main issue with this instrument is the exclusion restriction – the assumption that the bilateral exchange rate only affects institutional strength via the export share (influence). A major concern is that exchange rate movements affect institutional strength via economic growth. Rodrik (2008) shows that the exchange rate, and in particular, undervaluation, stimulates economic growth. Meanwhile, Schnabl (2007) finds a significant positive effect of exchange rate stability on growth in countries at the periphery of the eurozone. Nevertheless, the proposed instrument in this paper is the real bilateral exchange rate rather than the real effective exchange rate. The latter (the REER), which is the rate relative to a basket of other currencies, usually weighted by trade, is the measure of exchange rates that is most relevant to economic growth, and hence directly subject to endogeneity. A crude analysis yields a low correlation coefficient (0.31) between the bilateral exchange rate used in the sample and its REER counterpart. Additionally, assuming there is relatively low volatility in this bilateral exchange rate over the period under study, endogeneity will be less problematic. This introduces a trade-off since some variation in the instrument is required for consistent IV estimation.

Finally, lagged GDP per capita is proposed as an instrument in response to the endogeneity of contemporaneous per capita GDP. To accommodate the first differencing model, income per capita lagged two periods is used. In the literature, both Islam and Montenegro (2002) and Alonso and Garcimartin (2009) employ a cross-sectional approach and use GDP per capita outside the period under consideration to ameliorate the endogeneity problem. Here, the exclusion restriction may be problematic – twice-lagged GDP may affect institutional strength through channels other than current GDP. Therefore, in the empirical section, the IV regression is run with and without an instrument for GDP. If the instruments for trade share are strong, the influence estimator will be consistent anyway. This important argument applies for other potentially endogenous variables as well, such as trade openness. In fact, the model of institutional strength used here has several potentially endogenous explanatory variables, so the empirical analysis relies heavily on the strength of the instruments used.

RESULTS

This section presents the empirical results found, starting with a summary and then discussing each estimation technique used in turn. Table 1 presents summary statistics for the explanatory variables, sorted by membership of the Common-wealth of Independent States (CIS).

The differences between CIS and non-CIS data are striking. Within the CIS, the rule of law mean is substantially lower than outside it, but there is also less variance among the countries. This is in contrast to income, which has a higher variance among CIS countries, though again it is substantially lower than outside the organization. As expected, CIS countries have substantially higher trade shares with Russia, have a shorter independent history (all became independent around 1992), and are much more reliant on natural resources, although there is huge variation among them in this

Table 1. Summary Statistics.

	Non-CIS		CIS	
	Mean	sd	Mean	sd
RuleofLaw	0.24	0.60	−0.95	0.35
Exports	0.04	0.05	0.18	0.12
AveRussia	0.07	0.05	0.23	0.12
logpcapGDP	9.37	0.56	8.23	0.71
lag2GDP	9.25	0.58	8.08	0.71
Border	0.33	0.47	0.41	0.49
logdistance	7.30	0.32	7.48	0.52
TradeOpenness	111.56	31.10	103.20	29.35
Independence	57.33	37.69	22.00	0.00
eqdist	0.46	0.08	0.44	0.05
lnarea	4.18	0.72	5.32	1.31
natres	1.78	1.40	21.84	25.30
rer	0.07	0.09	2.70	4.47
checks	3.78	1.46	2.05	1.07
freedom	32.44	13.41	75.41	12.48
N	195		130	

respect. They also have fewer checks and balances on government and substantially less press freedom. A somewhat surprising result, however, is that CIS countries are on average, further from Russia when distance between capitals is used. These large discrepancies between the two groups are the basic motivation for this paper.

The first baseline regression run is pooled ordinary least squares (POLS) with robust standard errors. This is a 'naïve' approach in that it makes no use of the panel structure in the data and is likely to suffer from endogeneity problems. Nevertheless, it provides a good starting point for the analysis here. Table 2 contains the POLS estimates, with *t*-statistics in parentheses. The first two columns use export share to Russia and an average of export and import shares, respectively, and the third and fourth add the checks and balances and press freedom measures to check the robustness of the findings.

Table 2. Pooled OLS Results.

	RuleofLaw	RuleofLaw	RuleofLaw	RuleofLaw
Exports	−0.886		−0.899	0.421
	(2.15)**		(2.49)**	(2.40)**
logpcapGDP	0.504	0.454	0.383	0.223
	(10.74)***	(11.36)***	(8.18)***	(8.11)***
TradeOpenness	0.001	0.001	0.001	0.001
	(0.64)	(1.47)	(0.79)	(1.48)
Independence	0.003	0.002	0.003	−0.001
	(2.76)***	(1.66)*	(3.15)***	(1.83)*
natres	−0.005	−0.006	−0.001	0.004
	(3.08)***	(3.77)***	(0.96)	(5.59)***
lnarea	−0.154	−0.083	−0.142	−0.049
	(6.62)***	(3.08)***	(6.79)***	(2.85)***
eqdist	2.705	3.177	3.104	0.125
	(5.20)***	(6.57)***	(7.25)***	(0.48)
AveRussia		−1.921		
		(5.57)***		
checks			0.117	0.034
			(6.45)***	(2.55)**
freedom				−0.024
				(21.46)***
_cons	−5.172	−5.131	−4.781	−1.151
	(14.68)***	(17.68)***	(14.45)***	(4.99)***
R^2	0.79	0.82	0.82	0.91
N	300	300	300	300

* $p<0.1$; ** $p<0.05$; *** $p<0.01$.

The advantage of pooled OLS estimation is that along with dynamic variables, the effects of time invariant variables are also easily estimated. The baseline results show that both influence proxies have a statistically significant negative effect on institutions, at the 5% level for exports and the 1% level for the average. A 1% increase in export share to Russia leads to a decrease in the rule of law index of 0.009, or 0.019 in the case of the average of imports and exports, which is plausible given that the index ranges from −2.5 to +2.5. These results are robust to the inclusion of the checks variable (the AveRussia regressions are not included since they are very similar). Somewhat surprisingly, they are not robust to the inclusion of the freedom index. The large swing in the coefficient on exports is worrying and suggests that the freedom measure is highly endogenous. All of the controls have the expected signs, although trade openness is not significant. Another surprising result is that distance from the equator is highly significant – a plausible explanation is that the successful Baltic states, which are the northernmost countries in the sample, drive this result. Time dummies are included in the regression but left out here as only a small number are significant at the 10% level.

Next, to correct for endogeneity, the gravity instruments – distance and a border dummy – are introduced. Table 3 reports the results, with the second and third columns again adding the checks and freedom controls.

The results are similar to those obtained earlier. The Russian influence proxy, when instrumented for using distance and a border dummy, remains significant, but only at the 10% level. When the checks control is added, the coefficient decreases substantially and Russian influence becomes significant at the 1% level.

The press freedom control remains problematic, causing the proxy to lose significance, but in this case it does not switch signs. The rest of the controls retain their expected signs and remain highly significant, except trade openness. The average trade share proxy is used here as the instruments are relevant to both imports and exports, but the results are similar if the exports-only proxy is used.

Some statistics on the instruments are also discussed here. The first-stage F-statistic for the first (main) two-stage regression above is 28.37. This is far greater than the standard rule of thumb ($F \geq 10$) and suggests relevance is not problematic. Running the Hausman test for endogeneity yields a p-value of 0.0205 suggesting that the null hypothesis of exogeneity can be rejected and using instruments is justified. Finally, testing overidentifying restrictions yields a p-value of 0.4768, meaning that the null hypothesis of instrumental validity cannot be rejected.

Table 3. Pooled OLS with Instruments.

	RuleofLaw	RuleofLaw	RuleofLaw
AveRussia	−0.971	−1.715	−0.311
	(1.68)*	(3.93)***	(0.83)
logpcapGDP	0.510	0.363	0.201
	(9.72)***	(8.34)***	(7.91)***
TradeOpenness	0.001	0.001	0.001
	(0.78)	(1.60)	(2.09)**
Independence	0.002	0.002	−0.001
	(2.57)**	(2.15)**	(2.05)**
natres	−0.005	−0.003	0.003
	(3.37)***	(2.07)**	(3.45)***
lnarea	−0.129	−0.084	−0.035
	(4.65)***	(3.53)***	(1.92)*
eqdist	2.687	3.407	0.725
	(4.73)***	(7.40)***	(1.94)*
checks		0.100	0.039
		(5.99)***	(2.98)***
freedom			−0.022
			(13.05)***
_cons	−5.288	−4.833	−1.348
	(16.50)***	(17.60)***	(5.00)***
R^2	0.81	0.84	0.91
N	300	300	300

* $p<0.1$; ** $p<0.05$; *** $p<0.01$.

Although these results are promising, the underlying analysis fails to take into account the panel nature of the data, treating it instead as cross-sectional. To fully exploit the data, the model is estimated using the first differencing method and the results are shown in Table 4. The first two columns include the exports and average proxies as explanatory variables, respectively, while the third and fourth add the checks and freedom controls. Time dummies are included in the regression but excluded in the results – they are significant for 2005 and 2006 only.

Surprisingly, none of the explanatory variables appears significant and the coefficients on the Russian influence proxies decrease dramatically in magnitude. This suggests substantial bias due to fixed effects in the POLS results, yet the lack of significance on any of the variables also suggests potential endogeneity in this simple FD analysis. To correct for this endogeneity, the real exchange rate with the Russian rouble is used as a time-varying instrument. Twice-lagged per capita income is also added as an

Table 4. First Differenced Results.

	Druleoflaw	Druleoflaw	Druleoflaw	Druleoflaw
dexports	−0.422		−0.426	
	(1.30)		(1.30)	
dloggdp	0.222	0.212	0.226	0.215
	(1.64)	(1.60)	(1.68)*	(1.62)
dtrade	−0.001	−0.001	−0.001	−0.001
	(1.40)	(1.34)	(1.44)	(1.39)
dnatres	0.001	0.001	0.001	0.001
	(0.85)	(0.96)	(0.92)	(1.02)
daverussia		−0.249		−0.260
		(0.80)		(0.84)
dchecks			0.007	0.007
			(0.86)	(0.97)
dfreedom			−0.003	−0.003
			(0.84)	(0.81)
_cons	0.029	0.029	0.030	0.030
	(1.41)	(1.42)	(1.45)	(1.46)
R^2	0.12	0.11	0.12	0.11
N	250	250	250	250

* $p < 0.1$.

instrument for current income in the second and fourth columns. There is evidence for heteroskedasticity and serial correlation, so the standard errors are robust and clustered by country. The results are reported in Table 5.

The exports proxy for Russian influence is now highly negatively significant with a magnitude similar to the one found in the POLS case. This estimate is robust to using lagged GDP as an instrument for institutions and to the inclusion of the checks and freedom controls. In the first regression, with just the real exchange rate as an instrument, the first-stage (Cragg-Donald Wald) F-statistic is 61.86, while in the second, the Angrist-Pischke F-statistic for D.exports is 100.59. Again, weak instruments are not an issue here. However, since the model is exactly identified, there is no way to test validity. Indeed, these results need to be treated with caution since few variables are statistically significant. None of the expected results emerge from this FDIV model: surprisingly, trade openness is negatively related to institutional strength and natural resources are positively related, although both effects are extremely small. One reason for these unexpected results may be that there is very little variation in the variables between periods to exploit in estimation.

Table 5. FD with Instruments Results.

	D.RuleofLaw	D.RuleofLaw	D.RuleofLaw	D.RuleofLaw
D.Exports	−0.995	−0.990	−0.970	−0.967
	(2.78)***	(2.12)**	(2.82)***	(2.12)**
D.logpcapGDP	0.230	−0.382	0.235	−0.371
	(1.58)	(0.79)	(1.65)*	(0.77)
D.TradeOpenness	−0.001	−0.001	−0.001	−0.001
	(1.55)	(2.01)**	(1.58)	(2.03)**
D.natres	0.001	0.000	0.001	0.001
	(2.59)***	(0.75)	(2.76)***	(0.86)
D.checks			0.005	0.006
			(0.54)	(0.60)
D.freedom			−0.003	−0.003
			(1.16)	(0.88)
_cons	0.005	0.029	0.005	0.028
	(0.33)	(1.07)	(0.31)	(1.06)
R^2	0.09	0.02	0.10	0.03
N	250	250	250	250

* $p<0.1$; ** $p<0.05$; *** $p<0.01$.

ISSUES AND CONCLUSION

On balance, the results give some reason to believe that Russian influence is a significant factor in institutional development in the post-Soviet region. Nevertheless, the data and model used in this paper have a number of issues that mean that the results are simply a starting point for further, much more rigorous analysis. These problems, and potential solutions in future research, are discussed in this section.

First, the empirical analysis of this paper is heavily reliant on instrumental variables for identification. If these instruments are invalid or weak, the reported estimates are likely to be inconsistent. The exogeneity of the real exchange rate is not entirely convincing and a stronger substitute would strengthen the empirical findings. One possible alternative is a dummy variable for whether there is a Russian trade representative in the country. In addition, lagged GDP is also suspect as an instrument, again due to likely endogeneity. In this case, rainfall is a classic strong instrument that immediately comes to mind. Unfortunately, precipitation data is not readily available for this paper's sample, but a more detailed study should be able to compile these statistics.

Second, the proxy variable for Russian influence is central to the study. The goal of the trade share proxy is to capture the role of influence as closely as possible, yet in retrospect there are a couple of better alternative proxies. Energy dependence is a highly topical measure of Russian influence while Russian foreign direct investment (FDI) is also intuitively appealing. In the case of Russian FDI, it would have to be measured as a percentage of total FDI to rule out the general effect of a change in FDI.

Third, the sample selection is also imperfect. Ideally, the paper would examine the entire post-1992 period, but as discussed this was not possible. Further research might also limit the analysis to a specific region – the CIS seems to be a neat and interesting category to be studied on its own. Similarly, central and eastern Europe (excluding the former Yugoslav countries due to unbalanced panel issues) provides an interesting case study as well.

Finally, and perhaps most importantly, this empirical study was motivated by the large discrepancy in post-Soviet incomes, and so the natural question is the effect Russian influence has on income levels and growth rates themselves. Income is not used as a dependent variable, however, because of the difficulty of disentangling counteracting effects in a macroeconomic cross-country study. Institutions are assumed to affect growth as per the institutionalist thesis, but further research is required to confirm this link in the context of the post-Soviet region. A more micro-level approach might prove fruitful – for example, future research might conduct a difference-in-differences analysis after a policy change leading to decreased dependence on Russian natural gas in a certain country. In any case, institutional strength remains an important outcome variable in itself – after all, the rule of law index measures, among other things, the potential for crime and violence, which are directly relevant to individual welfare.

The policy implications of this paper are not immediately obvious. If a clear negative causal relationship between Russian influence and institutional strength can be confirmed in later work, this might suggest that external actors should contain Russian influence in the post-Soviet region where possible. Nevertheless, as the ongoing Ukrainian experience shows, this is a potentially dangerous proposition since the negative effects of ensuing conflict could far outweigh the gains from a rollback of Russian influence. Therefore, a safer approach would be to focus on economic and political development in Russia itself and softening the image of the EU within Russia. As Russia develops, one would expect its business climate to become more transparent and its ties to the EU to deepen. This would benefit not only Russian citizens, but the post-Soviet world as a whole, according to the results set out here.

This paper started out by contrasting the convergence thesis in theory with the lack of clear empirical evidence of convergence in the post-Soviet world. It then set out the link between institutions and growth and went on to focus on the determinants of institutional strength, one possible explanation for the continued discrepancies in income levels in the region. It introduced a new relevant variable for institutions – Russian influence – and presented empirical results showing that it is a significant negative factor. Yet the results were not always robust and it must be stressed that this is simply a starting point for deeper empirical research. Perhaps as the Ukraine crisis unfolds and Russia begins to re-assert itself as a major global player, policy changes will arise that allow for more precise identification of the role of Russian influence on post-Soviet political economy.

REFERENCES

Acemoglu, D., Johnson, S., & Robinson, J. A. (2001). The colonial origins of comparative development: An empirical investigation. *American Economic Review, 91*(5), 1369–1401.

Alonso, J. A., & Garcimartín, C. (2009). *The determinants of institutional quality. More on the debate*. Discussion Papers 09/04, University of Nottingham, CREDIT.

Aron, J. (2000). Growth and institutions: A review of the evidence. *World Bank Research Observer, 15*(1), 99–135.

Barro, R. J. (1998, January). *Determinants of economic growth: A cross-country empirical study* (1st ed., Vol. 1). Cambridge, MA: The MIT Press.

Beck, T. H. L., Clarke, G., Groff, A., Keefer, P., & Walsh, P. (2001). *New tools in comparative political economy: The database of political institutions*. Tilburg: Open Access Publications, Tilburg University.

Belke, A., Bordon, I., Melnykovska, I., & Schweickert, R. (2009). *Prospective NATO or EU membership and institutional change in transition countries*. Discussion Papers of DIW Berlin 915, DIW Berlin, German Institute for Economic Research.

Besley, T. (1995). Property rights and investment incentives: Theory and evidence from Ghana. *Journal of Political Economy*, 103(5), 903–937.

Borsi, M. T., & Metiu, N. (2013). *The evolution of economic convergence in the European Union*. Discussion Papers 28/2013, Deutsche Bundesbank, Research Centre.

Dragneva, R., & Wolczuk, K. (2012). Russia, the Eurasian Customs Union and the EU: Cooperation, Stagnation or Rivalry? Chatham House Briefing Paper.

Durlauf, S. N., & Johnson, P. A. (1995). Multiple regimes and cross-country growth behaviour. *Journal of Applied Econometrics, 10*(4), 365–384.

Epstein, R. A., & Sedelmeier, U. (2008). Beyond conditionality: Inter-national institutions in postcommunist Europe after enlargement. *Journal of European Public Policy*, *15*(6), 795–805.

Frankel, J. A., & Romer, D. (1999). Does trade cause growth? *American Economic Review*, *89*(3), 379–399.

Galor, O. (1996). Convergence? Inferences from theoretical models. *Economic Journal*, *106*(437), 1056–1069.

Glaeser, E. L., La Porta, R., Lopez-de-Silanes, F., & Shleifer, A. (2004). Do institutions cause growth? *Journal of Economic Growth*, 9(3), 271–303.

Grigas, A. (2012). *Legacies, coercion and soft power: Russian influence in the Baltic States*. Chatham House Briefing Paper.

Hall, R. E., & Jones, C. I. (1999). *Why do some countries produce so much more output per worker than others*? NBER Working Paper No. 6564, National Bureau of Economic Research, Inc.

Islam, N. (2003). What have we learnt from the convergence debate? *Journal of Economic Surveys*, *17*(3), 309–362.

Islam, R., & Montenegro, C. E. (2002). *What determines the quality of institutions?* Policy Research Working Paper Series 2764, The World Bank.

Kaufmann, D., Kraay, A., & Mastruzzi, M. (2010). *The worldwide governance indicators: Methodology and analytical issues*. Policy Research Working Paper Series 5430, The World Bank.

Libman, A., & Vinokurov, E. (2012a). Regional integration and economic convergence in the PostSoviet space: Experience of the decade of growth. *Journal of Common Market Studies*, *50*(1), 112–128.

Libman, A., & Vinokurov, E. (2012b). *Holding-together regionalism: Twenty years of Post-Soviet integration*. Basingstoke, Hampshire: Palgrave Macmillan.

North, D. C. (1990). *Institutions, institutional change, and economic performance*. Cambridge: Cambridge University Press.

Rapacki, R., & Prochniak, M. (2009). The EU Enlargement and Economic Growth in the CEE New Member Countries. European Commission Economic Papers 367, n.p., Web. Retrieved from http://ec.europa.eu/economy_finance/publications/publication 14295_en.pdf

Rodrik, D. (2008). The real exchange rate and economic growth. *Brookings Papers on Economic Activity*, *39*(2), 365–439.

Rodrik, D., Subramanian, A., & Trebbi, F. (2004). Institutions rule: The primacy of institutions over geography and integration in economic development. *Journal of Economic Growth*, 9(2),131–165.

Sachs, J., & Warner, A. (1997). Sources of slow growth in African economies. *Journal of African Economies*, *6*, 335–376.

Schnabl, G. (2007). *Exchange rate volatility and growth in small open economies at the EMU periphery*. Working Paper Series 0773, European Central Bank.

Siba, E. G. (2008). *Determinants of institutional quality in Sub-Saharan African countries*. Working Papers in Economics 310. University of Gothenburg, Department of Economics.

Szakacs, G. (2014). Hungary opposed to economic sanctions against Russia: PM. In M. Heinrich (Ed.). Reuters, March 28, n.p., Web. Retrieved from http://www.reuters.com/article/2014/03/28/us-ukraine-crisis-russia-hungary-idUSBREA2R0CD20140328

PART III
FINANCIAL SECTOR DEVELOPMENT

LENDING RATE PASS-THROUGH AND BANK HETEROGENEITY IN A HIGH INTEREST RATE ENVIRONMENT: EVIDENCE FROM AZERBAIJAN

Rustam Jamilov

ABSTRACT

I contribute to the ongoing policy discourse on the challenges of monetary policy transmission in environments with consolidated financial sectors and high credit rates. I empirically investigate the lending rate pass-through in Azerbaijan – a small resource-rich economy in transition – by taking advantage of a unique set of high-frequency bank-level data. My bottom-line policy message is the following. First, lending rates are considerably irresponsive to monetary policy shocks, and the interest rate channel ought to be somehow improved. Second, macroeconomic fundamentals and the concentrated bank sector are surprisingly not among the reasons behind the policy-market disconnect. Third, domestic commercial banks are able to exert substantial monopolistic pricing capacities and keep credit rates high, particularly when the central bank

Neo-Transitional Economics
International Finance Review, Volume 16, 193–217

ISSN: 1569-3767/doi:10.1108/S1569-376720150000016009

loosens its policy stance. Fourth, the underlying cause of both monetary policy inefficacy and high interest rate stickiness appears to be structural excess liquidity. In fact, empirical results show that pass-through is substantially higher for less liquid banks. Extraction of excess liquidity from the system should mitigate the banks' monopolistic pricing powers, improve the efficiency of the interest rate channel, and ultimately bring the credit rates down.

Keywords: Interest rate pass-through; bank heterogeneity; Pooled Mean Group panel cointegration; Azerbaijan

JEL classifications: E43; E52; N25

INTRODUCTION

Over the past five years, Central Bank of Azerbaijan has been systematically pursuing a softening strategy, lowering the key policy rates, and accommodating the economy amidst the Great Recession and falling oil prices. In the meantime, the country is enjoying solid growth prospects following a double-digit growth performance driven by the resource boom. The nominal economy is disinflating, price pressures are receding, and the domestic demand base is growing in both purchasing power and spending appetite. The financial sector, although still lacking competitiveness and considerably consolidated, has improved dramatically over the years, with the shares of total assets controlled by the top banks declining two-fold. The ratio of non-performing loans in the total credit pie is just over 2%, deeming the market risks associated with lending quite low. Despite all the aforementioned facts, however, domestic interest rates on credit remain stubbornly high. Although a phenomenon common to all transition economies, this is still continuously concerning both for regional policy makers and the various micro-economic stakeholders.

Why are the lending rates still high, and what can be done to mitigate this event? The present paper attempts to tackle this research question by focusing on the broader interest rate channel of monetary transmission in Azerbaijan. Within the interest rate channel, we specifically investigate the impact of innovations in the monetary policy rate on bank lending rates, i.e. the lending rate pass-through (LRPT). Our motive is, of course, driven by the disconnect between the central bank's low refinancing rates and the market's very high credit rates. Adopting the LRPT prism will allows us to build a complete picture by introducing the monetary policy maker, macroeconomic events (output and inflation), bank heterogeneities, sectoral differences, and bank sector consolidation all into one empirical framework.

The remaining of this paper is structured as follows. The section "The Lending Rate Pass-through" discusses the literature on the interest rate pass-through and the commonly employed methodologies. The section "The Azerbaijani Financial Sector" provides some background information on the Azerbaijani financial sector and the monetary policy framework. The section "Model Specification and Data Description" presents our econometric strategy and describes the data. The section "Empirical Results" reports the empirical results. Finally, the section "Concluding Remarks" concludes with some final remarks and policy recommendations.

THE LENDING RATE PASS-THROUGH

The basic logic behind the theory of LRPT is that faced with the monetary policy rate as a chief indicator of mainstream financing, financial institutions transmit the dynamics of policy rate innovations into their own rates on the retail level.[1] Lending rates for banks are essentially the borrowing rates for the other side of the bargain, and the transmission from policy rates to lending rates is justified both on economic and also on simple accounting grounds: banks, assuming they resort themselves mostly to mainstream financing, cannot issue loans at interest rates lower than their financing prices permit. In other words, retail and policy rates should be, in theory, congruent.

Of course, while we would expect some degree of pass-through to exist in any scenario, the extent would certainly differ across different cross-sections. Indeed, multiple arguments have been made to rationalize incomplete pass-through, which is very often the case for developing economies. The standard theory of credit rationing explains why interest rates are sticky with the presence of an underlying information asymmetry in the financial markets (Stiglitz & Weis, 1981). Another explanation for incomplete pass-through is high menu costs and the high opportunity cost of switching between retail interest rate regimes (Sharpe, 1997). For example, large clients of commercial banks, at least for the case of Azerbaijan or any country of this region, usually include state institutes or state-connected institutes or wealthy individuals. Large and important clients are protected from abrupt changes in main retail interest rates, as banks attempt to smooth the effect of transition from the old interest rate regime onto the new one, which in turn results in a sluggish and incomplete pass-through.

There are several popular strategies one could adapt for LRPT estimation.[2] Consider for example, the so-called cost-of-funds approach, which builds on a key assumption that banks consider money markets as a chief source of their financing (De Bondt, 2005). Unfortunately, the cost-of-funds method is impossible to implement in the context of Azerbaijan (and for the vast majority of countries in this region) since no functioning money market, or any other form of organized short-term financing, is in place. We will, in turn, focus on the monetary policy approach proposed in Sander and Kleimeier (2004). This method suggests to essentially bypass market rates and to model a relationship between central bank's policy rates and the retail rates on deposit and credit. We will adopt this method and target specifically the lending rates. Very broadly speaking, we will be following Egert et al. (2007) with regards to the econometric strategy of LRPT investigation. Although their paper was based on a cross-country study of the Eastern Europe states, the basic idea is essentially very similar when we apply it to a cross-section of heterogeneous banks within a single country framework.[3]

Apart from measuring the LRPT between the policy rate and the main bank-specific lending rates, we also perform a brief sectoral analysis. By that I mean a comparison of IRPT and speed of adjustment estimates for loan products directed at different sectors of the economy. Apart from the main, weighted average lending rate, we have data on interest rates on industrial, consumer, agricultural, and trade and services loans. This approach should eliminate any aggregation bias problems and improve the robustness of our bottom-line results. In addition, it can also identify sectors in which banks impose the stiffest monopolistic pricing powers (lowest pass-through), and for which the risks associated with lending and therefore hedging are the highest (largest pass-through).[4] Aziakpono and Wilson (2010) found that the speed of adjustment of market interest rates indeed varies across the rates, with the highest speed occurring for the lending rate, followed by Treasury bill rate and money market rate, and closely followed by commercial bank deposit rate, while the government bond yield has the slowest speed of adjustment. Rocha (2012) use bivariate and trivariate VECMs and confirm that heterogeneous adjustments exist among bank rates of different sector, maturity, and instrument type. A more complete long-run pass-through is found for corporate loans with far more rigidity in the personal loan sector.

A particular feature of this paper is that we will account for bank heterogeneity in quite a serious manner. Why should we believe that banks react to policy rate innovations heterogeneously? Banks with a diversified portfolio of activities (those which do not rely on formal operations as much as the median bank) may be less responsive to movements in policy rates (Sorensen & Werner, 2006). In the meantime, in a highly competitive environment, diversified banks may be able to exploit this by offering better rates to capture market shares, implying a faster pass-through. Further, banks with a large pool of deposit funding would be predicted to be less vulnerable to changes in market rates, thus leading to a relatively slower speed of adjustment (Sorensen & Werner, 2006). De Graeve et al. (2004) show that the higher the interest rate risk the banks are exposed to, the more they need to hedge, and the more they hedge the more they are exposed to the mainstream interest rate. Thus, speed of adjustment is positively correlated with interest rate risk, and that correlation will differ across banks with heterogeneous risk exposures. Finally, both banks' excess liquidity and excess capital may act as buffers against market fluctuations and would hence be expected to show a negative relationship with the speed of adjustment (Gambacorta, 2008). All in all, there are multiple criteria on which banks could and should differ among each other in terms of the degree of pass-through.

Unfortunately, most papers in the interest rate pass-through stream of literature do not conduct specific analyses of the importance of heterogeneous bank factors, and use simple bank dummies instead. De Graeve et al. (2007) and Horvath and Podpiera (2012) stand out as the most comprehensive examples of the bank heterogeneity analysis. For a better, more precise attack we propose to introduce the bank parameters directly into the baseline model. First, we will be setting up an array of bank characteristics including size, liquidity, capitalization, and profitability, and inserting them into the base regression as distinct covariates. Second, for each bank characteristic we will create a date-variant median and separate the banks into two groups: for those with below and above the median. Then we can run the baseline regression for both groups, thus identifying the transmission channel more correctly. For instance, if in the first stage of our analysis we obtain a statistically significant impact of liquidity on the pass-through, then segregation of cross sections into low- and high-liquid banks in the second stage should illustratively show a substantial differential in the pass-through estimates for banks with smaller and higher liquidity levels.

Both from academic curiosity and for policy relevance, we will conduct an asymmetric analysis.[5] We separate monetary policy shocks into instances of expansionary only and contractionary only interventions and observe how the pass-through alters across the two scenarios. First, lending rates are theoretically supposed to be stickier going downwards since banks are understandably reluctant to reduce their margins, for any given market-wise real interest rate level. Second, considering that the Central Bank of Azerbaijan is particularly concerned with overly high lending rates, the prospects of yet more expansionary policy in the future are quite realistic. Thus, it is healthy to essentially forecast a potential market response to a negative (policy rate decreases) shock to the domestic refinancing rate. Given that the domestic financial structure is unlikely to change in any drastic manner in the next few years, our asymmetric results can prove to carry very important implications for any shifts in Azerbaijan's monetary strategy in the foreseeable future.

It is striking that very few papers have analyzed the nexus between the interest rate pass-through and financial consolidation.[6] Some studies like Adams and Amel (2005), Olivero et al. (2011) have analyzed the effect that bank sector concentration has on the bank lending channel of monetary policy transmission. The consensus finding is that concentration in banking is negatively associated with the efficacy of this particular channel. Extrapolating these results to our work, we would therefore ex ante predict the same negative association between the interest rate pass-through and consolidation of the Azerbaijani banking sector. However, it must be noted that the bank lending channel is an issue substantially different from the pass-through prism that we are adopting in the present paper. In that regard, our a priori assumption is of course quite stretched. More broadly, analysis of consolidation performed in the present paper contributes with fresh results on the topic which is very much overlooked in the broader empirical monetary policy research stream.

THE AZERBAIJANI FINANCIAL SECTOR

Azerbaijan is a small open economy in transition with a quasi-fixed exchange rate regime;[7] relatively low degree of international capital mobility (Jamilov, 2013); financial sector over-reliant on commercial bank financing; a heavily concentrated bank sector which is dominated by a systemic state-owned bank and a small group of very large banks,[8] and which exhibits excess structural liquidity (IMF, 2012). As a brief rhetorical digression on transition studies, while the LRPT literature is sufficiently stuffed with papers on developed countries (such as the Eurozone), there are still not many cases of serious empirical works on the states in transition (Mishra, Montiel, & Spilimbergo, 2012). Azerbaijan's financial sector possesses all the strengths and weaknesses that a typical sector in a transition market would predictably display. Therefore, extrapolating our results to a broader cluster of economies in the Caucasus and the Commonwealth of Independent States should deem the paper very policy-relevant. Broadly speaking, apart from our contribution to the conduct of monetary policy in high interest rate environments, this paper also fills a considerable gap in the transition studies literature.

A few further words on the Azerbaijan's monetary policy practices and the financial sector. The primary monetary tool in the country is the main refinancing rate (RR) of the Central Bank of the Republic of Azerbaijan (Fig. 1). The money markets in the country are non-developed and the RR tool is the dominant component of the broader interest rate channel. The retail lending rates in Azerbaijan have been historically quite congruent across the banks and across different sectors (Fig. 2). It's peculiar that right from the start we can deduce that retail rates behave somewhat independently from the RR: retail rates on credit have been rising during the oil boom years and, although they have declined after the Financial Crisis,

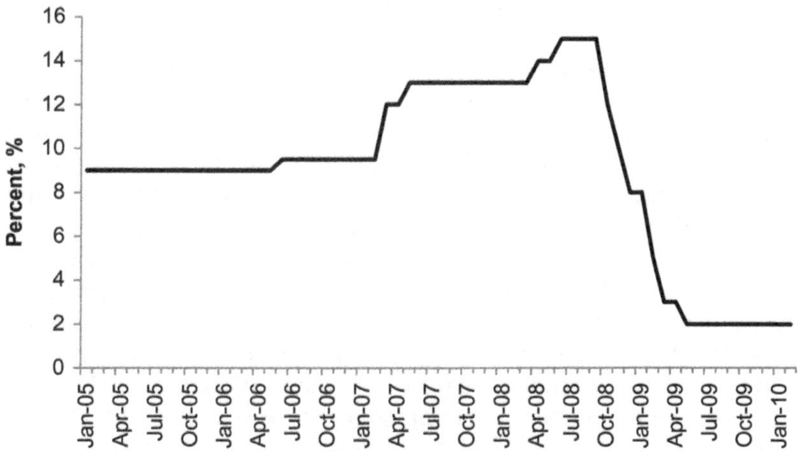

Fig. 1. Refinancing Rate.

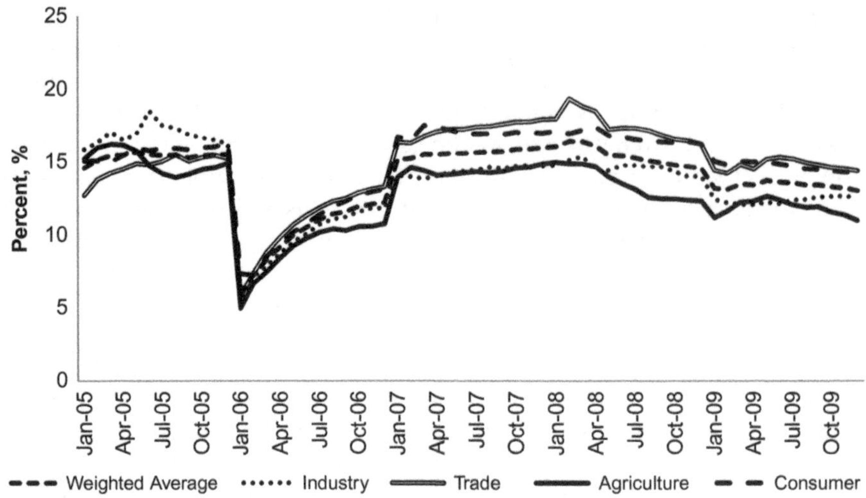

Fig. 2. Interest Rates on Credit.

the decrease has not been as apparent as the aggressive monetary policy intervention. Some degree of pass-through should be present, but imperfections in this channel should be already quite obvious. This is precisely where the natural interest in the subject culminates – why have the lending rates in Azerbaijan remained so high while the monetary policy stance has softened?

The national banking sector, much like every other sector of the economy, enjoyed a rapid and substantial growth during the oil boom era with total assets of the bank sector increasing more than 6-fold between 2004 and 2010 (Fig. 3). Interestingly, the ratio of the bank sector to Gross Domestic Product has risen by a more moderate extent and now stands at 30% of GDP. This points at the fact that, of course, the pre-crisis growth was not financial sector-driven and output generation in the country doesn't rely as much on financial services as it does on, say, oil prices. The narrative is quite similar with the case of total credits to the real economy (Fig. 4). Both total credits and total bank assets are quite pro-cyclical, reflecting the oil-dependent nature of the national growth formula. Among the total number of credit contracts issued in 2010, 25% were granted to regular physical agents – consumers. The rest are distributed among industrial, agricultural, trade, mortgage, electricity and utilities, and other loans.

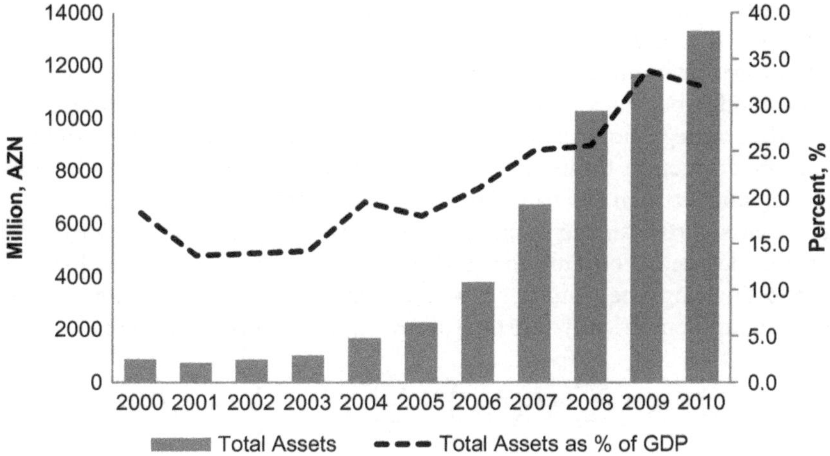

Fig. 3. Bank Sector Size.

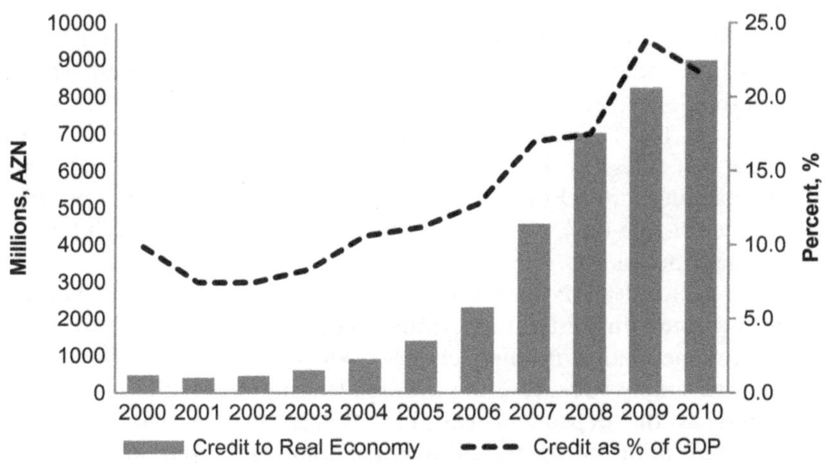

Fig. 4. Total Credit to the Real Economy.

MODEL SPECIFICATION AND DATA DESCRIPTION

The beauty of the Pooled Mean Group (PMG) approach, which we will employ, is in its applicability to both stationary and non-stationary heterogeneous dynamic panels. Pesaran, Shin, and Smith (1999) are able to prove asymptotic consistency of the PMG estimators for both when the covariates are $I(0)$ and $I(1)$ processes. Some of our series are $I(1)$ in levels but since we perform universal first-differencing of all regressors, every variable in the model becomes stationary, and hence the PGM technique can be applied. Cointegration testing is performed via a check on the stability of the error correction terms. If the term is consistently negative and statistically significant then we can claim that cointegration is achieved. This, in fact, occurs across all our estimation steps, so we can conclude with a considerable degree of certainty that our panels are cointegrated in the long run.

In estimating the lending rate pass-through for Azerbaijan, we will construct and empirically test the following reduced-form model:

$$D\left(i^r_{i,t}\right) = \alpha_0 + \sum_{j=1}^{p} \alpha_j D\left(i^r_{i,t-j}\right) + \sum_{k=0}^{q} \beta_k i^p_{t-k} + \sum_{k=0}^{q} \ln\left(\gamma_k D(\varphi_{t-k})\right) + \sum_{k=0}^{q} \delta_k D(\omega_{i,t-k}) + \varepsilon_{i,t} \quad (1)$$

where prefix $D(\ldots)$ indicates first-differencing, subscripts i and t are the bank and time indices, respectively, $i^r_{i,t}$ is the bank-specific retail response rate, i^p_t is the policy rate, φ_t is a vector of macroeconomic variables such as the GDP and the Consumer Price Index (CPI), and $\omega_{i,t}$ are the bank-specific deposit rates. In our analysis, the policy rate is the official central bank refinancing rate. For retail response rates we treat the weighted average interest rate on credit as the "main" rate on which we will base our bottom-line conclusions.

For our sectoral analysis purposes, we will use as dependent variables the lending rates on agricultural, industrial, consumer, and trade sector loans. Econometrically, nothing changes when we look at different loan products; we simply substitute the average lending rate with sector-specific instruments as the dependent variable. We emphasize that we are not talking about industry or period-average loan rates but are the *bank-specific* dynamic rates, the figures which are quite complicated to collect. As mentioned earlier, we are also particularly interested in looking at how lending rates would respond to an expansionary shock to the policy instrument. From the modeling standpoint, we simply create two sets of dummy variables, indicating a positive and a negative change in the policy rate. We then run our regression with the asymmetric policy variables in place of the normal symmetric variable.

The PMG method is very appealing because it respects the intertemporal dynamics of the pass-through transmission process. In the short run, bank pricing policies are usually heterogeneous, while in the long run they converge into a single homogeneous frame. Similarly, through the prism of the law of one price, banks must be free to conduct short-run policy in whichever way that their management wishes, but need to maintain the basic solvency requirement in the long run (Horvath & Podpiera, 2012). It turns out that the PMG method is, by the creators' own definition, a method which permits heterogeneity of the parameters in the short run but imposes the so-called "long-run homogeneity restriction." Short-run divergence and the long-run congruence between monetary policy and bank credit pricing is the major motivation for us to adopt the PMG approach, which is econometrically a perfect fit for our economic model. In other words, the coefficient of the impact of monetary policy shocks on retail lending rates will be homogenized across all the banks, while the short-term speeds of adjustment to the long-run equilibrating condition will be kept heterogeneous.[9]

Having estimated the long-run pass through and the error correction term (speed of adjustment to the long-run equilibrium), we will look at bank characteristics such as liquidity and capitalization to study the heterogeneity of pass-through estimates across banks. Fundamentally, this will be similar to the seminal analysis of Kashyap and Stein (1995, 2000). We emphasize that our study is an effort to investigate the interest rate pass-through, not the bank lending channel. We will proceed with this approach by analyzing the determinants of the estimated parameters in Eq. (1). Very generally speaking, we believe that the pass-through is some function of bank characteristics. As some of the characteristics change, such as size or liquidity, so does the degree of pass-through. The relationship can be formulated this very generic way:

$$\theta_i = f\left(\text{size}_i, \text{liquidity}_i, \text{capitalization}_i, \text{profitability}_i\right) \tag{2}$$

More concretely, building on the baseline model in Eq. (1), we can introduce bank characteristics into our regression in the form of distinct regressors:

$$\begin{aligned} D\left(i^r_{i,t}\right) = \alpha_0 + \sum_{j=1}^{p} \alpha_j D\left(i^r_{i,t-j}\right) + \sum_{k=0}^{q} \beta_k i^p_{t-k} + \sum_{k=0}^{q} \ln\left(\gamma_k D(\varphi_{t-k})\right) \\ + \sum_{k=0}^{q} \delta_k D(\omega_{i,t-k}) + \sum_{k=0}^{q} \theta_k(\tau_{i,t-k}) + \varepsilon_{i,t} \end{aligned} \tag{3}$$

where $\tau_{i,\ t}$ is the dynamic indicator of bank-specific characteristics.

We motivate the inclusion of *size* as a determinant of pass-through with the ability of larger banks to exploit their larger market share and charge higher rates, thus distorting competition and pass-through (Berger, 1995). *Liquidity* is an obvious member of this list because pass-through is typically worse for more liquid banks which are able to buffer themselves against policy shocks by a comfortable possession of liquid assets. We measure liquidity as the ratio of current assets over total assets. *Capitalization* should, in theory, be negatively associated with pass-through since less capitalized banks are more prone to market shocks and are more likely to exhibit a complete pass-through (Kashyap & Stein, 2000). Finally, *Profitability*, which we define as the basic Return on Assets (ROA) quotient, is an intuitive addition to our list. Banks, essentially, are in a constant process of risk-return tradeoff analysis, and more profitable banks should therefore be more aggressive risk-takers. In turn, risk exposure will raise the tendency for banks to hedge with the official refinancing rate, thus improving the pass-through effect.

We define our bank characteristics in the following way:

$$\text{Size}_i = \frac{\sum_i \text{TA}_{i,t} / \left(\sum_t \text{TA}_i / N_i\right)}{N_t}$$

$$\text{Liquidity Ratio}_i = \frac{\sum_i \text{CA}_{i,t} / \text{TA}_{i,t}}{N_t}$$

$$\text{Capitalization}_i = \frac{\sum_i \text{CAP}_{i,t} / \text{TA}_{i,t}}{N_t}$$

$$\text{Profitability}_i = \frac{\sum_i \text{ROA}_{i,t}}{N_t}$$

where TA is the measure of total assets, CA – current assets, CAP – capital stock, ROA – Return on Assets, i and t represent the bank and time indices, respectively. Our definitions are in line with the commonly accepted methodology in the literature.

Because, as has been mentioned earlier, Azerbaijan's financial sector is particularly consolidated, which probably leads to monopolistically high interest rates in the first place, we ought to check the impact of concentration on LRPT formally. Analysis of the effect of concentration will be performed by employing the Herfindahl-Hirschman Index (HHI). The HHI is simple and straightforward in its capacity to show how concentrated certain activity is in the hands of key market players. The HHI is computed the following way:

$$\text{HHI} = \sum_{i=1}^{N} S_i^2$$

where N is the number of banks, S is each bank's share of the sector's total assets, and i is bank-specific index. This specification will appreciate the shares of larger banks; the index will escalate faster if there are small large banks rather than many and small. An HHI index of below 0.01 indicates laisez-faire level perfect competition. Any number below 0.15 implies a generally unconcentrated sector; between 0.15 and 0.25 – moderate degree of concentration. Finally, an HHI higher than 0.25 suggests high concentration. The HHI will be introduced into the model via a normal variable, which will be common to all banks but differ across time periods. The interaction between the HHI and the policy variable will demonstrate whether monetary policy is indeed less effective in concentrated markets.

An alternative measure of concentration used in this paper is the combined share of total assets held by the three largest banks (CCR3). The CCR3 measure is quite common in literature. In the context of Azerbaijan, one bank controls up to 40% of the whole bank sector's assets at any given point in time. The remaining two top banks contribute each with between 5% and 10% of the total assets pie. The loan portfolio of the largest banks is crucial for the functioning of major domestic industrial entities and their deposit lists include some of the most important investors, government

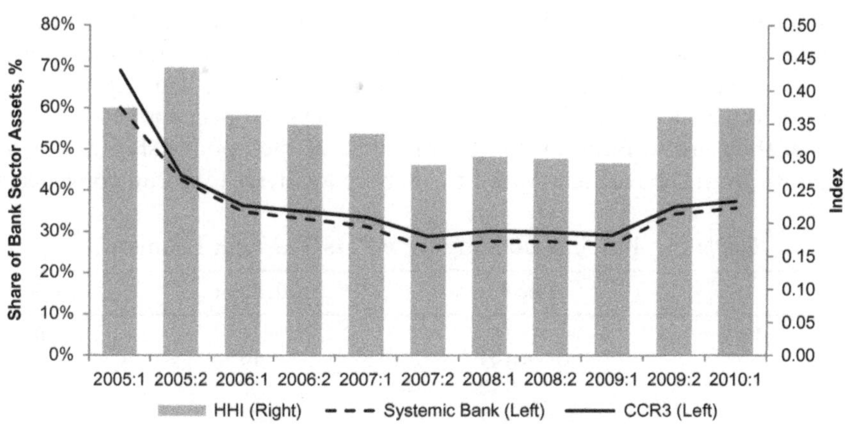

Fig. 5. Bank Sector Concentration Dynamics. *Note*: HHI refers to the Herfindahl-Hirschman Index of bank concentration. Systemic bank and CCR3 mean the asset shares of the state-owned systemic bank and of the three largest banks, respectively.

instiutions, and private sector firms. Fig. 5 displays the basic time dynamic of the measures of concentraion in the Azerbaijani bank sector. Note how concentration in the sector has declined over the past five years. In particular, the share of the top systemic bank has reduced dramatically from 70% to just over 40%. Yet, the time-average of the HHI index is about 0.25 which is on the borderline between moderate and extreme concentration.

For this study, I have assembled a dataset on 15 commercial banks of Azerbaijan for the period from 2005:1 till 2009:12. The sample constitutes over 75% of the overall bank sector's total assets, and doesn't only include large banks. In other words, if we only included the top 15 banks in the sample, then the analysis of bank heterogeneity (the impact of size or liquidity on LRPT) would be illogical. Instead, our sample includes the systemic bank, some large banks, and some smaller banks. All data is in a monthly format and has been collected from internal sources of the Central Bank of the Republic of Azerbaijan. Bank names have been coded on special request of authorities.

EMPIRICAL RESULTS

I now present the main findings of our research in Table 1. The table reports the combined panel coefficients of the interest rate pass-through in the long run, as well as the pooled short-run error correction terms (speed of adjustment measures). First, we notice an incomplete and statistically significant pass-through effect. A 1% innovation in the monetary policy rate triggers a 0.61% reaction in the weighted average lending rates for each bank, on average. This implies that for every open market intervention of the Central Bank of Azerbaijan, 40% of each policy shift causes no response from the real sector. We further see a perfect long-run congruence

Table 1. Baseline Lending Rate Pass-Through Estimates.

	Coefficient	Std. Error	*P*-Value
Monetary Policy	0.61	0.11	0.00
GDP	−0.93	0.19	0.00
CPI	−0.18	0.06	0.00
Deposit rate	1.19	0.08	0.00
EC term	−0.16	0.03	0.00

Note: Dependent variable is bank-specific weighted average lending rate. Estimation is based on Pesaran's (1999) Pooled Mean Group technique with a homogeneous long-run beta. The error-correction term is the unweighted pooled average across all banks.

between the lending and deposit interest rates; something to be expected. The coefficient for both macroeconomic indicators is negative. First, this suggests that as the economy grows (GDP increases), commercial banks tend to drive their credit rates down. This can be rationalized by the fact that a better growth atmosphere diminishes local market risks and instills confidence in the lenders. Second, it is surprising to see that lending rates decline as inflation rises. Finally, another important result is the error correction term which, standing at −0.16, implies an average period of full shock transmission of eight months. So, if the Central Bank of Azerbaijan raises its primary policy target by 1% in January, 2013, the average market response would be the increase in credit rates by 0.6% by August, 2013.

Of course, while the long-term pass-through estimate is forced to be homogeneous across the panel cross-sections, the short-term parameters are permitted to be heterogeneous across the banks. To have a first glimpse at the relationship between bank characteristics and the pass-through we present Table 2 which displays the bank-specific speed of adjustment terms and the four bank characteristics analyzed in this paper. Note that the shown bank characteristics are simple bank-specific time-averages of respective ratios. It is interesting to observe the heterogeneity of the error correction terms, which vary from as slow as −0.06 and as rapid as −0.43. Surely,

Table 2. Bank Heterogeneities in the Short Run.

Bank ID	ECT Term	Std. Error	*P*-value	Size	Liq	Cap	ROA
Bank 1	−0.22	0.07	0.00	0.54	0.17	0.10	2.86
Bank 2	−0.23	0.08	0.00	0.02	0.21	0.19	2.75
Bank 3	−0.04	0.01	0.00	0.03	0.22	0.15	2.63
Bank 4	−0.07	0.04	0.07	0.02	0.21	0.20	5.32
Bank 5	−0.17	0.06	0.01	0.02	0.14	0.19	3.41
Bank 6	−0.18	0.06	0.00	0.05	0.31	0.18	3.94
Bank 7	−0.04	0.04	0.36	0.01	0.19	0.24	1.77
Bank 8	−0.05	0.04	0.23	0.02	0.20	0.15	1.52
Bank 9	−0.13	0.07	0.06	0.01	0.14	0.21	1.02
Bank 10	−0.32	0.06	0.00	0.01	0.18	0.19	1.59
Bank 11	−0.07	0.03	0.05	0.08	0.15	0.16	3.06
Bank 12	−0.43	0.09	0.00	0.05	0.19	0.17	4.36
Bank 13	−0.27	0.08	0.00	0.05	0.20	0.13	2.43
Bank 14	−0.06	0.04	0.16	0.03	0.16	0.35	−1.91
Bank 15	−0.11	0.05	0.02	0.02	0.75	0.18	4.46

Note: ECT, Liq, Cap, ROA stand for the error correction term, liquidity ratio, capitalization ratio, and the return on average assets, respectively. The ECs are taken from the baseline PMG regression with heterogeneous bank-specific rates of adjustment. Bank characteristics are simple bank-specific time-averages of respective ratios.

the heterogeneity can be attributed to the bank-specific characteristics. A meticulous eye can already easily see some correlation between the liquidity and capitalization ratios and the degrees of adjustment. However, it is important to analyze bank heterogeneity in a formal manner and we therefore present the results (Table 4) of the baseline model with bank characteristics included as separate independent variables.

Table 3 presents the baseline results first and then the four cases with bank characteristics inserted one-by-one as covariates. First, we find that lending rates tend to be higher for banks of smaller size, higher capitalization, and better profitability levels (the latter effect is marginally significant at the 10% level). But far more importantly for our purposes are the interaction terms between the policy rate and the characteristics. We find that monetary policy efficiency is higher for banks with lower liquidity and capitalization levels. This is a fundamental finding for the Azerbaijani economy which has notably struggled with poor pass-through performance and structural excess liquidity. In order to improve monetary policy efficacy in this country's context it's important to control the level of liquidity and capital in the bank's sector. This finding is very much in line with existing literature postulations. We find no significant results in the case of either size or profitability.

Table 3. Pass-through with Bank Characteristics.

	Baseline	Bank Characteristics			
		Size	Cap	Liq	Profit
Policy	0.61	0.62	0.44	0.54	0.58
	0.00	*0.00*	*0.00*	*0.00*	*0.00*
GDP	−0.90	−0.87	−0.86	−0.85	−1.01
	0.00	*0.00*	*0.00*	*0.00*	*0.00*
CPI	−0.18	−0.17	−0.13	−0.17	−0.18
	0.00	*0.00*	*0.04*	*0.00*	*0.01*
Deposit	1.19	1.20	1.22	1.20	1.22
	0.00	*0.00*	*0.00*	*0.00*	*0.00*
Characteristic		−1.83	23.28	16.77	0.51
		0.01	*0.21*	*0.00*	*0.10*
Policy*Charact.		0.07	−3.76	−1.11	−0.03
		0.13	*0.04*	*0.03*	*0.32*

Note: Dependent variable is bank-specific weighted average lending rate. Bank characteristics are included into the baseline model one-by-one. For example, the regression for Size includes the monetary policy rate, GDP, CPI, deposit interest rate, the Size bank characteristic, and the interaction term between policy and Size all in the list of independent variables. Italics describe the estimates' *P*-values.

Now, for each bank characteristic we separate our baseline sample into groups of banks which are below and above the median threshold. Table 4 presents some very interesting results from this exercise. We see a considerable and statistically significant differential between the lending rate pass-through for banks with lower and higher levels of liquidity. This supports our previous finding that the interest rate channel (or the pass-through, to be more precise) is substantially more efficient for less liquid banks. The reason it is less effective for more liquid banks should be trivial. The same finding holds for the Size characteristic: banks of smaller size respond much more efficiently to a policy rate shock. This is particularly appealing since most banks in our sample which are large are also highly liquid, and vice versa, so the consistency of the observation across both characteristics is very healthy. For computational reasons it was impossible to do the calculations for capitalization and profitability characteristics.

Should the Central Bank of Azerbaijan decide to further expand its monetary policy base in an attempt to lower credit constraints on the domestic market, results from our asymmetric analysis should come in very beneficially. Table 5 reports the pass-through estimates for expansionary and contractionary policy shocks. Compared to the baseline case, the lending rate response to a negative change in the refinancing rate is now just

Table 4. Pass-through for Bank Sub-Samples.

	Baseline	Bank Characteristics			
		Size		Liq	
		Small	Large	Small	Large
Policy	0.61	1.22	0.60	1.54	0.34
	0.00	*0.00*	*0.00*	*0.00*	*0.00*
GDP	−0.90	0.37	−0.11	1.72	−0.14
	0.00	*0.03*	*0.62*	*0.00*	*0.48*
CPI	−0.18	−0.62	−0.15	−0.54	−0.02
	0.00	*0.00*	*0.06*	*0.00*	*0.67*
Deposit	1.19	1.17	1.36	−2.08	−0.19
	0.00	*0.00*	*0.00*	*0.00*	*0.29*
EC term	0.16	−0.16	−0.15	−0.11	−0.12
	0.00	*0.06*	*0.00*	*0.08*	*0.02*

Note: Dependent variable is bank-specific weighted average lending rate. For both Size and Liquidity, banks for which the corresponding characteristic is below or above the time-varying median are grouped under Small or Large, respectively. Singularity of the Hessian matrix prevents us from performing the same exercise for Capitalization and Profitability characteristics. Italics describe the estimates' *P*-values.

Table 5. Pass-through under Asymmetric Policy Shocks.

	Baseline	Asymmetric Policy	
		Expansion	Contraction
Policy	0.61	0.50	0.51
	0.00	*0.00*	*0.00*
GDP	−0.90	−0.96	−1.38
	0.00	*0.00*	*0.00*
CPI	−0.18	−0.20	−0.14
	0.00	*0.00*	*0.06*
Deposit rate	1.19	1.31	1.26
	0.00	*0.00*	*0.00*
EC term	−0.16	−0.15	−0.14
	0.00	*0.00*	*0.00*

Note: Dependent variable is bank-specific weighted average lending rate. Asymmetric extensions represent responses of retail rates to policy shocks when the shock is expansionary (Column 2) and contractionary (Column 3) only. Italics describe the estimates' *P*-values.

50%, about 100 basis points smaller. It is therefore crucial that policy makers will consider this particular downward stickiness when designing future intervention plans. The period of adjustment to long-run equilibrium is the same – the half-life is about four months.

For the purposes of our sectoral analysis, we propose to measure the impact of policy rate innovations on the interest rates on industrial, trade, agricultural, and consumer loans. Table 6 presents the results. First, lending rate pass-through is once again highly incomplete, and our conclusion from the aggregate case holds for industry-specific disaggregated data as well. Second, we notice that agricultural loan rates exhibit the weakest pass-through implying at least one possible explanation. About 95% of the domestic financial sector in Azerbaijan is commercial banking in the conventional sense. Capital markets are underdeveloped and access to quality financing is restricted to bank loans and, since half of the market is controlled by a hand-full of banks, the monopolistic power over agricultural clients becomes rather obvious. Regardless of the domestic macroeconomic climate and the policy strategy of the central bank, commercial lenders can still charge high rates because borrowers have very few (in fact, none) other alternatives. It simply appears that with the case of agricultural loans this rationale proves to be particularly stark. We also compute and present the half-lives for each of the four industrial cases. The quickest period of adjustment is recorded for consumer loans and the longest for the industrial loans.

Table 6. Sectoral Analysis of Lending Rate Pass-Through.

	Pass-through	*P*-value	EC Term	*P*-value	Half-Life
Industrial	0.57	0.00	−0.13	0.00	5.03
Trade	0.57	0.00	−0.19	0.00	3.24
Agro	0.34	0.00	−0.14	0.00	4.50
Consumer	0.43	0.00	−0.19	0.00	3.35
Average	0.61	0.00	−0.16	0.00	3.97

Note: These are estimates of the long-run pass-through and the short-run EC terms for different loan sectors. For example, "Industrial" indicates the pass-through from the refinancing rate to the rates on credit issued to borrowers from industry. Half-lives represent the time period required for transmission of 50% of the shock and are computed by the following formula: $\ln(0.5)/\ln(1+\alpha)$, where α is the sector-specific error correction.

Table 7. Pass-through and Bank Sector Consolidation.

	Baseline	Consolidation Indicators	
		CCR3	HHI
Policy	0.61	1.59	0.86
	0.00	*0.17*	*0.01*
GDP	−0.93	−0.89	−0.85
	0.00	*0.00*	*0.00*
CPI	−0.18	−0.23	−0.23
	0.00	*0.00*	*0.00*
Deposit	1.19	1.18	1.15
	0.00	*0.00*	*0.00*
Consolidation		5.33	3.07
		0.75	*0.76*
Policy*Comp		−1.30	−0.47
		0.44	*0.64*

Note: Dependent variable is bank-specific weighted average lending rate. CCR3 and HHI stand for the asset share of the top 3 banks and the Herfindahl-Hirschman index of consolidation, respectively. Consolidation indicators are included into the baseline model one-by-one. For example, the regression for HHI includes the monetary policy rate, the GDP, CPI, deposit interest rate, the H-H index, and the interaction term between policy and HHI all in the list of independent variables. Italics describe the estimates' *P*-values.

Finally, we complete our investigation with a look at the relationship between pass-through and bank consolidation. It has been noted on multiple occasions that the bank sector in Azerbaijan is dominated by selected few banks which control a significant portion of the total assets pie. Table 7 reports the results from the PMG regressions with the consolidation indicators included into the baseline case. Quite interestingly, we do not find any significant results either for the impact of plain concentration on lending rates or for the interaction term. This holds for both the HHI and the CCR3 indicators. It is unfortunate that we are not able to offer a policy recommendation with regards to sector consolidation and the interest rate pass-through, but this in itself can be viewed as an important discovery.

CONCLUDING REMARKS

This paper has laid out a systematic analysis of the lending rate pass-through in small open transition economies that are challenged by high lending rates and a consolidated bank sector. The Republic of Azerbaijan has been chosen as a country-model for our analysis, and our results have confirmed the selection as literature-consistent and policy-relevant. We have modeled the lending rate pass-through via the PMG method and have confirmed the presence of an imperfect pass-through in the long run and a sluggish adjustment to equilibrium in the short run. This finding is largely expected and is consistent with the literature on consolidated banking sectors with excess structural liquidity. Then, we have seen that pass-through remains incomplete when we disaggregate the weighted average lending rate into sector-specific loans. In particular, we found that agricultural loans deliver the weakest pass-through response among all other products. Finally, we have performed an analysis on the determinants of interest rate pass-through in order to account for heterogeneity in banking practices. Results have shown that liquidity has a consistently negative and significant effect on the interest rate pass-through. This finding is largely expected and confirms the detrimental impact of excess structural liquidity on the workability of the interest rate channel of monetary policy transmission.

With regards to policy implications, and in reaction to our main research question, our results lend to the following response. It is clear, although surprisingly so, that macroeconomic events do not explain the persistently high lending rates in any reasonable way. Likewise, the policy-market disconnect cannot be attributed to the concentration in the banking sector. The root of the problem lies in the considerably impaired operability of the domestic central bank, as evidenced by the sluggish and incomplete interest rate pass-through results, particularly for expansionary interventions. This incompleteness is apparently driven by the excess of structural liquidity in the financial market. It is hard to assign any blame to the central bank since its policy alternatives are limited substantially due to the country's resource-oriented growth design and a de facto fixed exchange rate regime. But if there is one policy recommendation that does require serious and immediate attention, then it is the withdrawal of excessive liquidity from the market for a better conduct of monetary policy. This recommendation is very much in line with the argument that the IMF has been pushing through for many years.

NOTES

1. Literature on the general interest rate pass-through dates back to the pioneering works of Neumark and Sharpe (1992) on the banking sector of the United States, and Cottarelli and Kourelis (1994) who conducted one of the first cross-country analyses of the LRPT. Mojon (2000) and De Bondt (2005) are among the many who studied the interest rate channel of monetary transmission in the European Union. De Graeve, De Jonghe, and Vander Vennet (2007), on the example of Belgium, introduced the analysis of specific bank effects into the mainstream LRPT literature. Egert, Crespo-Cuaresma, and Reininger (2007) provide a systematic treatment of the IRPT as well as asymmetric adjustment for the case of Eastern-European economies.
2. Some comparative examples of single-country studies of the interest rate pass-through include Cottarelli, Ferri, and Generale (1995) and Gambacorta (2005) for Italy, Burgstaller (2003) for Austria, Aydin (2007) for Turkey, Winker (1999) and Weth (2002) for Germany, De Graeve et al. (2004) for Belgium, Bogoev and Petrevski (2012) for Macedonia, Chionis and Leon (2006) for Greece, Wrobel and Pawlowska (2002) for Poland, Pereira and Maia-Filho (2012) for Brazil, Scholnick (1996) for Singapore and Malaysia, Hofmann and Mizen (2006) for UK, Iregui, Milas, and Otero (2002) for Colombia and Mexico, and Tieman (2004) for Romania.
3. I advise the interested reader to consult Egert and MacDonald (2009) for an excellent survey of the channels of monetary transmission in transition economies. No single-country empirical studies on the interest rate pass-through exist for the Caucasus and, to the best of my knowledge, for most Central Asian states. For Azerbaijan, I am completely certain than nobody has modeled interest rate pass-through before. Basically, apart from our systematic treatment of the LRPT methodology, this paper is unique in its precedent-setting work for the Caucasus and, presumably, for Central Asia as well.
4. In an important recent paper Zulkhibri (2012) find that the interest rate pass-through is incomplete and sluggish for the case of Malaysia – a country similar to Azerbaijan from the general development point of view. Pass-through is sluggish and incomplete for both lending and deposit interest rates. However, pass-through differs substantially across the retail rate instruments.

5. Asymmetry in the LRPT and short-run adjustment estimates has been studied extensively in the past years. Originating from the seminal empirical contribution of Scholnick (1996), asymmetric models of LRPT have extended mostly to the studies of the European Union (consider, for example, Egert et al., 2007; Sander & Kleimeier, 2004).

6. It is important to distinguish the notion "concentration" from "competition," since those are completely different concepts. Rich literature exists on the effect of bank sector competition on bank lending and credit interest rates. Most studies adopt either the Panzar-Rosse (Panzar & Rosse, 1987) methodology or construct the Boone competition indicator (Boone, 2008).

7. Bogoev and Petrevski (2012) examine Macedonia, as an example of a small open economy with a fixed exchange rate. They employ DOLS and ARDL models in their analysis and record an almost complete long-run adjustment. In the short run, however, adjustment is more sluggish. They conclude, much for the relevance to this paper's case, that the interest rate pass-through in small economies with fixed exchange rates is not of little effectiveness, contrary to what theory would predict.

8. Pereira and Maia-Filho (2012) argue that state-controlled banks, which are assets for crisis management purposes, have higher welfare costs than usually assumed. In the case of Azerbaijan, the systemic bank which controls more than 45% of the whole sector's assets, is also the only state-controlled bank in the country. At least one implication that must be drawn from Pereira and Maia-Filho (2012) is that the state-owned systemic bank in Azerbaijan could be privatized to minimize welfare costs for society.

9. I omit the more tedious technical details of the ML estimation step and advise to consult Pesaran, Shin, and Smith (1999) for a more thorough treatment of the subject.

ACKNOWLEDGMENTS

I am thankful to Peter Kugler of the University of Basel, Ulrich Camen of the Graduate Institute of International and Development Studies (IHEID), Carlos Lenz, Herman Werner, Marcel Savioz, and Gilbert Heim of the Swiss National Bank, and all participants of the monetary transmission seminar held at the Swiss National Bank in October, 2012, for very insightful comments. I am also grateful to Emin Huseynov, Vugar Ahmadov, Shaig Adigozalov, Nadir Ramazanov, Mehdi Mehdiyev, Ramiz Rahmanov, Salman Huseynov, Rashad Karimov, Leyla Yusifzadeh, and all other members of the Research Department at the Central Bank of Azerbaijan for numerous consultations and informal discussions. This paper was started when I was a researcher at the Central Bank of Azerbaijan and later a graduate student at the London School of Economics. Opinion expressed in this paper is solely my own and does not in any way represent the views of the State Oil Fund of Azerbaijan, the Central Bank of Azerbaijan, or any other institution or individual but myself. All errors are, of course, my own.

REFERENCES

Adams, R., & Amel, D. (2005). The effects of local banking market structure on the bank-lending channel of monetary policy. *Finance and Economics Discussion Series* 2005-16, Board of Governors of the Federal Reserve System.

Aydin, H. I. (2007). *Interest rate pass-through in Turkey*. The Central Bank of the Republic of Turkey Working Paper No. 07/05.

Aziakpono, M. J., & Wilson, M. K. (2010). Interest Rate Pass-Through and Monetary Policy Regimes in South Africa, Conference on Economic Development in Africa, St Catherine's College, Oxford University, Oxford, UK. March 21–23, 2010.

Berger, A. N. (1995). The profit-structure relationship in banking: Tests of market power and efficient structure hypothesis. *Journal of Money, Credit and Banking*, *35*, 1265–1306.

Bogoev, J., & Petrevski, G. (2012). Interest rate pass-through in a small open economy with a fixed exchange rate – The case of Macedonia. *Procedia – Social and Behavioral Sciences*, *44*, 125–133.

Boone, J. (2008). A new way to measure competition. *The Economic Journal*, *188*, 1245–1261.

Burgstaller, J. (2003). *Interest rate transmission to commercial credit rates in Austria*. Working Paper No. 0306, John Kepler University of Linz, Austria.

Chionis, D. P., & Leon, C. A. (2006). Interest rate transmission in Greece: Did EMU cause a structural break? *Journal of Policy Modeling*, *28*, 453–466.

Cottarelli, C., Ferri, G., & Generale, A. (1995). *Bank lending rates and financial structure in Italy: A case study*, IMF Working paper No. 95/38.

Cottarelli, C., & Kourelis, A. (1994). Financial structure, bank lending rates, and the transmission mechanism of monetary policy. *IMF Staff Papers*, *41*, 587–623.

De Bondt, G. (2005). Interest rate pass-through: Empirical results for the euro area. *German Economic Review*, *6*, 37–78.

De Graeve, F., De Jonghe, O., & Vander Vennet, R. (2007). Competition, transmission and bank pricing policies: Evidence from Belgian loan and deposit markets. *Journal of Banking and Finance*, *31*, 259–278.

Egert, B., Crespo-Cuaresma, J., & Reininger, T. (2007). Interest rate pass-through in central and Eastern Europe: Reborn from ashes merely to pass away? *Journal of Policy Modeling*, *29*, 209–225.

Egert, B., & MacDonald, R. (2009). Monetary transmission mechanism in central and Eastern Europe: Surveying the surveyable. *Journal of Economic Surveys*, *23*(2), 277–327.

Gambacorta, L. (2005). Inside the bank lending channel. *European Economic Review*, *49*(7), 1737–1759.

Gambacorta, L. (2008). How do banks set interest rates? *European Economic Review*, *52*, 792–819.

Horvath, R., & Podpiera, A. M. (2012). Heterogeneity in bank pricing policies: The czech evidence. *Economic Systems*, *36*(1), 87–108.

IMF. (2012). International Monetary Fund Country Memorandum on Azerbaijan, May.

Iregui, A. M., Milas, C., & Otero, J. (2002). On the dynamics of lending and deposit interest rates in emerging markets: A non-linear approach. *Studies in Nonlinear Dynamics and Econometrics*, *6*(3), Article 3.

Jamilov, R. (2013). Capital mobility in the caucasus. *Economic Systems*, *37*(2), 155–170.

Kashyap, A., & Stein, J. (1995). The impact of monetary policy on bank balance sheets. *Carnegie–Rochester Conference Series on Public Policy*, *42*, 151–195.

Kashyap, A., & Stein, J. (2000). What do a million observations on banks say about the transmission of monetary policy. *American Economic Review*, *90*(3), 407–428.

Mishra, P., Montiel, P. J., & Spilimbergo, A. (2012). Monetary transmission in low-income countries: Effectiveness and policy implications. *IMF Economic Review*, *60*(2), 270–302.

Mojon, B. (2000). *Financial structure and the interest rate channel of ECB monetary policy*. Working Paper Series 40, European Central Bank.

Neumark, D., & Sharpe, S. (1992). Market structure and nature of price rigidity: Evidence from the market for consumer deposits. *Quarterly Journal of Economics*, *107*, 657–680.

Olivero, M. P., Li, Y., & Jeon, B. N. (2011). Consolidation in banking and the lending channel: Evidence from bank-level data in Asia and Latin America. *Journal of International Money and Finance*, *30*(6), 1034–1054.

Panzar, J. C., & Rosse, J. N. (1987). Testing for monopoly equilibrium. *Journal of Industrial Economics*, *35*, 443–456.

Pereira, C. M., & Maia-Filho, L. F. (2012). Brazilian retail banking and the 2008 financial crisis: Were the government-controlled banks that important? *Journal of Banking and Finance*, *37*(7), 2210–2215. Retrieved from http://dx.doi.org/10.1016/j.jbankfin.2012.03.009

Pesaran, H., Shin, Y., & Smith, R. P. (1999). Pooled mean group estimation of dynamic heterogeneous panels. *Journal of American Statistical Association*, *94*, 621–634.

Rocha, M. D. (2012). Interest rate pass-through in Portugal: Interactions, asymmetries and heterogeneities. *Journal of Policy Modeling*, *34*(1), 64–80.

Sander, H., & Kleimeier, S. (2004). Convergence in Euro-zone retail banking? What interest rate pass-through tells us about monetary policy transmission, competition and integration. *Journal of International Money and Finance*, *23*(3), 461–492.

Scholnick, B. (1996). Asymmetric adjustment of commercial bank interest rates: Evidence from Malaysia and Singapore. *Journal of International Money and Finance*, *15*, 485–496.

Sharpe, S. A. (1997). The effect of consumer switching costs on prices: A theory and its application to the bank deposit market. *Review of Industrial Organization*, *12*, 79–94.

Sorensen, K. C., & Werner, T. (2006). *Bank interest rate pass-through in the Euro area: A cross country comparison*. ECB Working Paper No. 580.

Stiglitz, J., & Weis, A. (1981). Credit rationing in markets with imperfect information. *American Economic Review*, *71*, 393–410.

Tieman, A. F. (2004). *Interest rate pass-through in Romania and other central European economies, IMF* Working Paper No. 04/211.

Weth, M. A. (2002). *The pass-through from market interest rates to bank lending rates in Germany*, Deutsche Bundesbank Discussion paper 11/02.

Winker, P. (1999). Sluggish adjustment of interest rates and credit rationing: An application of unit root testing and error correction modeling. *Applied Economics*, *31*, 267–277.

Wrobel, E., & Pawlowska, M. (2002). *Monetary transmission in Poland: Some evidence on interest rate and credit channels*, NBP Bureau of Macroeconomic Research Working Paper No. 24/2002.

Zulkhibri, M. (2012). Policy rate pass-through and the adjustment of retail interest rates: Empirical evidence from Malaysian financial institutions. *Journal of Asian Economics*, *23*(4), 409–422.

THE INFLUENCE OF MACROECONOMIC RISKS ON CREDIT RISK IN THE SERBIAN BANKS' LOAN PORTFOLIO

Dragiša Otašević

ABSTRACT

Banking sectors in central, eastern and southeastern European (CESEE) countries have gone through a transformation from state-ownership and central planning to private ownership and market-oriented decision making during the first decade of the 21st century. However, financial markets in these countries are still developing and the private sector is highly exposed to changes in exchange rates, especially in terms of the balance sheet channel. The fact that these banking sectors are predominantly owned by eurozone banks makes them vulnerable to macroeconomic tensions in the European union. This analysis investigates macroeconomic determinants of the realisation of credit risk in the loan portfolio of banks in Serbia using a panel data set covering the period from 2008Q3 to 2012Q2. Three different panel methods were applied separately for loans to households and loans to enterprises.

Neo-Transitional Economics
International Finance Review, Volume 16, 219–243

ISSN: 1569-3767/doi:10.1108/S1569-376720150000016010

The results indicate that a deteriorating business cycle and exchange rate depreciation led to the worsening of the quality of banks' loan portfolio in Serbia in the period under review. In addition, statistical evidence indicates that the CPI inflation additionally affected the quality of loans. Furthermore, we find that household loan portfolios are also sensitive to changes in the short-run interest rates. As for policy implications, the importance of international cooperation between regulators is rising. A very important topic for such cooperation should be the risk-taking channel between countries with significant differences in interest rates and degree of riskiness. The interrelationship between the exchange rate and credit risk should be a major focus of both domestic macro- and micro-prudential policy – banks should be motivated to pay more attention to the possible negative spillovers when making credit decisions. Also, further development of the domestic primary and secondary T-bills market would help reducing unhedged FX risks.

Keywords: Loan portfolio; credit quality; economic activity; exchange rate; foreign currency induced credit risk; Serbia

JEL classifications: C33; E51; E58; G21; G32

INTRODUCTION

Since the onset of the crisis, credit quality in Central, Eastern and Southeastern Europe (CESEE) strongly deteriorated. High and rising levels of NPLs in many countries of the region continue to exert strong pressure on banks' balance sheets with possible (negative) repercussions on bank lending, financial stability and economic growth. The deterioration in the quality of banks' loan portfolio in Serbia following the spillover of the global financial crisis to our economy has been an important issue for national macro-prudential surveillance. Non-performing loans (NPLs) in the Serbian banking sector nearly doubled. A better understanding of the main drivers of ex post credit risk facilitates the identification of vulnerabilities in the banking sector.

The literature on credit quality and its relationship to macroeconomic conditions is vast and based on both theoretical and empirical analysis. The theoretical basis for approaching linkages between the macroeconomy and financial markets is the financial accelerator theory discussed in

Bernanke and Gertler (1989), Bernanke, Gertler, and Gilchrist (1999) and Kiyotaki and Moore (1997).

Comparable empirical results indicate a negative relationship between real GDP growth and the deterioration in the quality of banks' loan portfolio. Real GDP growth usually leads to more income which improves the capacity of borrowers to service their debt. As a result, credit quality should be higher. Contrarily, in the case of a slowdown in or even negative real GDP growth, credit quality could deteriorate. Changes in the key policy rate should affect credit quality through their pass-through to lending interest rates on domestic currency loans and changes in the borrowers' debt burden thereafter.

This analysis contributes to the assessment of the impact of realised macroeconomic and market risks, especially exchange rate risk, on the credit risk in the loan portfolio of banks in Serbia. It focuses on ex post credit risk, measured by the ratio of loan loss provisions to the value of total gross loans in the Serbian banking sector. It utilises a panel data set comprising 33 commercial banks and spans the period 2008Q3 to 2012Q2. This time period includes the financial crisis period, as well as the period of the sovereign debt crises and banking sector crisis in the eurozone. Banks' size, capitalisation and liquidity are also considered in the empirical analysis. These variables do not represent the focus of the analysis but are important to take into account the effect that bank-specific characteristics might have had on lending behaviour and the relationship between key macroeconomic variables and credit quality.

The findings indicate that a deteriorating business cycle and the exchange rate depreciation led to the worsening of the quality of banks' loan portfolio in Serbia in the period under review. In addition, statistical evidence indicates that the CPI inflation affected the quality of loans to enterprises and households. Furthermore, we find that household loan portfolios are sensitive to changes in the short-run interest rates (proxied by interbank money market rate, BELIBOR).

The structure of the rest of this text is organised as follows: the section 'A Brief Comparison of Literature' gives a comparative review of the relevant existing literature, section 'Serbia's Macroeconomy and Banking Sector' presents a short overview of the banking sector in Serbia and section 'Empirical Approach and Results' shows the empirical approach and discusses the results. Finally, concluding remarks and policy recommendations are given in the section 'Concluding Remarks and Policy Recommendations'.

A BRIEF COMPARISON OF LITERATURE

Keeton and Morris (1987) present one of the earliest studies to examine the drivers of loan losses within a specific country. The authors examine the loan losses (non-performing loans net of charge-offs) of commercial banks in the United States over the period 1979–1985 and show that local economic conditions along with the poor performance of certain sectors explain the variation in loan losses recorded by the banks. They also report that commercial banks with greater risk appetite tend to record higher losses. Subsequent studies offered similar as well as different explanations for the occurrence of loan losses in commercial banks' balance sheets in the United States. Louzis, Vouldis, and Metaxas (2010) examine the determinants of NPLs in the Greek banking sector. Their analysis covers the nine largest banks during 2003–2009 and NPLs broken down by type of loan – business, consumer and mortgage. Their findings indicate that, beside management quality, macroeconomic fundamentals explain NPLs (GDP, unemployment and interest rates). They find a positive relationship between NPL and real lending rates. Shijaku and Ceca (2011) concentrated on detecting a model of the response of credit quality to macroeconomic shocks in Albania, using banks' panel data. Though acknowledging the shortcomings related to lack of robustness in the results, they indicate evidence of a stronger response of credit quality to GDP shocks. They also found the exchange rates and EURIBOR to be important determinants of credit quality in foreign currency lending. This is not a complete review of relating literature. There are also one-country studies investigating the drivers of non-performing loans applying other econometric approaches than the panel data approach but with similar results.

One of the main focuses of several studies that deal with macro stress testing is a better understanding of the relationship of credit risk and the business cycle. Two analyses published by the IMF in the Global Financial Stability Report examine the deterioration of banks' loan portfolio after the financial crisis in emerging markets and in Central, Eastern and Southeastern Europe – Hartelius (2010) and De Bock and Demyanets (2012). De Bock and Demyanets (2012) assess the vulnerability of emerging markets and their banks to aggregate shocks. The authors find significant links between banks' asset quality, credit and macroeconomic aggregates. According to their results lower economic growth, an exchange rate depreciation, weaker terms of trade and a fall in debt-creating capital inflows reduce credit growth while loan quality deteriorates. Nkusu (2011) analyses the link between NPLs and the business cycle using two complementary approaches. First, she investigates the macroeconomic determinants of

NPLs in panel regressions and confirms that adverse macroeconomic developments lead to rising NPLs.

This analysis contributes to the existing literature on the empirical determinants of credit quality by employing a panel data analysis for the case of banks in Serbia.

SERBIA'S MACROECONOMY AND BANKING SECTOR

After the economic disaster in the 1990s, Serbia's economy has gone through a transformation process from central planning to market-orientated decision making. Real GDP growth was on a steady rise and the currency appreciated due to strong capital inflows from the eurozone. However, in the period after the global economic crisis hit in 2008, Serbia is faced with high and volatile inflation, strong depreciation of the local currency and a real GDP growth which is either negative or below pre-crisis levels (see Figs. 1–3). Slower growth in Serbia's main trading partners, especially in the eurozone, resulted in a flat or even negative GDP growth during the period after 2008. Prospects for a turnaround in the labour market remain dim. Bad agricultural seasons affected output and

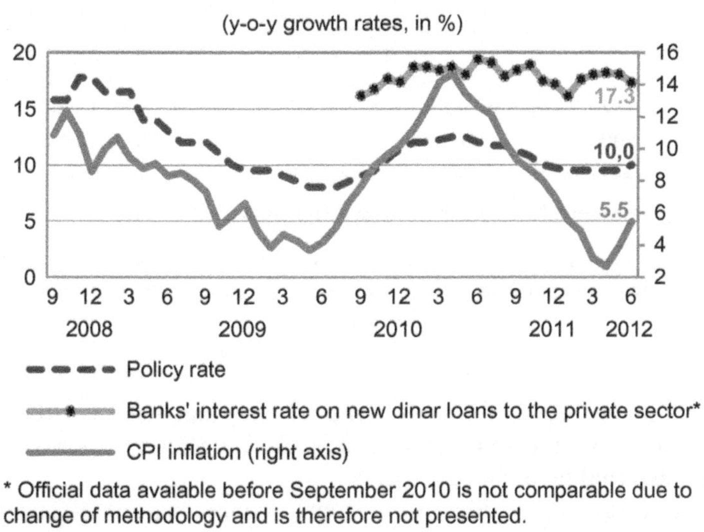

Fig. 1. CPI Developments and Interest Rates (in %). *Source*: National Bank of Serbia and Statistical Office of the Republic of Serbia.

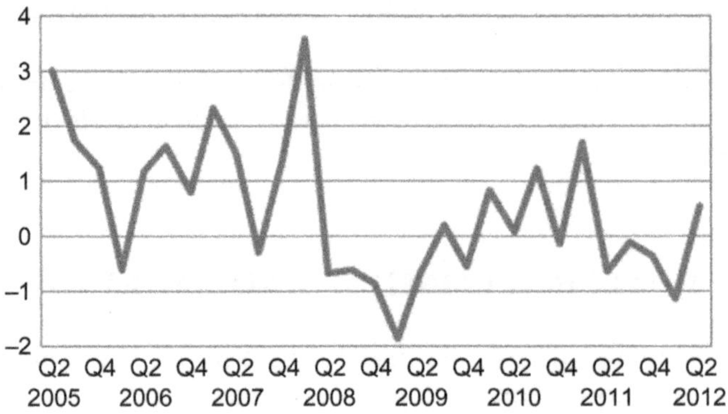

Fig. 2. GDP Developments (Seasonally Adjusted q-o-q Growth Rates in %). *Source*: National Bank of Serbia.

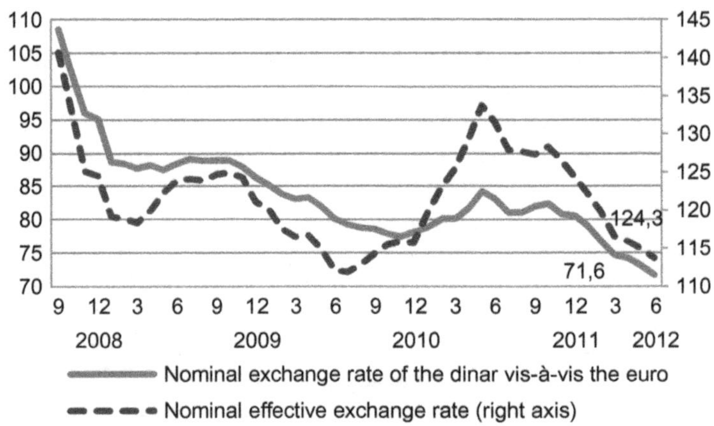

Fig. 3. Exchange Rate Developments (2005 = 100). *Source*: National Bank of Serbia and own calculations. *Note*: An increase represents the appreciation of the dinar.

price stability rather significantly. One of the main risks for the Serbian economy was lower capital inflows due to rising eurozone tensions that constrain external financing prospects.

Depreciations of the domestic currency could, instead of encouraging economic activity, contribute to defaults in the private sector through the balance sheet channel.

Serbia's banking sector has gone through a transformation from state-ownership and central planning to private (predominantly foreign) ownership and market-oriented decision making during the first years of the 21st century. In 2012Q2, 21 banks operating in Serbia were in foreign and 12 in domestic ownership at the end of June 2012. Foreign-owned banks accounted for around 74% of total assets. State- and privately owned domestic banks accounted for 26% of total banking sector assets.

The level of regulatory capital of Serbia's banking sector was adequate throughout the 2008–2011 period. It remained so after the harmonisation with Basel II requirements (end-2011). The capital adequacy ratio (CAR) was 17.2% in 2012Q2, which is significantly above both the minimum defined by Basel II standard (8.0%) and the regulatory minimum in Serbia (12%).

The Serbian banking sector is very liquid, hence the liquidity risk is not a serious threat. Banks in Serbia invest in government securities and NBS bills, which could be a form of liquidity hoarding due to heightened risk awareness. Having more liquid assets, banks are less sensitive to negative shocks and therefore might be motivated to engage in riskier behaviour. Thus a good liquidity outlook encourages banks to take more credit risks and not to screen their borrowers, which can lead to a worsening of credit quality. Profitability of the Serbian banking sector was sound.

Interest rates on both – RSD and foreign currency deposits and loans are much higher in Serbia than in the European Union where most of the shareholders of foreign-owned banks in Serbia come from.

After the crisis hit in 2008, the heightened risk awareness of banks in Serbia certainly had an impact on diminishing the real growth in lending activity. Government subsidy programmes led to temporary accelerations, but the trend of decelerating real growth rates continued until H1 2012 (see Figs. 4 and 5). Loans to enterprises, followed by loans to households, dominate in lending to nonmonetary sectors.

Foreign currency loans are dominant in the currency structure of total loans (see Figs. 6 and 7). Majority of foreign currency loans are dinar loans indexed to the euro. Such currency structure of the loan portfolio indicates an indirect foreign currency exposure of the banks through foreign currency induced credit risk of unhedged borrowers.

The quality of Serbian banks' loan portfolio deteriorated in the 2008–2012 period. The share of non-performing loans in total gross loans increased to 20% in H1 2012 from 11% in 2008 (see Fig. 8). Non-performing loans to enterprises account for the largest share of non-performing loans, followed by non-performing loans to households. The coverage of non-performing loans by allowances for impairment or

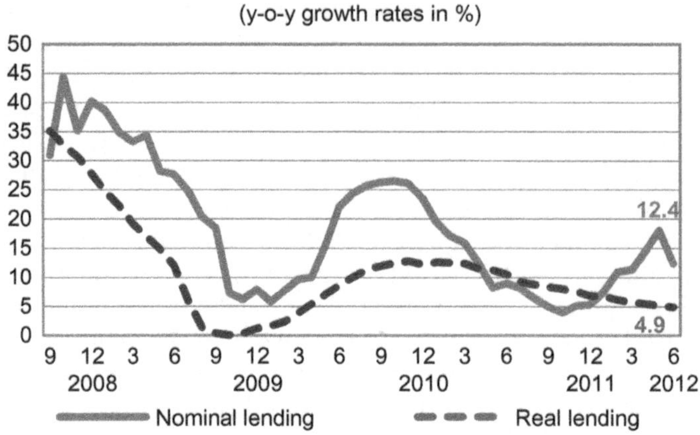

Fig. 4. Bank Lending to Households (y-o-y growth rates in %). *Source*: National Bank of Serbia and own calculations.

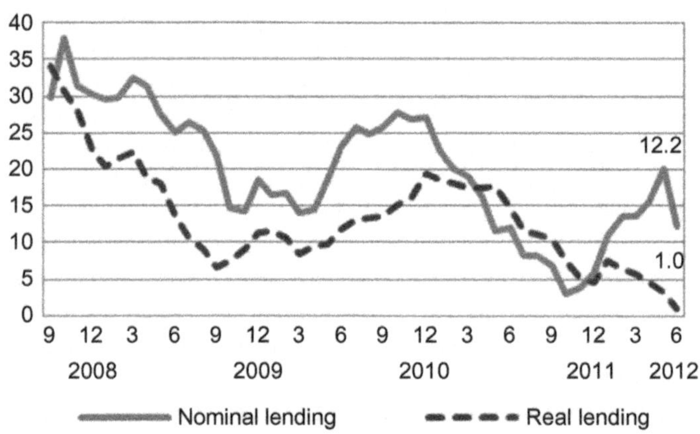

Fig. 5. Bank Lending to Enterprises (y-o-y growth rates in %). *Source*: National Bank of Serbia and own calculations.

regulatory reserves attests to the banking sector's capacity to absorb losses resulting from NPLs.

The ratio of loan loss provisions to total gross loans increased in the 2008–2012 period for both loan portfolios – loans to enterprises and loans to households (see Fig. 9). The ratio of loan loss provisions to non-performing loans was relatively stable during the period under consideration and equalled around 0.5 at the end of H1 2012.

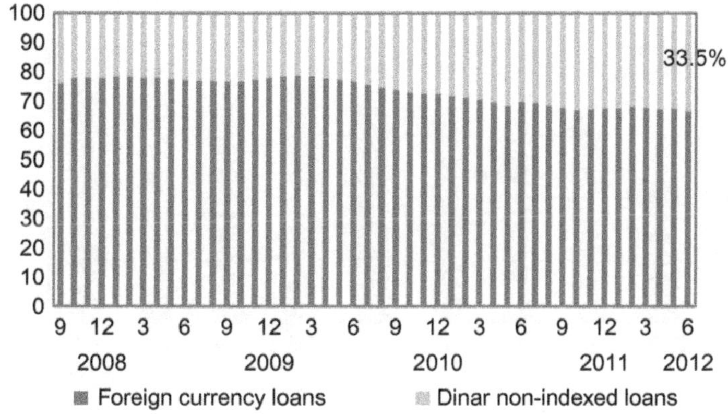

Fig. 6. Currency Structure of Loans to Households (in %). *Source*: National Bank of Serbia.

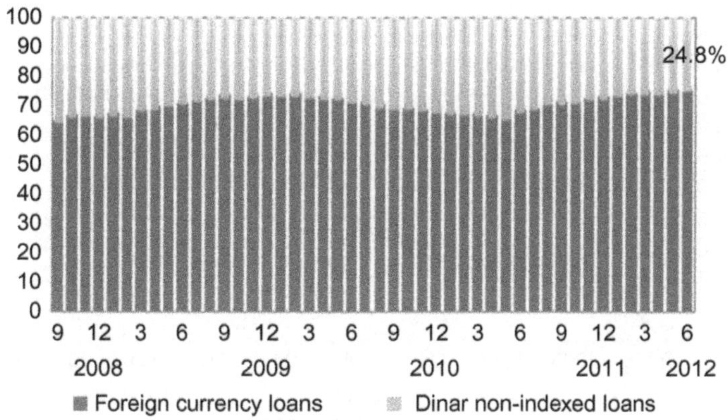

Fig. 7. Currency Structure of Loans to Enterprises (in %). *Source*: National Bank of Serbia.

EMPIRICAL APPROACH AND RESULTS

Econometric Specification

This analysis assesses the sensitivity of balance sheet items to the adverse change in relevant macroeconomic variables. The main advantage of

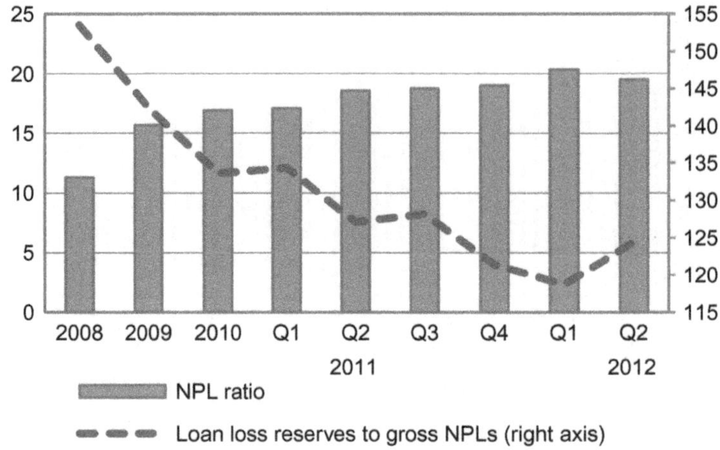

Fig. 8. Gross Non-Performing Loans to Total Gross Loans and their Coverage (in %). *Source*: National Bank of Serbia.

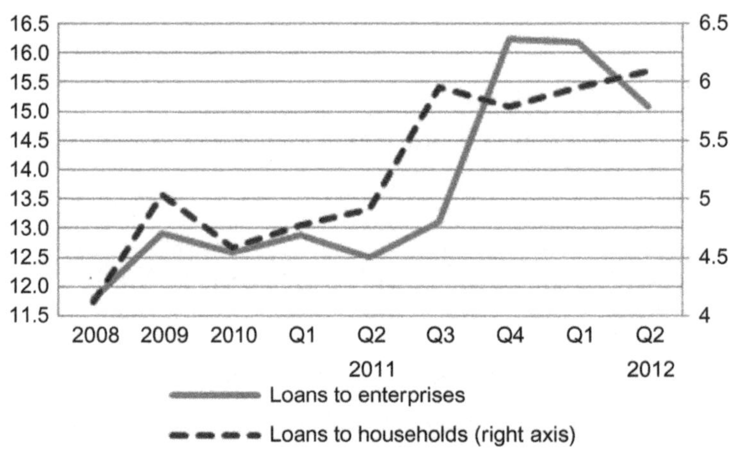

Fig. 9. Loan Loss Provisions in Total Gross loans (in %). *Source*: National Bank of Serbia and own calculations.

reduced form balance sheet models is that they are intuitive and easy to implement. The dependent variable (Credit Risk) is the logit transformation of the ratio of loan loss provisions (impairments) according to IFRS to total gross loans. This transformation is applied in order to allow for non-linearity. That measure should depend on the values of the macroeconomic variables, bank-specific characteristics and their interaction terms:

$$\text{Credit Risk}_{i,t} = \frac{e^{x_{it}}}{1 + e^{x_{it}}} \tag{1}$$

or equivalently:

$$\ln\left(\frac{\text{Credit Risk}_{i,t}}{1 - \text{Credit Risk}_{i,t}}\right) = x_{it} \tag{2}$$

More precisely, the full specification is given by the following expression:

$$\begin{aligned}
\Delta\text{logit(Credit Risk)}_{it} = \alpha_0 &+ \sum_{j=1}^{l} \beta_{1,j}\Delta\text{logit(Credit Risk)}_{i,\,t-j} \\
&+ \sum_{j=0}^{l} \beta_{2,j}\Delta\ln \text{GDP}_{t-1} + \sum_{j=0}^{l} \beta_{3,j}\Delta\ln \text{NEER}_{\,t-j} \\
&+ \sum_{j=0}^{l} \beta_{4,j}\Delta\ln \text{REPO}_{t-j} + \sum_{j=0}^{l} \beta_{5,j}\Delta\ln \text{CPI}_{\,t-j} \\
&+ \beta_{6,j}\text{Size}_{i,\,t-1} + \beta_{7,j}\text{Capitalisation}_{i,\,t-1} \\
&+ \beta_{8,j}\text{Liquidity}_{i,\,t-1} + \eta_i + \varepsilon_{i,t}
\end{aligned} \tag{3}$$

where $i = 1, 2, \ldots, N$ and $t = 1, 2, \ldots, T$ denote the cross section and time dimension of the panel, respectively. The constant term is not specified in the dynamic panel regression and the lagged dependent variable is omitted in the panel regression with fixed effects. The explanatory variables are explained in the section – Data description. The residual term consists of two parts: the first part η_i are unobserved and time invariant bank-specific effects and the second part $\varepsilon_{(i,t)}$ – i.i.d is the residual of bank i on a quarterly basis.

In order to also account for the time-constant unobserved heterogeneity between banks, the fixed effects model is applied. Then the assumption of independent and identically distributed disturbances is relaxed and a panel-corrected standard error (PCSE) model with unobserved bank-specific effects is estimated. This estimator accounts for heteroscedasticity and contemporaneously correlated disturbance terms across panels. The two-step generalised method of moments (GMM) developed by Arellano and Bond (1991) is also applied.

The applied two-step Arellano–Bond estimator (GMM) estimator assumes that the idiosyncratic disturbances are uncorrelated across individuals, which is not realistic. A possible solution to this problem is to include the GDP growth rate and inflation rate that may capture the relevant time effect. In this way the effects of period-specific and group invariant shocks are removed from the idiosyncratic error term into the systematic part of the model.

Data Description

The time period considered starts with 2008Q3 and covers the period until 2012Q2. This time-constraint is due to the availability of data for loan loss provisions and outstanding amounts of loans at the bank level.

The dependent variable (Credit Risk) is the logit transformation of the ratio of loan loss provisions (impairments) according to IFRS to total gross loans. It should indicate how much of the loans banks impair due to uncollectability and it is a reasonable ex post proxy measure for the realisation of credit risk.

The independent variables are macroeconomic and financial indicators which tend to affect the quality of bank loans. The data for q-o-q real GDP growth (GDP) and q-o-q CPI inflation (CPI) are obtained from the website of the Statistical Office of the Republic of Serbia. The data for the Belgrade interbank offer rate (BELIBOR) and nominal effective exchange rate (NEER), as well as bank-specific data for credit, loan loss provisions, assets (A_{it}), capital (C_{it}) and Liquidity (L_{it}) are obtained from the National Bank of Serbia, Directorate for Economic Research and Statistics. The nominal effective exchange rate (NEER) is included in the specifications in order to capture the effect that the depreciation of the local currency had on credit quality. The nominal effective exchange rate is calculated as the geometric weighted average of bilateral exchange rates of the dinar vis-à-vis the euro and the US dollar (weights are 80% and 20%, respectively).

In order to control for the existence of such distributional effects of changes in macroeconomic fundamentals across banks, bank-specific financial characteristics are introduced. These financial characteristics are size, capitalisation and liquidity. Large banks (in terms of their assets) can have easier access to non-deposit funds and are usually better positioned in the credit market which enables them make a better client selection. Therefore, large banks might differ in terms of their credit quality from smaller banks. Having more liquid assets, banks are less sensitive to negative shocks and therefore might be motivated to take more risks. Thus a good liquidity outlook might encourage banks to take more credit risks and not to mitigate them by screening their borrowers which can lead to a worsening of credit quality. Banks with high levels of capital relative to assets might be encouraged to embark on riskier activities leading to riskier credit portfolios (e.g. lending to FX risk unhedged borrowers). Measures for size, capitalisation and liquidity are given by the following equations:

$$\text{Size}_{i,t} = \log A_{it} - \frac{\sum_{i=1}^{N} \log A_{it}}{N_t} \tag{4}$$

$$\text{Capitalisation}_{i,t} = \frac{C_{i,t}}{A_{i,t}} - \frac{\sum_{i=1}^{T} \left(\sum_{i=1}^{N} \frac{(C_{i,t}/A_{i,t})}{N_t} \right)}{T} \tag{5}$$

$$\text{Liquidity}_{i,t} = \frac{L_{i,t}}{A_{i,t}} - \frac{\sum_{i=1}^{T} \left(\sum_{i=1}^{N} \frac{(L_{i,t}/A_{i,t})}{N_t} \right)}{T} \tag{6}$$

In order to adjust for distributional effects across banks and over time the measures for capitalisation and liquidity are normalised with respect to their mean across all banks in the sample and get indicators that sum to zero over all observations in the sample. By de-meaning the assets the upward trend that can be observed in banks' assets is removed.

Empirical Results

In Tables 1 and 2, the signs of the significant estimated coefficients are reported for the model for households and for enterprises, respectively. In Tables A2–A7 in the Appendix, the estimated coefficients and standard errors and a standard suite of diagnostic tests are reported.

At lag 1, the specification tests for first-order autocorrelation in the differenced error terms (AR(1)) reject the null hypothesis of first-order autocorrelation in the differenced error terms. The Arellano–Bond test for autocorrelation at lag 2 (AR(2)) accepts the null hypothesis of no second-order autocorrelation in the differenced terms. The Hansen test returns p-values higher than 0.10 confirming the joint validity of instruments.

Table 1. Results of Panel Estimation – Statistically Significant Coefficients for Loans to Households.

Explanatory Variable	Sign	Comment
Credit risk (LD)	+	High inertia
GDP (LD)	–	Strong business cycle effect
NEER (LD)	–	Exchange rate risk spillover
BELIBOR (LD)	+	Interest rate channel
CPI (D)	–	Reducing the real value of outstanding loans

Table 2. Results of Panel Estimation – Statistically Significant Coefficients for Loans to Enterprises.

Explanatory Variable	Sign	Comment
Credit risk (LD)	+	High inertia
GDP (LD)	–	Business cycle effect
NEER (LD)	–	Exchange rate risk spillover
CPI (D)	–	Reducing the real value of outstanding loans

The number of instruments in all dynamic panel regressions is smaller than the number of banks. Short-run elasticities of the models are also reported. Explanatory variables (except BELIBOR and bank-specific variables) are considered exogenous and are used as instruments in themselves.

With a small sample size (small number of both cross sections and time periods), caution should be applied in interpretation of the results. Also, it is important to bear in mind the possible bias in responses of credit quality to the chosen independent variables due to the fact that the time dimension corresponds to the period of global economic and financial crises. Credit quality deteriorated through the sample period and less than four years of data are not sufficient to capture the full credit cycle. Therefore only short-run relationships are analysed. However, having in mind these limitations, the estimated models are able to explain the development of credit risk in the Serbian banking sector reasonably well.

The coefficients of the lagged dependent variable are positive and statistically significant for loans to households and loans to enterprises. This might point to the persistence in credit risk but can also be observed from the viewpoint of inefficient bad debt write-off policies of banks.

As expected, a drop in real GDP growth led to a deterioration in the quality of bank loans to enterprises and households. Coefficients of lagged

GDP growth are negative and significant. This finding is robust across all considered specifications for loans to enterprises and for most specifications for loans to households. Recession or low GDP growth on average seems to precede the deterioration in credit quality.

The coefficients of the contemporaneous NEER are insignificant (except in one specification in the panel-corrected standard error model for loans to enterprises), but the coefficients of the lagged NEER are negative and significant in all specifications for loans to both households and enterprises. This leads to the conclusion that the depreciation of the dinar did not affect borrowers' payment ability within the same quarter but contributed to the deterioration in the quality of banks' loan portfolio after one quarter. Foreign exchange risk, which banks shifted to unhedged borrowers through foreign currency-indexation of loans, might have returned to the banking sector in the form of foreign exchange induced credit risk.

The coefficients of contemporaneous and lagged prices and the interbank money market rate differ for loans to households and loans to enterprises. Positive and significant coefficients of the lagged BELIBOR indicate that interbank money market interest rates affected the cost of borrowing of households through its pass-through to interest rates, thereby affecting households' credit burden. This is correlated with the fact that around one half of all non-performing household loans are loans in dinars. Also a significant portion of newly approved household dinar loans are loans with variable interest rates or initial period of interest rate fixation shorter than one year. In the case of loans to enterprises, all coefficients of the BELIBOR are insignificant so that there is no statistical evidence of the impact of changes in the money market interbank rate on credit risk in banks' loans to enterprises. There is statistical evidence that inflation affected credit quality in banks' loan portfolio. This evidence is stronger in the case of loans to enterprises. Negative coefficients of the contemporaneous inflation in all three models and all specifications suggest that inflation led to the lowering of credit risk in banks' loans to enterprises in the short-run. In the case of loans to households, the coefficients for contemporaneous inflation are negative and significant in all specifications of the panel-corrected standard error model and in two specifications of the fixed effects model. This lack of robustness may be correlated with the fact that growth in real net wages was rather low and sometimes even negative in the sample period. Overall, the results on CPI inflation suggest that higher inflation can make debt servicing easier by reducing the real value of outstanding loans and thus lead to a decrease of the credit risk ratio in the short-run.

The inclusion of the bank-specific variables does not appreciably change the statistical or economic significance of the macroeconomic variables. The coefficients of bank-specific characteristics themselves considered in this analysis are statistically insignificant in the case of loans to households. There is statistical evidence for a relationship between banks' size and capitalisation and the quality of loans to enterprises. However, this evidence is not robust to alternative methods and more research needs to be undertaken before the relationship between the revealed bank-specific characteristics and credit quality is more clearly understood.

CONCLUDING REMARKS AND POLICY RECOMMENDATIONS

This analysis investigates macroeconomic determinants of the realisation of credit risk in the loan portfolio of banks in Serbia using a panel data set covering the period from 2008Q3 to 2012Q2. Three different panel methods were applied separately for loans to households and loans to enterprises.

The main finding is that a worsening business cycle and exchange rate depreciation led to a deterioration in the quality of banks' loan portfolio in Serbia during the period of analysis. The statistical results are in line with economic theory. In the case of real GDP growth as explanatory variable, the results point to the dependence of the business and household sector's capacity to repay their debt on the state of the business cycle. After a negative GDP shock, the quality of both loans to enterprises and households deteriorates with a lag of one quarter. In the case of the results for the nominal effective exchange rate, the high share of foreign currency loans in total loans in the Serbian banking sector is relevant. In that context it is reasonable to assume that foreign exchange risk, which banks shifted to unhedged borrowers through foreign currency-indexation of loans, returned to the banking sector in the form of foreign exchange induced credit risk.

Changes in the interbank money market rate (BELIBOR) seem to have affected only the quality of loans to households through its pass-through to interest rates. With prevailing short-term loans to households, a significant portion of newly approved household dinar loans with variable interest rates or initial period of interest rate fixation shorter than one year, and approximately half of all non-performing loans to households being initially approved in dinars, such a conclusion seems to be reasonable. There is statistical evidence that CPI inflation affected the quality of loans to enterprises and households, which is stronger in the case of loans to enterprises. Such results suggest that higher inflation can make debt servicing easier by reducing the real value of outstanding loans and thus lead to a decrease of the credit risk ratio in the short-run.

These results are similar to the results of comparable studies on other CEESE banking sectors (Louzis et al., 2010 for Greece, Shijaku & Ceca, 2011 for Albania among others). This is reasonable due to the common characteristics of the countries of the region – foreign ownership of the banking sectors and high degree of financial Euroisation and strong economic dependence on the eurozone.

As for policy implications, international cooperation between regulators would help promote financial stability in future. As an example, the National Bank of Serbia (2010) played an important role in maintaining the stability of the banking sector during the period of the crisis. A very important topic of such cooperation should be the risk-taking channel between countries with significant differences in interest rates and degree of riskiness.

As Serbia is a country with less developed financial markets and a private sector which is highly exposed to changes in exchange rates, especially in terms of the balance sheet channel, the interrelationship between the exchange rate and credit risk should be a major focus of both domestic macro- and micro-prudential policy. Prudential regulations should motivate banks to pay more attention to possible negative spillovers when assessing the creditworthiness of individuals and corporations. Also, a successful continuation of the dinarisation strategy of the central bank would help reduce financial stability risks over the medium term, mainly by encouraging firms to avoid or hedge against foreign exchange risks. The further development of a primary and secondary T-bills market should promote dinarisation and thus strengthen monetary policy effectiveness and maintain financial stability by reducing unhedged foreign currency risks.

REFERENCES

Arellano, M., & Bond, S. (1991). Some tests of specification for panel data: Monte Carlo evidence and an application to employment equations. *Review of Economic Studies*, *58*, 277–297.

Bernanke, B., & Gertler, M. (1989). Agency costs, net worth and business fluctuations. *American Economic Review*, *79*, 14–31.

Bernanke, B., Gertler, M., & Gilchrist, S. (1999). The financial accelerator in a quantitative business cycle framework. In J. Taylor & M. Woodford (Eds.), *Handbook of macroeconomics* (Vol. 1C, pp. 1341–1393). Amsterdam: North-Holland.

De Bock, R., & Demyanets, A. (2012). *Bank asset quality in emerging markets: Determinants and spillovers*. IMF Working Paper 12/71. International Monetary Fund, Washington, DC.

Hartelius, K. (2010). Analyzing nonperforming loans in Central and Eastern Europe based on historical experience in emerging markets. Global Financial Stability Report. International Monetary Fund, Washington, DC.

Keeton, W., & Morris, C. S. (1987). Why do banks' loan losses differ? *Economic Review*, *72*(5), 3–21, Federal Reserve Bank of Kansas City.

Kiyotaki, N., & Moore, J. (1997). Credit cycles. *Journal of Political Economy*, *105*(2), 211–247.

Louzis, D. P., Vouldis, A. T., & Metaxas, V. L. (2010). *Macroeconomic and bank specific determinants of non-performing loans in Greece: A comparative study of mortgage, business and consumer loan portfolios*. Working Paper No. 118. Bank of Greece.

National Bank of Serbia. (2010). *Annual financial stability report, 37–38*, [online]. Retrieved from http://www.nbs.rs/export/sites/default/internet/english/90/90_2/financial_system_2010.pdf. Accessed on February 12, 2013.

Nkusu, M. (2011). *Nonperforming loans and macrofinancial vulnerabilities in advanced economies*. IMF Working Paper No. 11/161. International Monetary Fund, Washington, DC.

Shijaku, H., & Ceca, K. (2011). *A model for the credit risk in Albania using banks' panel data*. Working Paper No. 06 (29). Bank of Albania.

Windmeijer, F. (2005). A finite sample correction for the variance of linear efficient two-step GMM estimators. *Journal of Econometrics*, *126*(1), 25–51.

APPENDIX: VARIABLE DEFINITIONS AND REGRESSION RESULTS

Table A1. Variable Definitions.

Variable[a]	Definition
Credit Risk (households)	The logistic transformation of the ratio of loan loss provisions to total gross loans to households
Credit Risk (enterprises)	The logistic transformation of the ratio of loan loss provisions to total gross loans to enterprises
GDP	Real GDP growth rate (q-on-q) calculated as the log differenced real GDP
NEER[b]	Nominal effective exchange rate of the dinar against the euro and the US dollar
BELIBOR[b]	Three-month Belgrade Interbank Offer Rate
CPI	CPI inflation (q-o-q)
A_{it}^{**}	Total assets of a bank i in quarter t
$\frac{C_{it}^{**}}{A_{it}}$	The ratio of capital to total assets of bank i in quarter t
$\frac{L_{it}^{**}}{A_{it}}$	The ratio of liquid assets to total assets of bank i in quarter t Liquid assets comprise investment in government and other securities, NBS bills, current account, vault cash and deposit facilities with the NBS

[a]Except the dependent variable, all variables are taken in logs.
[b]Three-month averages were calculated.

Table A2. Results of Panel Regressions – Loan Loss Provisions to Total Gross Loans to Households.

Explanatory Variables	Fixed Effects			
	Model 1	Model 2	Model 3	Model 4
GDP				
LD.	−1.735*	−1.689*	−2.129**	−1.448
	(0.935)	(0.935)	(0.811)	(1.196)
NEER				
D1.	0.095	0.206	0.083	0.046
	(0.371)	(0.297)	(0.376)	(0.411)
LD.	−1.252***	−1.306***	−1.348**	−1.223***
	(0.429)	(0.433)	(0.525)	(0.399)
BELIBOR				
D1.	0.109	0.145	0.161	0.109
	(0.101)	(0.121)	(0.129)	(0.101)

Table A2. *(Continued)*

Explanatory Variables	Fixed Effects			
	Model 1	Model 2	Model 3	Model 4
LD.	0.339***	0.329**	0.386**	0.307**
	(0.122)	(0.124)	(0.156)	(0.119)
CPI				
D1.	−2.415	−2.158	−2.782	−2.306
	(1.470)	(1.146)	(1.850)	(1.357)
LD.	0.130	0.086	0.013	0.111
	(0.303)	(0.280)	(0.253)	(0.299)
Bank-specific control variables				
Size (L.)		0.366		
		(1.328)		
Capitalisation (L.)			0.941	
			(1.314)	
Liquidity (L.)				0.317
				(0.333)
Constant	0.048***	0.093*	0.052**	0.046***
	(0.017)	(0.053)	(0.022)	(0.016)
Number of observations	398	398	398	398
Number of banks	32	32	32	32
F-test for the significance of the whole regression (*p*-value)	10.33 (0.000)	10.78 (0.000)	8.46 (0.000)	7.01 (0.000)
R squared	0.094	0.098	0.069	0.049

Notes: D1. refers to the first difference of the variables in logarithms. LD. refers to the lagged differenced variables in logarithms.
Standard errors are given in parenthesis. Vce robust standard errors are reported.
***/**/* denote significance at 1%, 5% and 10% level of significance, respectively. Computations have been done in STATA 11.

Table A3. Results of Panel Regressions – Loan Loss Provisions to Total Gross Loans to Enterprises.

Explanatory Variables	Fixed Effects			
	Model 1	Model 2	Model 3	Model 4
GDP				
LD.	−2.855***	−2.734**	−3.081***	−2.708**
	(1.014)	(1.036)	(1.045)	(1.109)
NEER				
D1.	−0.272	−0.205	0.265	−0.293
	(0.440)	(0.427)	(0.444)	(0.430)
LD.	−0.876**	−0.910***	−0.949***	−0.860***
	(0.260)	(0.258)	(0.267)	(0.260)
BELIBOR				
D1.	0.050	0.046	0.037	0.048
	(0.132)	(0.128)	(0.126)	(0.131)
LD.	0.158	0.150	0.173	0.142
	(0.217)	(0.216)	(0.210)	(0.215)
CPI				
D1.	−3.311***	−3.247***	−3.597***	−3.247***
	(0.761)	(0.738)	(0.761)	(0.767)
LD.	1.102	−1.052	−1.138	−1.111
	(0.783)	(0.820)	(0.764)	(0.792)
Bank-specific control variables				
Size (L.)		−0.276**		
		(0.130)		
Capitalisation (L.)			−0.589	
			(0.524)	
Liquidity (L.)				0.163
				(0.289)
Constant	0.104***	0.103***	0.106***	0.102***
	(0.025)	(0.025)	(0.023)	(0.024)
Number of observations	399	399	399	399
Number of banks	32	32	32	32
F-test for the significance of the whole regression (*p*-value)	6.03 (0.000)	5.12 (0.000)	6.37 (0.000)	6.02 (0.000)
R squared	0.072	0.080	0.091	0.078

Notes: D1. refers to the first difference of the variables in logarithms. LD. refers to the lagged differenced variables in logarithms.
Standard errors are given in parenthesis. Vce robust standard errors are reported.
***/**/* denote significance at 1%, 5% and 10% level of significance, respectively.

Table A4. Results of Panel Regressions – Loan Loss Provisions to Total Gross Loans to Households.

Explanatory Variables	Xtpcse			
	Model 1	Model 2	Model 3	Model 4
Credit Risk (L.)	0.388***	0.355***	0.397***	0.386***
	(0.120)	(0.114)	(0.116)	(0.120)
GDP				
LD.	−0.977	−1.065*	−1.266*	−0.769
	(0.699)	(0.625)	(0.751)	(0.716)
NEER				
D1.	−0.331*	0.309	−0.291	−0.372*
	(0.193)	(0.190)	(0.206)	(0.191)
LD.	−0.686***	−0.716***	−0.781***	−0.660***
	(0.160)	(0.160)	(0.184)	(0.157)
BELIBOR				
D1.	0.009	0.000	0.008	0.006
	(0.070)	(0.072)	(0.079)	(0.067)
LD.	0.276***	0.273**	0.288***	0.248***
	(0.063)	(0.066)	(0.071)	(0.068)
CPI				
D1.	−1.464	−1.470***	−1.715***	−1.358***
	(0.472)	(0.472)	(0.551)	(0.458)
LD.	0.221	0.215	0.159	0.229
	(0.399)	(0.400)	(0.429)	(0.380)
Bank-specific control variables				
Size (L.)		−0.114		
		(0.139)		
Capitalisation (L.)			−0.591	
			(0.451)	
Liquidity (L.)				0.230
				(0.336)
Constant	0.069***	0.132*	0.069**	0.071***
	(0.027)	(0.075)	(0.027)	(0.027)
Number of observations	448	448	448	448
Number of banks	32	32	32	32
Wald statistic for the significance of the whole regression (*p*-value)	2.40e+07 (0.000)	1.87e+07 (0.000)	2.32e+06 (0.000)	68010101.44 (0.000)
R squared	0.305	0.305	0.330	0.305

Notes: D1. refers to the first difference of the variables in logarithms. LD. refers to the lagged differenced variables in logarithms.
Standard errors are given in parenthesis.
***/**/* denote significance at 1%, 5% and 10% level of significance, respectively.

Table A5. Results of Panel Regressions – Loan Loss Provisions to Total Gross Loans to Enterprises.

Explanatory Variables	Xtpcse			
	Model 1	Model 2	Model 3	Model 4
Credit Risk (L.)	0.307***	0.297***	0.311***	0.307**
	(0.083)	(0.087)	(0.082)	(0.083)
GDP				
LD.	−1.768*	−1.770*	−1.931**	−1.633*
	(0.931)	(0.923)	(0.986)	(0.935)
NEER				
D1.	−0.362	−0.365	−0.338	−0.388
	(0.289)	(0.287)	(0.300)	(0.294)
LD.	−0.566**	−0.568**	−0.702***	−0.546**
	(0.241)	(0.239)	(0.258)	(0.243)
BELIBOR				
D1.	0.070	0.069	0.043	0.069
	(0.115)	(0.114)	(0.122)	(0.115)
LD.	0.128	0.128	0.151	0.110
	(0.109)	(0.109)	(0.115)	(0.114)
CPI				
D1.	−3.065***	−3.070***	−3.469***	−2.995***
	(0.759)	(0.755)	(0.809)	(0.758)
LD.	0.541	−0.566	−0.581	−0.540
	(0.658)	(0.654)	(0.684)	(0.662)
Bank-specific control variables				
Size (L.)		−0.062**		
		(0.091)		
Capitalisation (L.)			−0.645*	
			(0.341)	
Liquidity (L.)				0.164
				(0.319)
Constant	0.158***	0.191***	0.158***	0.159***
	(0.043)	(0.065)	(0.043)	(0.044)
Number of observations	448	448	448	448
Number of banks	32	32	32	32
Wald statistic for the significance of the whole regression (*p*-value)	260850.16 (0.000)	126229.87 (0.000)	430080.03 (0.000)	73160.41 (0.000)
R squared	0.260	0.263	0.286	0.261

Notes: D1. refers to the first difference of the variables in logarithms. LD. refers to the lagged differenced variables in logarithms.
Standard errors are given in parenthesis.
***/**/* denote significance at 1%, 5% and 10% level of significance, respectively.

Table A6. Results of Panel Regressions – Loan Loss Provisions to Total Gross Loans to Households.

Explanatory Variables	Two-Stage (Arellano–Bond) Difference – GMM			
	Model 1	Model 2	Model 3	Model 4
Credit Risk (L.)	0.270**	0.120	0.177**	0.252**
	(0.136)	(0.110)	(0.097)	(0.132)
GDP				
LD.	−1.441*	−2.231*	−1.443*	−2.043*
	(0.847)	(1.113)	(0.784)	(1.082)
NEER				
D1.	0.220	0.281	0.115	0.292
	(0.260)	(0.279)	(0.211)	(0.242)
LD.	−0.402***	−0.500**	−0.402**	−0.464**
	(0.147)	(0.187)	(0.170)	(0.192)
BELIBOR				
D1.	−0.025	−0.051	−0.094	0.001
	(0.088)	(0.119)	(0.104)	(0.101)
LD.	0.196*	0.291**	0.257**	0.298*
	(0.103)	(0.131)	(0.106)	(0.162)
CPI				
D1.	−0.307	−0.498	−0.150	−0.378
	(0.521)	(0.522)	(0.509)	(0.579)
LD.	−0.183	0.181	−0.049	−0.487
	(0.367)	(0.374)	(0.309)	(0.401)
Bank-specific control variables				
Size (L.)		0.607		
		(0.490)		
Capitalisation (L.)			0.280	
			(0.731)	
Liquidity (L.)				0.309
				(0.705)
Number of observations	384	384	384	384
Number of banks	32	32	32	32
Number of instruments	15	16	16	17
F-test for the significance of the whole regression	5.33	4.47	4.31	6.10
(*p*-value)	(0.000)	(0.000)	(0.001)	(0.000)
AR(1)/(*p*-value)	0.088	0.079	0.084	0.095
AR(2)/(*p*-value)	0.149	0.182	0.127	0.148
Hansen (*p*-value)	0.278	0.370	0.423	0.514
Diff in Hansen cross sectional corr (*p*-value)	0.140	0.581	0.430	0.351

Notes: D1. refers to the first difference of the variables in logarithms. LD. refers to the lagged differenced variables in logarithms.
Windmeijer (2005) corrected standard errors are given in parenthesis.
***/**/* denote significance at 1%, 5% and 10% level of significance, respectively.

Table A7. Results of Panel Regressions – Loan Loss Provisions to Total Gross Loans to Enterprises.

Explanatory Variables	Two-Stage (Arellano–Bond) Difference – GMM			
	Model 1	Model 2	Model 3	Model 4
Credit Risk (L.)	0.312**	0.232***	0.355***	0.433***
	(0.128)	(0.052)	(0.087)	(0.095)
GDP				
LD.	−2.819*	−1.863*	−2.867*	−3.593*
	(1.505)	(1.035)	(1.524)	(2.080)
NEER				
D1.	0.679	0.135	0.591	0.286
	(1.004)	(0.579)	(0.399)	(0.431)
LD.	−0.654**	−0.667**	−0.542**	−0.705**
	(0.260)	(0.290)	(0.293)	(0.327)
BELIBOR				
D1.	0.224	0.186	0.167	0.251
	(0.364)	(0.118)	(0.210)	(0.170)
LD.	0.099	0.081	0.181	0.304
	(0.189)	(0.334)	(0.215)	(0.209)
CPI				
D1.	−3.306***	−3.278***	−3.880***	−3.666***
	(0.970)	(0.906)	(0.885)	(0.916)
LD.	0.532	−1.094	0.793	0.526
	(0.982)	(0.711)	(0.686)	(0.878)
Bank-specific control variables				
Size (L.)		−0.113		
		(0.914)		
Capitalisation (L.)			−2.964*	
			(1.719)	
Liquidity (L.)				2.273
				(1.384)
Number of observations	384	334	384	334
Number of banks	31	31	31	31
Number of instruments	16	20	16	16
F-test for the significance of the whole regression (*p*-value)	4.90 (0.000)	13.91 (0.000)	10.72 (0.000)	4.13 (0.000)
AR(1)/(*p*-value)	0.027	0.035	0.091	0.025
AR(2)/(*p*-value)	0.128	0.172	0.749	0.326
Hansen (*p*-value)	0.465	0.185	0.289	0.227
Diff in Hansen cross sectional corr (*p*-value)	0.236	0.145	0.451	0.304

Notes: D1. refers to the first difference of the variables in logarithms. LD. refers to the lagged differenced variables in logarithms.
Windmeijer (2005) corrected standard errors are given in parenthesis.
***/**/* denote significance at 1%, 5% and 10% level of significance, respectively.

DOES REGULATORY ENVIRONMENT AFFECT EARNINGS MANAGEMENT IN TRANSITIONAL ECONOMIES? AN EMPIRICAL EXAMINATION OF THE FINANCIAL REPORTING QUALITY OF CROSS-LISTED FIRMS OF CHINA AND HONG KONG

Matthias Nnadi, Kamil Omoteso and Yi Yu

ABSTRACT

This paper provides evidence on the impact of regulatory environment on financial reporting quality of transitional economies. This study compares the financial reporting quality of Hong Kong firms which are cross-listed in mainland China with those of Hong Kong firms cross-listed in China using specific earnings management metrics (earnings smoothing,

Neo-Transitional Economics
International Finance Review, Volume 16, 245–276

ISSN: 1569-3767/doi:10.1108/S1569-376720150000016011

timely loss recognition, value relevance and managing towards earnings targets) under pre- and post-IFRS regimes.

The financial reporting quality of Chinese A-share companies and Hong Kong listed companies are examined using earnings management measures. Using 2007 as base year, the study used a cumulative of −5 and +5 years of convergence experience which provide a total of 3,000 firm-year observations. In addition to regression analyses, we used the difference-in-difference analysis to check for the impact of regulatory environments on earnings management.

Through the lens of contingency theory, our results indicate that the adoption of the new substantially IFRS-convergent accounting standards in China results in better financial reporting quality evidenced by less earning management. The empirical results further shows that accounting data are more value relevant for Hong Kong listed firms, and that firms listed in China are more likely to engage in accrual-based earnings management than in real earnings management activities. We established that different earnings management practices that are seemingly tolerable in one country may not be tolerable in another due to level of differences in the regulatory environments.

The findings show that Hong Kong listed companies' exhibit higher level of financial reporting quality than Chinese listed companies, which implies that the financial reporting quality under IFRS can be significantly different in regions with different institutional, economic and regulatory environments. The results imply that contingent factors such as country's institutional structures, its extent of regulation and the strength of its investor protection environments impact on financial reporting quality particularly in transitional and emerging economies. As such, these factors need to be given appropriate considerations by financial reporting regulators and policy-makers interested in controlling earnings management practices among their corporations.

This study is a high impact study considering that China plays a significant role in today's globalised economy. This study is unique as it the first, that we are aware of, to compare real earnings activities against accrual-based earnings management in pre- and post-IFRS adoption periods within the Chinese and Hong Kong financial reporting environments, distinguishing between cross-listed and non-cross-listed firms.

Keywords: Financial; earning; quality; cash flow; emerging markets

INTRODUCTION

The effect of regulatory environment and the adoption of IFRS on financial reporting quality could vary across different countries. The mixed findings documented by prior studies can be explained by countries' institutional structures. Many studies argue that developing and transitional economies still have ineffective regulatory institutions despite any fast growth in their capital market. China is the largest developing country in the world, yet characterised with concentrated ownership structures, weak legal systems and highly politicised institutional arrangements (Piotroski & Wong, 2012). As a result, prior studies attribute low financial reporting quality to ineffective regulation and infrastructure (Ball, Kothari, & Robbin, 2000).

Whilst both countries share common cultural backgrounds, there is a significant difference in their interpretation of financial results and reporting. While Hong Kong analysts rely more on fundamental and technical analyses in their financial reporting (Wong & Cheung, 1999), the Chinese lean towards portfolio analysis. As a result of significant differences (in terms of the economy, regulatory and legal systems) between mainland China and Hong Kong, this study compares the financial reporting quality of Hong Kong firms which are cross-listed in mainland China with those of Hong Kong firms cross-listed in China using earnings management metrics under IFRS regime. Hong Kong has converged with IFRS since January 1, 2005. To match the post-convergence period with China, the accounting quality is compared for these two key emerging economies in the period from 2007 to 2011.

With the achievements of China's economic reform, their accounting system also has experienced tremendous changes. The earliest effort of converging Chinese domestic accounting system with international practices began in 1979, in which all joint ventures with foreign investments were required to be regulated under a set of accounting regulations. Subsequently, a set of accounting standards based on International Accounting Standards (IAS), known as Accounting Standards for Business Enterprises (ASBE), was released in 1992. This was a historic progress in the transitional reform of China's dogmatic accounting system. Between 1997 and 2001, China attempted to issue a series of new accounting standards to move towards International Accounting Standards (Chen & Peng, 2007).

As the Chinese come under increasing scrutiny by the international investment community, as well as their domestic capital markets, identifying acceptable financial measures of performance could guide benchmarking activities and regulatory monitoring (Avkiran, 2011). Our study provides evidence that substantial convergence of IFRS can improve financial reporting quality in a transitional and emerging economy such as China.

According to prior studies (Lang, Raedy, & Wilson, 2006; Leuz, Nanda, & Wysocki, 2003; Peng, 2005), accounting quality is higher in countries with a common law origin and high shareholder protection. However, in recent years, the Chinese government as well as Chinese listed firms have more incentives and pressures to enhance their financial reporting quality due to the rapid development of their equity markets and their desire to attract capital worldwide (Peng, 2005). By enhancing the efficiency of capital market infrastructure, China has made great efforts towards changing its accounting regulations (Chen, Wang, & Zhao, 2009). With the ongoing liberalisation of the Chinese economy and the increasingly competitive business environment, the need for Chinese firms to ensure greater efficiency and improve the quality of their financial reporting has become understandably very high (Laurenceson & Qin, 2008).

Specifically, government regulatory authorities have strengthened the regulation of information disclosure policies of listed companies. Chen and Peng (2007) find that such policy has helped in curbing earnings management opportunism in the application of Chinese accounting standards. This also indicates that effective regulatory enforcement is significant in the harmonisation of China's accounting practices with IFRS. Furthermore, Street and Gray (2002) provide the evidence that there is high compliance with accounting rules due to improved audit regulation and monitoring systems in China.

It is worth mentioning that the new Chinese Accounting Standards (CAS) are not complete translations of IFRS as there are few differences which represent China's unique environment and business practice. For example, in the new CAS, the reversal of asset impairment charges is prohibited, related party disclosure requirement is revised to reflect the context of state-ownership and the application of fair value is also tailor-made to reflect the need of the Chinese economy (Peng and Smith, 2010). Though there are scepticisms as to whether the Chinese authorities can effectively regulate some aspects of the IFRS (e.g. the fair value accounting – FVA), the convergence was regarded by both the Chinese government and the IASB as a significant move towards the development of the Chinese economy and its place in the world's global economy (Zhang, Andrew, & Rudkin, 2012).

Under the policy of one country-two systems, Hong Kong can be considered as a separate market from China. Prior to its IFRS adoption in 2005, Hong Kong applied its own accounting standards, which were independent of mainland China. The aim of the current study is to analyse, through the frame of contingency theory, the effect of the regulatory environments on earnings management and financial reporting quality of firms in the pre- and post-IFRS adoption periods in both countries. The remainder of this paper is organised as follows: The section 'Theoretical Framework: The Contingency Theory' discusses the study's theoretical framework, contingency theory; the section 'Earnings Management and Financial Reporting' provides a concise review of literature on earnings management within the context of financial reporting while the section 'Research Questions' explains how the current study differs from the previous ones on this subject. It also demonstrates how the study's three key research questions draw on the existing literature and attempt to fill some gaps inherent in the current body of knowledge in the subject area. The section 'Methodology' contains the research methods comprising details of sample selection used in the study, earnings metrics as used in the empirical work and how the study's hypotheses were developed. The section 'Discussion of Results' discusses the study's results including those of the sensitivity analyses and further tests conducted while the final section draws the conclusion, summarises the major findings and their implications, identifies the study's limitations and makes suggestions for future research in the subject area.

THEORETICAL FRAMEWORK: THE CONTINGENCY THEORY

Contingency theory was first popularised as a tool to explain organisational differentiation and integration through environmental factors (Lawrence & Lorsch, 1967). It is premised on a heuristic concept that oppose managers' tendency to adopt universalistic solutions and peddling panaceas (Wood, 1979). Contingency theory attempts to explain structural and process differences among organisations with respect to their operating environment, technology, size, strategy and culture among others (Scott, 1987). Therefore, within an organisational context, the following are the three basic principles of the contingency theory: (a) there is no one best way to organise; (b) different ways to organise are not equally effective; (c) the best way to organise depends on the nature of the environment to which the organisation relates (Bartol & Martin, 1994; Scott, 1987).

The intricacies of adopting, adapting and operating IFRS by different countries make contingency theory a potent framework to diagnose, understand and manage IFRS adoption. As this current study seeks to examine the effects of regulatory environments on earnings management within the context of two related but different countries (China and Hong Kong), the contingency theory is considered the most appropriate framework through which to gain an understanding of different contingent factors that could affect financial reporting quality under an IFRS regime.

The use of the theory is not strange in accounting research as it has been adopted in different areas of the subject because of its versatility. These areas include management accounting (Gul & Chia, 1994; Hayes, 1977; Hopwood, 1983; Otley, 1980); governmental accounting (Gupta, Dirsmith, Fogarty, 1994; Lüder, 1992); accounting information systems (Gordon & Miller, 1976; Nicolaou, 2000; Rayburn & Rayburn, 1991); accounting education (Lopez-Gavira & Omoteso, 2013) accounting ethics (Schweikart, 1992); auditing (Omoteso, 2013) and financial reporting (Thomas, 1986, 1991; Xiao, Dyson, & Powell, 1996).

EARNINGS MANAGEMENT AND FINANCIAL REPORTING

Leuz et al. (2003) defined earnings management as the alteration of a firm's financial reports by insiders in order to either mislead some stakeholders or to influence contractual outcomes that are dependent on numbers in the financial reports. This can be in the form of a deliberate attempt to distort financial data which may not be very apparent to investors. Earnings management is generally understood to mean attempts by company insiders to protect their positions and benefits by manipulating the financial information provided to outsiders. This often takes the form of income smoothing or income manipulation.

However, measuring the degree of earnings management has presented challenges (Dechow & Skinner, 2000; Dechow, Sloan, & Sweeney, 1995; Healy & Wahlen, 1999), as it is difficult to establish such manipulation. In practice, insiders can 'smooth', that is reduce the variability of reported earnings, by altering the accruals of revenues and expenses. Thus any indication of a reduction in the variability of earnings (often called earning smoothing) would suggest that the firm is involved in earnings management. Conversely, a higher earnings smoothing implies that a firm is less likely to manage its earnings effectively.

As Gopalan and Jayaraman (2012) indicate, if the fluctuation of operating earnings is small in comparison to the fluctuation of cash flow from operations, it is likely that management has used discretionary accruals to smooth reported operating earnings. This measure is based on the idea that insiders may attempt to hide reductions in cash flow by manipulating the accruals. The indication is that accruals for firms that wish to manipulate their reported earnings will be large compared to the cash flow from operations (Dechow & Skinner, 2000). As Leuz et al. (2003) argue, firms operating in regulatory environments can retain their ability to consume private benefits by keeping firm disclosures obscure. This allows them to not only extract benefits when the firm performs well but also to keep a poorly performing firm active (Fang & Zhou, 2012; Wang & Campbell, 2012).

The above earnings management practice is usually accrual-based which are otherwise discretionary accruals. In other words, management use their discretion to manipulate the earning in order to avoid reporting huge losses. In practice though, management also engages in real earnings manipulations such as acceleration of the timing of sales through price discounts, reporting of lower cost of costs sold through increased production and decrease in discretionary expenses such as advertising cost and research and development (Cohen, Dey, & Lys, 2008; Dechow & Skinner, 2000). Interestingly, Roychowdhury (2006) adds that some of the real earnings management activities are departures from normal operations activities which do not necessarily contribute to the firm value but may help managers meet up with their reporting goals. Our study makes a significant contribution by examining both earning management practices among Chinese and Hong Kong cross-listed firm. To the best of our knowledge, none of the existing studies on earnings management among Chinese and Hong Kong financial reporting systems have covered both practices.

RESEARCH QUESTIONS

Although several studies have been conducted on the impact of adoption of IFRS on financial reporting quality and earnings management in China, our current study differs substantially in approach and scope in several ways. First, our study examines the effect of regulatory environment on earnings management by comparing firms in one country,[1] but under two regulatory environments. This is important because firms operating in China are highly regulated by the state whilst Hong Kong is seen as market oriented with strong equity and transparent reporting environment (Loh, 2006; Wong & Cheung, 1999). Prior studies have established that benefits from mandatory adoption of IFRS are found in countries and regions with certain characteristics such as legal enforcement and transparent reporting environment, none of such studies (Barth, Landsman, & Lang, 2008; Gordon, Loeb, & Zhu, 2012; Peng & Bewley, 2010) have tested such hypotheses on regions with dual regulatory environments for example China and Hong Kong.

Second, our study compares real earnings activities against accrual-based earnings management in the pre- and post-IFRS adoption periods in both regulatory environments. This helps to examine whether firms in the regions are more likely to engage in real or discretionary accruals earnings manipulations in any or both countries, and the impact of IFRS adoption in regulating such practices. Most studies on accounting quality and earnings management among Chinese firms apply the commonly used metrics such as earning smoothing, timely loss recognition and value relevance. In addition to these commonly used measures, our study further adds real earnings management activities metrics such as manipulations in the revenue or sales, production costs and discretionary expenses.[2] We use the abnormal cash flows, abnormal production cost and discretionary expenses by firms in both regions to compare with the accrual-based earnings managements using discretionary accrual metric. This approach allows us to control for any industry-wide changes in economic conditions across the regions. Prior studies on China such as Liu, Yao, Hu, and Liu (2011), Lin and Chen (2005), Li (2010) did not consider discretionary accruals and real earnings activities of firms in their studies but used the commonly accrual-based measures only. Although these studies focused on Chinese firms, none compared the earnings management activities with Hong Kong firms. Our study therefore fills the gap.

Third, in contrast to previous studies, we distinguish between cross-listed firms and non-cross-listed firms. This is important because state controlled firms in China which are not cross-listed are often subjected to government control. Lee (2001) finds that firms receiving more government financial support will have a lower incentive to improve financial reporting even after IFRS adoption. In such cases, government directives are often of more importance than the interest of investors (Kim, 2012).

Such political influence has been found to have far reaching effect on Hong Kong firms that are cross-listed in China (Piotroski, Wong, & Zhang, 2014). Finally, we apply difference-in-difference analysis to compare the impact of differences in regulatory environments on earnings management between China and Hong Kong firms before and after IFRS adoption. These distinctions in our approach and techniques differentiate our paper from previous studies and thus make significant contributions to the earnings management literature.

We formulate three research questions: the first question helps to establish and identify the level of earnings management practices in both countries and to consider the influence of IFRS adoption in reducing such practices. The research questions are formulated thus:

RQ1. To what extent are the management of earnings by cross-listed firms affected by the adoption of IFRS in the two countries?

Some empirical studies suggest that firms are less likely to manage reported earnings towards a positive target after converging with IFRS (Lang et al., 2006; Leuz et al., 2003; Liu et al., 2011). If this argument is correct, it is imperative to distinguish between real and accrual-based earnings management by firms. The distinction between both forms of earnings management is important as this may be influenced by the regulatory environment of both countries. We argue that firms from stronger regulatory environments may curb accrual-based earnings management but may or may not allow real earnings management. Previous studies on China IFRS adoption (Chin, Chen, & Hsieh, 2009; Liou & Yang, 2008; Liu et al., 2011) have not considered such comparisons in earnings management in their sampled firms. Thus, our second research question addressed the following question:

RQ2. To what extent do the regulatory environments affect both real earnings and discretional accruals management by firms in China and Hong Kong?

The study takes into consideration the uniqueness of Chinese adoption of IFRS and compares the effect of IFRS adoption in both environments. Unlike China, Hong Kong is a market-oriented economy, with strong equity market and transparent reporting environment. According to prior studies, benefits from mandatory adoption of IFRS are found only in countries and regions with strong legal enforcement and transparent reporting environment characteristics. For example, Bailey, Harte, and Sugden (2000) argue that for financial reporting to be more credible, it should contain complete picture of corporate activity such as the management of earnings, role of accounting information and regulation. This is correct to the extent that accounting reports play important roles in shaping investors views and ideology. Therefore, to investigate the influence of such institutional factors on financial reporting quality, this study also examines the third research question:

> **RQ3.** To what extent does the Chinese financial reporting quality differ from the Hong Kong listed firms under IFRS?

METHODOLOGY

Sample Selection

To compare the financial reporting quality for Chinese A-share firms and Hong Kong firms under IFRS regime, we first obtained a sample of all Hong Kong cross-listed firms in China and also Chinese A-share firms that are cross-listed in Hong Kong markets. Although Hong Kong commenced full convergence with IFRS in 2005, we used 2007 as the base year to allow a matched sample for Chinese A-share firms with same mandatory convergence period. We chose cross-listed firms to enable us to check for the impact of regulatory environments on the behaviour of the firms in the management of earnings. We also tested our results on a set of non-cross-listed firms of both nations. Further, we selected a matched sample of firms based on key characteristics such as total assets, market capitalisation, sales growth and return on assets. Our final sample consists of 250 Chinese firms listed in Hong Kong market and 100 Hong Kong firms listed in China A-share market.

The empirical analysis straddles two separate periods. The first period is defined as the post-convergence period from 2007 to 2011 and the other is defined as pre-convergence period from 2002 to 2006. The two periods provide a cumulative of −5 and +5 years of convergence experience with 3,000 firm-year observations for the study. All financial and accounting data are collected from Thomson One databases. The sample firms are from a wide range of industries, with most in consumer discretionary, financials, industrials, IT and energy among others.

Research Design

Our design comprises of both accrual-based earnings measures and real earnings activities between the two countries and across the IFRS adoption periods. We differentiate between discretionary accruals and real earnings as these activities may be affected by the regulatory environments existing in both countries. We further applied the difference-in-difference analysis to check the impact of the regulatory environments on earnings management between the two countries. We also mitigated for the impact of cross-listing activities on our result by composing a control group of firms that are indigenous to both China and Hong Kong which are not cross-listed in both countries. This enables us to check for any other factors that might be correlated with cross-listing decision which might affect accounting data (Lang et al., 2006).

Earnings Management Metrics

We apply earnings smoothing, timely loss recognition, value relevance as well as managing towards earnings targets as measures of earnings management (Ball & Shivakumar, 2005; Barth et al., 2008; Lang et al., 2006).

According to prior research, higher earnings quality is an indication of less earning management or less earnings smoothing. Earnings management can be evaluated from two perspectives: earnings smoothing and managing reported earnings towards a positive objective. Based on Barth et al. (2008), we chose control variables that are associated with China convergence with IFRS and that might affect financial reporting. These include firms' size, growth, capital structure, debt and equity issuing and auditors.

Earnings Smoothing: The first earnings smoothing approach is to measure the volatility of earnings. If firms maximise their earnings opportunities, their earning variability should be lower than firms with less earning management. Therefore, following prior studies, the fluctuation in reported earnings is measured by the change in annual net income (scaled by annual total assets). The reported earnings can be sensitive to a series of other factors that are non-attributable to mandatory introduction of IFRS. Although in this study, a number of control variables and industry fixed effects identified in previous studies (Barth et al., 2008; Christensen, Lee, & Walker, 2008; Lang et al., 2006) can mitigate these confounding factors to some extent, the effect of those factors may still remain. Therefore, the analysis is mainly focused on the residuals generated from the relevant regression rather than on the reported earnings themselves. This approach further differentiates our study from previous research in earnings management.

Industry fixed-effect regression is conducted in the estimation (Eqs. (1)–(6)). The firm-year observations are first pooled for the periods between 2002 and 2006 (pre-convergence) and the period between 2007 and 2011 (post-convergence). Then, the regression (Eq. (1)) is run separately for the firms in both time periods to obtain a set of residuals. Finally, the variance of the residuals (ΔNI*) are computed for the firms in the two periods and the difference compared with the variance ratio *F*-test (Lang et al., 2006).

Regression of ΔNI on the control variables is stated as:

$$\Delta NI_{it} = \alpha_0 + \alpha_1 SIZE_{it} + \alpha_2 GROWTH_{it} + \alpha_3 EISSUE_{it} + \alpha_4 DISSUE_{it} + \alpha_5 TURN_{it} + \alpha_6 LEV_{it} + \alpha_7 CFO_{it} + \alpha_8 AUD_{it} + \varepsilon_{it} \quad (1)$$

where for firm *i* in year *t:* ΔNI = change in annual net income scaled by total assets; SIZE = natural logarithm of total assets; GROWTH = percentage change in revenues; EISSUE = percentage change in common shareholders' equity; DISSUE = percentage change in total liabilities; TURN = revenues divided by total assets; LEV = total liabilities divided by book value of equity; CFO = annual net cash flow from operating activities divided by total assets; AUD = dummy variable taking the value of 1 when the firm's auditor is one of the Big Four accounting firms, that is, PwC, KPMG, E&Y, or D&T, and 0 otherwise.

Despite a wide range of control variables included in Eq. (1), the variability of earnings may not be captured by those variables. As suggested by Lang et al. (2006), firm-specific factors connected with the underlying volatility of cash flow may still impact on the variance of earnings. Typically, when there are more fluctuated cash flows, firms should expect a more volatile net income. Therefore, the second earnings smoothing measure extends the analysis of the first measure by benchmarking it against the volatility of cash flows. This involves calculating the ratio of the variability of the change in net income to the variability of cash flow.

Similar to the first measure, the regression of the change in net income scaled by total assets (ΔNI) and the regression of change in operating cash flow scaled by total assets (ΔCF) is run on the same set of control variables identified in the first metric separately. Then, residuals from these two regressions are obtained accordingly. The ratio is based on the variance of those residuals. ΔNI* is residuals from the regression of ΔNI on the control variables (Eq. (1)) and ΔCF* is residuals from the regression of ΔCF on the control variables (Eq. (2)). The regression of ΔCF on the control variables is represented as:

$$\Delta CF_{it} = \alpha_0 + \alpha_1 SIZE_{it} + \alpha_2 GROWTH_{it} + \alpha_3 EISSUE_{it} + \alpha_4 DISSUE_{it} + \alpha_5 TURN_{it} + \alpha_6 LEV_{it} + \alpha_7 CFO_{it} + \alpha_8 AUD_{it} + \varepsilon_{it} \quad (2)$$

As proposed by Leuz et al. (2003), firms are expected to manipulate reported earnings by utilising accruals and smooth fluctuations of cash flow streams. A negative relationship between accruals and cash flows should exist due to this effect on accounting accruals. Thus, the third earning smoothing metric is the Spearman correlation between accruals and cash flows. Correlations between cash flow residuals (CF*) and accruals residuals (ACC*), rather than correlations between cash flow and accruals, are used in this study. Consistent with the previous two measures, the residuals are regressed from Eqs. (3) and (4) on the similar control variables. *Ceteris paribus*, a larger magnitude of negative correlation between accruals and cash flows means earnings smoothing and poor earnings quality.

Regression of CFO on the control variables is represented as:

$$\begin{aligned}\mathrm{CFO}_{it} = {} & \alpha_0 + \alpha_1 \mathrm{SIZE}_{it} + \alpha_2 \mathrm{GROWTH}_{it} + \alpha_3 \mathrm{EISSUE}_{it} + \alpha_4 \mathrm{DISSUE}_{it} \\ & + \alpha_5 \mathrm{TURN}_{it} + \alpha_6 \mathrm{LEV}_{it} + \alpha_7 \mathrm{CFO}_{it} + \alpha_8 \mathrm{AUD}_{it} + \varepsilon_{it} \end{aligned} \tag{3}$$

Regression of ACC on the control variables is represented as:

$$\begin{aligned}\mathrm{ACC}_{it} = {} & \alpha_0 + \alpha_1 \mathrm{SIZE}_{it} + \alpha_2 \mathrm{GROWTH}_{it} + \alpha_3 \mathrm{EISSUE}_{it} + \alpha_4 \mathrm{DISSUE}_{it} \\ & + \alpha_5 \mathrm{TURN}_{it} + \alpha_6 \mathrm{LEV}_{it} + \alpha_7 \mathrm{CFO}_{it} + \alpha_8 \mathrm{AUD}_{it} + \varepsilon_{it} \end{aligned} \tag{4}$$

where $\mathrm{ACC}_{it} = \mathrm{NI}_{it} - \mathrm{CF}_{it}$.

After generating the residuals of CFO and ACC from above regressions, Spearman correlation *rho* can be computed for the firms in the two periods. Then, the study compares the correlations to evaluate a change in the earnings smoothing behaviour after IFRS convergence and further assesses the level of earnings smoothing in the different economies.

Managing Earnings towards a Positive Target: The last earnings management metric is to test managing towards small positive earnings (SPOS). It is argued that managers have incentive to report small positive earnings instead of negative earnings. Moreover, the frequency of reporting small positive net income is higher for firms operating in poor investor protection environment (Leuz et al., 2003). Following prior studies (Barth et al., 2008; Lang et al., 2006), we examine the frequency of small positive earnings. Dummy variable for SPOS is set to one if annual net income (scaled by total assets) is between 0 and 0.01, and equal to zero otherwise. We examine the probability of firms reporting small positive earnings change after transiting to IFRS, by interpreting the SPOS coefficient from the following regressions:

$$\text{Period}(0, 1)_{it} = \alpha_0 + \alpha_1 \text{SIZE}_{it} + \alpha_2 \text{GROWTH}_{it} + \alpha_3 \text{EISSUE}_{it} + \alpha_4 \text{DISSUE}_{it} + \alpha_5 \text{TURN}_{it} + \alpha_6 \text{LEV}_{it} + \alpha_7 \text{CFO}_{it} + \alpha_8 \text{AUD}_{it} + \alpha_9 \text{SPOS}_{it} + \varepsilon_{it} \quad (5)$$

$$\text{IFRS}(0, 1)_{it} = \alpha_0 + \alpha_1 \text{SIZE}_{it} + \alpha_2 \text{GROWTH}_{it} + \alpha_3 \text{EISSUE}_{it} + \alpha_4 \text{DISSUE}_{it} + \alpha_5 \text{TURN}_{it} + \alpha_6 \text{LEV}_{it} + \alpha_7 \text{CFO}_{it} + \alpha_8 \text{AUD}_{it} + \alpha_9 \text{SPOS}_{it} + \varepsilon_{it} \quad (6)$$

When comparing pre-convergence and post-convergence period, we analyse the regression of an indicator variables period and IFRS (0, 1) equals one for the pre-convergence period and zero for post-convergence period (Eqs. (5) and (6)). A negative coefficient on SPOS would indicate the level at which firms report small positive earnings. When comparing for A-share firms and Hong Kong listed firm in the post-convergence period, IFRS (0, 1) is set to one for Hong Kong listed firms and zero for A-share firms.

Timely Loss Recognition: Timeliness implies that once the managers notice economic losses, they should report the losses as soon as possible rather than wait passively and allowing the effect to spread over time. This is an important measurement for accounting quality. Based on Basu (1997) and Lang et al. (2006), our study focus on investigating the relationship between timeliness of accounting income and stock return to determine the timely loss recognition. The underlying concern is to measure whether accounting income can capture the market information in a timely fashion.

Thus, we examine the reverse regressions of reported earnings on a series of independent variables, which include stock return, an indicator variable for negative return and the interaction of return with the indicator variable (Eq. (7)). The magnitude of the coefficient on the interaction of stock return with indicator variable can be explained as measurement for timeliness of loss recognition (Lang et al., 2006). Comparing pre- and post-periods, a larger coefficient of the firms will indicate that such firms recognise losses more timely. The regression of earnings on returns is expressed as:

$$\text{NIPS}_{it} = \alpha_0 + \alpha_1 \text{RETURN}_{it} + \alpha_2 \text{BAD}_{it} + \alpha_3 \text{RETURN}_{it} * \text{BAD}_{it} + \varepsilon_{it} \quad (7)$$

where NIPS = net income per share deflated by the price at the beginning of the period; BAD (0, 1) = dummy variable taking on 1 for firm i with negative returns in year t and 0 otherwise; RETURN = the natural logarithm of the ratio of the stock price six months after fiscal year-end to the stock price six months before fiscal year-end, adjusted for dividends and stock splits.

Value Relevance: High value relevance should be reflected as higher association between accounting numbers such as net income, equity book value and market-based information such as share prices, which suggests that accounting data is informative. Following Barth, Beaver, and Landsman (2001), value relevance is constructed in two metrics; price model and return model.

The first value relevance metric is based upon the explanatory power of the regression of share price on net income and equity book value. This is measured by R^2 value of the price regression (Eq. (8)). In order to provide sufficient time for accounting and financial information absorbed by market, six months share price after the fiscal year-end is used following prior studies (Barth et al., 2001). Furthermore, to control the effect of differences across industries which may influence the explanatory power, share price is first regressed on industry fixed effects (SIC codes) to derive the price residuals. Then the regression of price residuals P^* is run on equity book value per share (BVEPS) and net income per share (NIPS) separately in the pre- and post-IFRS convergence periods. *Ceteris paribus*, a higher R^2 value would suggest that firms are expected to have a higher association between share price and accounting data. The regression of price residuals P^* on BVEPS and NIPS is:

$$P^*_{it} = \beta_0 + \beta_1 \text{BVEPS}_{it} + \beta_2 \text{NIPS}_{it} + \varepsilon_{it} \quad (8)$$

where P = share price six months after the fiscal year-end date; P^* = residuals from a regression of P on industry fixed effects; BVEPS = book value of equity per share; NIPS = annual net income per share.

The second value relevance metric, the return model, is based on the approach of timely loss recognition to test the association between earnings and returns. In Eq. (9), accounting earnings are defined as dependent variable and returns are defined as independent variable. The relationship between these two variables may be strong if firms report losses in timely manner, indicating that more earning information reflects in the market when the losses occur. As suggested by prior studies (Ball et al., 2000; Barth et al., 2008; Basu, 1997), the analysis is not limited to the case of losses (negative return). Stock returns are separated into two cases:

negative return and non-negative return. Thus, value relevance is examined by comparing explanatory power (R^2 value) from regressions of net income per share on annual stock return for both cases.

Similar to the price model, net income per share divided by beginning of year price (NI/*P*) is first regressed on industry fixed effects to obtain the residuals of NI/*P* ([NI/*P*]*). Then, regressions are run separately for companies with 'good news' (non-negative annual share returns) and companies with 'bad news' (negative annual share returns) (Ball et al., 2000; Barth et al., 2008; Basu, 1997). Good news observations represent those for which RETURN is non-negative while bad news observations represent those for which RETURN is negative. After pooling all observations in relevant groups, regressions are run separately for A-share companies and Hong Kong listed companies for both 'good news' and 'bad news' in the two respective periods. Higher R^2 values for both cases imply higher level of value relevance.

Where the regression of [NI/*P*]* on RETURN:

$$[\mathrm{NI}/P]^*_{it} = \beta_0 + \beta_1 \mathrm{RETURN}_{it} + \varepsilon_{it} \tag{9}$$

where NI/*P* = annual net income per share scaled by share price at the beginning of fiscal year; [NI/*P*]* = residuals from a regression of NI/*P* on industry fixed effects; RETURN = the natural logarithm of the ratio of the stock price six months after fiscal year-end to the stock price six months before fiscal year-end, adjusted for dividends and stock splits.

Real Earnings Management and Discretionary Accrual Management

We further examined whether regulatory environment has an impact on real and accrual-based earnings management of firms in China and Hong Kong by comparing the financial results in pre and post-adoption periods. We argue that firms from stronger regulatory environments may curb accrual-based earnings management but may or may not allow real earnings management. Roychowdhury (2006) finds that firms engage in real earnings management to avoid reporting losses. Using similar variables in Roychowdhury (2006) and Cohen and Zarowin (2010), we estimate real earning manipulations using abnormal cash flows from operation, production cost, and discretionary expenses. The cash flow from operation include the annual revenue, the production costs is the sum of goods sold while the discretional expenses comprise advertising expenses, research and development, selling, general and administrative expenses. The abnormality is measured by the deviations in the predicted values of the industry.

We measured discretionary accrual as the difference between total accruals (earnings before extraordinary items and discontinued operations[3]) less normal accruals, defined as

$$\mathrm{DA}_{it} = \left(\frac{\mathrm{TA}_{it}}{\mathrm{Assets}_{i,t-1}}\right)^{-} \mathrm{NA}_{it} \tag{10}$$

where TA_{it} = is the total accruals which is defined as the $\mathrm{EBXI}_{it} - \mathrm{CFO}_{it}$ of firm i and time t; DA_{it} = discretionary accrual of firm i and time t. EBXI is the earnings before extraordinary items and continued operations, CFO is the operating cash flows from continuing operations and $\mathrm{Assets}_{i,t-1}$ represents total assets.

NA_{it} = normal accruals is measured as

$$K_1 \frac{1}{\mathrm{Assets}_{i,t-1}} + K_2 \frac{\Delta \mathrm{Sales}_{it}}{\mathrm{Assets}_{it}} + K_3 \frac{\mathrm{PPE}_{it}}{\mathrm{Assets}_{i,t-1}}$$

Thus, our combined discretionary accrual model is:

$$\mathrm{DA}_{it} = \left(\frac{\mathrm{EBXI}_{it} - \mathrm{CFO}_{it}}{\mathrm{Assets}_{i,t-1}}\right) - \left(K_1 \frac{1}{\mathrm{Assets}_{i,t-1}} + K_2 \frac{\nabla \mathrm{Sales}_{it}}{\mathrm{Assets}_{it}} + K_3 \frac{\mathrm{PPE}_{it}}{\mathrm{Assets}_{it}}\right) + \mathrm{SC}_{i,t} \tag{11}$$

Using discretionary accruals allows us to control for industry-wide changes in economic conditions that affect total accruals. Prior studies on earnings management (Cohen & Zarowin, 2010; Dechow, Kothari, & Watts, 1998) have shown that these areas are susceptible to manipulation by firms. For example, Roychowdhury (2006) finds that unusually low cash flow and discretionary expenses (which includes advertising cost) and unusually high production costs exhibited by firms are likely signals of earnings manipulations.

Hypotheses Development

Given the rapid development of Chinese economy and capital market, IFRS can be expected to be relevant to China. Regulators expect that

IFRS adoption can contribute to great advantages, one of which is improved financial reporting quality.[4]

As there are significant differences in terms of economy, regulatory and legal systems between mainland China and Hong Kong, we compare the financial reporting quality of Hong Kong firms listed in mainland China with Chinese listed firms in Hong Kong and examine whether there are significant differences in financial reporting quality under IFRS regime operating in different regulatory environments.

According to prior studies, accounting quality is higher in countries with a common law origin and high protection of shareholder. In sum, it is reasonable to hypothesise that the financial reporting quality in terms of earning management, timely loss recognition and value relevance will improve after substantially converging with IFRS. Therefore, the hypotheses are formulated as follows:

H1. Earning management has significantly decreased following substantial convergence with IFRS in China and Hong Kong.

H2. The regulatory environments have significant impact on firms' manipulations of real earnings and discretionary accruals in China and Hong Kong.

H3. Financial reporting quality is higher for Chinese companies cross-listed in the Hong Kong stock exchange than for Hong Kong companies that are cross-listed in mainland China.

DISCUSSION OF RESULTS

Descriptive Results

Table 1 presents the descriptive statistics of the sample variables for Chinese A-share firms and Hong Kong listed firms in the convergence period. A comparison of the sample firms reveals that the mean and median for all non-dummy test variables are significantly different, with the exception of change in operation cash flows (ΔCF). The change in net income (ΔNI) decreases in Hong Kong listed firms with negative mean and median, which are −0.0141 and −0.0028, respectively. On the contrary, A-share firms have experienced an increase in ΔNI (positive mean). It can be seen also that the book value of equity per share

Table 1. Descriptive Statistics of A-Share Firms in Pre- and Post-Period.

	Chinese A-Shares Firms			Hong Kong Listed Firms		
	Mean	Median	Std. Dev.	Mean	Median	Std. Dev.
Test variables						
ΔNI	0.0005	−0.0003	0.1563	−0.0141*	−0.0028*	0.2083***
ΔCF	−0.0051	−0.0058	0.1295	0.0001	−0.0009	0.0975***
CFO	0.0424	0.0441	0.1030	0.0306	0.0289***	0.0855***
ACC	−0.0044	−0.0131	0.1283	0.7155***	0.0041***	4.0143***
SPOS	0.1330	0.0000	0.3397	0.1425	0.0000	0.3498
Price	11.8801	9.3050	8.2173	15.0745**	2.7200***	26.6984***
BVEPS	3.3512	2.8050	2.1672	14.6308***	3.2012	25.8241***
NIPS	0.3046	0.2050	0.4278	1.4776***	0.1766	13.1752***
NI/P	0.0242	0.0236	0.0517	1.7059***	0.0713***	12.4935***
RETURN	−0.0151	−0.0326	0.3757	−0.0168	−0.0140**	0.3903
Control variables						
SIZE	8.4664	8.4033	1.1976	8.7979	8.4212	2.1624***
GROWTH	0.2618	0.1393	0.9417	0.3870	0.0691***	2.5063***
EISSUE	0.2416	0.0783	2.0944	0.2210	0.0885	1.0666***
DISSUE	0.3150	0.1259	2.6644	0.5560	0.0582***	3.9273***
TURN	0.7650	0.5762	0.7534	0.3916***	0.1947***	0.5097***
LEV	1.4280	1.1860	2.9218	0.9688**	0.4723***	6.3831***
CFO	0.0424	0.0441	0.1030	0.0306	0.0289***	0.0855***
AUD	0.1250	0.0000	0.3309	0.6800***	1.0000***	0.4671***

*, **, *** indicate significant difference from pre-adoption and post-adoption at the 10%, 5% and 1% confidence level, respectively (one-sided).

(BVEPS) is substantially larger for Hong Kong sample firms that for A-share sample firms. Both the Hong Kong listed firms and the Chinese A-share firms have negative stock returns of −0.0168 and −0.0151, respectively, in the post-convergence period, though the mean difference is not significant.

Although the size of both groups of sample firms is similar, the Hong Kong listed firms have higher growth than the A-share firms. However, the test statistics do not uncover significant difference in growth between the two groups. Further, the result demonstrates that A-shares firms have higher probability to issue debt than Hong Kong listed firms (median difference is significant). At the same time, it is highly leveraged for the A-shares firms compared to the Hong Kong firms, and the mean of leverage ratio is 1.4280 and 0.9688, respectively (both mean and median differences are significant). Finally, the Hong Kong listed firms are more likely to be audited by the Big four auditors (AUD), which implies that Hong Kong has more professionals and better audit environment.

Empirical Results

Table 2 presents a comparison of financial reporting quality metrics using earnings management, timely loss recognition and value relevance for firms listed in Chinese A-share market before and after substantial convergence with IFRS. The results reveal that the firms exhibit less earnings management, more timely loss recognition. Furthermore, the reported accounting and financial figures are more value relevant since 2007 (i.e. after convergence), which is consistent with the predictions. This result makes IFRS adoption itself a contingent factor for obtaining a high quality financial reporting system.

Panel A (Table 2) compares earnings management metrics of A-share firms between pre- and post-convergence periods. The first three earnings management measures report on the residuals after regressing each dependent variable on a specific set of control variables. The first finding suggests that Chinese A-share firms exhibit a substantially higher volatility in net income (ΔNI*) than in the post-period, that is 0.0236 versus 0.0058 and the

Table 2. Financial Reporting Quality Measures Analysis of Chinese A-Share Firms.

	Predict	Pre	Post	Diff.
Panel A: Earning management metrics				
Variability of ΔNI*	Post > Pre	0.0236	0.0058***	0.0178
Variability of ΔNI*/ΔCF*	Post > Pre	0.7749	2.3561	1.5812
Correlation of ACC* and CFO*	Post > Pre	−0.7568	−0.8214	−0.0646
Small positive net income (SPOS)		−0.0881##		
Panel B: Timely loss recognition metrics				
RETURN*BAD coefficient	Post > Pre	0.0069	0.0292**	0.0223
Panel C: Value relevance metrics (R^2)				
Price model	Post > Pre	0.1260	0.2437*	0.1177
RETURN model				
Good news	Post > Pre	0.0009	0.0573*	0.0564
Bad news	Post > Pre	0.0018	0.0039	0.0021

*, **, *** indicate significant difference from pre-adoption and post-adoption at the 10%, 5% and 1% confidence level, respectively (one-sided). ## indicates significantly different from zero at the 5% level (one-sided).

difference is statistically significant at the 0.01 level. This finding is consistent with the prediction that the reporting earnings for Chinese A-share firms are more volatile since 2007.

The second earnings management metric, the volatility of change in operating cash flow is examined on the same controlled variable as the first metric. Similar to the first result, the finding indicates that the ratio of the variability of change in net income, ΔNI*, to the variability of the change in cash flow, ΔCF*, is higher in the post-convergence period than that in pre-convergence period. The ratio changes from 0.7749 in pre-adoption period to 2.3561 and cash flow variability is similar for the two samples, which suggests that it is not the higher volatility in cash flows that leads to the higher earnings variability in the post-convergence period. The high difference of 1.5812 confirms the existence of earnings smoothing in the earlier result.

However, the third metric, the correlation between accruals and cash flows after convergence (−0.8214) is more negative than before adoption (−0.7568), though the difference is not significant. This finding contrasts with the prediction that A-shares firms have a significantly less negative correlation between accruals and cash flows in the post-convergence period. This result however indicates that A-firms engage in smoothing as managers increase accruals to make up for poor cash flow (Liu et al., 2011).

Finally, the fourth earning management metric analyses the regression of small positive net income on control variables. The result reveals that there is a significant negative coefficient (−0.0881) for small positive net income, SPOS, which suggests that A-share firms are more likely to manage earnings towards positive target after substantially converging with IFRS.

Taken together, these results are consistent with our predictions, that Chinese listed firms engage less in earnings smoothing in the post-convergence period than in the pre-convergence period. The results depict the positive impact of IFRS in improving the quality of financial reporting.

Panel B (Table 2) compares measures of timely loss recognition between two periods. Based on Lang et al. (2006), reported earnings are regressed on returns, a bad news earnings indicator, and the interaction of the two variables. It is suggested that more timely loss recognition will result in a larger coefficient estimate on bad news earnings in the regression. The coefficient of RETURN*BAD is 0.0292 in the post-period, significantly higher than that in pre-period (0.0069). This finding indicates that managers in A-shares firms are more likely to report large losses in timely fashion since the companies adopt substantially IFRS-convergent standard.

Panel C presents the results of value relevance tests. The price model is to test the level of association between accounting number and share price. The regression of share price on earnings per share and book value of equity demonstrates a significantly higher R^2 in post-adoption period (24.37%) than pre-convergence period (12.60%). For the return model, the sample is separated into two categories based on good news and bad news. The R^2 of the regression of earnings per share on good news (bad news), 5.73% (0.39%), is also higher in post-adoption period than that in pre-adoption period, 0.09% (0.18%). These findings indicate that value relevance of accounting data has improved after substantially convergent with IFRS for Chinese A-shares firms, which is consistent with our prediction.

Table 3 presents results comparing the quality of financial reporting for firms listed in Hong Kong before and after the IFRS regime. The results are mostly consistent with the prediction that the accounting quality is higher for Hong Kong listed firms than A-share firms. It reveals that Hong Kong listed firms experience less earning management, more timely loss recognition and more value relevance of accounting and financial information.

In terms of earnings management, Hong Kong listed firms exhibit a significantly low variability of change in net income, ΔNI*, a negligible difference of 0.0018 after the IFRS convergence. The second metric of earning management is the ratio of the variance of change in net income, ΔNI*,

Table 3. Financial Reporting Quality Analysis of Hong Kong Firms.

	Predict	Pre	Post	Diff.
Panel A: Earning management metrics				
Variability of ΔNI*	Post > Pre	0.0218	0.0236***	0.0018
Variability of ΔNI*/ΔCF*	Post > Pre	2.3561	2.3871	0.031
Correlation of ACC* and CFO*	Post > Pre	−0.0821	−0.0830***	−0.0009
Small positive net income (SPOS)		−0.03898##		
Panel B: Timely loss recognition metrics				
RETURN*BAD coefficient	HK > A share	0.0292	0.7171***	0.6879
Panel C: Value relevance metrics (R^2)				
Price model	HK > A share	0.2437	0.6208***	0.3771
RETURN model				
Good news	HK > A share	0.0573	0.0023	−0.055
Bad news	HK > A share	0.0039	0.0002	0.0037

*** indicate significant difference from pre-adoption and post-adoption at the 1% confidence level, respectively (one-sided). ## indicates significantly different from zero at the 5% level (one-sided).

to variance of change in cash flow, ΔCF*, which shows a difference of 0.031. The negligible figure of the difference indicates that firms engage less in earnings management. This is consistent with the first finding of low volatility in earnings. The correlation between accruals, ACC*, and cash flow, CFO*, for firms listed in Hong Kong firms is −0.0830, significantly less negative than the pre-adoption ratio (−0.0821). The coefficient on SPOS, −0.3898, is negative, which suggests that Hong Kong firms are less likely to manage earnings in both periods. Overall, the findings for earning management provide evidence that firms listed in Hong Kong have higher accounting quality than A-share firms in the form of less earnings smoothing behaviour.

Lang et al. (2006) argue that more timely loss recognition will result in a larger coefficient estimate on bad news earnings in the regression of earnings on returns. The coefficient of RETURN*BAD is larger for Hong Kong listed firms in the post-convergence period, 0.7171 versus 0.0292, suggesting that large losses are reported in timely manner by Hong Kong listed firms in the post-convergence period.

In terms of value relevance, regression of price on net income and equity book value reveals that the R^2 for firms listed in Hong Kong is significantly larger than that for A-shares firms, which are 62.08% and 24.37%, respectively. However, contrary to the prediction, the R^2 value for good news and bad news in return model is lower for firms listed in Hong Kong. Thus, the price regression suggests that accounting data are more value relevant for firms listed in Hong Kong than A-share firms while the return model findings do not. Overall, these result lay credence to the contingency theory as the effective management of earnings is, as observed above, contingent upon the regulatory environment and IFRS adoption (post-IFRS).

Sensitivity Analyses – Real versus Accrual-Based Earnings Management

The consideration for the sensitivity analyses is that the regulatory environment may be influential in the earnings management behaviour of firms. Prior studies argue that firms may engage in real earnings management to avoid reporting annual losses (Roychowdhury, 2006), but may not manipulate earnings through discretionary accruals. We argue that firms from stronger regulatory environments may curb accrual-based earnings management and intolerant to real earnings management, which can also be affected by the regulatory environment.

Therefore, segmenting the firms into two regulatory environments that is Chinese firms in Hong Kong and vice versa and differentiating the earnings management practices into real and accrual-based will help to clarify whether such practices are influenced by the regulatory environments.

The results shown in Table 4 indicate that firms listed in China are more likely to engage in accrual-based earnings management than in real earnings management activities even after the converging with IFRS. Abnormal cash flows from operations and discretionary expenses are significantly negative (−0.025 and −0.040) in both periods indicating that real earnings manipulations are less tolerated particularly after the convergence. Conversely, Hong Kong firms tolerate some forms of real earnings management such as abnormal cash flows from operations and abnormal discretionary expenses as both show positive significance of 0.579 and 0.088 but would not condoned accrual-based manipulations such as discretionary accruals. These results indicate that the leverage on forms of earnings manipulations used by firms in the two regions is affected by the operational and regulatory environment. For Hong Kong firms, the negative significance with discretionary accruals earning management activities indicates that such practices remotely occur.

The results demonstrate that different earnings management practices that are tolerable in one country may not be the case in another which is largely affected by the level of regulations. Cross-listed firms tend to imbibe the earnings management culture of their environment. For instance, firms

Table 4. Result of the Real versus Accrual-Based (Discretionary) Earnings Management of China and Hong Kong Firms.

Cross-Listed Firms	China		Hong Kong	
	Pre	Post	Pre	Post
Discretionary (accrual-based) accruals	0.018***	0.322***	−1.241**	−0.010**
	(0.019)	(0.153)	(−0.012)	(−0.003)
Abnormal cash flows from operations	−0.005*	−0.025*	0.102**	0.579***
	(−0.214)	(−0.002)	(0.017)	(0.196)
Abnormal production costs	−0.060	−0.077	−0.060	−0.102
	(−0.008)	(−0.007)	(−0.201)	(−0.187)
Abnormal discretionary expenses	−0.032**	−0.040**	0.11**	0.088**
	(−0.014)	(−0.172)	(0.015)	(0.098)

Notes: The accrual-based earnings are discretionary accruals while the real earnings activities include abnormal cash flows from operations, production cost and discretionary expenses of the firms.

***significant at the 1% level, **significant at the 5% level, *significant at the 10% level.

from countries where the regulations are strict, if cross-listed in weakly regulated environments are likely to lower their financial reporting quality. Therefore, we can conclude that the control of earning management practices is contingent upon the strength of a country's regulatory environment.

Further Robust Check

To check that our results on real and discretionary earnings management are consistent with our prediction that regulatory environment influence earnings management practices, we run the same regression on set of non-cross-listed firms. Lin and Liu (2009) show that regulatory controls can be critical in adhering to financial reporting standards or engaging in earnings manipulation activities. Thus, we argue that non-cross-listed Chinese firms are more likely to engage in accrual-based earnings manipulation as they operate under a less strict control environment. As such, Chinese firms, cross-listed in Hong Kong and therefore outside the Chinese regulatory authorities are expected to conform to the standards measurable with Hong Kong firms and thus likely to engage in some forms of real earning management.

The results as presented in Table 5 are consistent with our hypothesis that Chinese indigenous firms are more likely to engage in discretionary accruals than in accrual-based earnings management. Conversely, we find that Hong Kong firms are more prone to engaging in real earnings management though at a lesser degree since the IFRS convergence.

Table 5. Robust Check – Non-Cross-Listed Firms.

Non-Listed Firms	China		Hong Kong	
	Pre	Post	Pre	Post
Discretionary (accrual-based) accruals	0.272***	0.283***	−1.287***	−3.686***
	(0.052)	(0.035)	(−0.186)	(−0.363)
Abnormal cash flows from operations	−0.235**	−0.203*	0.405**	0.579**
	(−0.023)	(−0.031)	(0.063)	(0.196)
Abnormal production costs	0.142**	0.526**	0.046*	0.121*
	(0.047)	(0.057)	(0.020)	(0.037)
Abnormal discretionary expenses	−0.282**	−0.625***	0.014**	0.015**
	(−0.024)	(−0.093)	(0.078)	(0.028)

*, **, *** indicate significant difference from pre-adoption and post-adoption at the 10%, 5% and 1% confidence level, respectively (one-sided).

Table 6. Difference-in-Difference Analysis.

	Pre-IFRS Adoption	Post-IFRS Adoption	Mean Difference
China	17.56	20.21	2.65
Hong Kong	13.74	15.03	1.29
	3.82	5.18	0.36*

*significant at the 10% level and indicates the difference in regulatory environment of China and Hong Kong after the adoption period.

Difference-in-Difference Analysis

To further examine the impact of the regulatory environment on IFRS adoption between China and Hong Kong, we conduct a difference-in-difference (DID) test. The DID test is applied here for three reasons: first to compare the influence of IFRS on the management of earnings in the pre- and post-IFRS adoption in both countries. Second, it allows us to cater for differences in regulatory environments in the two countries and third, it is used to check for the endogeneity problem of omitted variables associated with our sample selection.[5]

The DID analysis is based on the mean aggregate of the earnings management variables and the result presented in Table 6 shows a greater reduction in the earnings management of Chinese firms more than in Hong Kong firms. This is remarkable as the mean difference shows a remarkable significance of 0.36, indicating the positive influence of IFRS on the quality of financial reporting in China than in Hong Kong.

CONCLUSION

Our results reveal that Chinese firms exhibit less earning management, more timely loss recognition and the reported accounting and financial figures are more value relevant since 2007, which is consistent with the predictions. The results are consistent with prior studies which indicate that Chinese listed firms engage less in earnings smoothing in the post-convergence period than in the pre-convergence period. The results depict the positive impact of IFRS in improving the quality of financial reporting thereby making IFRS adoption (post-IFRS) a strong contingent factor for high quality financial reporting (with effective control of earning management). This is also consistent with prior studies which suggest that there is more earning management and lower value relevance in weaker investor protection environments (Leuz et al., 2003).

The findings are also consistent with the prediction that the accounting quality is higher for Hong Kong listed firms than for Chinese firms. It shows that Hong Kong listed firms experience less earning management, more timely loss recognition and more value relevance of accounting and financial information. Our results suggest that large losses are reported in timely manner by Hong Kong listed firms in the post-convergence period. Similarly, the results of real and discretionary accrual measures reveal that different earnings management practices can be tolerable in one country and not in another, largely due to the level of regulations. In addition, cross-listed firms tend to follow culture in their environment.

Our study reveals that the regulatory environment influence earnings management practices as firms from strong and stricter regulatory environments are seen to be tolerant to certain earnings manipulations if cross-listed in less regulatory environments. The DID analysis indicates a greater reduction in the earnings managements of Chinese firms after the IFRS convergence indicating the positive impact of the IFRS on the quality of financial reporting in China than in Hong Kong. Through the frame of the contingency theory, therefore, these results confirm a country's institutional structures, its extent of regulation and the strength of its investor protection environments as strong contingent factors that determine the quality of financial reporting capable of effectively controlling earning management practices. The foregoing results and the emerging contingent factors should be able to guide financial reporting regulators and standard setters as well as policy-makers within relevant government agencies in their efforts in curbing the incidence of earnings management practices. They will also guide government policies, as in the case of China, towards strengthening financial reporting systems.

Notwithstanding the relevance and adoption of the contingency theory in this study, the theory has been criticised by a number of writers. For example, Schoonhoven (1981) opined that contingency theory is an orienting strategy (or meta-theory) rather than a theory in the conventional sense. He therefore suggested its use as an underlying conceptual framework upon which other perspectives can be applied. Similarly, Scott (1987, pp. 507–509) observed that unless combined with another theory, contingency theory standing alone cannot offer a whole understanding of the different roles carried out by various management practices (in the forms of control and coordination) that are used in modern organisations. As such, we suggest that future research could explore combining institutional theory with the contingency theory with a view to drawing out institutional factors that may influence the effectiveness of the contingent factors identified in the current study. Also, it will be interesting to see how these results might change if the earning management metrics are altered – an idea that might worth exploring by future studies on the subject.

NOTES

1. Hong Kong and China operate a 'one country, two systems' governance model. Although Hong Kong is considered relatively dependent of China, they both have different and independent regulatory, political and institutional frameworks (Loh, 2006).
2. For details on real and accrual-based earnings management activities metrics by firms, see Cohen et al. (2008).
3. The discretionary accrual approach applied in our study is consistent with Cohen and Zarowin (2010), we have presented the abridged cross-sectional model (see also Jones, 1991).
4. See EC Regulation No. 1606/2002.
5. Gordon et al. (2012) apply similar approach in testing the endogeneity issues of self – selection of adoption of IFRS adoption between developed and developing economies.

ACKNOWLEDGEMENTS

We wish to thank Abu Shiraz Abdul-Rahaman of Haskayne School of Business, University of Calgary; Marcia Annisette of Schulich School of Business, York University, Canada and Sailesh Tanna of Coventry University Business School for their supports and suggestions which have improved the current version of the paper.

REFERENCES

Avkiran, N. K. (2011). Association of DEA super-efficiency estimates with financial ratios: Investigating the case for Chinese banks. *Omega*, *39*(3), 323–334.

Bailey, D., Harte, G., & Sugden, R. (2000). Corporate disclosure and the deregulation of international investment. *Accounting, Auditing & Accountability Journal*, *13*(2), 197–218.

Ball, R., Kothari, S. P., & Robbin, A. (2000). The effect of international institutional factors on properties of accounting earnings. *Journal of Accounting and Economics*, *29*, 1–51.

Ball, R., & Shivakumar, L. (2005). Earnings quality in UK private firms: Comparative loss recognition timeliness. *Journal of Accounting and Economics*, *39*, 83–128.

Barth, M., Landsman, W., & Lang, M. (2008). International accounting standards and accounting quality. *Journal of Accounting Research*, *46*, 467–498.

Barth, M. E., Beaver, W. H., & Landsman, W. R. (2001). The relevance of the value relevance literature for accounting standard setting: Another view. *Journal of Accounting & Economics*, *39*, 77–104.

Bartol, K. M., & Martin, D. C. (1994). *Management* (2nd ed.). New York, NY: McGraw-Hill.

Basu, S. (1997). The conservatism principle and the asymmetric timeliness of earnings. *Journal of Accounting and Economics*, *24*, 3–37.

Chen, J., & Peng, C. (2007). The impact of regulatory enforcement on harmonization of accounting practices: Evidence from China. *Journal of Contemporary Accounting and Economics*, *3*(1), 58–71.

Chen, S., Wang, Y., & Zhao, Z. (2009). Regulatory incentives for earnings management through assets impaired reversals in China. *Journal of Accounting, Auditing and Finance*, *24*, 589–620.

Chin, C. L., Chen, Y. J., & Hsieh, T. J. (2009). International diversification, ownership structure, legal origin, and earnings management: Evidence from Taiwan. *Journal of Accounting, Auditing and Finance*, *24*, 233–362.

Christensen, H. B., Lee, E., & Walker, M. (2008). *Incentives or standards: What determines accounting quality changes around IFRS adoption*? Working Paper. Manchester Business School. Retrieved from https://research.mbs.ac.uk/investment-risk/Portals/0/docs/ChristensenLeeWalker2008-IncentivesStandards.pdf. Accessed on September 13, 2013.

Cohen, D., Dey, A., & Lys, T. (2008). Real and accrual based management in the pre and post Sarbanes Oxley periods. *The Accounting Review*, *83*, 757–787.

Cohen, D. A., & Zarowin, P. (2010). Accrual-based and real earnings management activities around seasoned equity offerings. *Journal of Accounting and Economics*, *50*, 2–19.

Dechow, P., Kothari, S. P., & Watts, R. (1998). The relationship between earnings and cash flows. *Journal of Accounting and Economics*, *25*, 133–168.

Dechow, P. M., & Skinner, D. J. (2000). Earnings management: Reconciling the views of accounting academics, practitioners, and regulators. *Accounting Horizons*, *14*, 235–250.

Dechow, P. M., Sloan, R. G., & Sweeney, A. P. (1995). Detecting earnings management. *The Accounting Review*, *70*(2), 193–225.

Fang, F., & Zhou, H. (2012). Institutional ownership, internal control, and disclosure transparency. In J. Jay Choi & H. Sami (Eds.), *Transparency and governance in a global world* (Vol. 13, pp. 11–37). International Finance Review. Bingley, UK: Emerald Group Publishing Limited.

Gopalan, R., & Jayaraman, S. (2012). Private control benefits and earnings management: Evidence from insider controlled firms. *Journal of Accounting Research*, *50*(1), 117–159.

Gordon, L. A., Loeb, M. P., & Zhu, W. (2012). The impact of IFRS adoption on foreign direct investment. *Journal of Accounting and Public Policy*, *31*(4), 374–398.

Gordon, L. A., & Miller, D. (1976). A contingency framework for the design of accounting information systems. *Accounting, Organizations and Society*, *1*(1), 59–69.

Gul, F. A., & Chia, Y. M. (1994). The effects of management accounting systems, perceived environmental uncertainty and decentralization on managerial performance: A test of three-way interaction. *Accounting, Organizations and Society*, *19*(4–5), 413–426.

Gupta, P. P., Dirsmith, M. W., & Fogarty, T. J. (1994). Coordination and control in a government agency: Contingency and institutional perspectives on GAO audits. *Administrative Science Quarterly*, *39*(2), 264–285.

Hayes, D. C. (1977). The contingency theory of managerial accounting. *The Accounting Review*, (January), *52*(1), 22–39.

Healy, P. M., & Wahlen, J. M. (1999). A review of the earnings management literature and its implications for standard setting. *Accounting Horizons*, *13*(4), 365–383.

Hopwood, A. G. (1983). On trying to study accounting in the contexts in which it operates. *Accounting, Organizations and Society*, *8*(2–3), 287–305.

Jones, J. (1991). Earnings management during import relief investigations. *Journal of Accounting Research*, *29*, 193–228.

Kim, M. S. (2012). Corporate transparency of business group firms in the absence of internal market benefits. In J. Jay Choi & H. Sami (Eds.), *Transparency and governance in a global world* (Vol. 13, pp. 39–67). International Finance Review. Bingley, UK: Emerald Group Publishing Limited.

Lang, M., Raedy, J., & Wilson, W. (2006). Earnings management and cross-listing: Are reconciled earnings comparable to US earnings? *Journal of Accounting and Economics*, *42*, 255–283.

Laurenceson, J., & Qin, F. (2008). Has minority foreign investment in China's banks improved their cost efficiency? *China & World Economy*, *16*, 57–74.

Lawrence, P. R., & Lorsch, J. W. (1967). Differentiation and integration in complex organizations. *Administrative Science Quarterly*, *12*(1), 1–47.

Lee, C. W. (2001). Financial restructuring of state owned enterprises in China: The case of Shanghai Sunve Pharmaceutical Corporation. *Accounting, Organisation and Society*, *26*, 673–689.

Leuz, C., Nanda, D., & Wysocki, P. D. (2003). Earnings management and investor protection: An international comparison. *Journal of Financial Economics*, *69*, 505–527.

Li, S. (2010). Does mandatory adoption of international financial standards in the European Union reduce the cost of equity capital? *The Accounting Review*, *85*(2), 607–636.

Lin, Z. J., & Chen, F. (2005). Value relevance of international accounting standards harmonisation: Evidence from A-and B-share markets in China. *Journal of International Accounting, Auditing and Taxation*, *14*, 79–103.

Lin, Z. J., & Liu, M. (2009). The impact of corporate governance on auditor choice: Evidence from China. *Journal of International Accounting, Auditing, and Taxation*, *18*, 44–59.

Liou, F. M., & Yang, C. H. (2008). Predicting business failure under the existence of fraudulent financial reporting. *International Journal of Accounting and Information Management*, *16*, 74–86.

Liu, C. H., Yao, L. J., Hu, N., & Liu, L. (2011). The impact of IFRS on accounting quality in a regulated market: An empirical study of China. *Journal of Accounting, Auditing and Finance*, *26*(4), 659–676.

Loh, C. (2006). Hong Kong's relationship with China: The future of 'one country, two systems'. *Social Research*, *7*(1), 293–299.

Lopez-Gavira, R., & Omoteso, K. (2013). Perceptions of the use of virtual learning environments in accounting education: A comparative evaluation of undergraduate accounting students in Spain and England. *Accounting Education: An International Journal*, *22*(5), 445–466.

Lüder, K. G. (1992). A contingency model of governmental accounting innovations in the political administrative environment. *Research in Governmental and Nonprofit Accounting*, *7*, 99–127.

Nicolaou, A. I. (2000). A contingency model of perceived effectiveness in accounting information systems: Organizational coordination and control effects. *International Journal of Accounting Informational Systems*, *1*(2), 91–105.

Omoteso, K. (2013). *Audit effectiveness: Meeting the IT challenge*. Hampshire: Gower.

Otley, D. T. (1980). The contingency theory of management accounting: Achievement and prognosis. *Accounting Organizations and Society*, *5*(4), 413–428.

Peng, S. (2005). *The harmonization of Chinese accounting standards with international accounting standards: An empirical evaluation*. Doctor dissertation, Virginia Commonwealth University.

Peng, S., & Bewley, K. (2010). Adaptability to fair value accounting in an emerging economy. *Accounting, Auditing & Accountability Journal*, *23*(8), 982–1011.

Peng, S., & Smith, J. L. (2010). Chinese GAAP and IFRS: An analysis of the convergence process. *Journal of International Accounting, Auditing and Taxation*, *19*, 16–34.

Piotroski, J., & Wong, T. J. (2012). Institutions and the information environment of Chinese listed firms. In J. Fan & R. Morck (Eds.), *Capitalizing China* (pp. 201–248). Chicago, IL: NBER and University of Chicago Press.

Piotroski, J., Wong, T. J., & Zhang, T. (2014). Political incentives to suppress negative financial information: Evidence from Chinese listed firms. *China-Europe Conference: Transparency, economic institutions and governance* (July 2014). Hosted by Erasmus University, Rotterdam.

Rayburn, J. M., & Rayburn, L. G. (1991). Contingency theory and the impact of new accounting technology in uncertain hospital environments. *Accounting, Auditing and Accountability Journal*, *4*(2), 55–75.

Roychowdhury, S. (2006). Earnings management through real activities manipulation. *Journal of Accounting and Economics*, *42*, 335–370.

Schoonhoven, C. B. (1981). Problems with contingency theory: Testing assumptions hidden within the language of contingency 'Theory'. *Administrative Science Quarterly*, *26*(3), 349–377.

Schweikart, J. A. (1992). Cognitive-contingency theory and the study of ethics in accounting. *Journal of Business Ethics*, *11*(5–6), 471–478.

Scott, W. R. (1987). *Organisations, rational, natural and open systems* (2nd ed.). London: Prentice Hall.

Street, D. L., & Gray, S. J. (2002). Factors influencing the extent of corporate compliance with international accounting standards: Summary of a research monograph. *Journal of International Accounting, Auditing and Taxation*, *11*, 51–76.

Thomas, A. P. (1986). The contingency theory of corporate reporting: Some empirical Evidence. *Accounting, Organizations and Society*, *11*(3), 253–270.

Thomas, A. P. (1991). Towards a contingency theory of corporate financial reporting systems. *Accounting, Auditing & Accountability Journal*, *4*(4), 40–57.

Wang, Y., & Campbell, M. (2012). Earnings management comparison: IFRS vs. China GAAP. *International Management Review*, *8*(1), 5–11.

Wong, M. C., & Cheung, Y. L. (1999). The practice of investment management in Hong Kong: Market forecasting and stock selection. *Omega, International Journal of Management Science*, *27*, 451–465.

Wood, S. (1979). A reappraisal of the contingency approach to organization. *Journal of Management Studies*, *16*(October), 334–354.

Xiao, J. Z., Dyson, J. R., & Powell, P. L. (1996). The impact of information technology on corporate financial reporting: A contingency perspective. *The British Accounting Review*, *28*(3), 203–227.

Zhang, Y., Andrew, J., & Rudkin, K. (2012). Accounting as an instrument of neoliberalisation? Exploring the adoption of fair value accounting in China. *Accounting, Auditing & Accountability Journal*, *25*(8), 1266–1289.

PART IV
FISCAL POLICY AND DEBT MANAGEMENT

DEBT SUSTAINABILITY ANALYSIS FOR EMERGING AND DEVELOPING MARKETS: AN APPLICATION ON TRANSITION COUNTRIES

İbrahim Ünalmış

ABSTRACT

In this paper, we derive debt sustainability conditions for emerging and developing countries. Since most of these countries have foreign debt, that is, they have the so-called original sin problem, our calculations take into account both domestic and foreign debt. Our setup can be used to evaluate the short-term fiscal stance of a government. Using this setup, we analyze the post crisis fiscal adjustment in transition countries, namely Armenia, Azerbaijan, Georgia, Kazakhstan, Kyrgyz Republic, Moldova, Tajikistan, Turkmenistan, Ukraine, and Uzbekistan. Our findings suggest that country performances are rather mixed and the pace of debt accumulation in some of these countries should be monitored closely.

Keywords: Fiscal policy; emerging markets; sustainability analysis; transition countries

Neo-Transitional Economics
International Finance Review, Volume 16, 279–297

ISSN: 1569-3767/doi:10.1108/S1569-376720150000016012

INTRODUCTION

In the literature on debt sustainability analysis, the common approach to assess the sustainability of the debt stock of a country is the stationarity tests on fiscal debt and deficits. However, these tests are backward looking and they don't represent the future policy stance of the governments. As pointed out by Polito and Wickens (2005), fiscal sustainability tests are relying on the dynamic properties of debts and deficits and assume that these processes will continue in the infinite future and compare the present value of the future primary surpluses with the current debt stock of the government. As they point out, there are certain problems with this approach. First of all, there is a possibility that using the long data series may lead to the rejection of sustainability in the tests when the current fiscal policy is sustainable. Therefore, a test result which indicates an unsustainable fiscal policy doesn't necessarily mean that the current fiscal policy of the government is unsustainable. In addition, while tests indicate an unsustainable fiscal policy, if the markets believe that the government will eventually take the necessary measures for sustainable fiscal policies, the government can continue to borrow. Therefore, practical relevance of these tests is questionable. In particular, there is a problem with this approach for emerging and developing countries. Since these countries do not have long time series of data, this methodology is not suitable for them.

In line with these arguments, we use a more transparent and forward looking approach adopted from Polito and Wickens (2005) to assess the fiscal stance of a government. The method that they propose is easy to compute and does not depend on a particular theoretical model. However, the approach used by Polito and Wickens (2005) is more relevant for advanced economies since the government obligations of those countries are generally in domestic currency. However, most of the emerging market governments borrow in both foreign and domestic currencies. Obviously, having obligations in foreign currency, called "original sin," makes the total debt stock of the government vulnerable to exchange rate movements. Therefore, we modify the Polito and Wickens approach by separating the total debt stock into foreign and domestic components.

Using the framework that we develop, we test fiscal stance of the countries that are members of the Commonwealth of Independent States (CIS). At the early development stages, many emerging markets have faced with debt sustainability problems, such as Brazil, Mexico, and Turkey. CIS countries are no exception. During the early times of the transition process, they have accumulated significant amount of foreign debt. Fig. 1 shows

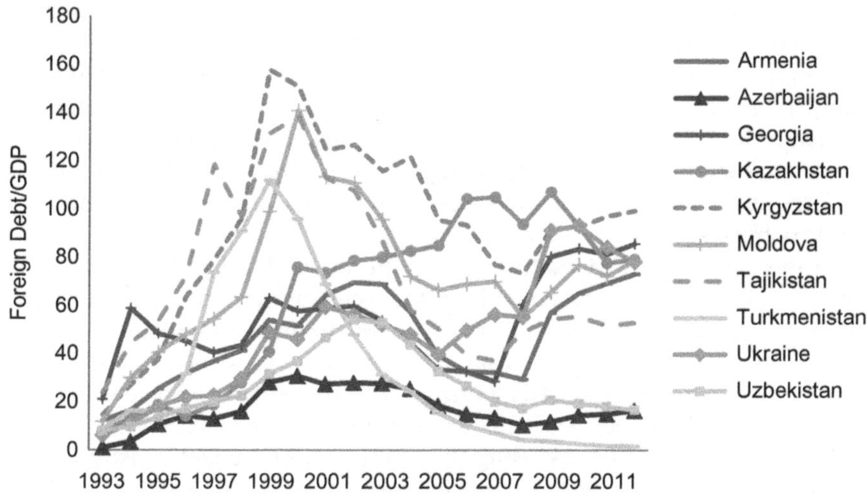

Fig. 1. Foreign Debt/GDP Ratio in CIS Countries.

that CIS countries had almost zero foreign debt in 1992 but they rapidly increased their foreign debt to finance current account deficits. Remarkably, foreign debt stock of Kyrgyzstan, Moldova, Tajikistan, and Turkmenistan has exceeded 100 percent of their GDP in 2000. Azerbaijan is an exception as it exports natural resources to finance its current imports. Although these countries have reduced their foreign debt stock in the later period, their rapid debt accumulation process in the 1990s shows that fiscal stance of these countries should be monitored closely to control the excessive debt accumulation which in turn could prevent them from a fiscal crisis. In addition, these countries would probably adopt in the near future rather complicated monetary policies, that is, inflation targeting (Armenia has already been implementing inflation targeting policy since 2006). As indicated by Benigno and Woodford (2006), appropriateness of the inflation targeting as a policy recommendation may depend critically on the nature of fiscal policy. Sims (2003) argues that fiscal policies of some of the emerging market countries might lead to a failure of the inflation targeting policy. This is due to the existence of fiscal dominance in some emerging market countries which prevent the achievement of rational expectations equilibrium and the inflation target. He also asserts that in such a case, trying to implement inflation targeting policy may lead to less stability than could have been achieved through other alternative policies. The reason is basically the following: If there is a certain degree of fiscal dominance in the country, then any interest rate rise to control the inflation will bring an additional cost to the Treasury. Therefore, fiscal authorities should be ready to raise enough primary budget surpluses in order to finance the burden of higher borrowing cost. Otherwise, rising debt stock could lead to the deterioration of inflation expectations since higher debt stock ultimately requires even higher price increases than would have been needed for stable debt stock levels.

In this paper, we first outline the conditions under which domestic and foreign debt stocks are sustainable in the long run. Second, using forward looking framework, we show how to assess the fiscal stance of a government in the short run. Third, using this framework, we analyze the fiscal developments in some the CIS countries after the global financial crisis.

The rest of the paper is organized as follows. In the next section, we set up the analytical framework using the intertemporal budget constraint. We outline the possible cases of constant and variable discount rates. After this, we analyze short-term debt dynamics of transition countries. The last section concludes.

THE ANALYTICAL FRAMEWORK

The analytical framework depends on the nominal intertemporal government budget constraint (GBC). We assume that primary budget deficit is financed by domestic and foreign borrowing and money creation.

$$P_t g_t + \left(1 + R_t^d\right) B_{t-1}^d + \left(1 + R_t^f\right) B_{t-1}^f S_t = B_t^d + B_t^f S_t + \Delta M_t + P_t T_t \qquad (1)$$

where P_t is the price level, g_t is the real government expenditure including real transfers to households, T_t is the total real taxes, and M_t is the nominal money stock, B_t^d is the nominal value of government bonds issued in domestic currency at the end of period t, B_t^f is the nominal value of government bonds issued in foreign currency at the end of period t, S_t is the nominal exchange rate, R_t^d and R_t^f are average interest rate on domestic and foreign currency bonds, issued at the end of period $t-1$ respectively. $R_t^d B_{t-1}^d$ represents the total interest payments of the domestic debt stock for the period t and $R_t^f B_{t-1}^f S_t$ represents the total interest payments of the foreign debt stock in domestic currency for the period t. Hence, the left-hand side of the equation shows the nominal expenditures in period t and the right-hand side of the equation shows the available resources for the government to pay its expenditures.

In order to find the real GBC, we divide Eq. (1) by P_t:

$$g_t + \left(1+R_t^d\right)\frac{P_{t-1}}{P_t}\frac{B_{t-1}^d}{P_{t-1}} + \left(1+R_t^f\right)\frac{P_{t-1}}{P_t}\frac{B_{t-1}^f}{P_{t-1}}S_t = \frac{B_t^d}{P_t} + \frac{B_t^f}{P_t}S_t + \frac{M_t}{P_t} - \frac{P_{t-1}}{P_t}\frac{M_{t-1}}{P_{t-1}} + T_t \tag{2}$$

We define inflation as $\pi_t = \frac{\Delta P_t}{P_{t-1}}$, real stock of domestic and foreign government debts as $b_t^d = \frac{B_t^d}{P_t}$ and $b_t^f = \frac{B_t^f}{P_t}$, real money stock as $m_t = \frac{M_t}{P_t}$, and real interest rate as $(1+r_t) = \frac{(1+R_t)}{(1+\pi_t)}$. We can write Eq. (2) as:

$$g_t + \left(1+r_t^d\right)b_{t-1}^d + \left(1+r_t^f\right)b_{t-1}^f S_t = b_t^d + b_t^f S_t + m_t - \frac{1}{(1+\pi_t)}m_{t-1} + T_t \tag{3}$$

Dividing Eq. (3) by y_t, we get the GBC proportional to the real GDP:

$$\frac{g_t}{y_t} + \frac{\left(1+R_t^d\right)}{(1+\pi_t)(1+\gamma_t)}\frac{b_{t-1}^d}{y_{t-1}} + \frac{\left(1+R_t^f\right)(1+\%\Delta S_t)}{(1+\pi_t)(1+\gamma_t)}\frac{b_{t-1}^f}{y_{t-1}}S_{t-1} = \frac{b_t^d}{y_t} + \frac{b_t^f}{y_t}S_t + \frac{m_t}{y_t} - \frac{1}{(1+\pi_t)(1+\gamma_t)}\frac{m_{t-1}}{y_{t-1}} + \frac{T_t}{y_t} \tag{4}$$

We define the nominal public sector borrowing requirement (PSBR) as

$$P_t D_t = P_t g_t + R_t^d B_{t-1}^d + R_t^f B_{t-1}^f S_t - P_t T_t - \Delta M_t \tag{5}$$

Dividing Eq. (5) by $p_t y_t$, we get the real PSBR:

$$\frac{D_t}{y_t} = \frac{g_t}{y_t} + \frac{\left(1+R_t^d\right)}{(1+\pi_t)(1+\gamma_t)}\frac{b_{t-1}^d}{y_{t-1}} + \frac{\left(1+R_t^f\right)(1+\%\Delta S_t)}{(1+\pi_t)(1+\gamma_t)}\frac{b_{t-1}^f}{y_{t-1}}S_{t-1} - \frac{m_t}{y_t} + \frac{1}{(1+\pi_t)(1+\gamma_t)}\frac{m_{t-1}}{y_{t-1}} - \frac{T_t}{y_t} \tag{6}$$

In addition, PSBR is equal to the change in government debt stock between time t and $t-1$. Hence:

$$\frac{D_t}{y_t} = \frac{b_t^d}{y_t} + \frac{b_t^f}{y_t} S_t - \frac{1}{(1+\pi_t)(1+\gamma_t)} \frac{b_{t-1}^d}{y_{t-1}} + \frac{(1+\%\Delta S_t)}{(1+\pi_t)(1+\gamma_t)} \frac{b_{t-1}^f}{y_{t-1}} S_{t-1} \tag{7}$$

If we subtract the interest payments of domestic and foreign debt stock from the nominal PSBR, we get the primary balance:

$$P_t d_t = P_t D_t - R_t^d B_{t-1}^d - R_t^f B_{t-1}^f S_t \tag{8}$$

Dividing the nominal primary balance with the nominal GDP, we get:

$$\frac{d_t}{y_t} = \frac{D_t}{y_t} - \frac{R_t^d}{(1+\pi_t)(1+\gamma_t)} \frac{b_{t-1}^d}{y_{t-1}} - \frac{R_t^f(1+\%\Delta S_t)}{(1+\pi_t)(1+\gamma_t)} \frac{b_{t-1}^f}{y_{t-1}} S_{t-1} \tag{9}$$

By using Eqs. (7) and (9), primary balance to output ratio can be written as

$$\begin{aligned}\frac{d_t}{y_t} = {} & \frac{b_t^d}{y_t} + \frac{b_t^f}{y_t} S_t - \frac{1}{(1+\pi_t)(1+\gamma_t)} \frac{b_{t-1}^d}{y_{t-1}} - \frac{(1+\%\Delta S_t)}{(1+\pi_t)(1+\gamma_t)} \frac{b_{t-1}^f}{y_{t-1}} S_{t-1} \\ & - \frac{R_t^d}{(1+\pi_t)(1+\gamma_t)} \frac{b_{t-1}^d}{y_{t-1}} - \frac{R_t^f(1+\%\Delta S_t)}{(1+\pi_t)(1+\gamma_t)} \frac{b_{t-1}^f}{y_{t-1}} S_{t-1}\end{aligned} \tag{10}$$

Rewriting Eq. (10) gives us

$$\frac{b_t^d}{y_t} + \frac{b_t^f}{y_t} S_t = \frac{d_t}{y_t} + \frac{(1+R_t^d)}{(1+\pi_t)(1+\gamma_t)} \frac{b_{t-1}^d}{y_{t-1}} + \frac{\left(1+R_t^f\right)(1+\%\Delta S_t)}{(1+\pi_t)(1+\gamma_t)} \frac{b_{t-1}^f}{y_{t-1}} S_{t-1} \tag{11}$$

This is a nonlinear difference equation in $\frac{b_t^d}{y_t}$ and $\frac{b_t^f}{y_t}$. If we define

$$(1+\rho_t^d) = \frac{(1+R_t^d)}{(1+\pi_t)(1+\gamma_t)} \quad \text{and} \quad (1+\rho_t^f) = \frac{\left(1+R_t^f\right)(1+\%\Delta S_t)}{(1+\pi_t)(1+\gamma_t)}$$

then Eq. (11) becomes

$$\frac{b_t^d}{y_t} + \frac{b_t^f}{y_t}S_t = \frac{d_t}{y_t} + \left(1+\rho_t^d\right)\frac{b_{t-1}^d}{y_{t-1}} + \left(1+\rho_t^f\right)\frac{b_{t-1}^f}{y_{t-1}}S_{t-1} \tag{12}$$

Fiscal Sustainability

Conventional methods use Eq. (12) while assessing the sustainability of fiscal policies of a country. The idea is that whether the total debt, $\frac{b_t^d}{y_t} + \frac{b_t^f}{y_t}S_t$, remains finite or explodes over time. These methods can be divided into two, according to their assumption on whether the discount rate is constant or time varying.

Constant Discount Rate

Suppose discount rates are constant and domestic and foreign debts evolve according to following equations:

$$\frac{b_t^d}{y_t} = \frac{d_t^d}{y_t} + \left(1+\rho^d\right)\frac{b_{t-1}^d}{y_{t-1}} \tag{13}$$

$$\frac{b_t^f}{y_t} = \frac{1}{S_t}\frac{d_t^f}{y_t} + \left(1+\rho^f\right)\delta^f\frac{b_{t-1}^f}{y_{t-1}} \tag{14}$$

where $\delta^f = \frac{S_{t-1}}{S_t}$ and constant over time.

Since they are first-order difference equations, sustainable solutions for $\frac{b_{t-1}^d}{y_{t-1}}$ and $\frac{b_{t-1}^f}{y_{t-1}}$ depend on their coefficients.

Case 1a: $\left(1+\rho^d\right)<1$ and $\left(1+\rho^f\right)\delta^f<1$ (stable case)

If $\frac{\left(1+R_t^d\right)}{(1+\pi_t)(1+\gamma_t)}<1$, then Eq. (13) is a stable difference equation and can be solved backwards by successive substitution. Then, the expected value of the debt-GDP ratio in *n* period's time conditional on information at time *t* is

$$E_t\left(\frac{b_{t+n}^d}{y_{t+n}}\right) = \left(1+\rho^d\right)^n\frac{b_t^d}{y_t} + \sum_{s=0}^{n-1}\left(1+\rho^d\right)^{n-s}E_t\left(\frac{d_{t+s}^d}{y_{t+s}}\right) \tag{15}$$

We take the limit of Eq. (15) as $n \to \infty$.

Since $lim_{n\to\infty}\left(1+\rho^d\right)^n \frac{b_t^d}{y_t}=0$,

$$\lim_{n\to\infty} E_t\left(\frac{b_{t+n}^d}{y_{t+n}}\right) = \lim_{n\to\infty}\sum_{s=0}^{n-1}\left(1+\rho^d\right)^{n-s}E_t\left(\frac{d_{t+s}^d}{y_{t+s}}\right) \tag{16}$$

Eq. (16) can be interpreted as follows: The evolution of debt stock doesn't depend on the current debt stock but future primary balances. Suppose that $\frac{d_t^d}{y_t}$ is stochastic but is expected to grow at the rate λ such that

$$E_t\left(\frac{d_{t+s}^d}{y_{t+s}}\right) = (1+\lambda)^s\frac{d_t^d}{y_t} \tag{17}$$

Then

$$\begin{aligned}\lim_{n\to\infty} E_t\left(\frac{b_{t+n}^d}{y_{t+n}}\right) &= \lim_{n\to\infty}\sum_{s=1}^{n}\left(1+\rho^d\right)^{n-s}(1+\lambda)^s\frac{d_t^d}{y_t}\\ &= \lim_{n\to\infty}\left(\frac{(1+\lambda)^n-\left(1+\rho^d\right)^n}{\lambda-\rho}\right)(1+\lambda)\frac{d_t^d}{y_t}\end{aligned} \tag{18}$$

For example, if $\lambda=0$ then

$$= -\frac{1}{\rho}\frac{d_t^d}{y_t} \tag{19}$$

If both ρ and λ are less than zero, then $lim_{n\to\infty}E_t\left(\frac{b_{t+n}^d}{y_{t+n}}\right)=0$. When $\lambda<0$, $\frac{d_t^d}{y_t}$ will be $I(0)$ process and expected value of the long run debt to GDP ratio is zero. If $\lambda>0$, as can be seen from Eq. (18), debt to GDP ratio will explode. However, when $\lambda=0$, $\frac{d_t^d}{y_t}$ is a non-stationary process; hence, $\frac{b_t^d}{y_t}$ will also be $I(1)$ process. As indicated by Polito and Wickens, $\frac{b_t^d}{y_t}$ and $\frac{d_t^d}{y_t}$ will be cointegrated with the cointegrating vector $\left(1,\frac{1}{\rho}\right)$. As the debt to GDP ratio doesn't grow over time, it can be said that fiscal policy is sustainable.

Case 1b: $\left(1+\rho^f\right)\delta^f<1$

If $\frac{\left(1+R_t^f\right)(1+\%\Delta S_t)}{(1+\pi_t)(1+\gamma_t)}\frac{S_{t-1}}{S_t}<1$, then Eq. (14) is a stable difference equation and can be solved by backwards induction.

$$E_t\left(\frac{b^f_{t+n}}{y_{t+n}}\right) = ((1+\rho^f)\delta^f)^n \frac{b^f_t}{y_t} + \sum_{m=1}^{n} ((1+\rho^f)\delta^f)^{n-m} E_t\left(\frac{1}{S_{t+m}}\frac{d^f_{t+m}}{y_{t+m}}\right) \quad (20)$$

Taking the limit of Eq. (20) as $n \to \infty$, we get

$$\lim_{n\to\infty} ((1+\rho^f)\delta^f)^n \frac{b^f_t}{y_t} = 0$$

Hence

$$\lim_{n\to\infty} E_t\left(\frac{b^f_{t+n}}{y_{t+n}}\right) = \lim_{n\to\infty} \sum_{m=1}^{n} ((1+\rho^f)\delta^f)^{n-m} E_t\left(\frac{1}{S_{t+m}}\frac{d^f_{t+m}}{y_{t+m}}\right) \quad (21)$$

Again, the long run debt stock is not related with the current debt stock. However, in foreign debt stock case, the primary balances in terms of foreign currency determines the evolution of debt stock. Suppose that $\frac{d^f_t}{y_t}$ is stochastic but is expected to grow at the rate λ such that

$$E_t\left(\frac{d^f_{t+m}}{y_{t+m}}\right) = (1+\lambda)^m \frac{S_{t+m}}{S_t}\frac{d^f_t}{y_t} \quad (22)$$

$$\begin{aligned}
\lim_{n\to\infty} E_t\left(\frac{b^f_{t+n}}{y_{t+n}}\right) &= \lim_{n\to\infty} \sum_{m=1}^{n} ((1+\rho^f)\delta^f)^{n-m} (1+\lambda)^m \frac{1}{S_t}\frac{d^f_t}{y_t} \\
&= \lim_{n\to\infty} \sum_{m=1}^{n} ((1+\rho^f)\delta^f)^n \left(\frac{(1+\lambda)}{((1+\rho^f)\delta^f)}\right)^m \frac{1}{S_t}\frac{d^f_t}{y_t} \\
&= \lim_{n\to\infty} ((1+\rho^f)\delta^f)^n \frac{(1+\lambda)}{((1+\rho^f)\delta^f)} \sum_{m=0}^{n-1} \left(\frac{(1+\lambda)}{((1+\rho^f)\delta^f)}\right)^m \frac{1}{S_t}\frac{d^f_t}{y_t} \\
&= \lim_{n\to\infty} (1+\lambda)\left[\frac{((1+\rho^f)\delta^f)^n - (1+\lambda)^n}{((1+\rho^f)\delta^f - (1+\lambda))}\right] \frac{1}{S_t}\frac{d^f_t}{y_t}
\end{aligned} \quad (23)$$

If $\lambda = 0$, then

$$\lim_{n\to\infty} E_t\left(\frac{b^f_{t+n}}{y_{t+n}}\right) = -\frac{1}{\delta^f - \rho^f \delta^f - 1}\frac{1}{S_t}\frac{d^f_t}{y_t} = -\frac{1}{\rho^f}\frac{1}{S_{t-1}}\frac{d^f_t}{y_t} \tag{24}$$

If $\delta^f + \delta^f \rho^f < 1$ and λ is less then whatever the initial exchange rate and primary balance is, in the long run foreign debt stock goes to zero, $lim_{n\to\infty} E_t\left(\frac{b^f_{t+n}}{y_{t+n}}\right) = 0$. If $\lambda > 0$, as can be seen from Eq. (23), debt to GDP ratio will explode. However, $\frac{d^f_t}{y_t}$ is a non-stationary process when $\lambda = 0$; hence, $\frac{b^f_t}{y_t}$ will also be $I(1)$ process. As indicated by Polito and Wickens, $\frac{b^f_t}{y_t}$ and $\frac{d^f_t}{y_t}$ will be cointegrated with the cointegrating vector $\left(1, \frac{1}{\rho S_{t-1}}\right)$. As the debt to GDP ratio doesn't grow over time, it can be said that fiscal policy is sustainable.

Case 2a: $(1 + \rho^d) > 1$ (unstable case)

When $0 < \frac{(1+\pi_t)(1+\gamma_t)}{(1+R^d_t)} < 1$, then Eq. (13) is an unstable difference equation; hence, it must be solved forwards as follows.

$$\frac{b^d_t}{y_t} = -\frac{1}{(1+\rho^d)}E_t\left(\frac{d^d_{t+1}}{y_{t+1}}\right) + \frac{1}{(1+\rho^d)}E_t\left(\frac{b^d_{t+1}}{y_{t+1}}\right) \tag{25}$$

$$\frac{b^d_t}{y_t} = \left(1+\rho^d\right)^{-n} E_t\left(\frac{b^d_{t+n}}{y_{t+n}}\right) - \sum_{s=0}^{n}\left(1+\rho^d\right)^{-s} E_t\left(\frac{d^d_{t+s}}{y_{t+s}}\right) \tag{26}$$

If we take the limit of Eq. (26) as $n\to\infty$

$$\lim_{n\to\infty}\left(1+\rho^d\right)^{-n} E_t\left(\frac{b^d_{t+n}}{y_{t+n}}\right) = 0 \tag{27}$$

Eq. (27) represents the transversality condition and if it holds then

$$\frac{b^d_t}{y_t}\sum_{s=1}^{n}\left(1+\rho^d\right)^{-s} E_t\left(\frac{-d^d_{t+s}}{y_{t+s}}\right) \tag{28}$$

Eq. (28) can be interpreted as follows: If a country's fiscal policy is sustainable then the present value of current and future primary surpluses must be equal to or higher than the current debt stock.

Suppose, again, that $\frac{d_t^d}{y_t}$ evolves according to Eq. (17).

$$\frac{b_t^d}{y_t} = \sum_{s=1}^{\infty} (1+\rho^d)^{-s}(1+\lambda)^s\left(-\frac{d_t^d}{y_t}\right)$$

If λ and ρ meet the requirements of $-1<\lambda<\rho, \rho>0$

$$= \frac{(1+\lambda)}{\rho-\lambda}\left(-\frac{d_t^d}{y_t}\right) \tag{29}$$

Eq. (29) implies that present value of future primary surpluses is sufficient to pay off the current debt stock. However, debt stock grows at the same rate of primary surplus.

Case 2b: $(1+\rho^f)\delta^f>1$ (unstable case)

If $\frac{(1+R_t^f)(1+\%\Delta S_t)}{(1+\pi_t)(1+\gamma_t)}\frac{S_{t-1}}{S_t}>1$, then Eq. (14) is an unstable difference equation and can be solved by forwards.

$$\frac{b_t^f}{y_t} = ((1+\rho^f)\delta^f)^{-n}E_t\left(\frac{b_{t+n}^f}{y_{t+n}}\right) - \sum_{m=1}^{n} ((1+\rho^f)\delta^f)^{-m}E_t\left(\frac{1}{S_{t+m}}\frac{d_{t+m}^f}{y_{t+m}}\right) \tag{30}$$

In order to get the transversality condition, we take the limit of Eq. (30) as $n\rightarrow\infty$; hence, as long as $(1+\rho^f)\delta^f>1$, the following transversality condition holds:

$$\lim_{n\rightarrow\infty} ((1+\rho^f)\delta^f)^{-n}E_t\left(\frac{b_{t+n}^f}{y_{t+n}}\right)=0$$

As a result, we have the following relation between current foreign debt stock and future primary surpluses in terms of foreign currency:

$$\frac{b_t^f}{y_t} = \sum_{m=1}^{\infty} ((1+\rho^f)\delta^f)^{-m}E_t\left(-\frac{1}{S_{t+m}}\frac{d_{t+m}^f}{y_{t+m}}\right) \tag{31}$$

Eq. (31) implies that present value of future primary surpluses in terms of foreign currency must be equal to the current foreign debt stock. Unlike the usual debt stock analysis, we have currency mismatch problem here. In other words, assuming that the country earns enough foreign exchange in order to pay the foreign debt, generating enough primary surpluses is not the only parameter in sustainability analysis. However, we assume that exchange rate is purely forecastable in this case. If the future exchange rate is not certain, assessing sustainability of foreign debt stock will get more complicated.

Suppose that $\frac{d_t^f}{y_t}$ follows the rule in Eq. (22). Then,

$$\frac{b_t^f}{y_t} = \frac{(1+\lambda)}{((1+\rho^f)\delta^f)} \sum_{m=0}^{\infty} \left(\frac{(1+\lambda)}{((1+\rho^f)\delta^f)} \right)^m \left(-\frac{1}{S_t} \frac{d_t^f}{y_t} \right)$$

$$\frac{b_t^f}{y_t} = \left(\frac{(1+\lambda)}{(1+\rho^f)\delta^f - (1+\lambda)} \right) \left(-\frac{1}{S_t} \frac{d_t^f}{y_t} \right) \tag{32}$$

In this case, ratio of exchange rates between t and $t-1$ is a variable together with the growth rate of the primary surplus and discount rate. If $-1 < \lambda$, $(1+\rho^f)\delta^f > 0$, and $(1+\rho^f)\delta^f > (1+\lambda)$, then the present value of future primary surpluses meets the current debt obligations.

Time-Varying Discount Rate

These tests are invalid due to the fact that discount rate is time varying. As long as $\rho_t^d < 0$ and $\frac{d_t^d}{y_t}$ is stationary, then the domestic debt stock will remain finite. However, in the case of foreign debt, discount rate, $(1+\rho^f)\delta^f$, must be less than one and primary surplus in terms of foreign currency must be stationary. In the following sections, we analyze the sustainability of foreign and domestic debt when the Eqs. (13) and (14) are unstable difference equations.

Case 1: $\rho_t^d > 0$

Again we solve Eq. (13) forwards.

$$\frac{b_t^d}{y_t} = E_t\left(\left(\prod_{m=1}^{n} \frac{1}{(1+\rho_{t+m}^d)} \right) \frac{b_{t+n}^d}{y_{t+n}} \right) - E_t\left[\sum_{m=1}^{n} \left(\prod_{i=1}^{m} \frac{1}{(1+\rho_{t+i}^d)} \right) \left(\frac{d_{t+m}^d}{y_{t+m}} \right) \right] \tag{33}$$

Here, the critical question is whether $\prod_{m=1}^{n} \frac{1}{(1+\rho_{t+m}^d)}$ is less than or equal to one, $\prod_{m=1}^{n} \frac{1}{(1+\rho_{t+m}^d)} \leq 1$, for all $m \geq 1$. If it is the case, the transversality condition holds. Hence,

$$\lim_{n\to\infty} E_t\left(\left(\prod_{m=1}^{n}\frac{1}{(1+\rho^d_{t+m})}\right)\frac{b^d_{t+n}}{y_{t+n}}\right)=0 \tag{34}$$

As a result, Eq. (33) can be written as

$$\frac{b^d_t}{y_t}=E_t\left[\sum_{m=1}^{n}\left(\prod_{i=1}^{m}\frac{1}{(1+\rho^d_{t+i})}\right)\left(-\frac{d^d_{t+m}}{y_{t+m}}\right)\right] \tag{35}$$

Interpretation of Eq. (35) is very similar to Eq. (28). Sustainability of fiscal policy requires that present value of current and future primary surpluses must be sufficient to pay back the current debt stock. As indicated by Polito and Wickens (2005), the difference between Eqs. (28) and (35) is that the discount rate is compounded from time-varying rate.

Case 2: $\left(1+\rho^f_t\right)\delta^f_t>1$

Solving Eq. (13) forwards gives us the following equation:

$$\begin{aligned}\frac{b^f_t}{y_t}=&E_t\left[\prod_{m=1}^{n}\left(\frac{1}{\left(1+\rho^f_{t+m}\right)\delta_{t+m}}\right)\frac{b^f_{t+n}}{y_{t+n}}\right]\\&-E_t\left[\sum_{m=1}^{n}\left(\prod_{i=1}^{m}\frac{1}{(1+\rho^d_{t+i})\delta_{t+m}}\right)\left(\frac{1}{s_{t+m}}\frac{d^f_{t+m}}{y_{t+m}}\right)\right]\end{aligned} \tag{36}$$

As $\left(1+\rho^f_t\right)\delta^f_t>1$, transversality condition holds. Hence,

$$\lim_{n\to\infty} E_t\left[\prod_{m=1}^{n}\left(\frac{1}{\left(1+\rho^f_{t+m}\right)\delta_{t+m}}\right)\frac{b^f_{t+n}}{y_{t+n}}\right]=0 \tag{37}$$

Then, we can write Eq. (36) as

$$\frac{b^f_t}{y_t}=E_t\left[\sum_{m=1}^{n}\left(\prod_{i=1}^{m}\frac{1}{(1+\rho^d_{t+i})\delta_{t+m}}\right)\left(-\frac{1}{s_{t+m}}\frac{d^f_{t+m}}{y_{t+m}}\right)\right] \tag{38}$$

Eq. (38) indicates that the current and discounted future primary surpluses in terms of foreign currency must be equal to the current debt obligations of the government in foreign currency. Different from the domestic sustainability case, here we have a currency mismatch problem. Although government revenues are in domestic currency, some parts of the obligations of the government are in foreign currency, which makes analyzing the long-term sustainability of government debt in foreign currency a tough task. A sudden currency outflow may cause a rapid depreciation of the domestic currency which in turn raises the amount of primary surpluses needed for paying off the foreign debt obligations. Since it is not easy to generate revenues for government in the short run, options for the government are either borrowing more in domestic currency or printing money. While the former option puts pressure on domestic interest rates, the latter one raises inflation expectations. Celasun, Gelos, and Prati (2004) report that the primary balance is significantly linked to inflationary expectations especially during periods of disinflation from chronically high inflation rates. As the inflation targeting policy is proposed as a cure to the emerging market countries that have chronic inflation problems, management of expectations about fiscal policy becomes more important.

AN APPLICATION ON TRANSITION COUNTRIES

In this section, we use Eq. (12) to conduct short-term fiscal policy analyses of some transition countries, namely Armenia, Azerbaijan, Georgia, Kazakhstan, Kyrgyz Republic, Moldova, Tajikistan, Turkmenistan, Ukraine, and Uzbekistan.

After the collapse of the Soviet Union in 1992, these countries have increased their debt stock rapidly. Helbling, Mody, and Sahay (2004) argue that three factors contributed to swift debt accumulation processes. First, transfers from Moscow stopped and they faced with negative terms of trade shocks. In other words, these countries started to produce large current account deficits that need to be financed. Second, positive effects of fiscal reforms on the economy have been seen later than expected. Therefore, low growth and very high inflation were very common in these countries. Third, multilateral institutions (especially the IMF and the World Bank) were highly optimistic about the future of these countries; hence, they provided large amount of loans in a very short period of time. A rapid debt accumulation process obviously raised the issue of debt sustainability in these countries.[1] Although at the beginning of the 2000s some of the CIS countries' fiscal policies were considered unsustainable, Aristovnik and Berčič (2007) show that CIS countries' foreign debt position could be considered as sustainable in the late 2000s. In other words, in the pre global financial crisis period CIS countries' fiscal policies were seen healthy. As can be seen in Fig. 1, CIS countries' debt stocks were declining except for Kazakhstan and Ukraine. However, global financial crisis was a turning point and debt stocks of Armenia, Georgia, Kyrgyzstan, Moldova, Tajikistan, and Ukraine started to increase rapidly. It should be noted that important parameters of debt sustainability, budget deficit, interest rate, economic growth, and inflation in these countries are much more healthier compared with the 1990s. For example, average inflation of CIS countries between 1993 and 2000 was 238 percent, but it declined to 10 percent during the 2008–2013 period (see Table 1). However, in case of an external shock they could deteriorate quickly. In 2008, average inflation jumped to 16.8 percent while it was 13 and 10.1 percent in the 2000–2008 and 2008–2013 periods, respectively. As initial debt accumulation experience of CIS countries was still in minds, we argue that fiscal stance of these newly developing countries should be monitored closely.

We especially focus on short-term fiscal dynamics of CIS countries first, because we are particularly interested in post global financial crisis debt dynamics of these countries and secondly these countries do not have long enough data to conduct long-term analysis. We are aware of the fact that the number of transition countries is higher but unfortunately we eliminate some of them due to lack of data problem of these countries. We collect data from IMF and World Bank data bases. Starting point of data set for each country is different because of data availability and data end in 2013. We report historical averages of variables in Table 2.

Table 1. Inflation in Selected CIS Countries.

	Inflation			
	1993–2000 (Average)	2008	2000–2008 (Average)	2008–2013 (Average)
Armenia	512.9	8.9	3.6	6.1
Azerbaijan	298.6	20.8	7.8	7.1
Belarus	511.7	14.8	39.9	27.7
Georgia	33.7	10.0	6.8	4.3
Kazakhstan	305.5	17.2	9.4	8.5
Kyrgyz Republic	17.4	24.5	8.8	10.9
Moldova	20.5	12.9	13.3	6.2
Ukraine	203.7	25.2	14.2	9.8
CIS average	238.0	16.8	13.0	10.1

Table 2 shows that CIS countries' domestic debt stocks spread between 15.1 percent and 78 percent and foreign debt stocks spread between 16.9 percent and 91 percent. While Azerbaijan has the lowest foreign debt stock, Kazakhstan has the lowest domestic debt stock. The share of government spending and income in output also varies among CIS countries. Azerbaijan's total government income is almost 45 percent of the GDP and the government spending of the Uzbekistan constitutes almost 36 percent of the GDP. In addition, growth performances of these countries differ significantly. For example, with 11.7 percent Armenia has the highest average growth rate and with 0.6 percent Moldova shows the weakest growth performance among CIS countries.

In Table 3 we present average discount factors for domestic and foreign debt. It shows that since their discount factors are less than one, debt dynamics are in favor of Armenia and Azerbaijan both for domestic and foreign debt. In Kyrgyz Republic, Moldova and Tajikistan debt dynamics

Table 2. Historical Averages of Variables.

	b/y	b^*/y	v/y	g/y	r	r^*	pi	Change in S	G
Armenia	31.6	46.2	22.1	24.2	13.1	1.2	4.1	−1.7	11.7
Azerbaijan	15.1	16.9	44.8	32.5	5.9	2.7	5.1	−0.6	6.4
Georgia	32.9	53.9	18.8	20.5	20.0	2.5	6.7	2.3	6.0
Kazakhstan	10.5	63.6	22.9	20.7	22.2	4.4	8.5	2.1	3.9
Kyrgyz Republic	78.2	91.6	26.7	31.1	25.0	1.8	7.9	0.3	1.8
Moldova	61.8	71.5	30.5	32.6	10.3	3.0	9.0	1.6	0.6
Tajikistan	60.0	71.7	19.4	22.5	19.4	1.9	10.7	5.7	3.2
Turkmenistan	20.5	33.1	20.9	17.9	6.0	2.8	4.0	0.0	7.4
Ukraine	32.7	48.2	32.9	35.1	12.0	5.5	11.5	4.0	4.4
Uzbekistan	20.4	26.3	36.2	36.2	16.0	3.7	15.0	9.2	4.8
CIS average	36.4	52.3	27.5	27.3	15.0	3.0	8.3	2.3	5.0

Table 3. Discount Factors for Domestic and Foreign Debt Stocks.

	Armenia	Azerbaijan	Georgia	Kazakhstan	Kyrgyz Republic
Domestic debt stock	0.97	0.95	1.19	1.17	1.18
Foreign debt stock	0.86	0.91	1.04	1.02	0.96

	Moldova	Tajikistan	Turkmenistan	Ukraine	Uzbekistan
Domestic debt stock	1.02	1.05	1.09	1.05	1.06
Foreign debt stock	0.97	0.94	1.06	1.03	1.03

are in favor of foreign debt. In other words, these countries could be better off by issuing foreign debt in this period.

We are basically interested in three empirical questions. First, how far the debt stock of a transition country is away from its historical average debt stock and in five years how much primary surplus is needed to reduce the debt stock to its historical average level? Second, how much primary surplus is needed in five years for a transition country to reduce its debt stock to transition countries' average debt stock? Here, we are interested in the required relative fiscal adjustment in each transition country. Last but not least, how much primary surplus is required to reduce the current debt stock to pre-crisis level in five years? The last question is related with the degree of fiscal adjustment after 2008 global financial crisis and required fiscal tightening to reduce the debt stock to pre-crisis levels.

We outline our results in Table 4. First, there is no homogeneity in results. For example, as an answer to our first question, debt stocks of

Table 4. Fiscal Adjustment Experiments on Transition Countries.

(% of GDP, Minus Indicate Surplus)	Armenia	Azerbaijan	Georgia	Kazakhstan	Kyrgyz Republic
Required primary balance for each year to reach historical average debt stock in five years	−4.48	1.21	−8.11	−4.19	3.32
Required primary balance for each year to reach average debt stock of transition countries in five years	−2.88	11.99	−8.31	−1.85	−13.47
Required primary balance for each year to reach the pre-crisis debt stock in five years	−11.28	−1.67	−7.92	0.05	−6.31

	Moldova	Tajikistan	Turkmenistan	Ukraine	Uzbekistan
Required primary balance for each year to reach historical average debt stock in five years	6.49	9.63	6.43	−7.65	4.10
Required primary balance for each year to reach average debt stock of transition countries in five years	−3.01	0.47	12.87	−6.68	11.92
Required primary balance for each year to reach the pre-crisis debt stock in five years	−5.34	−0.95	−2.92	−8.72	0.74

Armenia, Georgia, Kazakhstan, and Ukraine are above their historical average; hence, they should produce enough primary surpluses to return back to their historical debt stock. Especially in Ukraine and Georgia, very large fiscal tightening is needed to reduce the debt stock to its historical average. On the other hand, debt stocks of Moldova, Tajikistan, and Turkmenistan are well below their historical average. One should be aware of the fact that due to very high debt stocks in certain periods, average debt stock could be calculated very high so that current debt stock level could be seen as comfortable. In order to avoid such a misleading conclusion, average debt stock could be calculated for different time periods or years of very high debt stock could be eliminated from the sample. Among the CIS countries, Azerbaijan and Uzbekistan have the most comfortable debt levels.

Second, current debt stocks of Armenia, Georgia, Kazakhstan, Kyrgyz Republic, Moldova, and Ukraine are above the transition countries' average of 88.7 percent. Among these countries, highest adjustment is needed in Georgia, Kyrgyz Republic, and Ukraine as they have the highest divergence from the average debt stock of CIS countries and also they have relatively weak debt dynamics.

Third, we analyze the effects of global financial crisis on the debt dynamics of transition countries. Our results show that almost all countries need to produce primary surplus to reduce their debt to pre-crisis levels in five years. Exceptions are Kazakhstan and Uzbekistan. In other words, fiscal position of 8 countries out of 10 has deteriorated after the financial crisis. The highest primary surpluses are needed in Armenia and Ukraine. This means that the worst deterioration happened in these countries. The pace of increase in debt stock of Armenia is especially remarkable since Armenia has a very favorable debt dynamics, that is, discount factors for both domestic and foreign debt are smaller than one. However, increase in government expenditure in this period was so high that (g/y ratio was 22.7 percent in 2007 and 30 percent in 2009), a rapid rise in debt stock was inevitable.

CONCLUSION

This study outlines requirements for fiscal policy sustainability especially for emerging and developing countries. Our framework is also useful for conducting short-term fiscal policy analysis. Using our framework, we analyze CIS countries' debt dynamics. We are particularly interested in the effect of global financial crisis on the debt dynamics of transition countries and to show that worst effect of the crisis is seen in Armenia and Ukraine.

The considerable increase in these countries' government expenditures is the main reason behind the rapid rise in their debt stock. Lastly, Armenia, Georgia, Kazakhstan, and Ukraine have been accumulating debt stock quite fast. Although Armenia has very favorable debt dynamics, these dynamics could change in a very short period of time. In such a situation, Armenia would need considerable fiscal adjustment. In addition, Georgia and Kazakhstan's pace of debt accumulation should be monitored closely.

NOTE

1. For a detailed debt sustainability analysis see Islamov (2001), Helbling, Mody, and Sahay (2004), Aristovnik and Berčič (2007).

REFERENCES

Aristovnik, A., & Berčič, B. (2007). Fiscal sustainability in selected transition countries. *Journal of Economics*, *55*(7), 659–675.

Benigno, P., & Woodford, M. (2006). *Optimal inflation targeting under alternative fiscal policy regimes*. NBER Working Paper Series No. 12158.

Celasun, O., Gelos, R. G., & Prati, A. (2004). *Obstacles to disinflation: What is the role of fiscal expectations*? IMF Working Paper No. 04/111.

Helbling, T. F., Mody, A., & Sahay, R. (2004). *The low-income countries of the commonwealth of independent states: Progress and challenges in transition*. IMF Working Paper No. 04/93.

Islamov, B. (2001). *The central Asian states ten years after: How to overcome traps of development, transformation and globalisation?* Tokyo: Maruzen.

Sims, C. (2003). Limits to inflation targeting. In B. S. Bernanke & M. Woodford (Eds.), *The inflation targeting debate*. Cambridge, MA: National Bureau of Economic Research Studies in Business Cycles.

Vito, P., & Wickens, M. R. (2005). *Measuring fiscal sustainability*. CDMA Conference Paper Series 0503, Centre for Dynamic Macroeconomic Analysis.

TWIN DEFICITS IN EUROPEAN TRANSITION ECONOMIES

Rajmund Mirdala

ABSTRACT

Deficits in fiscal and current account balances in a large number of countries reveal interesting implications of the causal relationship between internal and external imbalances. Empirical evidence about the occurrence of so-called twin deficits or twin surpluses provides crucial information about the validity of an intertemporal approach. However, most recent dynamic cyclical changes during the crisis period revealed many questions about the direct interconnection between macroeconomic performance and twin imbalances. In the paper we observe substantial features of twin imbalances in European transition economies. Event study (identification of large fiscal and current account changes and their parallel occurrence) and vector auto-regression methods will be employed to examine key aspects of twin imbalances. Our results suggest that current account deteriorations were predominately associated with negative public investment and savings balances (fiscal deficits), while current account improvements were predominately associated with positive private investment and savings balances, confirming empirical evidence about twin deficits in European transition economies.

Neo-Transitional Economics
International Finance Review, Volume 16, 299–333

ISSN: 1569-3767/doi:10.1108/S1569-376720150000016013

Keywords: Fiscal imbalances; current account adjustments; economic crisis; vector autoregression; impulse-response function

JEL classifications: C32; E62; F32; F41; H60

INTRODUCTION

Twin deficits represent one of the most discussed areas of open economy macroeconomics. Liberalization of external trade and capital flows since the beginning of the 1980s clearly intensified dynamic expenditure shifting and capital flow allocation on a cross-country basis. As a result, persisting internal and external imbalances in many advanced as well as advancing, emerging, and low-income economies, seemingly without direct association with the phase of the business cycle or trends in key fundamental indicators, has been obvious for decades (Gruber & Kamin, 2005). However, capital flows resulting from persistent external imbalances, followed by the periods of excessive current account imbalances, have revealed a crucial need to examine the contribution of internal and external sources of current account imbalances to associated foreign debt accumulation (Chinn & Prasad, 2003). The origins and implications of fiscal and current account imbalances, their parallel occurrence, and their mutual relationship in a large number of countries thus drew the attention of policy makers as well as academics (Caldara & Camps, 2008).

The parallel occurrence of fiscal and current account imbalances, as well as investigation of their mutual relationship in countries with varying per capita incomes represent one of the most challenging areas of open economy macroeconomics. Many theoretical and empirical studies have focused on the determinants and dynamics of current accounts over the last few decades. One of the most productive conceptual approaches to current account determination, highlighting consumption smoothing over time by countries through the cross-border exchange of the current and future consumption and associated lending and borrowing abroad, was elaborated by an intertemporal approach (Obstfeld & Rogoff, 1995). The key contribution of this approach is based on revealing a conditional relationship between current account adjustments and the gap between domestic investments and savings. Moreover, internal imbalances between investments and savings can be conventionally decomposed into their public and private components. Provided that the current account imbalance originates in the existing investment-savings gap, the country with the current account deficit either suffers from a lack of domestic savings to cover its investments and/or has a fiscal deficit (Corsetti & Muller, 2006). It is then suggested that governments willing to reduce a current account deficit can find this objective quite challenging without accompanying fiscal deficit reduction (Corsetti & Gernot, 2006).

At the beginning of the 1990s, European transition economies clearly suffered from low levels of domestic savings affected especially by the initial transition shock, poor macroeconomic performance, a series of exchange rate devaluations, and high inflation pressure followed by sharp price liberalization. Due to restrictions on current account transactions and international capital flows, it seems that the initial negative investments-savings balance was not associated with excessive current account deficits. However, expected European integration efforts and gradual liberalization of current and capital account transactions soon resulted in negative current account pressure (Arghyrou & Chortareas, 2008). As a result, all European transition economies experienced significant deterioration in their current accounts until the end of the first decade of their transition process.

Structural reforms employed by governments up to the end of the 1990s intensified the convergence process of the European transition economies toward western European countries. As a result, countries in this group experienced periods of improved macroeconomic performance over the last decade. However, while the sustainability of generally high real output growth rates became clearly conditional to keeping the internal and external disequilibria within reasonable limits, the reality of persistent investment-savings gaps and associated current account deficits continued to weaken overall macroeconomic stability. Despite relatively high rates of growth in export performance, all countries from the group experienced current account deficits through most of the pre-crisis period. In addition to existing differences in the contribution of public and private components to the overall investment-savings disequilibrium, individual countries in the group employed different exchange rate arrangements that seem to affect their external competitiveness and in the direction of their current account balances (Obstfeld & Rogoff, 2005).

The crisis period affected both the fiscal stance of government budgets and their current accounts levels and trends in all ten European transition economies. As a result, the direction of both indicators changed significantly. The economic crisis intensified redistributive effects (cross-country expenditure shifting) that imposed diverse and spurious effects on current account balances (Glick & Rogoff, 1995). Immediately after the beginning of the crisis period, current accounts in all countries temporarily deteriorated (with different intensities the various countries). However, we soon observed a positive trend (either improvement or a stable outlook) in almost all countries, reflecting intensified redistributive effects of the crisis on cross-country expenditure shifting.

The negative implications of the economic and debt crisis also revealed questions associated with disputable implications of fiscal incentives that seem contrary to the crucial need for the effective fiscal consolidation that is necessary to reduce excessive fiscal deficits and high sovereign debt (Soyoung & Roubini, 2008). While challenges to the fiscal policy and its anti-cyclical potential have risen steadily (though not desperately) since the beginning of the economic crisis, the call for fiscal consolidation became urgent almost immediately, and this need significantly strengthened after the debt crisis contagion flooded Europe. The overall fiscal budgetary stance thus became determined by mutually contradictory discretionary fiscal forces even as they remained affected by lagging recession (Hassan, 2004).

In this paper we observe substantial features of the twin imbalances in European transition economies. An event study (identification of large fiscal and current account changes and their parallel occurrence) approach will be employed to examine key aspects of the twin imbalances. Our results suggest that current account deteriorations were predominately associated with negative public investment-savings balances (fiscal deficits), while current account improvements were predominately associated with positive private investments-savings balances, confirming empirical evidence about twin deficits in the European transition economies.

OVERVIEW OF MAIN TRENDS IN TWIN DEFICITS

Early in the 1990s, during the first decade of the transition process, the European transition economies experienced periods of excessive current account deficits. This negative trend is obvious especially at the end of the first decade and corresponds to the finalization of the process of current account liberalization. The initial transition shock, sharp real output decline, insufficient dynamics in the accumulation of savings, the investment-intensive process of the economic transition, and low international competitiveness represent key causes that led to the generally expected international financial position of these countries as net debtors.

Significant foreign capital inflows, followed by successful capital account liberalization up to the end of the century helped the European transition economies to fill their persistent investments-savings gap. However, and despite generally improved macroeconomic performance since the beginning of the 2000s, European transition economies still experienced negative trends in their current account balances. In line with the intertemporal approach (Roubini, 1988), we observed clear evidence of a mutual relationship between imbalances in current accounts and the domestic investment-savings balances in all countries in the group. An overview of the main trends in the current account and private, public, and overall investment-savings balances in the European transition economies is summarized in Fig. 1.

In line with an intertemporal approach, it is clear that observed current account imbalances reflected a negative trend in the investment-saving ratio. While current account adjustments revealed crucial and generally expected implications of the continuously increasing international economic and financial integration of European transition economies (increased indebtedness, lagging competitiveness, fiscal imbalances, foreign capital inflows, etc.), there seems to be still enough room to investigate partial effects of dynamic changes in the key current account determinants to observe associated current account adjustments.

The intertemporal approach clearly suggests that current account imbalances originate in the corresponding savings-investment gap (Kim & Roubini, 2008). Despite some differences, we have observed quite similar trends in the trajectories of current accounts and savings-investment gaps in all countries in the group. However, an expenditure shifting effect associated with current account imbalances in each country does not seem to be solely determined by the savings-investment gap in the public and private sectors. We suggest that use of an appropriate methodology that identifies subperiods with significant mutual relationships between public and private sector balances and associated current account adjustments is necessary to provide rigorous insight into the problem. It seems that small and short-term changes in the savings-investment gaps in both sectors do not initiate corresponding current account adjustments (Kumhof & Laxton, 2009).

Considering the relative heterogeneity of individual countries in our sample, we can conventionally identify key fundamental determinants that have induced different patterns in the general scenario of the negative current account development and its origins over most of the observed period.

The first group of countries, represented here by Bulgaria and the Baltic countries (Estonia, Latvia, and Lithuania), employed rigid exchange rate

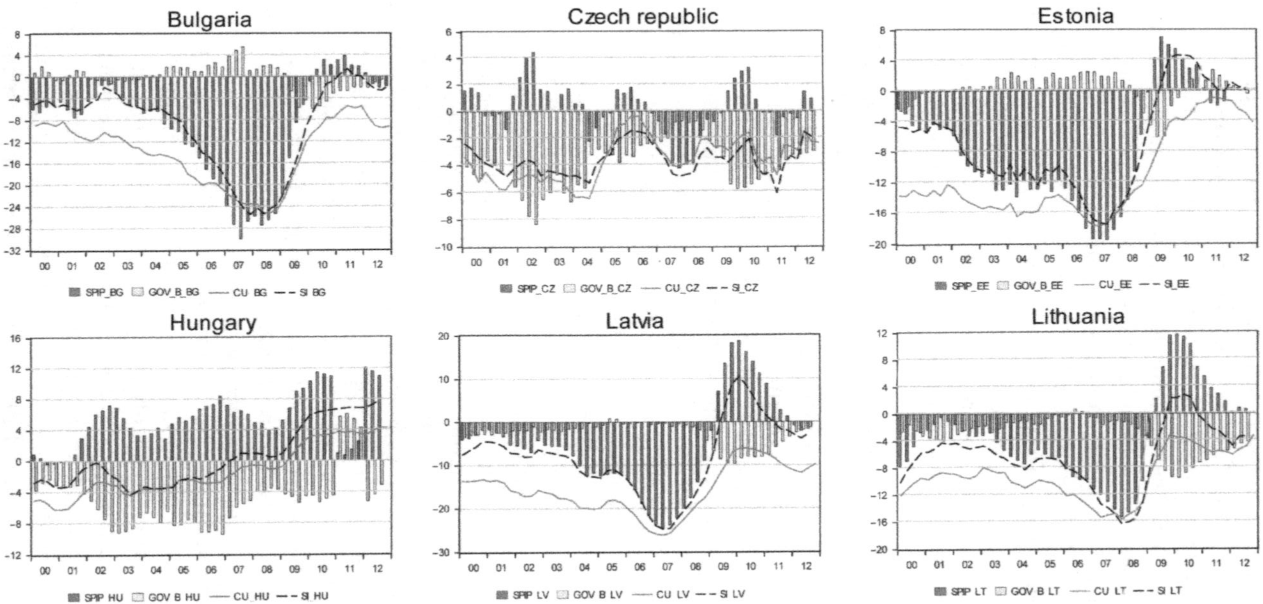

Fig. 1. Overview of Current Account and Private, Public, and Overall Net Savings-Investments Positions (2000Q1–2012Q4). *Source*: Compiled by author based on data taken from IMF – International Financial Statistics (October 2014). *Note*: Variables: Private savings less private investments (SPIP), primary balance (GOV_B), current account (CU), and overall savings less investments (SI) are expressed as percentage share of GDP.

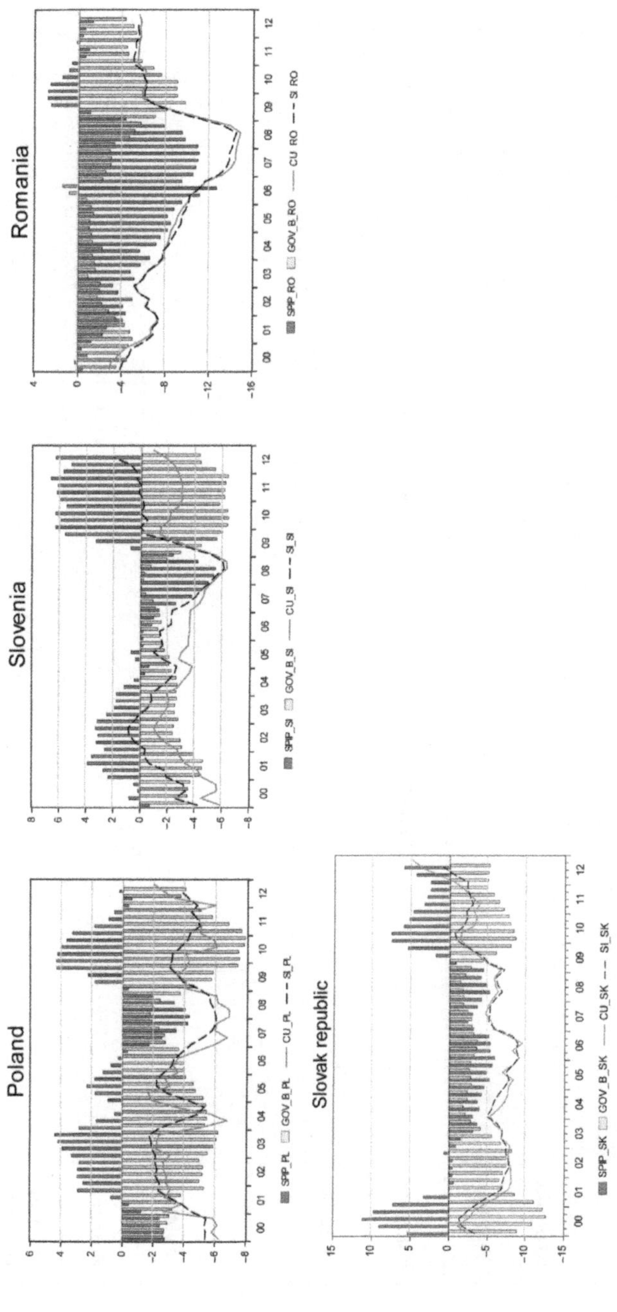

Fig. 1. (*Continued*)

Table 1. Exchange Rate Arrangements in European Transition Economies.

	Exchange rate regime
Bulgaria	(shaded, unlabelled) 1990; Managed floating 1991–1997; Currency board 1998–2013
Czech Republic	Peg with horizontal bands 1990–1996; Managed floating 1997–2013
Estonia	(shaded, unlabelled) 1990–1991; Currency board 1992–2004; ERM2 2005–2010; Eurozone 2011–2013
Hungary	Adjustable peg 1990–1994; Crawling peg 1995–1999; Peg with horizontal bands 2000–2007; Managed floating 2008–2013
Latvia	(shaded, unlabelled) 1990–1991; Floating 1992–1993; Conventional fixed peg 1994–2005; ERM2 2006–2013
Lithuania	(shaded, unlabelled) 1990–1991; Floating 1992–1993; Currency board 1994–2004; ERM2 2005–2013
Poland	(shaded, unlabelled) 1990; Crawling peg 1991–1999; Free floating 2000–2013
Romania	Free floating 1990–1997; Managed floating 1998–2013
Slovak Republic	Peg with horizontal bands 1990–1998; Managed floating 1999–2005; ERM2 2006–2008; Eurozone 2009–2013
Slovenia	(shaded, unlabelled) 1990; Managed floating 1991–2001; Crawling band 2002–2004; ERM2 2005–2006; Eurozone 2007–2013
	1990 1991 1992 1993 1994 1995 1996 1997 1998 1999 2000 2001 2002 2003 2004 2005 2006 2007 2008 2009 2010 2011 2012 2013

Source: IMF AREAER 1990–2011, author's processing.

Note: Exchange rate regime evolution in the European transition economies: *Bulgaria* – after 1991 floating (pegged exchange rate regime undesirable due to possible low credibility), currency board since 1997 [after 1996–1997 financial crisis (public debt, bad commercial banks loans)]. *Czech Republic* – exchange rate pegged to currency basket with narrow but continuously widen horizontal bands; since May 1997, after currency attacks, switched to managed floating with no predetermined path for the exchange rate with DEM (EUR) as reference currency. *Estonia* – currency board from 1992 to 2011 (euro adoption), plan to adopt in 2008 but delayed due high inflation; since 2011 eurozone membership. *Hungary* – managed floating until February 1995, from March 1995 to the end of 1999 crawling peg with continuously decreased rate of periodical devaluation and widened horizontal bands; since January 2000 exchange rate pegged to euro combined with wide horizontal bands (since May 2001); since May 2008 managed floating with EUR as reference currency. *Latvia* – since February 1994 exchange rate pegged to SDR [fixing the exchange rate to a basket of currencies (SDR) instead of a single currency serves to promote long-term stability]; after January 2005 pegged to EUR; since 2014 eurozone membership. *Lithuania* – after April 1994 currency board (exchange rate pegged to USD, in February 2002 pegging switched to EUR). *Poland* – since the end of 1991 crawling peg with continuously decreased rate of periodical devaluation and widen horizontal bands; after April 2000 free floating. *Romania* – free floating, since 1998 exchange rate arrangement reclassified as managed floating. *Slovak Republic* – exchange rate pegged to currency basket with narrow but continuously widening horizontal bands; after October 1998, after currency attacks, switched to managed floating with no predetermined path for the exchange rate with DEM (EUR) as reference currency; since 2009 eurozone membership. *Slovenia* – managed floating with no predetermined path for the exchange rate (since February 2002 crawling band – the monetary authority manages the float of the domestic currency within certain fluctuating margins around a depreciating path – a heavily-managed crawling band with pragmatic monetary, real, external, and financial indicators).

ERM2:

– June 2004 – Estonia (left in January 2011 after euro adoption), Lithuania, Slovenia (left in January 2007 after euro adoption).

– May 2005 – Latvia (left in January 2014 after euro adoption).

– November 2005 – Slovak Republic (left in January 2009 after euro adoption).

regimes over most of the period. Exchange rate anchoring obliged fiscal authorities to observe more prudent fiscal discipline in comparison with the remaining countries (Obstfeld & Rogoff, 2005). Fiscal sustainability thus represents one of the key commitments of government to maintain a fixed exchange rate (Sek & Chuah, 2013). However, countries in this group experienced excessive current account deficits over most of the period. Fig. 1 clearly suggests that current account imbalances originated mostly in the high investment-savings imbalances of the private sector.

The second group of countries, represented here by the Czech Republic, Hungary, Poland, Romania, the Slovak Republic, and Slovenia, enjoyed the effects of relative exchange rate flexibility during most of the period. It seems that the absence of a commitment to preserve fiscal discipline was associated with generally higher fiscal deficits and thus a greater contribution of the fiscal imbalances to current account determination.

It seems that countries with rigid exchange rate arrangements (Bulgaria, Estonia, Latvia, and Lithuania – the group of so-called "peggers") experienced periods with generally higher discrepancies in GDP shares of both indicators, though the trajectories of both indicators seem to be quite similar, revealing some common patterns in the main trends. However, the beginning of the crisis period (2008–2009) clearly reduced differences in the shares. We suggest that the absence of exchange rate flexibility and persisting real exchange rate appreciation contributed to deterioration of overall competitiveness and thus accelerated a negative trend in the current account imbalances, even more than we would expect from the savings-investment gaps (Lee & Chinn, 2006). A brief overview of the evolution of exchange rate regimes in the European transition economies is provided in Table 1.

Prudential fiscal discipline and excessive current account deficits in countries with rigid exchange rate arrangements (this negative trend accelerated in the second half of the pre-crisis period) revealed significant imbalances between private savings and private investment. As a result, fiscal discipline tightening, together with exchange rate–based anchoring, provided a convenient vehicle for spreading internal imbalances in the private sector across the borders, causing high current account deficits. In countries with flexible exchange rate arrangements (Czech Republic, Hungary,[1] Poland, Slovenia, and Slovak Republic – the group of so-called "floaters"), the situation during the pre-crisis period seems to have been quite different, though not uniform. In the Czech Republic, Hungary, Poland, and Slovenia, persistent negative savings-investment imbalances originated in excessive fiscal deficits. The situation in Romania changed over time. The negative trend in savings-investment GDP shares initially originated in fiscal imbalance, though it was soon replaced by private sector expansion. A similar scenario, though with higher initial fiscal deficits and less imbalanced growth in the private sector, was observed in the Slovak Republic.

The crisis period significantly affected not only the direction of the savings-investment gap and current account development, but also the relative contributions of the public and private sectors to both internal and external imbalances. Even countries with prudential pre-crisis fiscal policies could not avoid the trend of significant divergence in the public (deterioration) and private (large improvement) savings-investment gaps associated with significant improvement in the current account stance and overall savings-investment balances. It seems that this sudden turn was induced by the general trend of debt accumulation in both the public and private sectors before the crisis. While the debt of the private sector (households and enterprises) steadily increased over the whole pre-crisis period, the debt of the public sector (as the GDP ratio) was generally stable in the whole group of countries. The significant accumulation of private debt during the pre-crisis period initiated intensive hoarding of savings in the private sector. When one (private) sector saves more, the other (public) sector has to spend more, otherwise a savings paradox may occur. As a result, sovereign debt crisis and related deterioration in public finance may be considered the implication, not the origin of the debt crisis in Europe.

OVERVIEW OF LITERATURE

Bussiere, Fratzscher, and Muller (2004) analyzed the current account determination in 33 countries employing an intertemporal approach via regression analysis, considering effects of the fiscal stance of governments as well as real exchange rate deviations. The authors suggest that current account balances of countries included in the model are close to their structural current account positions, confirming the validity of the intertemporal approach. Abbas, Bouhga-Hagbe, Fatás, Mauro, and Velloso (2011) examined the relationship between fiscal policy and current account of a large sample of advanced and emerging economies using a variety of statistical methods: panel regressions, an analysis of large fiscal and external adjustments, and VAR. These authors suggest that a strengthening of the fiscal balance by 1 percentage point of GDP is associated with a current account improvement of 0.3–0.4 percentage point of GDP. The evidence is stronger, especially in emerging and low-income countries, when the exchange rate is flexible, when the economies are more open, when output is above potential, and when initial debt levels are above 90 percent of GDP. Javid, Javid, and Arif (2010) investigated the effects of fiscal policy and government budget deficit shocks on the current account and other macroeconomic variables for Pakistan over the period 1960–2009 by employing an SVAR model. They suggest that expansionary fiscal policy shock improves the current account and depreciates the exchange rate. A rise in private savings and a fall in investment contribute to the current account improvement as the exchange rate depreciates. Schnabl and Wollmershäuser (2012) considered the role of diverging fiscal policy stances on current account (im)balances in Europe since the early 1970s under alternative institutional monetary arrangements by employing pooled panel regressions. They concluded that divergent fiscal policy stances are an important determinant of intra-European current account imbalances both before and after the introduction of the euro. The authors highlighted that there is evidence that current account imbalances were encouraged by an expansionary ECB monetary policy stance after the year 2001. Fidrmuc (2002) defined twin deficits as a cointegrating relationship between the current account, the fiscal balance, and investment. This author found that both current accounts and fiscal balances have displayed a significant degree of hysteresis. His paper shows that while twin deficits emerged in the 1980s, there seems to be a lack of evidence for twin deficits in the 1990s. In a sample of both OECD and emerging economies with data between 1970 and 2001, the author found that the countries which pursue sustainable fiscal policies also display a high flexibility in the current account.

LARGE CHANGES IN FISCAL POLICY AND EXTERNAL BALANCES (EVENT STUDY)

Methodological Notes to Large Changes in CAPB and Current Account

Observation of periods associated with large changes in cyclically adjusted primary balance (CAPB) and current account requires some introduction to the methodology that will be employed. Changes in CAPB as well as the current account are usually associated with adjustments on one of the sides determining their overall balance (or dynamics), or both at the same time. The balance of the government budget is determined by the set of fiscal arrangements on the side of revenues and/or expenditures followed by improvement or deterioration in the fiscal stance (Lane, 2010). The balance of the current account is determined by competitiveness effects associated with cross-country expenditure shifting via export (inflows) and/or import (outflows) dynamics.

There seem to be several approaches to measuring large fiscal changes and to evaluating the effects of fiscal episodes. For example, Alesina and Ardagna (2009) identify three types of fiscal adjustment episodes to analyze episodes of fiscal consolidation. For purposes of our study we employ this methodology as adapted by Abbas et al. (2011), who investigated episodes of large fiscal and current account changes. However, we have slightly adjusted key measures to better suit our sample of countries. It is important to emphasize that we focus on large and continuous changes in fiscal stances and current accounts. The durability of adjustments is thus crucial to avoid misleading effects of short-term volatility. At the same time, no sharp reversal movements[2] against the main trend are allowed during identified episodes of significant changes in order to presume continuity of fiscal or current account adjustments. We suggest that investigation of key features of large and continuous changes in both indicators may provide some insights into the empirical validity of the intertemporal approach.

Extracted episodes of large fiscal stance and current account changes will be identified by the following measures: (1) continuous cumulative improvement (deterioration) in CAPB or current account by at least 2 percent of GDP share; and (2) improvement (deterioration) of real output by at least 1.5 percent on an annual basis within identified episodes of large CAPB or current account adjustment. However, we have observed a relatively low connection between rates of real output growth and dynamics in CAPBs and current accounts, which is why we separately identify episodes of large changes in CAPB and current account with and without real output growth rate interference. We also investigate large changes in ratios of overall savings-investment gap to GDP as well as ratios of private savings-investment gap to GDP following measure (1) to observe more detailed mechanisms of intertemporal approach in the European transition economies during the pre-crisis and crisis periods.

Cyclically Adjusted Primary Balance

To assess a detailed overview of large fiscal policy changes and their effects, it is necessary to estimate the influence of fiscal adjustments based on tax and/or expenditures changes on fiscal balance. However, it seems to be necessary to reveal changes in the revenue and expenditure sides of government balances associated with automatic effects induced by changes in the macroeconomic environment and effects of discretionary fiscal policy actions. In the first case, a cool-down of real output growth may be followed by a cut in government revenues (due to reduced tax capacity of an economy in a time of crisis) and an increase in government expenditures (due to higher unemployment benefits). As a result, deterioration of the fiscal balance will occur. At the same time, similar effects on the fiscal balance will be followed by discretionary tax cuts or expenditure increases. The fiscal stance of a government budget may thus reflect mixed effects of automatic changes in budgetary revenues and expenditures associated with business cycle fluctuations, as well as discretionary changes on both sides of the budgets associated with discretionary fiscal policy actions.

To eliminate the effects of a business cycle on the fiscal stance of a government budget it is necessary to eliminate the influence of cyclical movements of fiscal variables. As a result of filtered business cycle impacts, together with some other adjustments (i.e. exclusion of interest payable on the side of government expenditures), a CAPB will be calculated. The empirical literature provides many approaches to calculating CAPB. In general, the main algorithm follows the same procedure: (1) estimation of potential GDP, (2) determination and calculation of key revenue and expenditure categories' responses to the fluctuations in cyclical GDP, (3) adjustments in budgetary revenues and expenditures according to the cyclical effects in both sides of the budget. As a result we obtain a cyclically adjusted structural or primary balance. On the other hand, we have found some differences in step (2) in the current empirical literature reflecting a diversity of approaches employed to estimate income elasticity of the main budgetary variables (on both revenue and expenditure sides). At the same time, most studies have calculated cyclical components in real output by estimating potential output (and output gap) using a simple HP filter[3] or potential employment based on detrending NAIRU calculations.

Bouthevillain et al. (2001) calculated fiscal elasticity using econometric regressions or derivation from tax or expenditure laws and from detailed information on the distribution of income and revenue. Altăr, Necula, and Bobeică (2010) estimated tax and revenue elasticity by applying methodology similar to that employed by the OECD and by the European Commission. These authors decomposed the main components of revenue and expenditure budgetary sides using a linear system of equations. Girouard and André (2005) calculated the income elasticity of four different types of taxes, while on the expenditure side there is only a single item –

unemployment-related transfers – that the authors treated as cyclically sensitive.

Günaydın and UğraşÜlkü (2002) employed a vector-error correction (VEC) model to estimate income elasticity of budgetary components. Provided there is a long-run equilibrium (cointegration) between GDP and budgetary variables, expected elasticity coefficients are represented by normalized cointegrating coefficients derived from cointegrating equations.

To cyclically adjust a government budget – that is, to estimate the underlying fiscal position when cyclical and/or automatic components are removed – we follow a VEC methodology implemented by Günaydın and UğraşÜlkü (2002).

Cyclically adjusted primary balance (CAPB) is calculated by subtracting the cyclical component (B^C) from the primary government balance (PB):

$$\text{CAPB}_t = \text{PB}_t - B_t^C = \text{PB}_t - \sum_{i=1}^{n} B_{t,i}^C \tag{1}$$

where (PB) represents actual government budget balance (B) less interests payable (E^I):

$$\text{PB}_t = B_t - E^I \tag{2}$$

and $\left(B_{t,i}^C\right)$ represents a cyclical component of each of n revenue and expenditure budgetary categories included in the model given by the following equation:

$$B_{t,i}^C = B_{t,i}.e_i.Y_t^{\text{gap}} \tag{3}$$

where (e_t) represents the individual elasticity of each particular budget category (that responds automatically to real output fluctuations) included in the model and (Y^{gap}) represents the output gap expressed as a percentage of GDP.

Income Elasticity of Budgetary Categories

In our model we include three types of budget revenues (revenues from direct taxes, indirect taxes, and social contributions) and one budget expenditure category (unemployment-related transfers) that seem to respond to short-run (cyclical) movements in real output. As a result, we expect that selected fiscal variables automatically respond to the cyclical fluctuations in real output.

To estimate the income elasticity of budgetary categories, we expect that there is a long-run equilibrium relationship (cointegration) between each included fiscal variable and real output. Cointegration methodology, introduced by Johansen (1988, 1991) and Johansen and Juselius (1990), will be employed to estimate the long-rum equilibrium relationships between different types of budgetary variables and real output in the European transition economies. Johansen's method is applied to the unrestricted vector autoregression (VAR) model, which can be written by the following moving average representation of n non-stationary variables containing p lagged values:

$$Y_t = \mu + A_1 Y_{t-1} + A_2 Y_{t-2} + \ldots + A_p Y_{t-p} + \varepsilon_t \tag{4}$$

where Y_t is an $n\ x\ 1$ vector of the contemporaneous endogenous variables, μ is an $n\ x\ 1$ vector of the constants, A_t is an $n\ x\ n$ polynomial variance-covariance matrix, $\varepsilon_t \sim N_n(0, \sum_\varepsilon)$ is an $n\ x\ 1$ normalized vector of exogenous shocks (innovations) to the model representing unexplained changes in the variables.

If at least two of the variables are cointegrated on the order one [$I(1)$], the VAR representation in Eq. (4) can be rewritten by subtracting Y_{t-1} from the following vector error correction model (VECM):

$$\Delta Y_t = \mu + \Pi Y_{t-p} + \sum_{i=1}^{p-1} \Gamma_i \Delta Y_{t-i} + \varepsilon_t \tag{5}$$

where ΔY_t is an $n\ x\ 1$ vector of the first differences of stochastic variables Y_t, $\Pi = \sum_{i=1}^{p} A_i - I$, and $\Gamma_i = -\sum_{j=i+1}^{p} A_j$, I is an $n\ x\ n$ identity matrix.

The VECM presented contains information on both short-term and long-term adjustments to changes in Y_t included in estimated Γ and Π, respectively. Γ is an $n\ x\ n$ matrix that represents the short-term dynamic – adjustments to changes in Y_t. Π is an $n\ x\ n$ matrix consisting of the long-run coefficients – the cointegrating relationships (cointegrating vectors) and of the error correction term. Π can be decomposed as follows:

$$\Pi = \alpha\beta' \tag{6}$$

where α represents an $n\ x\ r$ a loading matrix containing coefficients that describe the contribution of the r long-term (cointegrating) relationships in the individual equations and denotes the speed of adjustment from disequilibrium, while β is an $n\ x\ r$ matrix of long-run coefficients and represents the r

linearly independent cointegrating vectors (each column of β is the cointegrating vector). The number of cointegrating relations among variables of Y_t is the same as the rank (r) for the matrix Π. If it has a full rank, the rank $r = n$ and it means there are n cointegrating relationships and that all variables are $I(0)$. If a vector Y_t is a vector of endogenous variables that are $I(1)$, then all terms in Eq. (5) are $I(0)$, and ΠY_{t-1} must be also stationary for $\varepsilon_n \sim I(0)$ to be white noise. If the matrix Πhas reduced rank, $r<n$, there are $n-1$ cointegrating vectors, and even if all endogenous variables in the model are $I(1)$, the level-based long-run component would be stationary. VECM requires that there exist at least one cointegrating relationship.

In order to find the presence of cointegrating (long-run) relationships, we use a trace test and maximum eigenvalue test. Determination of rank and estimation of the coefficients are computed as maximum likelihood estimations. The corresponding likelihood-ratio test statistics are:

$$\lambda_{\text{trace}}(r) = -T \sum_{i-r+1}^{n} \ln(1 - \frown\lambda_i) \quad \lambda_{\max}(r, r+1) = -T\ln(1 - \frown\lambda_{r+1}) \tag{7}$$

where r is the number of cointegrating vectors under the null hypothesis and $\frown\lambda$ is the estimated value for the ith ordered eigenvalue from the Πmatrix. Under the trace statistic, the null hypothesis that the number of cointegrating vectors is less than or equal to r is tested against the alternative that there are more than r vectors. Under the maximum eigenvalue test, the null hypothesis that there are r cointegrating vectors is tested against the alternative of $r + 1$ cointegrating vectors.

Provided that time series for direct tax revenues, indirect tax revenues, social contributions, unemployment-related transfers, and real output are $I(1)$,[4] we estimate four different VEC models employing quarterly data for the period 2000Q1–2012Q4 (52 observations) for government expenditures, real output, inflation, tax revenues, and short-term interest rates drawn from IMF database (International Financial Statistics, October 2014). Time series for direct tax revenues, indirect tax revenues, social contributions, unemployment-related transfers, and real output were seasonally adjusted. Tests for cointegration were computed using two lags, as recommended by the AIC (Akaike Information Criterion).

Results of both the Johansen cointegration procedures (trace statistics and maximum eigenvalue statistics) confirmed our hypothesis about the existence of one long-run equilibrium (cointegrating) relationship between each fiscal variable and real output. Normalized cointegrating coefficients derived from each cointegrating equation represent elasticity coefficients of each fiscal category with respect to real output.

Episodes of Large Current Account and Fiscal Changes

In this section we analyze the occurrence as well as substantial features of episodes containing large current account and fiscal changes in the European transition economies since 2000. Substantial changes in current accounts and CAPBs will be identified according to associated trends in real output to observe possible interference with the performance of the countries. At the same time we identify large changes in the private savings-investment gap to GDP ratio and the overall savings-investment gap to GDP ratio[5] and indicate possible causalities and implications according to an intertemporal approach.

Identified episodes of large current account changes are summarized in Fig. 2. Individual countries in the group experienced several episodes of continuous current account adjustments that in total represent 66 episodes, of which 35 refer to current account improvement and 31 to current account deterioration. We found that during more than 62 percent of episodes the current account adjustments did not interfere with the real output trajectory (either positively or negatively). This result is contrary to conclusions proposed by, among others, Abbas et al. (2011).

Bulgaria experienced 8 large continuous current account changes: 4 improvements (2 episodes with and 2 episodes without GDP interference) and 4 deteriorations (3 episodes with and 3 episodes without GDP interference). Episodes of large current account changes were associated with corresponding SPIP and SI episodes. Large CAPB episodes were less frequent and were partially associated with large current account changes during the crisis period.

The Czech Republic experienced 6 large continuous current account changes: 4 improvements (3 episodes with and 1 episode without GDP interference) and 2 deteriorations (both 2 episodes without GDP interference). Large and durable current account improvement in the first half of the period was associated with a corresponding CAPB episode. In the second half of the period (and especially during the crisis period), large current account changes were followed by lagged corresponding episodes of SPIP adjustments.

Estonia experienced 7 large continuous current account changes: 4 improvements (3 episodes with and 1 episode without GDP interference)

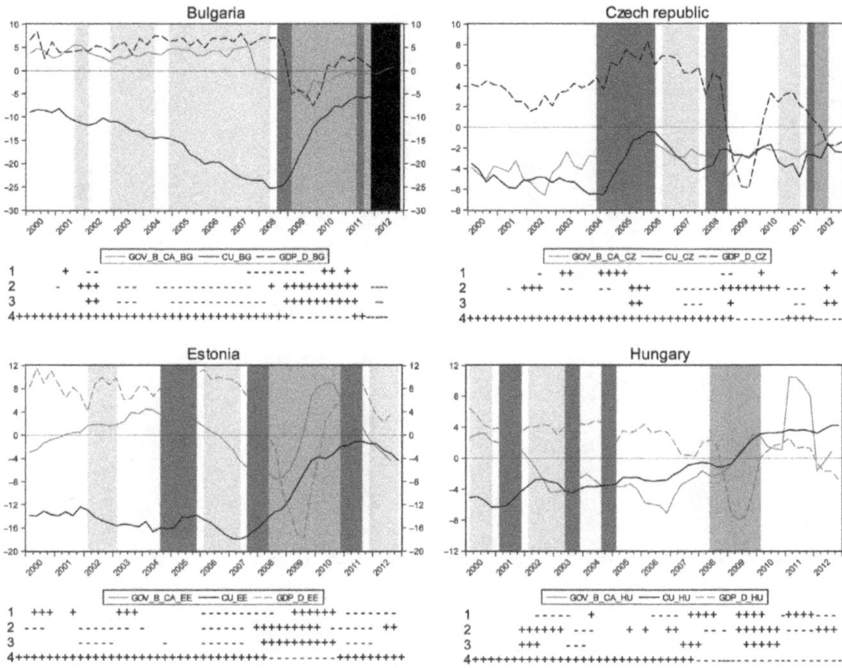

Fig. 2. Episodes of Large Current Account Changes (2000Q1–2012Q4). *Source:* Author's calculation. *Note:* Variables – cyclically adjusted primary balance – CAPB (GOV_B_CA) and current account (CU) are expressed as percentage share of GDP. Real output growth rate (GDP_D) is expressed as percentage change in annual real GDP over the corresponding period in the previous year. Data in tables below each figure represent large changes (+ for improvement, – for deterioration) in (1) cyclically adjusted primary balance (CAPB), (2) private savings-investment gap to GDP ratio (SPIP), and (3) overall savings-investment gap to GDP ratio (SI). The last row represents (4) annual changes in real output. For (1), (2), and (3), each individual sign (+ or –) represents a large change during one year (four quarters) backward.

CAPB (–) (with negative real GDP interference)

CAPB (–) (w/o negative real GDP interference)

CAPB (+) (with positive real GDP interference)

CAPB (+) (w/o positive real GDP interference)

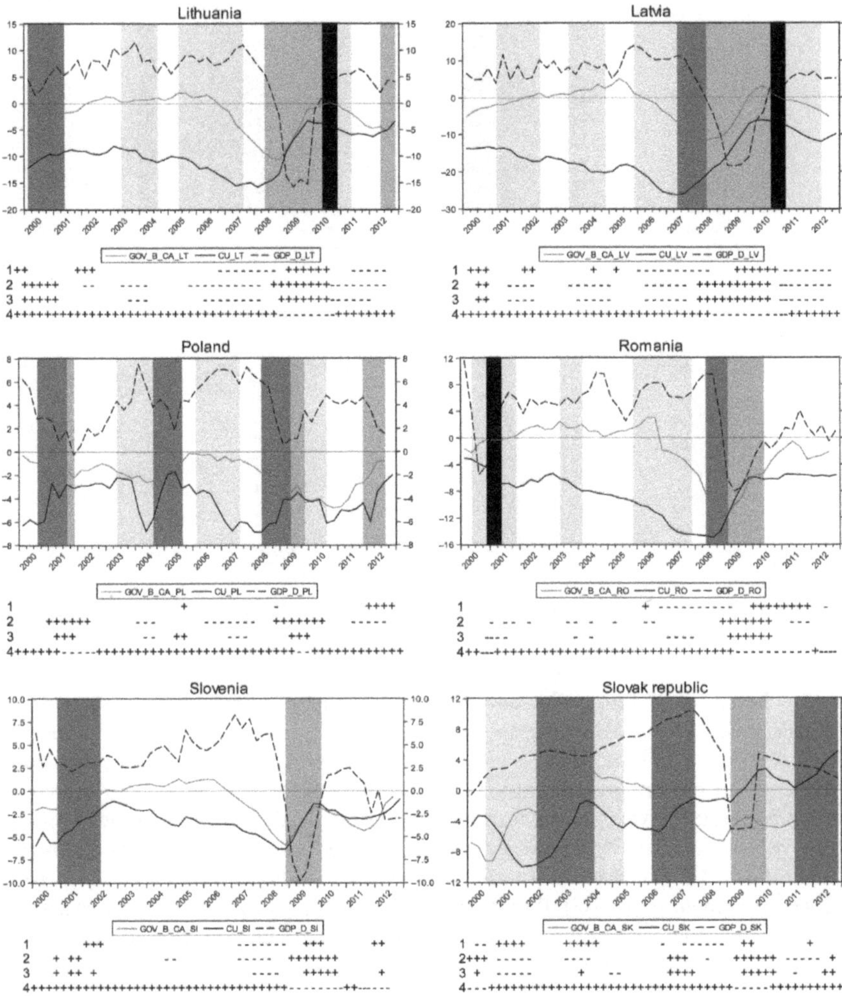

Fig. 2. (*Continued*)

and 3 deteriorations (all 3 episodes without GDP interference). During the first half of the period, we observed a parallel occurrence of current account deterioration SPIP and SI episodes, while CAPB episodes don't seem to have affected current account adjustments (similarly, as in Bulgaria – we suggest it is especially due to tightened fiscal discipline conducted under strict exchange rate anchoring). The crisis period seems to have strengthened an occurrence of current account episodes and CAPB, SPIP, SI episodes, though with persistent lags.

Hungary experienced 6 large continuous current account changes: 4 improvements (3 episodes with and 1 episode without GDP interference) and 2 deteriorations (both episodes without GDP interference). Episodes of large current account changes in the middle of the first half of the period were associated with a lagged occurrence of SPIP, SI, and CAPB episodes. At the same time, it seems that large changes in domestic (private and public) components of SI adjustments followed contrary trends, with a dominance in SPIP effects. The only crisis period current account episode was associated with slightly lagged continuous changes in both CAPB and SPIP.

Lithuania experienced 7 large continuous current account changes: 3 improvements (1 episode with and 2 episodes without GDP interference) and 4 deteriorations (1 episode with and 3 episodes without GDP interference). Despite an initial short CAPB episode, we found that large current account adjustments were not associated with continuous CAPB changes during most of the pre-crisis period (the last pre-crisis one was followed by a significant lag). On the other hand, current account episodes strictly corresponded to SPIP episodes. Parallel occurrence of corresponding current account and CAPB, SPIP, and SI episodes became much more frequent during the crisis period (similar to Bulgaria and Estonia).

Latvia experienced 7 large continuous current account changes: 2 improvements (1 episode with and 1 episode without GDP interference) and 5 deteriorations (1 episode with and 4 episodes without GDP interference). Similarity with Lithuania's pre-crisis current account episodes scenario is obvious. The connection between current account and SPIP (as well as SI) episodes is clear. Situation changes during the crisis period though CAPB episodes slightly lagged behind large and continuous current account changes.

Poland experienced 9 large continuous current account changes: 6 improvements (3 episodes with and 3 episodes without GDP interference) and 3 deteriorations (all 3 episodes without GDP interference). During the first half of the period, we observed a parallel occurrence of current account deterioration and SI episodes. However, only 1 current account episode (2005) was associated with a short CAPB episode, while the rest occurred in parallel with large SPIP changes. Despite general improvement in parallel occurrence of current account episodes as well as SPIP and

CAPB changes, SPIP and CAPB episodes tended toward divergent adjustments.

Romania experienced 7 large continuous current account changes: 2 improvements (1 episode with and 1 episode without GDP interference) and 5 deteriorations (1 episode with and 4 episodes without GDP interference). Deteriorating current account episodes during the whole pre-crisis period were associated purely with large SPIP changes, causing SI adjustments (except for the last, which clearly preceded CAPB deterioration at its beginning). While an episode of continuous current account improvement at the beginning of the crisis period occurred, again in parallel with a large positive SPIP episode, there also seemed to be a substantial, though lagged, occurrence of the episode with large CAPB improvement.

The Slovak Republic experienced 7 large continuous current account changes: 4 improvements (3 episodes with and 1 episode without GDP interference) and 3 deteriorations (all 3 episodes without GDP interference). Large changes in CAPB and SPIP followed contrary trends during the pre-crisis period. However, episodes of large SI changes generally reflected associated large continuous current account changes and thus appear to be clearly parallel. The occurrence of volatile current account episodes (shifting of positive and negative episodes) intensified during the crisis period and occurred in parallel with SPIP episodes.

Slovenia experienced 2 large continuous current account changes: 2 improvements (1 episode with and 1 episode without GDP interference) and no deteriorations. The rare occurrence of continuous large current account episodes reflects a relative SI stability during the pre-crisis period. The episode of current account improvement at the beginning of the period occurred in parallel with positive SPIP and SI changes as well as a subsequent, though lagged, CAPB episode (this scenario happened again at the beginning of the crisis period). However, negative CAPB, SPIP, and SI episodes don't seem to be associated with corresponding current account episodes.

Identified episodes of large fiscal changes are summarized in Fig. 3. Individual countries from the group experienced several episodes of continuous fiscal adjustment (represented by adjustments in CAPB) that in total represent 55 episodes, of which 32 refer to fiscal stance improvement and 23 to fiscal stance deterioration. We found that in almost 53 percent of episodes, adjustments in CAPB did not interfere with the real output trajectory (either positively or negatively).

Bulgaria experienced 5 large continuous fiscal changes: 2 improvements (1 episode with and 1 episode without GDP interference) and 3

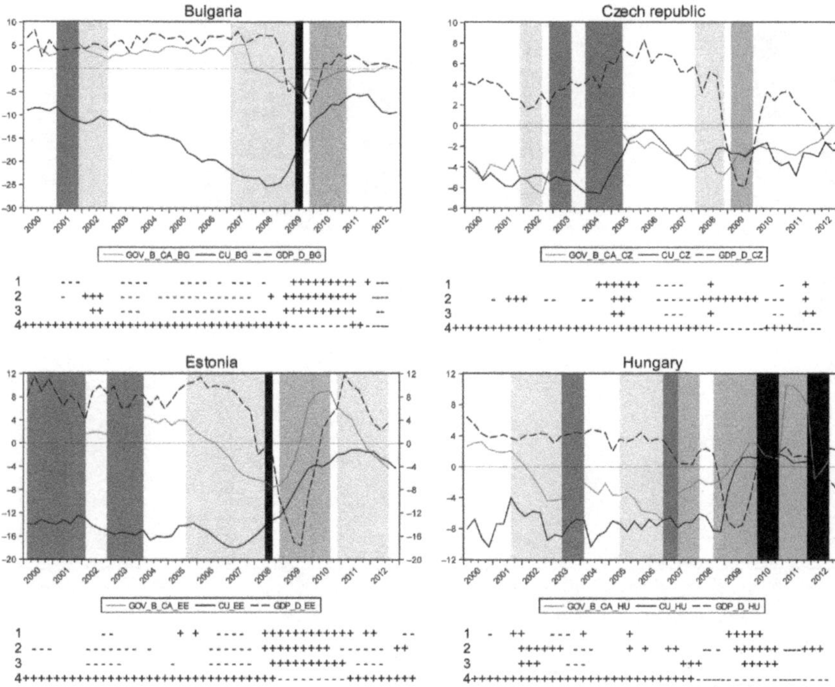

Fig. 3. Episodes of Large Fiscal Policy Changes (2000Q1–2012Q4). *Source:* Author's calculation. *Note:* Variables – cyclically adjusted primary balance – CAPB (GOV_B_CA) and current account (CU) are expressed as percentage share of GDP. Real output growth rate (GDP_D) is expressed as percentage change of annual real GDP over the corresponding period in the previous year. Data in the tables below each figure represent large changes (+ for improvement, – for deterioration) in (1) current account (CU), (2) private savings-investment gap to GDP ratio (SPIP), and (3) overall savings-investment gap to GDP ratio (SI). The last row represents (4) annual changes in real output. For (1), (2), and (3), each individual sign (+ or –) represents a large change during one year (four quarters) backward.

CAPB (–) (with negative real GDP interference)

CAPB (–) (w/o negative real GDP interference)

CAPB (+) (with positive real GDP interference)

CAPB (+) (w/o positive real GDP interference)

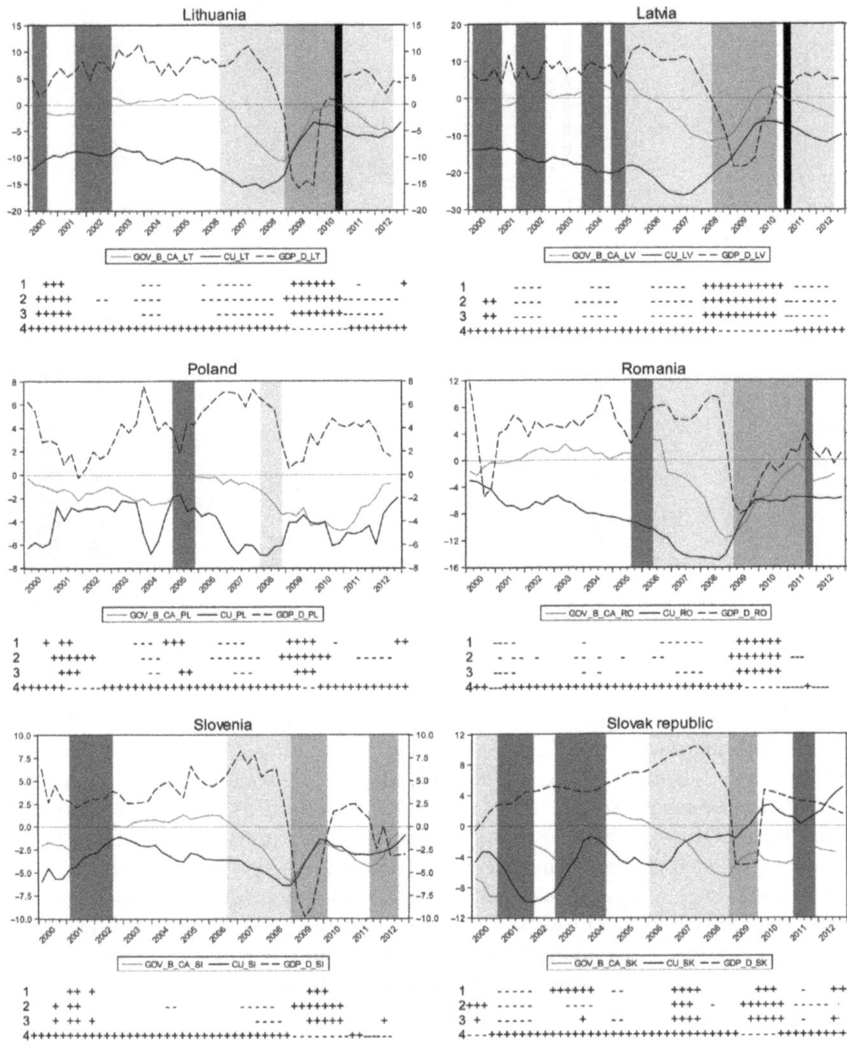

Fig. 3. (*Continued*)

deteriorations (1 episode with and 2 episodes without GDP interference). CAPB episodes seem to be rare during the pre-crisis period, and their interference with either GDP or current account was generally low. Large CAPB changes intensified during the crisis period. The parallel occurrence of CAPB episodes and current account, SPIP, and SI episodes became obvious.

The Czech Republic experienced 5 large continuous fiscal changes: 3 improvements (2 episodes with and 1 episode without GDP interference) and 2 deteriorations (both episodes without GDP interference). Fiscal episodes occurred with a few quarters lag behind SPIP episodes, which seems to neutralize these mutually contrary trends on the overall SI balance (we have observed no large SI episode during the first half of the period) during the pre-crisis period. Effects associated with the beginning of the crisis period resulted in the parallel occurrence of CAPB, current account, SPIP, and SI episodes of the same direction, though with different intensity and durability.

Estonia experienced 6 large continuous fiscal changes: 3 improvements (2 episodes with and 1 episode without GDP interference) and 3 deteriorations (1 episode with and 2 episodes without GDP interference). Despite the relatively high occurrence of CAPB episodes, associated interactions with large current account adjustments were not obvious, though deteriorating CAPB episodes were followed by corresponding SPIP and SI episodes. However, the situation significantly changed during the crisis period. We identified large continuous CAPB changes with parallel occurrence of current account as well as SPIP and SI episodes.

Hungary experienced 9 large continuous fiscal changes: 5 improvements (2 episodes with and 3 episodes without GDP interference) and 4 deteriorations (2 episodes with and 2 episodes without GDP interference). Negative large CAPB episodes were associated with lagged (first) or nonsignificant (second) current account deteriorations. The remaining pre-crisis continuous CAPB changes were not followed by equivalent current account adjustments. At the same time, all pre-crisis CPAB episodes were associated with opposite SPIP and SI changes that probably neutralize the effects of fiscal stance changes. Only the initial CAPB episode during the crisis period was parallel with large current account, SPIP, and SI changes. The remaining CAPB episodes were followed only by lagged SPIP episodes.

Lithuania experienced 6 large continuous fiscal changes: 3 improvements (2 episodes with and 1 episode without GDP interference) and 3 deteriorations (1 episode with and 2 episodes without GDP interference). The occurrence of large CAPB episodes (except the initial one) was not strictly parallel with continuous current account changes during the pre-crisis period. However, we observed a significant intersection of current account, SPIP, and SI episodes. Parallel occurrence significantly improved during the crisis period, though the last large CAPB change was associated with less dynamic current account deterioration.

Latvia experienced 8 large continuous fiscal changes: 5 improvements (4 episodes with and 1 episode without GDP interference) and 3 deteriorations (1 episode with and 2 episodes without GDP interference). Large CAPB episodes were not associated with continuous current account changes during the most of the pre-crisis period (except the last one). However, we observed a clear improvement in the parallel occurrence of episodes in all indicators (CAPB, current account, SPIP, SI) during the crisis period.

Poland experienced 2 large continuous fiscal changes: 1 improvement with GDP interference and 1 deterioration without GDP interference. Large fiscal episodes in Poland were quite rare. Neither continuous fiscal change occurred in strict parallel with current account episodes. The first CAPB episode lagged slightly, and the second one significantly behind large current account changes. We did not observe any large CAPB episode during the crisis period.

Romania experienced 4 large continuous fiscal changes: 3 improvements (2 episodes with and 1 episode without GDP interference) and 1 deterioration without GDP interference. The country did not experience any parallel occurrence of large CAPB or current account episodes during the pre-crisis period. However, the situation significantly changed during the crisis period. We observed a parallel occurrence of two large CAPB and current account changes (1 deterioration and 1 improvement).

The Slovak Republic experienced 6 large continuous fiscal changes: 4 improvements (3 episodes with and 1 episode without GDP interference) and 2 deteriorations (both episodes without GDP interference). We identified mixed results of CAPB and current account episode occurrence during the pre-crisis period. The first large CAPB change (deterioration) was followed by a current account change of the same direction but with a significant lag, clearly interfering with the following CAPB episode (improvement). The parallel occurrence of CAPB and current account changes was observed only during the second episode of CAPB improvement. During the crisis period we identified only 1 large current account improvement, though clearly lagging behind CAPB episode. For the rest of the crisis, continuous CAPB and current account changes followed contrary trends.

Slovenia experienced 4 large continuous fiscal changes: 3 improvements (1 episode with and 2 episodes without GDP interference) and 1 deterioration without GDP interference. Both pre-crisis CAPB episodes occurred in parallel with current account episodes. While the first large CAPB change was followed by the lagged current account episode, the second CAPB episode was not associated with a significant current account adjustment.

Examination of current account episodes in the European transition economies revealed some crucial implications of large and continuous current account changes. We have observed strong evidence of large current account (CU) changes and overall savings-investment gap to GDP ratio (SI) in parallel occurrence. While changes in public (CAPB[6]) and private (SPIP) savings-investment gap to GDP ratio generally corresponded with large current account adjustments, in minor cases we have observed either a contrary trend in both categories or the magnitude of change did not meet condition (1) to be considered a large continuous change. SPIP episodes seem to be generally more frequent than CAPB episodes, and thus afford a more accurate interpretation of a causal relationship between large and continuous current account changes and corresponding adjustments in SI balance. This investigation is even more relevant in countries with strong exchange rate anchors (in countries from the group of "peggers") and more prudential fiscal policy. The lower occurrence of large changes in the fiscal stance in these countries during the pre-crisis period thus corresponds with our general expectations.

Examination of fiscal episodes in the European transition economies revealed some crucial implications of large and continuous fiscal changes. The low impact of large CAPB changes on real output was caused by reduced GDP interference with internal (fiscal) imbalances due to high real output growth rates, followed by an intensified convergence during the first half of the period. At the same time, it seems that the crisis period, associated with deterioration effects on overall demand (both internal and external), reduced exposure of GDP to internal (fiscal) imbalances as well. We also observed persistent disproportions between CAPB and SGSI, revealing substantial effects of the business cycle on the budgetary components.

Table 2 summarizes the revealed episodes of large continuous current account and CAPB changes in the European transition economies since 2000. The number of episodes with improved current accounts was slightly higher than the number of episodes with improved CAPB. This difference is significantly higher in the case of deteriorating episodes.

The occurrence of current account episode types is clearly distributed between the crisis and pre-crisis periods. Most episodes associated with large current account deteriorations occurred during the pre-crisis period, revealing the generally expected proposition of an intertemporal approach

Table 2. Episodes of Large Current Account and Fiscal Changes (2000Q1–2012Q4) (Brief Overview of Episodes Types Occurrence).

	Current Account Changes					Fiscal Changes				
	Improvement		Deterioration		Total	Improvement		Deterioration		Total
	With GDP interference	W/o GDP interference	With GDP interference	W/o GDP interference		With GDP interference	W/o GDP interference.	With GDP interference	W/o GDP interference	
Bulgaria	2	2	1	3	8	1	1	1	2	5
Czech Republic	3	1	0	2	6	2	1	0	2	5
Estonia	3	1	0	3	7	2	1	1	2	6
Hungary	3	1	0	2	6	2	3	2	2	9
Lithuania	1	2	1	3	7	2	1	1	2	6
Latvia	1	1	1	4	7	4	1	1	2	8
Poland	3	3	0	3	9	1	0	0	1	2
Romania	1	1	1	4	7	2	1	0	1	4
Slovak Republic	3	1	0	3	7	3	1	0	2	6
Slovenia	1	1	0	0	2	1	2	0	1	4
Total	*21*	*14*	*4*	*27*	*66*	*20*	*12*	*6*	*17*	*55*
Average durability (in quarters)	*5.15*	*6.07*	*3.36*	*5.04*		*4.89*	*6.42*	*2.67*	*7.63*	

Source: Author's calculation.
Note: Data represent a number of episodes of large current account and fiscal changes.

for converging economies catching up to western European countries. All countries experienced episodes of large current account improvement at the beginning of the crisis period as an immediate result of deteriorating effects affecting domestic demand. However, the subsequent higher occurrence of contrary large current account episodes demonstrates the accelerated redistributive effects of the crisis associated with short-term expenditure shifting across countries, causing higher volatility in current account balances.

The occurrence of CAPB episodes seems to be distributed across the whole period more uniformly. However, episodes of large CAPB improvements tend to be more frequent during the pre-crisis period. Moreover, the durability of continuous CAPB improvements is clearly higher in the Baltic countries (with rigorous exchange rate anchoring), highlighting a commitment to conduct prudential fiscal policies necessary to maintain sustainability of a tough exchange rate arrangement. At the same time, episodes of large fiscal policy improvements helped to reduce the persistent SI disequilibrium caused by deteriorating SPIP imbalances in the whole group of "peggers." In countries with flexible exchange rate arrangements ("floaters"), we observed some sort of alteration in episodes of CAPB improvement and deterioration in the medium-term period. All countries (except for Hungary) experienced a large deteriorating episode at the beginning of the crisis period followed by an improving episode (except for Poland), with differing lags, revealing a crucial need for fiscal consolidation.

Table 3 summarizes a detailed overview of intertemporal effects associated with episodes of large continuous current account and CAPB changes and associated adjustments in SI, SPIP, and SGIG balances in the European transition economies since 2000. The average length of the current account episode was more than 5.2 quarters [episodes of current account improvement (5.4 quarters) were slightly more durable than episodes of current account deterioration (5.16 quarters)] and the CAPB episode more than 5.6 quarters [episodes of CAPB deterioration (6.95 quarters) were significantly more durable than episodes of CAPB improvement (4.85 quarters)]. The average change in the current account was −0.96 percent of GDP, consisting of 3.38 percent of GDP for positive episodes and −4.34 percent of GDP for negative episodes. Average change of CAPB is −1.41 percent of GDP, consisting of 3.16 percent of GDP for positive episodes and −4.57 percent of GDP for negative episodes.

The relative contribution of private and public savings-investment balances to the overall SI stance reflected in current account improvement and deterioration episodes seems to be quite different. Around 78 percent of the average current account balances during large current account

Table 3. Episodes of Large Current Account and Fiscal Changes (2000Q1–2012Q4) (Detailed Overview of Intertemporal Effects).

Type of Episode	Number of Episodes	Duration (Quarters)	Δ	NX			SI			SPIP			SGIG		
				+	–	Net	+	–	Net	+	–	Net	+	–	Net
CU	66	5.20	–0.96	6.51	–7.47	–0.96	6.36	–7.31	–0.95	4.24	–3.09	1.16	2.18	–4.29	–2.11
CU (+)	35	5.40	3.38	4.89	–1.51	3.38	4.85	–1.56	3.29	3.93	–1.31	2.62	0.91	–0.26	0.65
CU (–)	31	5.16	–4.34	1.62	–5.96	–4.34	1.51	–5.76	–4.25	0.31	–1.78	–1.46	1.26	–4.03	–2.77
CAPB	55	5.65	–1.41	3.51	–4.62	–1.11	2.86	–4.00	–1.14	1.18	0.18	1.36	1.64	–4.10	–2.46
CAPB (+)	32	4.85	3.16	2.26	–0.20	2.06	2.14	–0.12	2.02	–1.01	0.31	–0.70	3.15	–0.39	2.76
CAPB (–)	23	6.95	–4.57	1.25	–4.42	–3.17	0.72	–3.88	–3.16	2.19	–0.13	2.06	–1.51	–3.71	–5.22

Source: Author's calculation.

Note: Data in the first column represent a number of large CU (current account) and CAPB (cyclically adjusted primary balance) changes (episodes); the second column shows the average duration in quarters followed by estimated changes, expressed as GDP shares.

improvements is associated with positive SPIP balances and thus a minor contribution of SGIG balances. On the other hand, the contribution of SPIP to the average current account balances during large current account deteriorations is only 34 percent, revealing a much higher impact of SGIG balances. Our findings seem to be contrary to the key outcomes proposed by Abbas et al. (2011),[7] who revealed that changes in the current account during average episodes are driven almost exclusively by SPIP balances in advanced economies, while in emerging and low-income countries it is around three-fourths of the change in current account. The much higher contribution of SGIG to current account deterioration reveals a substantial causal relationship between deteriorating fiscal episodes and current account deteriorations. We suggest that this observation originates in the weaker fiscal discipline in countries from the group of "floaters" during the pre-crisis period and associated crowding-out effects that contributed to current accounts deterioration. A significant contribution also refers to the intensive deterioration in the fiscal stance in most countries in the group at the beginning of the crisis period. The lack of fiscal discipline in countries without explicit strong nominal anchors also reveals questions associated with fiscal sustainability after euro adoption.

Large CAPB improvements and deteriorations revealed a significant responsiveness of large current account adjustments to fiscal incentives (0.65 +). The ratio is slightly higher for CAPB deteriorating episodes. The responsiveness of the current account is slightly higher during deteriorating episodes that, in our sample of countries, typically occurred at the beginning of the crisis period. Deterioration in overall demand (for domestic as well as foreign goods), together with accelerated negative trends in CAPB, intensified contrary trends in current account and fiscal balances. Large CAPB changes were associated with contrary adjustments in SPIP balances. As a result, private savings offset around 32 percent of CAPB changes (fiscal impulse) for episodes of CAPB improvements and around 48 percent of CAPB changes for episodes of CAPB deteriorations. Offsetting effects are clearly visible in most countries during the initial effects of the crisis period.

CONCLUSION

Current account adjustments revealed crucial implications of the continuously rising international economic and financial integration of this group of countries (increased indebtedness, lacking competitiveness, fiscal imbalances, foreign capital inflows, etc.). However, there is still enough room to investigate partial effects of dynamic changes in key current account determinants to observe associated current account adjustments.

Changes in the fiscal policy stance associated with changes in CAPB affected current accounts in the European transition economies. Despite some differences, we have observed similar trends in the trajectories of current accounts and savings-investment gaps that clearly follow the main outcomes of an intertemporal approach. However, expenditure shifting effects associated with current account imbalances in each individual country do not seem to be determined solely by the internal balance between savings and investments. Countries from the group of "peggers" experienced periods with generally higher discrepancies in CAPB and current account balances. The beginning of the crisis period clearly reduced these misalignments. In the group of "floaters," we examined persistent negative SI imbalances, originating in excessive fiscal deficits.

The occurrence of episodes of large CAPB change seems to be uniformly distributed across the whole period. The durability of continuous CAPB improvements is clearly higher in the Baltic countries (with rigorous exchange rate anchoring), highlighting a commitment to prudential fiscal policies necessary to maintain the sustainability of tough exchange rate arrangements. In countries with flexible exchange rate arrangements ("floaters"), we observed some sort of alteration in episodes of CAPB improvement and deterioration in the medium-term period. All countries (except for Hungary) experienced a large deteriorating episode at the beginning of the crisis period, followed by improving episodes (except for Poland), with differing lags, revealing the crucial need for fiscal consolidation. Large CAPB improvements and deteriorations revealed a significant responsiveness of large current account adjustments to fiscal incentives (0.65 +) in the whole group of countries. The ratio is slightly higher for CAPB deteriorating episodes.

NOTES

1. The Hungarian forint operated during the pre-crisis period in de facto fixed peg regime, but due to the substantial range for fluctuations provided by wide horizontal bands, it was included in the group of so-called "floater" countries.

2. However, small reversals are allowed (up to 20 percent in reverse direction against the main trend) to preserve a substantial quantity of identified periods. In the original study by Abbas et al. (2011) no reversals in the trend are allowed at all.

3. Despite wide criticism of the Hodrick-Prescott (HP) filter for inducing a spurious cycle in the time series (i.e. it cannot reflect an impact of structural breaks) as well as for poor approximation near the endpoint (so-called endpoint bias), it still represents one of the most frequently used filters in the current empirical literature.

4. Detailed results of the unit root test are not reported here to save space. As with any other results, they are available upon request from the author.

5. The rule for identification of large changes in the private savings-investment gap to GDP ratio and the overall savings-investment gap to GDP ratio follows just condition (1) from Section 5.1 for a proposed identification scheme. Otherwise, we would have identified a much lower occurrence of both episodes.

6. While CAPB is not an accurate measure for calculation of overall net public (savings-investment) position, it was employed in this section to reveal intertemporal effects of discrete changes in fiscal policy stance.

7. However, the authors covered the period 1970–2007 in their study, avoiding effects of the crisis period on the fiscal balances.

ACKNOWLEDGMENT

This paper was written in connection with scientific project VEGA no. 1/0892/13. Financial support from the Ministry of Education's scheme is also gratefully acknowledged.

REFERENCES

Abbas, S. M. A., Bouhga-Hagbe, J., Fatás, A., Mauro, P., & Velloso, R. C. (2011). Fiscal policy and the current account. *IMF Economic Review*, *59*(4), 603–629.

Alesina, A., & Ardagna, S. (2009). *Large changes in fiscal policy: Taxes vs. spending*. [National Bureau of Economic Research Working Paper No. 15438]. National Bureau of Economic Research, New York, p. 37.

Altăr, M., Necula, C., & Bobeică, G. (2010). Estimating the cyclically adjusted budget balance for the romanian economy. A Robust Approach. *Romanian Journal of Economic Forecasting*, *13*(2), 79–99.

Arghyrou, M. G., & Chortareas, G. (2008). Current account imbalances and real exchange rates in the Euro area. *Review of International Economics*, *9*(5), 747–764.

Bouthevillain, C., Cour-Thimann, P., Van Den Dool, G., Hernández De Cos, P., Langenus, G., Mohr, M., ... Tujula, M. (2001). *Cyclically adjusted budget balances: An alternative approach*. [European Central Bank Working Paper No. 77/2001]. European Central Bank, Frankfurt am Main, p. 73.

Bussiere, M., Fratzscher, M., & Muller, G. J. (2004). *Current account dynamics in OECD and EU acceding countries – An intertemporal approach*. [European Central Bank, Working Paper No. 311/2004] Frankfurt, European Central Bank, 38 p.

Caldara, D., & Camps, C. (2008). *What are the effects of fiscal policy shocks*. [European Central Bank Working Paper No. 877/2008] Frankfurt am Main, European Central Bank, 47 p.

Chinn, M. D., & Prasad, E. S. (2003). Medium-term determinants of current accounts in industrial and developing countries: An empirical exploration. *Journal of International Economics*, *59*(1), 47–76.

Corsetti, G., & Gernot, J. M., (2006). Budget deficits and current accounts: Openness and fiscal persistence. *Economic Policy*, *21*(48), 597–638.

Corsetti, G., & Müller, G. (2006). Twin deficits: Squaring theory, evidence and common sense. *Economic Policy*, *48*, 597–638.

Fidrmuc, J. (2002). Twin deficits: Implications of current account and fiscal imbalances for the accession countries. *Focus on Transition*, *2*, 72–83.

Girouard, N., & André, C. (2005). *Measuring cyclically-adjusted budget balance for EOCD countries*. [Organization for Economic Cooperation and Development Working Paper No. 21/2005] Paris, Organization for Economic Cooperation and Development, 42 p.

Glick, R., & Rogoff, K. (1995). Global versus country-specific productivity shocks and the current account. *Journal of Monetary Economics*, *35*(1), 159–192.

Gruber, J. W., & Kamin, S. (2005). *Explaining the global pattern of current account imbalances, board of governors of the federal reserve system*. International Finance Discussion Papers, 846.

Günaydın, E., & UğraşÜlkü, Z. (2002). Cyclically Adjusted Primary Balance: The Case of Turkey, VI. International Conference in Economics, September 11th–14th, Ankara, Turkey, 52 p.

Hassan, M. (2004). Budget deficits and the current account balance: New evidence from panel data. *Journal of Economics and Finance*, *28*(1), 39–45.

IMF. (2014). International Financial Statistics (October 2014), CD-ROM.

Javid, A. Y., Javid, M., & Arif, U. (2010). Fiscal policy and current account dynamics in case of Pakistan. *The Pakistan Development Review*, *49*(4), 577–592.

Johansen, S. (1988). Statistical analysis of cointegrating vectors. *Journal of Economic Dynamic & Control*, *12*(2–3), 231–254.

Johansen, S. (1991). Estimation and hypothesis testing of cointegrating vectors in Gaussian Vector autoregressive models. *Econometrica*, *59*(6), 1551–1580.

Kim, S., & Roubini, N. (2008). Twin deficit or twin divergence? Fiscal policy, current account and real exchange rate in the US. *Journal of International Economics*, *74*, 362–383.

Kumhof, M., & Laxton, D. (2009). *Fiscal deficits and current account deficits*. [International Monetary Fund, Working Paper No. 237/2009] Washington, International Monetary Fund, 35 p.

Lane, P. R. (2010). *External imbalances and fiscal policy*. [Institute for International Integration Studies, Working Paper No. 314/2010] Dublin, Trinity College Dublin and CEPR, 24 p.

Lee, J., & Chinn, M. D. (2006). Current account and real exchange rate dynamics in the G7 countries. *Journal of International Money and Finance*, *25*(2006), 257–274.

Obstfeld, M., & Rogoff, K. (1995). *The intertemporal approach to the current account.* [National Bureau of Economic Research Working Paper No. 4893] New York, National Bureau of Economic Research, 75 p.

Obstfeld, M., & Rogoff, K. S. (2005). Global current account imbalances and exchange rate adjustments. *Brookings Papers on Economic Activity*, *36*(1), 67–123.

Roubini, N. (1988). *Current account and budget deficits in an intertemporal model of consumption and taxation smoothing. A solution to the feldstein-horioka puzzle?* [National Bureau of Economic Research Working Paper No. 2773] New York, National Bureau of Economic Research, 52 p.

Schnabl, G., & Wollmershäuser, T. (2012). *Fiscal divergence and current account imbalances in Europe*. [CESifo, Working Paper No. 4108] Munich, CESifo, 38 p.

Sek, S. K., & Chuah, C. L. (2013). The dynamic of the current account in emerging East-Asian: Does exchange rate matter? *International Journal of Trade, Economics and Finance*, *2*(4), 293–299.

Soyoung, K., & Roubini, N. (2008). Twin deficit and twin divergence? Fiscal policy, current account, and real exchange rate in the U.S. *Journal of Economic Literature, 74*, 362–383.

PART V
INTERNATIONAL TRADE AND ECONOMIC INTEGRATION

ESTIMATING REMITTANCES IN THE FORMER SOVIET UNION: METHODOLOGICAL COMPLEXITIES AND POTENTIAL SOLUTIONS

Jakhongir Kakhkharov and Alexandr Akimov

ABSTRACT

Remittances in the former Soviet Union have increased rapidly over the past decade. In some countries of the former Soviet Union, remittances have reached staggering levels. For example, in Armenia, Kyrgyzstan, Moldova, Tajikistan, and Uzbekistan remittances now account for over 10% of GDP, with Tajikistan leading the pack with annual remittances of approximately 40% of GDP. Remittances in this group of economies now exceed foreign direct investment and foreign assistance. Because this rapid rise in remittances is a relatively recent trend and obtaining reliable data is difficult, this area of research has been underexplored.

The aim of this paper is to provide a comprehensive review of existing remittance measurement methodologies. Moreover, we propose practical methods to adjust the Central Bank of Russia data to derive more

Neo-Transitional Economics
International Finance Review, Volume 16, 337–362

ISSN: 1569-3767/doi:10.1108/S1569-376720150000016014

accurate remittances estimates in selected countries of the former Soviet Union. These selected economies are major recipients of remittances among transition economies and account for as much as 10% of remittances worldwide. There have been attempts to provide this type of estimation in individual countries; however, there have been no studies, to our knowledge, that propose a general methodology for the region.

Keywords: Remittances; international migration; labor migration; macroeconomic data

JEL classifications: F24; F22; C82

INTRODUCTION

Migrant remittances in the former Soviet Union are a relatively recent trend. However, they became an important element of neo-transitional economies from the beginning of the 2000s. The growth rate of remittances over the past decade is remarkable. In some countries of the former Soviet Union, remittances have reached staggering levels. For example, in Armenia, Kyrgyzstan, Moldova, Tajikistan, and Uzbekistan remittances now account for over 10% of GDP, with Tajikistan leading the pack with annual remittances of approximately 40% of GDP. Remittances in this group of economies now exceed foreign direct investment (FDI) and foreign assistance. Because this rapid rise in remittances is a relatively recent trend and obtaining reliable data is difficult, this area of research has been underexplored.

Data availability improved in 2006 when the Central Bank of Russia (CBR) began publishing data on money transfers from Russia through money transfer operators (MTOs) by recipient country. Moreover, the CBR publishes the cross-border transactions of individuals (both residents and non-residents) conducted through all credit institutions (including MTOs). The statistics demonstrate that the largest proportion of remittances is channeled through MTOs. In 2012, the total volume of cross-border flows to the CIS (Commonwealth of Independent States) countries via all credit institutions equaled $19.2 billion, whereas money transfers through MTOs amounted to $18.2 billion. Approximately 80% of this $1 billion difference is due to transfers to Ukraine, Armenia, and Georgia – countries with more developed financial systems.[1] Remittances to these countries are often sent using bank wire transfers. The fact that the majority of remittances are conducted via MTOs is unfortunate because remittances sent through the banking sector are more likely to be retained within the banking sector in the form of deposits and therefore possess greater potential for economic development.

The datasets published by the CBR allow estimation of the volume of remittances from Russia to the former Soviet republics. Because Russia is the major source of remittances for these economies, the estimation and analysis of these flows is very important for economic policy making in neo-transitional economies. The aim of this paper is to undertake a comprehensive review of existing knowledge on the scope, scale, and estimation methodologies applicable to ex-Soviet republics, as well as contemporary challenges. Moreover, we suggest a potential method to improve the accuracy of remittances estimation, by adjusting data published by the CBR. Global financial crisis had a significant term impact on remittances from Russia. However, despite its continuous drag on the global financial markets, decline in remittances from Russia was very brief. In 2009, remittances from Russia bounced back and currently greatly exceed pre-crisis levels. Some post-Soviet economies are major recipients of remittances and as a group account for as much as 10% of remittances worldwide. There have been attempts to provide this type of estimation in individual countries; however, there have been no studies, to our knowledge, that provide a comprehensive analysis of remittances and their estimation problems that propose ways to improve estimation accuracy for the region. Remittances in this region frequently flow through unofficial channels. Moreover, a large share of petty trade is disguised as remittances which makes the accurate estimation of remittances difficult (Ibragimova, Burzhubaev, & Temirov, 2008; Mughal, 2007; Rustamov, 2008). Therefore, we propose adjusting the official statistics to account for informal remittances and petty trade.

This paper consists of seven sections. The next section briefly introduces the institutional setting in which the flow of remittances to the post-Soviet region takes place. This section also describes the trends, magnitude, and importance of these flows for the economies of the former Soviet Union. The section "Review of Remittances Measurement Methodologies" reviews the concept of remittances as defined in the fifth and sixth editions of the IMF Balance of Payments (BoPs) Manuals. Although the most recent sixth edition significantly revised the concept of remittances, its definition is still hampered by practical and methodological problems. The section "Remittances and Remittance Transfer Channels in the Former Soviet Union" describes the problems involved in the estimation of remittances in the former Soviet Union. The section "Estimation Methods" analyzes and briefly evaluates some alternative methods to estimate remittances utilized by practitioners and researchers. In the section "The Adjustment Methodology and Its Application to Remittances in the Former Soviet Republics," we propose adjustments to more accurately estimate remittances from Russia to selected former Soviet countries. The last section summarizes the major findings of the paper. This section also provides suggestions to improve the remittance measurement framework.

THE INSTITUTIONAL SETTING FOR REMITTANCES IN THE POST-SOVIET REGION

In 2012, the Russian Federal Migration Service (FMS) estimated the number of labor migrants entering the country to be approximately 11–14 million people per year. According to the FMS, 77% of these migrants come from the CIS (Rossiyskoe Informatsionnoe Agentstvo – Novosti, 2012). Following this migration flow in the 2000s, the scale of remittances in the post-Soviet region has also increased dramatically. Russia is the largest migrant receiving country and the main source of remittances into the other members of the CIS. According to the CBR, the total amount of money transfers sent from Russia to other CIS states increased by a factor of 36 between 1999 and 2012, that is, from $0.5 billion to $19.205 billion (Central Bank of Russia [CBR], 2012).

The main recipients of remittances in the post-Soviet region are Uzbekistan, Tajikistan, Ukraine, Kyrgyzstan, Moldova, Armenia, Georgia, and Azerbaijan. Although there are no precise estimates, it is a stylized fact that remittances from Russia constitute the majority of remittances in these economies. Financial transfer channels between the major remittance recipient countries in the former Soviet Union and Russia can be divided into two categories: "formal" or "official" and "informal" or "unofficial" remittance channels. The official channels utilize banks and MTOs. Unofficial channels utilize friends, relatives, methods similar to "hawala,"[2] exchange through electronic accounts and transporting money themselves.

Armenia provides a good example of the disarray in the estimation of remittances. Tumasyan, Manukyan, Torosyan, Terzikyan, and Mnatsakanyan (2008), based on a survey of 3,000 respondents in Armenia, estimated total remittances to Armenia at $381 million in 2006. However, IMF BoPs statistics estimated total remittances at $505 million in the same year. The CBR reported that Russia alone transferred $604 million in remittances via MTOs and postal offices to Armenia in 2006[3] (Shelburne & Palacin, 2007). The survey conducted by Tumasyan et al. (2008) indicated that 58% of all remittances were received through banks and MTOs. That same survey reported that 76.9% of all remittances originated in Russia. However, another survey conducted by Central Bank of Armenia in 2005 suggests that 78% of all remittances were received via banks and MTOs (Central Bank of Armenia, 2006).

Different estimates of remittances to Azerbaijan are also difficult to reconcile. A survey conducted with funding from the Asian Development Bank (ADB) estimated total remittances to Azerbaijan at $428 million in 2006, whereas the balance of payments data for Azerbaijan suggests workers' remittances and migrant transfers through MTOs and banks of $679 million (Rustamov, 2008). The same survey found that transfers through MTOs and banks accounted for 32% of remittances to Azerbaijan in 2006, which increases the total amount of remittances to Azerbaijan to $2.1 billion. Data from the Russian Central Bank suggest remittances from Russia through MTOs and postal offices alone of $440 million (Shelburne & Palacin, 2007). Russia was the source of 83% of all remittances to Azerbaijan in 2006 (Rustamov, 2008).

Despite the aggravation of political relations between Georgia and Russia in 2006, Russia continues to generate a significant flow of remittances to Georgia. The Russian Federation accounted for 56% of remittances to Georgia in 2010 (Melkadze, 2012). This same study noted data from the National Bank of Georgia estimating that the total amount of remittances sent through official channels to Georgia in 2011 reached $940 million, which represents approximately 8.1% of the GDP of Georgia. The CBR estimated remittances to Georgia via MTOs and banks of $754 million (CBR, 2011).

An ADB funded study by Ibragimova et al. (2008) estimated remittances in 2006 to Kyrgyzstan at $253 million, whereas the Kyrgyz National Bank estimate for the same year indicates that remittances exceeded $730 million. The Russian Central Bank reported remittances to Kyrgyzstan from Russia for the same year of $438 million (Shelburne & Palacin, 2007). Russia accounted for 82% of remittances to Kyrgyzstan in 2006 (Ibragimova et al., 2008). This report also found that nearly 78% of all remittances to Kyrgyzstan were transferred through banks and MTOs in 2006. Mogilevsky and Atamanov (2008) noted that large ($10,000–50,000) and very large (more than $50,000) transactions made up 22% and 72% of all remittances, respectively, and concluded that the majority of funds in these types of transactions are actually the revenues of shuttle traders and repayments of loans for trade deals.

Luecke, Mahmoud, and Steinmayr (2009) estimated that the total value of remittances to Moldova was approximately $1.5 billion and $1.9 billion in 2007 and 2008, respectively. The Russian Central Bank report on cross-border transfers via MTOs and postal offices estimated remittances from Russia to Moldova of $832 million and $1.143 billion in 2007 and 2008, respectively (CBR, 2007, 2008a).

Brown, Olimova, and Boboev (2008), utilizing data from the National Bank of Tajikistan (NBT), estimated that the value of remittances through official channels to Tajikistan was $1.13 billion in 2006. The data from the Russian Central Bank suggest that the value of remittances from Russia through MTOs and postal offices was equal to $957 million in the same year (Shelburne & Palacin, 2007). Brown et al. (2008) estimated that Russia was the source of 83% of total remittances to Tajikistan in 2006, and approximately 10–15% of remittances via official channels were related to shuttle trade. Citing NBT representatives, Brown et al. (2008) note that 10–15% of remittances were transferred to Tajikistan informally in 2006. Mughal (2007) estimates a slightly higher share, 18.5%, of informal transfers based on Khatlon Living Standards Survey and notes that this share should be further adjusted for in-kind transfers valued at approximately 7% of total transfers.

The following balance of payments data from the National Bank of Ukraine, presented in Table 1, was prepared according to the sixth edition of the IMF BoPs and International Investment Manual of IMF.

Kupets (2012) reports estimates of remittances to Ukraine ranging from $1.7 billion to $54 billion and highlights alternative estimates of the proportion of transfers occurring through informal channels, which range from 15% to 200% of official remittances. Table 2 presents the data from the Russian Central Bank for remittances to Ukraine originating in Russia.

Table 1. Remittances to Ukraine in Millions of $.

Description	2008	2009	2010	2011	2012
Total remittances	6,177	5,370	5,862	7,019	7,526
Through informal channels	805	713	777	963	1,035
From the Russian Federation	NA	NA	1,619	1,988	2,350
Remittances as a % of GDP	3.4	4.6	4.3	4.3	4.3

Source: National Bank of Ukraine [NBU] (2013).

Table 2. Remittances from Russia to Ukraine in Millions of $.

Description	2010	2011	2012
Remittances from Russia to Ukraine	2,201	2,758	3,162

Source: CBR (2010, 2011, 2012).

The State Committee for the Republic of Uzbekistan on Demonopolization (2006) draws data from the Ministry of Labor to note that approximately 75% of the total workforce migrating from Uzbekistan traveled to the Russian Federation (State Committee for the Republic of Uzbekistan on Demonopolization, 2006). Uzbekistan has been the top recipient of remittances from Russia through MTOs since the CBR began publishing these data in 2006.

REVIEW OF REMITTANCES MEASUREMENT METHODOLOGIES

To understand the challenges encountered in measuring remittances, it is useful to define the major concepts. The sixth edition of the IMF BoPs and International Investment Position Manual (International Monetary Fund [IMF], 2009, p. 272) notes that "remittances represent household income from foreign economies arising mainly from the temporary or permanent movement of people to those economies." Remittances include cash and noncash items that flow through formal channels, such as wire transfers, or through informal channels, such as money or goods carried across borders. Remittances consist primarily of funds and noncash items from individuals who have migrated to a new country and became residents there; these funds also include the net compensation of border, seasonal, or other short-term workers who are employed in an economy in which they are not resident. According to the IMF (2009, p. 272), "The two items in the balance of payments framework that substantially relate to remittances are 'compensation of employees' and 'personal transfers'. Both of these standard components are recorded in the current account."

Total remittances encompass personal remittances, which consist of the compensation of employees, personal transfers, and capital transfers between households and social benefits. Social benefits include "benefits payable under social security funds and pension funds. They may be in cash or in kind" (IMF, 2009, p. 213). Thus, the total amount of remittances includes income from individuals working abroad for short periods, from individuals residing abroad and sending transfers, and from social benefits from abroad.

The most notable change in the new edition of BPM6 that is relevant to remittances is in "personal transfers," which replaces the concept "workers' remittances" in the BPM5. In addition, the new manual includes transferrable social benefits in the definition of remittances.

Many authors have previously criticized the definition of "workers' remittances" for its link to the UN's concept of a long-term migrant, which consists of residents staying for 12 months or more (Alfieri, Havinga, & Hvidsten, 2006). This concept excluded seasonal migrants and second-generation migrants. The exclusion of seasonal migrants and their remittances in the former Soviet Union was especially misleading because labor migration in this region is predominantly seasonal. Furthermore, the previous definition of remittances included only officially recorded migrants and their families. However, it is estimated that majority of labor migrants from former Soviet Union countries working in Russia are not frequently given formal labor agreements by their employers. In some cases, remittances might be channeled through employers and acquaintances in Russia. Therefore, these payments are not captured in the BoP statistics on remittances.

The distinctive feature of the IMF's new definition is the absence of the concept of "migrant." Rather, new definitions are based on the concept of "residence," a broader concept that incorporates a larger migration process. The manual stipulates that personal remittances include transfers originating from individuals who are not migrant workers. In other words, transfers from second-generation and naturalized citizens are included in the new version of the manual. Another improvement is that the definition of personal transfers, consistent with the 1993 System of National Accounts' definition, encompasses all transfers from residents to non-residents whatever the source of income, the relationship between them, and the purpose of the transfer. In addition, the BPM6 also extends the concept of total remittances and transfers to non-profit institutions serving households (NPISHs). This item is the sum of personal remittances, social benefits (defined as "disposable income from abroad"), and current transfers to NPISHs. The BPM6 significantly broadens and improves the conceptualization of remittances in previous definitions. However, the revision further complicates the measurement of remittances. For instance, practical problems in identifying particular population groups, such as second-generation migrants, utilizing survey data often prevent their inclusion in measurement (Lerch, Wanner, & Haug, 2008). Therefore, many countries either do not report remittances in BoP or provide extremely inaccurate estimates.

As noted above, some migrant workers (in the case of labor migration in the CIS, most likely the majority of workers) reside in a recipient country temporarily and seasonally. Upon returning home, many migrants bring personal assets that will be owned by the household of origin. However, this type of asset is nearly impossible to account for in balance of payments transactions; therefore, these are not recorded as transfers. These in-kind transfers resemble imports of foreign goods. Unlike cash transfers that can be invested or utilized to purchase locally produced goods, these imports have, at best, no effect on GDP. In some cases, they may even have a negative substitution effect.

Furthermore, the new definitions include the compensation of employees in the measure of remittances and do not suggest a methodology for separating the part of compensation of short-term workers sent or returned to the country of origin. Obviously, not all of the income that individuals earn while working abroad will be transferred to the country of origin, and some of this money will be spent in the recipient country. For instance, Shelburne and Palacin (2007), referring to a 2005 World Bank survey, note that workers from Tajikistan spent approximately half of the income they earned in Russia for living expenses in Russia.

The propensity to spend in a host country might differ for migrants from various countries. Migrants from countries with levels of higher per capita income might be inclined to spend more in a host country compared to those from a country with a lower level of per capita income.

The underreporting of received remittances in surveys is observed in many countries (Shonkwiler, Grigorian, & Melkonyan, 2011). Possible reasons for this underreporting include: (i) the perceived risk of taxation of remittance income by the less educated population and (ii) the fear that a substantial amount of remittances may affect eligibility to receive payments or benefits from state and foreign aid organizations. Shonkwiler et al. (2011) note another potential reason – understating wealth/income to limit the demands of poorer relatives and neighbors for informal loans and advances to support their livelihood.

Thus, despite major improvements to the definition of remittances in the IMF (2009) Manual on the BoPs, additional room for improvement exists. More precise measurement of remittances requires some adjustments. This precision is important to the proper evaluation of the impact of remittances on various types of economic activities in countries receiving these remittances. Current remittance measurement tools, econometric models, and worldwide surveys suffer from serious problems. These methods are unlikely to measure remittances with a high degree of accuracy not only because migration and remittances are an infrequent, although growing phenomena, but also because of various complex issues entailed in migration and remittances (Lerch et al., 2008).

In cases where the data is sufficient to produce reliable estimates of the size of official transfers (e.g., Russia-CIS remittances where the outflow of workers' remittances is calculated utilizing data provided by MTOs and special banks), it is possible to estimate the total amount of remittances if the ratio of informal to formal remittances is known. This calculation is based on the assumption that labor migrants and their families have little incentive to lie about which channel they utilize to remit funds (Mughal, 2007). However, even in such cases, not all of the transfers are related to migrants' transfers because some of them could be related to trade. In other words, part of the transfers via MTOs must be classified as the export receipts of shuttle traders. This ratio may vary significantly for transfers from different migrant receiving countries. The proportion of remittances transferred through MTOs for neighboring countries such as Kazakhstan-Uzbekistan or Russia-Belarus might seem insignificant because migrants prefer to carry cash themselves when returning to their country of origin. The ratio of informal to formal remittances is unlikely to remain constant over time and is very sensitive to transfer commission fees charged by MTOs, MTO branch network both in host and home countries, migrants literacy in using financial services, as well as legal complexity/documentation requirements for sending and receiving funds using MTOs.

In general, our definition of remittances encompasses both transfers through financial system as well as cash returned to the home country. In-kind transfers appear to be associated with a small-scale trade, and a sizeable share of small-scale trade is disguised as remittances in the CIS, which we exclude from estimates of total remittances. In the next section, we discuss the relationship between formal and informal transfers in the former Soviet Union in greater detail.

REMITTANCES AND REMITTANCE TRANSFER CHANNELS IN THE FORMER SOVIET UNION

Until very recently, it was customary to transfer money through a network of relatives and acquaintances, train and airplane crews, bus drivers, and delivery services. However, evidence from the Khatlon Living Standards Survey (KLSS) in Tajikistan analyzed by Mughal (2007), as well as research conducted by Ibragimova et al. (2008), Luecke et al. (2009), Poghossian, Hakobyan, and Saidov (2010), Tumasyan et al. (2008) and a small-scale survey in Uzbekistan conducted by the authors reveals that the utilization of informal channels is gradually decreasing.

According to the CBR (2012), Uzbekistan and Tajikistan are the two largest recipients of remittances from Russia. It is believed that the greater volume of remittances from Russia is transferred through MTOs today than a few years ago. For example, a survey conducted by one of the authors in 2009 as part of a consulting project with the assistance of the Tashkent Regional Bureau of Employment of Citizens Abroad revealed that 74.8% of funds transferred home by respondents are transmitted through formal channels and only 25.2% of funds are transmitted through informal channels. The data from this survey were collected via contact interviews based on a standard questionnaire. A standard questionnaire was used because it is a more effective method to cover a large scope of migrants and it was less time-consuming. The questionnaires were distributed to the migrants in the Tashkent area (mainly at the airport and train stations) through the Tashkent Regional Bureau of Employment of Citizens Abroad. Some interviews were conducted by phone or face-to-face. In total, 85 people were interviewed in Tashkent. Sixty eight percent (59 people) of the sample group were urban residents and 32% (26 people) were from a rural population. Sixty four percent of respondents were male and 36% female. In terms of regional distribution, the respondents represented a good mix from all 12 regions of Uzbekistan and Karakalpakstan Autonomous Republic, although 51% of people interviewed were from the Tashkent or Tashkent region. The average age of respondents was 34 years and 29% of respondents possessed university degree qualifications.

Post-Soviet Republics, with the exception of Georgia, do not tax remittances, which combined with the favorable regulation of MTOs, encouraged the development of the remittances market. MTOs offer near to instant transactions (de Luna-Martinez, 2005). They promise the receipt of funds in another country within a few minutes to a few hours.

Migrant workers from the former Soviet Republics rarely utilize bank accounts because opening a bank account is often costly and time-consuming. Moreover, many migrant workers may face legal obstacles to opening an account in the host country due to their undocumented status there. Therefore, account-to-account transfers are less convenient than instant cash money transfers.

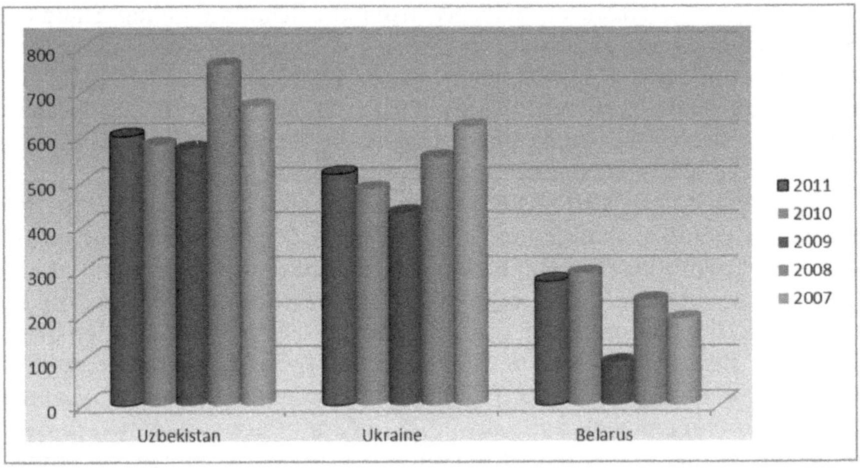

Fig. 1. Average Remittance Value for Uzbekistan, Belarus, and Ukraine.

Fig. 1 provides a comparison of transfer patterns within the CIS. This figure indicates that the average amount transferred to Uzbekistan is significantly higher than the average amount transferred to Ukraine and Belarus. Ukraine and Belarus were selected for this comparison because these countries have migrants who are typically more skilled than those from Uzbekistan and consequently earn higher wages than Uzbek migrants.

Several explanations exist for this phenomenon. Transfers to Uzbekistan are frequently consolidated, that is, several persons combine their savings and transfer the funds to a person who distributes this amount among several beneficiaries (Gusman, 2007; Zykova, 2008). Gusman (2007) observes that migrants utilize two primary channels to remit funds: documented migrants transfer money themselves, whereas undocumented migrants utilize the assistance of an intermediary. This logic implies that the level of undocumented migration can be estimated by comparing the number of senders and the number of recipients. At the beginning of 2009, the number of recipients per sender decreased, which indicates a decrease in the level of undocumented migration (RusSlavBank, 2009). In other words, the GFC-related crisis in Russia and job losses mainly affected undocumented migrants and a significant number of these workers returned home. Most documented migrants were unaffected and continued to work in Russia. This difference could also result from the process described by the gravity model of workers' remittances developed by Lueth and Ruiz-Arranz

(2006). These authors find that reported remittances through MTOs to a country that shares a border are approximately 50% of the level of remittances for the equivalent country that does not share a border. In other words, reported remittances are usually lower because a higher percentage of transfers are conducted through informal channels.[4] The higher level of remittances from Russia to Uzbekistan compared to Ukraine and Belarus could reflect differences in the levels of per capita income in these countries. The higher the per capita income in a country, the lower the amount transferred home (Lueth & Ruiz-Arranz, 2006).

Toward the end of the 1990s and the beginning of the 2000s, the majority of transfers from Russia were made through informal channels. Tyuryukanova (2005) found in a study sponsored by the International Labor Organization that 75% of surveyed migrants transmitted money through informal channels and only 10% utilized services provided by MTOs and banks. A survey conducted in Moldova in 2004 reported that 30% of labor migrants utilized official channels and 70% utilized unofficial channels. This survey also indicated that 70% of migrants from Moldova were undocumented (Black, Pantiru, & Sabates-Wheeler, 2007).

Recent reductions in rates by MTOs could be a competitive response to the global economic slowdown in 2009. For example, the average fee for remittances was slightly over 10% in 2002 when only three MTOs were operating in Uzbekistan. By 2005, 10 companies were operating and the average fee dropped to 4–5% (State Committee for the Republic of Uzbekistan on Demonopolization, 2006). By 2009, the average transfer fees

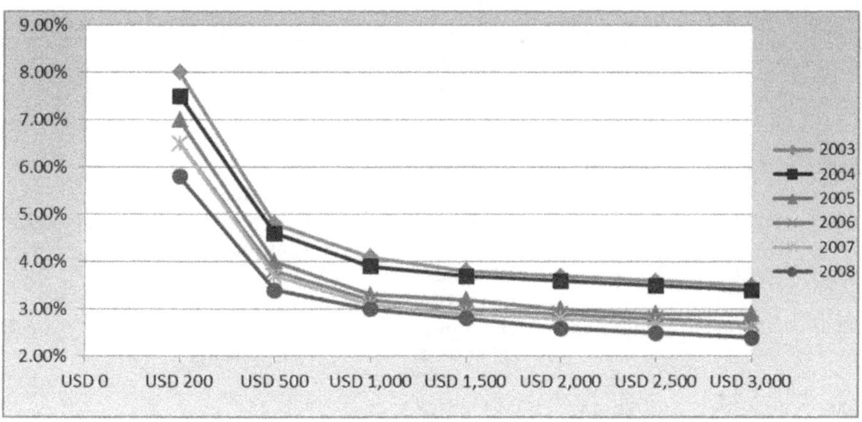

Fig. 2. Average Fee (for Remittances from Russia via MTOs). *Source*: CBR (2008b).

had decreased to 2–3%. The total value of transfers from Russia to Uzbekistan in 2009 was approximately $3 billion, and Uzbek migrants saved approximately $90 million in fees in 2009 compared to 2005. These savings provided a good incentive to switch from informal to formal channels of transferring funds. However, 15% of respondents continued to cite high transfer fees as the single most important reason for not utilizing MTO services in 2009. Fig. 2 depicts the downward trend in fees for different sizes of transfers.

Thus, surveys and research in various countries of the former Soviet Union, despite differing from each other in terms of their focus, suggest that informal remittances as a percentage of formal remittances are decreasing over the years. Table 3 sums up these surveys and their results.

Table 3. Survey Data on Use of Formal versus Informal Channels for Remitting Money in the CIS.

	% Formal Remittances in Total Remittances	Country	Source	Share of Households Receiving via MTO/Bank	Migrant (%)	Third Party (%)
2003	56	Moldova	Ghencea and Gudumac (2004)	48% (72.2% informally)		
2004		Tajikistan	Migration, Remittances and Living Standards in Tajikistan (Mughal, 2007)	59% (41% informally)		
2005		Tajikistan	Migration, Remittances and Living Standards in Tajikistan (Mughal, 2007)	64% (36% informally)		
2006	58	Armenia	ADB (Tumasyan et al., 2008)	69% (31% informally)	27.9	12
2006	29.91	Azerbaijan	ADB (Rustamov, 2006)	32.12% (68% informally)	47.23	22.92
2006	77.8	Kyrgyzstan	ADB (Ibragimova et al., 2008)		3.3	18.6
2006	58.7	Tajikistan	ADB (Brown, Olimova, & Boboev, 2008)	80.3% (74% informally)	34.6	6.7
2006		Moldova	IOM-CBSAXA (Lucke et al., 2009)	49% (51% informally)		

Table 3. (*Continued*)

	% Formal Remittances in Total Remittances	Country	Source	Share of Households Receiving via MTO/Bank	Migrant (%)	Third Party (%)
2006		Georgia	Georgia's National Public Opinion Survey	64% (total for world), 76% (from Russia)		
2007		Armenia	CRRC Migration and Remittances, Data from CRRC DI Surveys (2007c)	85% (33% informally)		
2007		Azerbaijan	CRRC Migration and Remittances, Data from CRRC DI Surveys (2007c)	62% (90% informally)		
2007		Georgia	CRRC Migration and Remittances, Data from CRRC DI Surveys (2007c)	72% (45% informally)		
2008		Moldova	IOM-CBSAXA (Lucke et al., 2008)	63% (37% informally)		
2009		Tajikistan	ILO Migrant remittance to Tajikistan (Poghossian et al., 2010)	87% (13% informally)		
2009	75	Uzbekistan	GIZ small-scale survey			
2011						
2012		Moldova	Fetiniuc (2013)	76.76% of migrants used formal channels (23.23% informal)		

ESTIMATION METHODS

The goal of this section is to undertake the analysis of the remittances estimation challenges in post-Soviet countries and discuss applicability of existing remittances estimation methods that may help us to overcome some of those challenges. Ultimately, we aim to arrive with a method which will provide us more accurate data on remittances in the former Soviet republics.

Both the small-scale survey conducted by an author and other studies in this area indicate that most funds are currently transferred through MTOs. However, there is still a significant fraction of remittances made using informal channels, which is not captured by official statistics. Moreover, inaccuracies may arise by treating some transfers as remittances whereas they are, in fact, payments for small-scale shuttle trade. Therefore, a researcher attempting to study the effects of remittances on these economies should make appropriate adjustments to the data to improve its accuracy.

Accurate estimation of remittances in this region is further hampered by the fact that the majority of the former Soviet economies do not publish remittance data consistent with IMF methodological guidelines. On the contrary, some countries, such as Uzbekistan and Turkmenistan, either publish very limited statistics or do not publish remittances statistics at all. In other cases, data quality is questionable, and different methodologies hamper verification of the data on remittances from other sources (Shelburne & Palacin, 2007). This problem is not limited to this region; the quality of remittance data is poor globally (Kapur, 2004; Lerch et al., 2008; Shelburne & Palacin, 2007). In contrast, some of the former Soviet republics, such as Kazakhstan, Tajikistan, Moldova, and Russia, provide more statistics on remittance senders and recipients than most countries in the world. However, data problems exist and policy makers, central banks, and scholars examining remittances resort to particular measurement methods or surveys to produce estimations.

One estimation methodology, a gravity model, traditionally utilized to explain trade and FDI, can also be applied to explain variations in bilateral remittances as presented in the work by Lueth and Ruiz-Arranz (2006). Elaborating on concepts developed by Zipf (1946) and utilizing data for 11 countries in Asia and Europe, Lueth and Ruiz-Arranz (2006) found that flows are larger between larger countries. Larger countries receive and send larger volumes of remittances in dollar terms. They also find that the greater the distance between two countries, the smaller the flow of remittances. In addition, the study found that other variables such as the partner countries' GDP, a common border, and a common language explain over 50% of the variation in remittance flows across time and countries. Thus, the study predicts that remittance flows increase as the source country gets richer and recipient country gets poorer. Specifically, the empirical results of the gravity model argue that doubling the per capita GDP of the recipient country is likely to reduce remittances by a factor of four. If this finding holds after controlling for other factors (such as GDP, distance), Uzbekistan would receive 16 times the remittances from Russia than are received by Kazakhstan from Russia because Uzbekistan's per capita income is one-eighth that of Kazakhstan. In addition, as noted above, remittances transmitted through formal channels to a country that shares a border are one-half of what they would be otherwise. Note that this prediction in the gravity framework is confirmed for the Kazakh-Uzbek remittance corridor. Todoroki, Celik, and Kholmatov (2011), utilizing data from the National Bank of Kazakhstan, note that total transfers via MTOs from Kazakhstan to Uzbekistan in 2009 and 2010 were $189 million and $212 million, respectively. Todoroki et al. (2011) estimate at least 330,000 migrants from Uzbekistan were working in Kazakhstan in 2010. Makhmutova et al. (2008) estimate that remittances to Uzbekistan from Kazakhstan amount to approximately $1,522 per migrant per year, an amount equal to at least $500 million a year in remittances to Uzbekistan. This estimate is consistent with the (Makhmutova et al., 2008) estimate for total remittances to Uzbekistan per year in 2003–2004. Therefore, remittances to Uzbekistan via MTOs constitute approximately 40% of total remittances. The small scale-survey conducted by one of the authors indicates that informal remittances from Russia (which does not share a border with Uzbekistan), constitute approximately 25% of total remittances to Uzbekistan from Russia. Thus, the estimates based on the gravity model are roughly consistent with the proportion of formal to total remittances ratio for remittances from Russia and Kazakhstan to Uzbekistan.

The World Bank methodology for estimating remittances is based on migration data (Ratha & Shaw, 2007). However, data on migration within the former Soviet Union are of poor quality for both estimating yearly flows and the stocks from each country. Moreover, data on the stock of migrants in the former Soviet Union include a large number of permanent migrants. These are people returning to their country of origin rather than labor migrants. Permanent migrants have little motivation to remit unless some family remains in the home country. The majority of migrants in the former Soviet Union enjoy visa-free travel and can reside and work without undergoing a proper registration process, which makes the estimation of their numbers very difficult. These might explain why the World Bank did not provide an estimate of remittances for some Central Asian countries until recently, when the Russian Central Bank began to publish datasets on remittances in the CIS and the rest of the world, including transfers via MTOs.

Mughal (2007) estimates remittance flows to Tajikistan in 2004 and 2005 utilizing the ratio of informal to formal transfers. Data on formal worker remittances were drawn from the NBT. The author made a 10% adjustment to these formal workers' remittances because these data include small-scale trade. The ratio of informal to formal transfers is identified from the Khatlon[5] Living Standards Survey conducted in 2005. According to Mughal (2007), Russia was the destination for 99% of migrants from Tajikistan. However, Brown et al. (2008) find that 83% of incoming remittances from abroad were sent from Russia. The ratio of informal to formal transfers in Tajikistan had been declining since the Mughal (2007) research was conducted because of lower transfer costs, better access to MTO services, and simpler transaction procedures.

Lerch et al. (2008) described other methodologies utilized to account for remittances by agencies in Switzerland and in the United States. For example, the Swiss National Bank (SNB) utilizes extrapolation to calculate the outflow of remittances from Switzerland. The number of documented foreign workers is multiplied by mean wage to calculate the earnings of migrants. Residents are divided into those who reside and work in Switzerland with short-term, one-year, and permanent permits. Then, the SNB, without providing a justification, assigns fixed percentages of the average wage that these three groups of migrants send home – 25%, 12%, and 5%. In addition, border workers are assumed to remit 100% of their earnings. Thus, this very simple model does consider differences in the transfer behavior of migrants from various countries. According to Lerch et al. (2008), the US Bureau of Economic Analysis utilizes a more sophisticated model based on data from the US Census and the annual American Community Survey. These two sources collect data on all foreign-born residents, including undocumented migrants. This model incorporates many other factors important to the remittance decision, such as duration of residence, presence of children, and macroeconomic data for the recipient countries.

THE ADJUSTMENT METHODOLOGY AND ITS APPLICATION TO REMITTANCES IN THE FORMER SOVIET REPUBLICS

The previous section of this paper reviewed several methodologies for estimating remittances. Some of these methodologies, for example, the gravity model and the model of the US Bureau of Economic Analysis, yield quite reasonable estimates of remittances but fail to include shocks such as economic crises and differences in remittance transferring behavior of labor migrants from different countries; most importantly, these estimates lack precision. Other methodologies (the World Bank and Swiss National Bank methodologies) are not applicable to the former Soviet Union where migration data are unreliable and borders are porous. However, the importance of remittance flows for many countries of the former Soviet Union is increasing. Thus, to increase the effectiveness of policy-making decisions, there is a need for a more precise methodology to estimate remittances in the former Soviet Union.

This section provides sample applications of how adjustments to the CBR may produce more accurate estimates of remittances from Russia to the selected countries of the former Soviet Union. In particular, the adjustments are made for small-scale trade, informal transfers, and the border effect discussed previously.

The example of remittances from Russia to Uzbekistan in 2012 is utilized for illustration. According the CBR, remittances to Uzbekistan from Russia through MTOs and banks reached $5.693 billion in 2012 (CBR, 2012). Based on the authors' interviews with migrants and their families, policy makers, and representatives of international organizations, approximately 10% of this amount represents small-scale trade. To adjust for small-scale trade, we subtract 10% from the amount of total remittances reported by the CBR. After this adjustment, remittances to Uzbekistan drop to $5.1 billion. The next step is to make adjustments for informal remittances and the border effect. Because Russia and Uzbekistan do not share a border, we do not make adjustments for the border effect; however, we adjust for informal remittances so that they constitute 13.91% of total remittances. This estimate of informal remittances is based on the small-scale survey conducted by the authors in Uzbekistan in 2009 and further decrease in the share of informal remittances after 2009. This decrease in the share of informal remittances is associated with decrease in remittance fees, rapidly expanding branch network, and improved literacy of migrants in relation to MTO procedures, which have been taking place simultaneously. Table 4 summarizes the remittance fees applicable for average amount of transfer for respective years based on data from CBR and associated with it decrease in the share of informal remittances estimated by authors. We sourced the data for share of informal remittances from existing surveys (see Table 3) and link the rate of annual decline in the share of informal remittances with the reduction in transfer fees.

Table 4. Estimated Decrease in the Share of Informal Remittances Associated with Decrease in Remittance Fees.

Year	Remittance Fees for Average Amount of Remittance (%)	Informal Remittances as a Share of Total Remittances (%)
2006	3.7	40
2007	3.3	33.48
2008	3.03	29.08
2009	2.78	25
2010	2.44	19.46
2011	2.3	17.17
2012	2.1	13.91

Table 5. Remittances from Russia to Uzbekistan in Millions of US$.

Year	Reported Remittances	Share of Small-Scale Trade in Reported Remittances	Share of Informal Transfers in Total Remittances (%)	Adjustment for Border Effect	Remittances Adjusted for Small-Scale Trade, Informal Transfers, and Border Effect
2006[a]	1,080	−10%	40	–	1,620
2007	1,693	−10%	33.48	–	2,291
2008	3,007	−10%	29.08	–	3,816
2009	2,071	−10%	25	–	2,485
2010	2,858	−10%	19.46	–	3,194
2011	4,276	−10%	17.17	–	4,646
2012	5,693	−10%	13.91	–	5,952

Sources: Data from 2007 to 2012 are from the Central Bank of Russia (CBR, 2007, 2008a, 2009, 2010, 2011, 2012).

[a]Data for the last three quarters of 2006 are also from the Central Bank of Russia. However, the first quarter data for 2006 are not available and were estimated to add to the available three quarters data for 2006.

These adjustments produce an estimate of $5.952 billion in remittances to Uzbekistan in 2012. Because remittance transfer fees have decreased over time and awareness of the decrease spread gradually, the adjustment factor for informal channels has fallen gradually from 40% in 2006 to 13.91% in 2012. Table 5 summarizes these calculations for Uzbekistan.

Consider the example of remittances from Russia to Azerbaijan. Based on a survey of 3,900 households, Rustamov (2008) estimates that only 32% of total remittances were received via banks and MTOs in 2006. Thus, approximately 68% of all remittances to Azerbaijan occurred through informal channels in 2006. The share of informal transfers in Azerbaijan is much higher than Uzbekistan. This difference is consistent with the gravity model, which predicts higher volumes of informal transfers for countries with common borders. In fact, consistent with the gravity model estimates of Lueth and Ruiz-Arranz (2006), remittances to a country that shares a border are one-half of what would be expected. Because transfer fees have fallen in the former Soviet Union in the same pattern, it is assumed that the share of informal transfers has also been changing in a fashion similar to the pattern observed in Uzbekistan. Table 6 summarizes the calculations for Azerbaijan. Note that, according to our calculations, the share of reported remittances through banks and MTOs in 2006 was 40% of total remittances – a number that is very close to the estimate from the survey conducted by Rustamov (2008).

We realize that our estimation methods are not perfect. For example, in case of Azerbaijan, despite having a common border with Russia, anecdotal evidence suggests that the majority of Azerbaijani labor migrants reside in Moscow or Saint Petersburg which is far away from the border of Russia with Azerbaijan. Therefore, it is probably more convenient for them to transfer funds to Azerbaijan than bringing cash home in their pockets. However, the fact that the results of our estimations coincide with the

Table 6. Remittances from Russia to Azerbaijan in Millions of US$.

Year	Reported Remittances	Share of Small-Scale Trade in Reported Remittances (%)	Share of Informal Transfers in Total Remittances (%)	Adjustment for Border Effect (%)	Remittances Adjusted for Small-Scale Trade, Informal Transfers, and Border Effect
2006[a]	645	−10	40.00	200	1,935
2007	814	−10	33.48	200	2,203
2008	1,061	−10	29.08	200	2,693
2009	748	−10	25.00	200	1,795
2010	881	−10	19.46	200	1,969
2011	1,159	−10	17.17	200	2,519
2012	1,230	−10	13.91	200	2,572

Sources: Data from 2007 to 2012 are from the Central Bank of Russia (CBR, 2007, 2008a, 2009, 2010, 2011, 2012).

[a]Data for the last three quarters of 2006 are also from the Central Bank of Russia. However, the first quarter data for 2006 are not available and were estimated to add to the available three quarters data for 2006.

survey estimations of Rustamov (2008) suggests that our methodology is good enough to make meaningful estimations. All in all, it seems that in the case of remittances from the CIS, this methodology makes quite precise estimations.

Similar estimates were produced for other countries of the former USSR (except Baltic countries). They are available from the authors upon request.

We made substantial adjustments to the estimates of remittances produced by Shelburne and Palacin (2007) prior to 2007 and to the data published by the CBR. These new estimates substantially change the value of remittances in some cases and could be used to analyze the impact of remittances in the economies of major recipients. Because remittances from Russia are by far the most significant source of remittances within the CIS, these data approximate the total amount of remittances that these countries receive.

CONCLUSION

This study has provided a comprehensive review of existing remittance measurement methodologies relevant to the countries of the former Soviet Union. This study also discussed problems with the IMF BoP framework and inaccuracies and weaknesses in other data sources.

The empirical evidence suggests that the share of formal remittance channels is growing at the expense of informal channels in the CIS. Labor migrants understand that carrying cash is risky – the money could be stolen or corrupt customs and passport control officers could expropriate part or all of this money. If a migrant sends earnings with another person, there is a risk that the money courier may deceive the sender.

The utilization of formal and informal channels also varies according to the distance separating the sending and receiving countries. Interviews and surveys also suggest that other factors can determine the choice of formal over informal channels: the education level of the migrant, the nature of employment, the presence of a migrant community/network, the average salary level, etc. More educated and white-collar migrants tend to send more money via MTOs.

The sheer size and significance of remittances make harnessing this economic phenomenon to benefit the economy reasonable. Policies to increase the share funds transferred through formal channels rather than informal channels would be a first step in this direction. However, the eventual success of this first step depends on the institutional capacity of the financial/banking sector to transform the development potential of remittances into benefits for the country.

The aim of this paper was to review the remittance estimation methodologies and challenges in post-Soviet region as well as to propose some adjustments that may improve accuracy of remittance estimations. We believe this goal has been achieved. Despite its deficiencies, the methods have reasonable empirical confirmation from existing surveys. This new methodology has a potential to be utilized in other regions and countries experiencing similar data challenges.

NOTES

1. As measured by EBRD banking sector development indicators (European Bank for Reconstruction and Development [EBRD], 2012).
2. Hawala is an alternative informal transfer method utilized parallel to official channels and implies the use of brokers (hawaladars), family and regional ties and connections.
3. Data for remittances via MTOs is utilized for 2006 because data for total remittances in 2006 are not available by country for the entire year. Data are available for the last three quarters of 2006 only.
4. Carrying cash upon returning home is considered to be an informal channel of remittance.
5. One of five regions, and the poorest, in Tajikistan.

REFERENCES

Alfieri, A., Havinga, I., & Hvidsten, V. (2006). Issue paper: Definition of remittances. *Meeting/conference of the United Nations Technical Subgroup on Movement of Persons–Mode 4*, New York.

Black, R., Pantiru, M. C., & Sabates-Wheeler, R. (2007). *Migration and poverty reduction in Moldova.* Working Paper C 10. Sussex Centre for Migration Research and Institute for Development Studies, Falmer.

Brown, R., Olimova, S., & Boboev, M. (2008). *Country report on remittances of international migrants in Tajikistan.* Study on International Migrants' Remittances in Central Asia and South Caucasus, Asian Development Bank, Manila.

Central Bank of Armenia. (2006). *Analytical study based on the survey on money transfers received from abroad by the households in Armenia in 2005*. Yerevan: Central Bank of Armenia.

Central Bank of Russia. (2007). *Cross-border transactions of individuals (residents and nonresidents) in breakdown by countries* Retrieved from http://www.cbr.ru/eng/statistics/print.

aspx?file=CrossBorder/C-b_trans_countries_07_e.htm&pid=svs&sid=TGO_sp. Accessed on September 13, 2013.

Central Bank of Russia. (2008a). *Cross-border transactions of individuals (residents and nonresidents) in breakdown by countries*. Retrieved from http://www.cbr.ru/eng/statistics/print.aspx?file=CrossBorder/C-b_trans_countries_08_e.htm&pid=svs&sid=TGO_sp. Accessed on September 13, 2013.

Central Bank of Russia. (2008b). *Cross-border remittances via money transfer operators and post offices in breakdown by countries*. Retrieved from http://www.cbr.ru/eng/statistics/CrossBorder/Cross-border_08_e.pdf?pid=svs&sid=TGO_obz. Accessed on May 13, 2013.

Central Bank of Russia. (2009). *Cross-border transactions of individuals (residents and nonresidents) in breakdown by countries*. Retrieved from http://www.cbr.ru/eng/statistics/print.aspx?file=CrossBorder/C-b_trans_countries_09_e.htm&pid=svs&sid=TGO_sp. Accessed on September 13, 2013.

Central Bank of Russia. (2010). *Cross-border transactions of individuals (residents and nonresidents) in breakdown by countries*. Retrieved from http://www.cbr.ru/eng/statistics/print.aspx?file=CrossBorder/C-b_trans_countries_10_e.htm&pid=svs&sid=TGO_sp. Accessed on September 13, 2013.

Central Bank of Russia. (2011). *Cross-border transactions of individuals (residents and nonresidents) in breakdown by countries*. Retrieved from http://www.cbr.ru/eng/statistics/print.aspx?file=CrossBorder/C-b_trans_countries_11_e.htm&pid=svs&sid=TGO_sp. Accessed on September 13, 2013.

Central Bank of Russia. (2012). *Cross-border transactions of individuals (residents and nonresidents) in breakdown by countries*. Retrieved from http://www.cbr.ru/eng/statistics/print.aspx?file=CrossBorder/C-b_trans_countries_12_e.htm&pid=svs&sid=TGO_sp. Accessed on September 13, 2013.

CRRC Data Initiative Team. (2007c). CRRC Data Initiative Survey – Armenia. Caucasus Research Resource Centers. Retrieved from http://www.crrccenters.org/index.php/en/11. Accessed on May 15, 2014.

de Luna-Martinez, J. (2005). *Workers' remittances to developing countries: A survey with central banks on selected public policy issues*. World Bank Policy Research Working Paper 3638, World Bank Publications, Washington, DC.

European Bank for Reconstruction and Development. (2012). Transition Report, EBRD, London.

Fetiniuc, A. (2013). *Labor migration and remittances in the Republic of Moldova: Are the remittances efficiently used by the migrants' households?* Dissertation, Dublin Business School.

Ghencea, B., & Gudumac, I. (2004). *Labour migration and remittances in the republic of Moldova*. Moldova Microfinance Alliance and Soros Foundation in Moldova.

Gusman, N. (2007). Denezhnie perevody kak otrazhenie processov migratsii. *Economicheskoe Obozrenie EvrAzES*, *4*(3), 17–20.

Ibragimova, S., Burzhubaev, T., & Temirov, A. (2008). *Country report on international migrants' remittances and poverty in the Kyrgyz Republic*. Manila: A Study on International Migrants' Remittances in Central Asia and Southern Caucasus, Asian Development Bank.

International Monetary Fund. (2009). *Balance of payments and international investment position manual* (6th ed.). Washington, DC: International Monetary Fund.

Kapur, D. (2004). *Remittances-the new development mantra*. G-24 Discussion Paper Series No. 29. United Nations, New York/Geneva.

Kupets, O. (2012). *The development and the side effects of remittances in the CIS countries: The case of Ukraine*. Research Report CARIM-East RR2012/02, European University Institute Badia Fiesolana.

Lerch, M., Wanner, P., & Haug, W. (2008). *The measurement of remittances in industrialized countries – or how to limit multiple biases*. Background Paper for the Joint UNECE/World Bank/US Census Bureau Expert Group Meeting on the Contribution of Household Surveys to Measuring Remittances, Suitland, USA.

Luecke, M., Mahmoud, T. O., & Steinmayr, A. (2009). *Labour migration and remittances in Moldova: Is the boom over*. Chisinau: International Organization for Migration, Moldova Office.

Lueth, E., & Ruiz-Arranz, M. (2006). *A gravity model of workers' remittances*. IMF Working Paper WP/06/290. International Monetary Fund, Washington, DC.

Makhmutova, M., Makatova, A., Kourmanova, A., Abdullaev, U., Dienova, M., & Bakas Uuly, B. (2008). *Country report on remittances of international migrants and the financial sector in Kazakhstan*. Manila: Study on International Migrants Remittances in Central Asia and South Caucasus, Asian Development Bank.

Melkadze, G. (2012). *Macroeconomic determinants of remittances in Georgia: A dynamic panel data approach*. Tbilisi: International School of Economics at Tbilisi State University.

Mogilevsky, R., & Atamanov, A. (2008). *Country report on remittances of international migrants and the financial sector in the Kyrgyz republic*. Manila: A Study on International Migrants' Remittances in Central Asia and South Caucasus, Asian Development Bank.

Mughal, A. G. (2007). *Migration, remittances, and living standards in Tajikistan*. Dushanbe: International Organization for Migration.

National Bank of Ukraine. (2013). *Remittances in Ukraine*. Retrieved from http://www.bank.gov.ua/doccatalog/document?id=80651. Accessed on May 19, 2013.

Poghossian, A., Hakobyan, I., & Saidov, F. (2010). *Migrant remittances to Tajikistan: The potential for savings, economic investment and existing financial products to attract remittances*. Moscow: ILO Subregional Office for Eastern Europe and Central Asia.

Ratha, D., & Shaw, W. (2007). *South-South migration and remittances*. Working Paper No. 102. World Bank, Washington, DC.

Rossiyskoe Informatsionnoe Agentstvo – Novosti. (2012). Ezhegodno v Rossiyu vezzhayut 14 millionov migrantov. *Demoscope Weekly*, pp. 531–532. Retrieved from http://demoscope.ru/weekly/2012/0531/rossia01.php. Accessed on May 17, 2013.

RusSlavBank. (2009). *Denezhnie perevody kak metod otsenki migratsionnih protsessov*. Press-release. Retrieved from http://www.russlavbank.com/prcenter/newsdetail/642.html. Accessed on May 15, 2013.

Rustamov, V. (2008). *Country report on remittances of international migrants and poverty in Azerbaijan*. Manila: A Study on International Migrants' Remittances in Central Asia and South Caucasus, Asian Development Bank.

Shelburne, R., & Palacin, J. (2007). *Remittances in the CIS: Their economic implications and a new estimation procedure*. Discussion Paper Series No. 2007.5. United Nations Economic Commission for Europe, Geneva.

Shonkwiler, J. S., Grigorian, D., & Melkonyan, T. (2011). Controlling for the underreporting of remittances. *Applied Economics*, *43*(30), 4817–4826.

State Committee for the Republic of Uzbekistan on Demonopolization, Support of Competition and Entrepreneurship. (2006). International money transfer services market in Uzbekistan. Development competition, and trends. In Antimonopoly Policy Improvement Center, Tashkent.

Todoroki, E., Celik, K., & Kholmatov, M. (2011). *Alternative remittance systems in Kazakhstan*. Washington, DC: World Bank.

Tumasyan, M., Manukyan, Y., Torosyan, G., Terzikyan, G., & Mnatsakanyan, V. (2008). *Country report on remittances of international migrants and poverty in Armenia*. Manila: A Study on International Migrants' Remittances in Central Asia and South Caucasus, Asian Development Bank.

Tyuryukanova, E. (2005). *Forced labour in the Russian federation today: Irregular migration and trafficking in human beings*. Geneva: International Labour Organization.

Zipf, G. K. (1946). The P 1 P 2/D hypothesis: On the intercity movement of persons. *American Sociological Review*, *11*(6), 677–686.

Zykova, T. (2008). Rubl v perevode. *Rossiyskaya Gazeta*, March 22, p. 1.

NO CONVERGENCE IN THE CENTRAL EASTERN EUROPEAN NEW MEMBER STATES: A MULTI INDICATOR ANALYSIS

Zoltán Pogátsa

ABSTRACT

This paper looks at the convergence of CEE economies to North-western Europe (Austria, Belgium, Denmark, France, Germany, Ireland, Netherlands, Norway, the United Kingdom, Sweden, and Switzerland, simplified in this study as 'Western Europe') in terms of indicators other than GDP, which are more relevant reflections of the welfare level of everyday citizens. It finds that contrary to the results of studies concentrating solely on GDP, a multi indicator analysis reveals a slow but definite divergence rather than convergence.

Keywords: Convergence; GDP; wages; productivity

Neo-Transitional Economics
International Finance Review, Volume 16, 363–376

ISSN: 1569-3767/doi:10.1108/S1569-376720150000016015

The 25th anniversary of transition and the 10th anniversary of European Union membership provide a reason for reflections on the extent of convergence between former state socialist economies and the developed capitalist economies of North-Western Europe. Frequently, these assessments of convergence[1] have been based on a single indicator, primarily the per capita Gross Domestic Product. They usually arrive at the conclusion that Central Eastern European (CEE) enlargement has been successful, since convergence can be demonstrated for most economies of the region. This leads to triumphalism from the part of regional governments and the EU institutions[2] alike. Their optimism is in sharp contrast with the actual political economic developments on the ground. Most states in the region face rampant corruption, political crises, social unrest, low fertility rates and increasing outward migration. What explains this apparent contradiction between the supposed economic success and the weak socioeconomic performance experienced by citizens?

In this paper we argue that if we take a more holistic approach and base our analysis on more than a single economic output indicator, we can understand why the superficial phenomenon of convergence is in fact a mirage. While GDP/capita is obviously a valid and important figure, it demonstrates only a single element of a very complex picture: how much new value is produced in an economy in a given year. It says nothing about how that new value is distributed in society between profits, wages and taxes, which is not a trivial question in a region where owners of capital are often foreign investors, and where 'dependent competition states'[3] race each other to the bottom with low taxes and low wages. The GDP figure also says nothing about how many wage earners there actually are (the employment rate), or the distribution of income between those households earning wages. How fast have prices caught up? How are these indicators converging with the developed states of North-western Europe? (The 'EU average' served well as a convergence anchor initially, but since the economic collapse of the Southern European periphery this average is too low a benchmark for the CEE region.) To arrive at a complete picture we must examine all these dimensions of convergence, and more.

EMPLOYMENT

After the GDP/capita indicator, the first and most important question for the CEE countries is how many citizens actually hold a job in these economies? What percentage of the adult population are taxpayers, and thereby contribute to the sustainability of the national budget and the social redistributive systems? (We take the view that state employed taxpayers are in no way less inferior to private sector ones. While it is true that their salaries are paid from tax revenues, the private sector would in turn be unable to produce any wealth without state and local government services. A hypothetical separation ignores the intimate real life symbiosis between them, and how one would collapse without the other.) How does their level of employment compare to 'Western Europe'?

It can be seen from Fig. 1 that in 2012 no CEE country reached the Western European average. Their employment levels were in the 62–72% range, with North-Western Europe continuously averaging around 75% (with roughly a 67–82% spread). Employment in certain countries by and large stagnated (Hungary, Romania, Czech Republic). The only two countries that had levels of employment comparable to Western Europe were the Czech Republic and Slovenia. The latter is the only former socialist country that transformed itself not into a dependent FDI based but a coordinated, corporative Rhineland model[4] economy.

As is visible from the chart, the three Baltic economies and Bulgaria played roller coaster with the jobs of their citizens: they show significant increase, then decline. This is likely to be related to their significant levels of outward migration of guest workers to Western Europe before the Great Recession. The small size of the individual Baltic labour markets also might

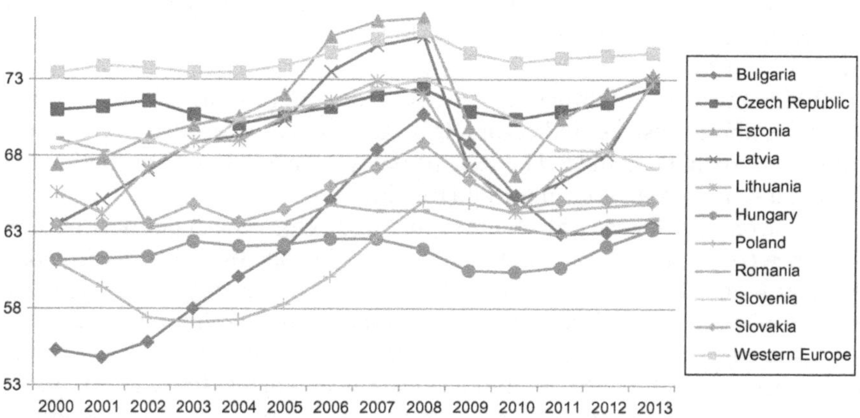

Fig. 1. Employment Rates in the CEE and the North-Western European Average (Own Calculation). *Source*: Eurostat code t2020_10.

serve to explain the phenomenon, as the collapse of even a single industrial sector can have a dramatically greater effect on the entirety of a small economy. Western European economies have significantly higher employment stability compared to these unstable labour markets.

As for Slovakia, before the 2008 crisis it basically caught up with its pre restructuring levels employment that characterised the country before the Dzurinda reforms (1998 = 67.4%) before the 2008 crisis. Slovak employment decreased, finishing the period only slightly higher than at the turn of the millennia. These empirical data contrast with the buoyant narrative that had surrounded the Slovak economy before Poland took over as the star student of the region during the crisis years. Poland itself, in spite of its alleged economic miracle during the Great Recession years, never again managed to reach its 1998 employment rate of 65.4%.

All in all, significantly, the new member states as a group remain decidedly below the Western European levels of employment. It is difficult to observe a convergence process in this group.

INCOMES

For those holding a job in the CEE region, actual incomes are the next most important issue. In addition, national and local budgets are financed to no small degree from the tax base of those with an actual income. It is therefore important to ask how much wage earners in the CEE region actually earn. How does this compare with North-western European levels of income over time?

While Eurostat publishes up to date, sometimes quarterly or monthly statistics about business indicators, it is far less helpful as a source of social indicators such as income. The best proxy we can work with is total actual individual household consumption (Fig. 2).

At current prices, the only country that had achieved a slight positive convergence (of about €367) with North-western Europe by 2013 was Slovakia. Hungary and Poland had suffered considerable divergence (€2,133 and €1,833, respectively), while all the others gone through a slight divergence.

Naturally, consumption levels cannot be accounted for current prices, they need to be brought to purchasing power parity. Price levels play a decisive role in how much these earnings are worth in a given economy. Here, however we run into difficulties because the officially published price level indices of Eurostat are contestable.

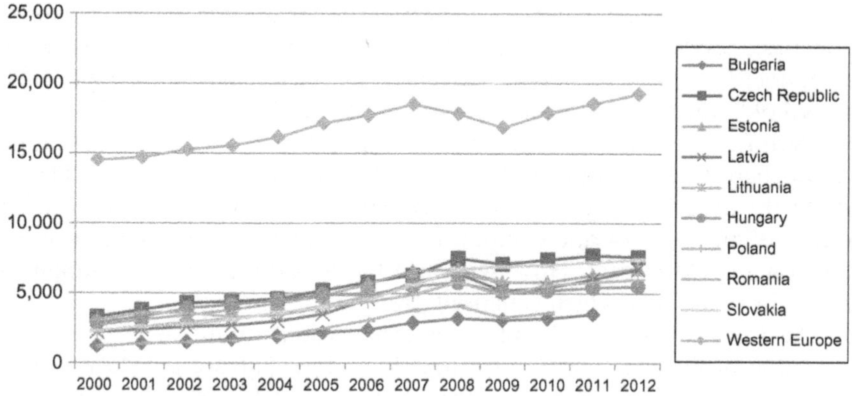

Fig. 2. Total Household Consumption Expenditure at Current Prices, CEE and North-Western Europe (Own Calculation). *Source*: Eurostat code nama_co3_c.

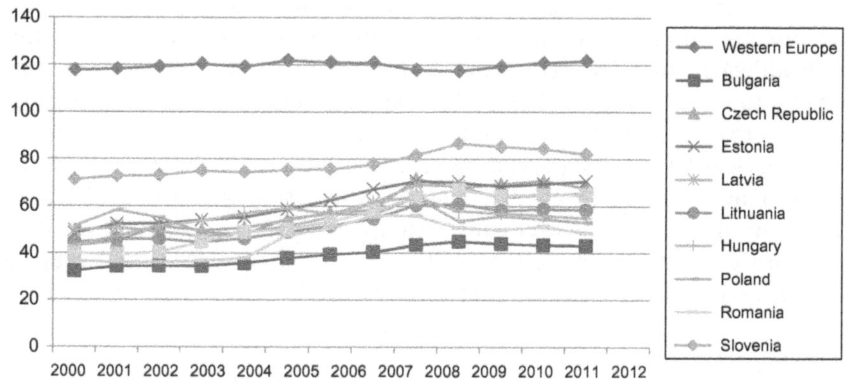

Fig. 3. Actual Individual Consumption Price Level Indices of CEE and North-Western European EU Member States (Latter Own Calculation), EU27 = 100%. *Source*: Eurostat code prc_ppp_ind.

Even the official 'actual individual consumption' price level statistics of Eurostat indicate a very rapid price convergence, much faster than that of consumption itself (Fig. 3).

Thus if we base our assessment on these official figures, we can conclude that while there was a mild divergence in nominal consumption, there was simultaneously a very rapid convergence in prices from about a third of Western European prices to about half. However, it is questionable whether this indicator is really a correct approximation of actual consumption price levels. It is very likely that it undershoots it, if we look at its components. A simple weighted average of the dominant elements of a household consumption basket yields a price level closer to two-thirds of Western European levels rather than half (Table 1).

It is hard to see what component of what supposed consumption basket yields the official overall 'actual individual consumption' price level index when its most important components are higher in value. One possible candidate could be rent. However, Eurostat does not publish a component index for rent alone, which is in itself problematic.

The Eurostat handbook[5] provides explanations about these discrepancies. One problem is that the methodology does not use simple weighted averages, which means that services such as 'hotels and restaurants' are over weighted in the price indices. (CEE citizens usually hardly spend any nights in hotels in their own countries, and a major proportion of them cannot afford to regularly dine in restaurants.) Even more significantly, the official price indices contain price levels for government services that are not directly purchased by households from the market, such as education or healthcare. In CEE economies, prices in these sectors are very low, mostly due to low wages. The underlying assumption of this methodology is that cross county comparability is only ensured with countries where these services have to be purchased on a market basis if the cost of services is taken into account even in countries where they are provided free of charge by the state. However, this assumption is flawed. First of all, there are almost no such extreme market based economies within the European Union, as health and educational services are available free of charge in

Table 1. Component Price Level Indices, EU27 = 100% 2012.

	CZ	HU	PL	SK	EE	LV	LT
A. Actual individual consumption	*67.7*	*54.9*	*53*	*64.8*	*70.5*	*65.4*	*58.4*
B. Food and non-alcoholic beverages	83.7	80.8	61.6	86.7	86.6	87.1	77.4
C. Electricity gas and other fuels	90.8	81.3	71.1	96.4	74.3	76.1	81.4
D. Transport services	66.4	65	57.3	55.1	73	68.1	58.7
E. Communication	112.6	111.9	70.1	125.4	72.4	81.2	58.3
F. Hotels and restaurants	58.2	50.1	74.9	70.9	76.3	80.7	63.6
Average B-E	*88.375*	*84.75*	*65.025*	*90.9*	*76.575*	*78.125*	*68.95*
Average B-F	82.34	77.82	67	86.9	76.52	78.64	67.88
Residential buildings	65.1	49.6	56.7	64.2	70.5		

Source: Eurostat code prc_ppp_ind.

most EU member states, or at least operate in a parallel manner, in that one can buy supposedly higher quality services privately, alongside free public service. Even more importantly, it is mistaken to assume, as the 'no free lunch' argument often does, that public services are at the end of day financed by households through taxation. There are plenty of other sources of state revenue that can finance 'free' government services. They include taxes on profits, wealth, excise, environmental degradation and others. Considerably lowering the price indices by including these governmental services therefore introduces an unjustifiable downward bias. The actual consumption price indices are more likely to be in the range of 80–85%, as represented by the direct market based household expenditure components published by Eurostat.

DISTRIBUTION OF INCOMES

Given that Visegrad and Baltic citizens nominally earn on average around a third of what Westerners earn, yet their prices are half to two-thirds of Western ones, we have a situation where a typical Eastern household is forced to spend almost all of its income on basic consumption. This average Eastern household is about the seventh decile of society. This means that only the top deciles really have savings in the CEE region (Fig. 4).

The Eastern European average corresponds to the lowest two deciles of Western European income distribution. These are the only two deciles of Western society that do not have significant savings after basic consumption on food, energy, housing and transport. The lowest tenths of CEE societies continue to live in extreme physical poverty, which is almost non-existent in North-western Europe.

As far as minimum wages are concerned, they provide no more than a facade of a welfare arrangement in the region. As can be seen from Fig. 5, statutory CEE minimum wages are around 1/4–1/5 of Western European minimum wages. Many Western European countries, such as Scandinavia, do not have general minimum wage levels. Instead, they agree on industry specific wage floors, which fulfil the same purpose, only in a more differentiated way. These industrial wage floors are mostly higher than even the statutory Western European minimum wage levels. Therefore, taking these countries into account, minimum wage levels in Eastern member states, approximate more a 1:5 rather than the 1:4 ratio. Given that the price levels can be approximated at around 2:3 of Western price levels, it becomes clear

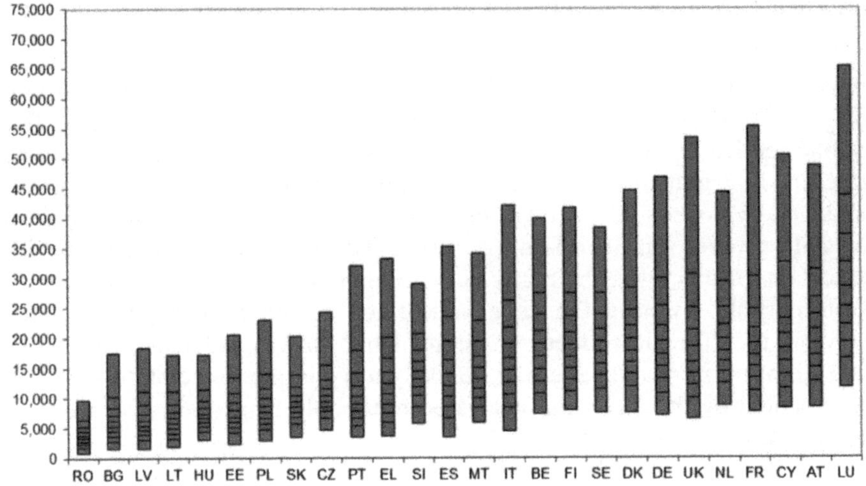

Fig. 4. Income Distributions across EUROPE, in € at Official Eurostat PPS, 2010. *Source*: European Commission, Eurostat, cross-sectional EU-SILC 2011, UDB August 2013 Social Situation Monitor.

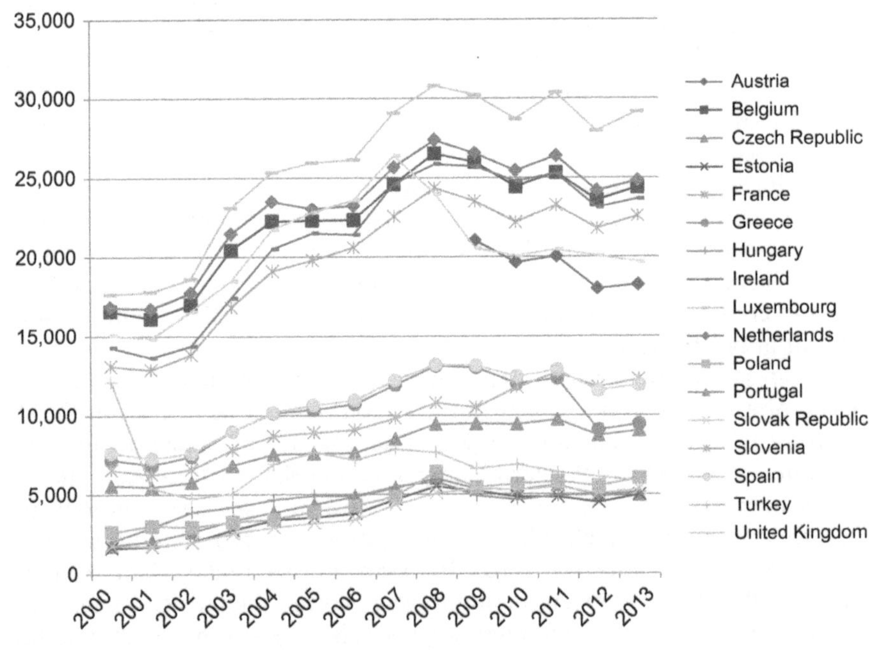

Fig. 5. Official Statutory Minimum Wages in European Countries. *Source*: OECD Labour Statistics.

that CEE minimum wage levels are so extremely low that they become meaningless in terms of social protection. In fact in almost all cases they fall below the official subsistence minimum published by National Statistical Offices.

PRODUCTIVITY DIVERGENCE AS A BASIS FOR WAGE DIVERGENCE

It is also important what defines the dynamics of wage growth. The central prospect of both economic transition and EU accession was the gradual convergence of incomes with Western Europe in the medium time range (i.e. within a generation or so). There was no expectation of full convergence, which would have been insensible from an economic point of view. What was expected was a noticeable gradual process, much like what has actually been taking place in terms of GDP. (It is telling how in spite of Eastern GDP levels actually approximating and in some cases overtaking Southern member state levels, actual household income levels remain far lower.) Since the populations of the region are not experiencing this convergence, it is important to examine the underlying factors. Apart from negotiation between employers and employees, it is productivity that determines wages. Extreme and continued wage increases beyond productivity increases price out an economy in international competition.

Naturally, productivity in a given economy is distributed across a range. This in itself is significant. Why do Eastern European societies have such flat income distributions, when their productivity distributions are quite likely to be wider? That is a question that begs for an answer. Productivity distributions, however, are not available, only national averages. Economy wide average productivity is estimated by dividing aggregate GDP by the number of employed, or the number of hours worked in the given economy.

What can be observed from Fig. 6 is that the productivity gap between CEE and Western Europe actually increased before the crisis, only to drop slightly between 2007 and 2009. After that, divergence resumed. Over the whole period the region diverged by some €1–3. The worst performer, Bulgaria, an outlier, diverged by €4.3 in this period.

Productivity is a crucial underlying factor because it determines wages. Therefore it is extremely important to understand what we are measuring, and its dynamics. The first key precondition is that because it is calculated

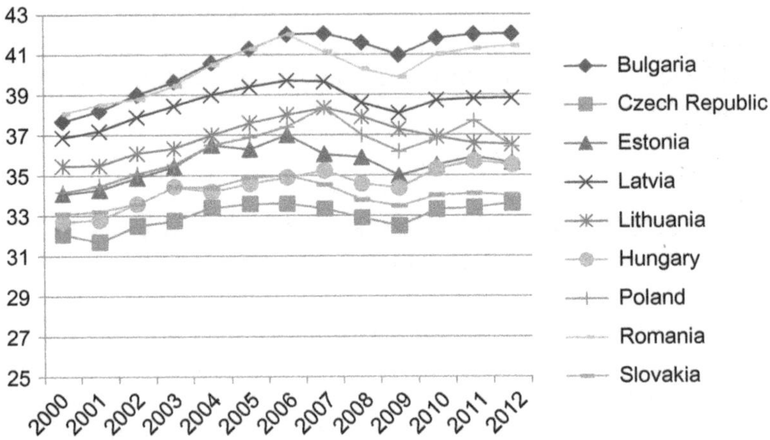

Fig. 6. The Productivity Gap between CEE Economies and Western European Economies, Euro per Hour Worked. *Source*: Own calculations based on Eurostat code [nama_aux_lp].

by using the aggregate GDP figure, the GDP figure should be accurate. However, we can be sure that this is not the case. Since the region is dependent on transnational foreign investment, we must calculate with the massive effects of transfer pricing by these transnationals. According to a well-respected report[6] by an NGO dealing with offshore leakages, The Tax Justice Network, several of the economies of the region are amongst the greatest losers of the global offshore network. Thus the actual GDP of these countries, and by inference their actual productivity levels must in fact be higher than the official statistics suggest. If wages are to conform to real productivity levels, the existing wages are too low (Fig. 7).

What we see on this regression line is that there seems to be a very close correlation between productivity and wages. As we have already mentioned, if an economy moves too far above the trend line, it is going to price itself out. Seemingly the economies of region lie close to the regression line, which suggests that all is well with incomes. (Slovakia is a noticeable outlier.) This regression line, however, is not an explanation for diverging productivity levels of the CEE economies, but a graphical representation of it. There is still a need to explain what it is that accounts for the productivity divergence.

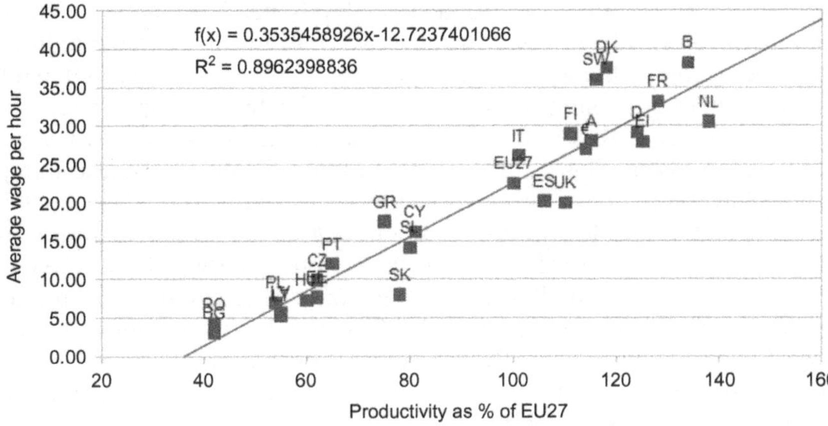

Fig. 7. Linear Regression Trend Line between Productivity as a Percentage of EU27 Average, and Average Wage per Hour in €, 2010. *Source*: Own calculation based on Eurostat.

Productivity is related to both labour and capital.[7] It is often assumed that it is the human capital of the region that explains the level of productivity. This claim can now be empirically tested with the help of the OECD's Programme for the International Assessment of Adult Competencies (PIACC). Like its better known sister programme, PISA, it measures the same numerical, computational and problems solving capacities. It does so, however, amongst those already employed, rather than students. This means that PIACC is an optimal tool for assessing the human capital of the region, as it measures exactly what we are seeking to find. If the productivity of the region was lower because of weaker labour market skills of local employees, we would expect to find these characteristics reflected in the PIACC study. The 2013 report,[8] however, does not confirm these expectations. High productivity North-western European, North American and CEE economies are mixed in terms of all three competencies. These results seem to indicate that it is not the human skills of labour in this region that serves as an explanation for lower levels of overall average productivity.

Numerous alternative explanations could be offered, but it is high time economists dealing with the region addressed these issues. Here we offer one possible explanation. As we have already mentioned, Western European economies have minimum wage levels (or industrial wage floors) that are around €10–16 per hour. It is economically unfeasible to employ labour in those countries at productivity levels per hour that are below these levels of regulated pay. Incidentally, this north-western minimum wage level is above the average income level of the dependent FDI based dependent market economies in Central and Eastern Europe. The minimum wage levels of these countries are as far lower, at around 2 euros per hour, or even lower. This leads to what is often referred to as social dumping: the low value added production phases of multinational production chains,[9] which create less than this amount of value, migrate towards the low wage East, lowering the average there, thus lowering the country on the regression line. All in all, the East-West wage differential is institutionalised across the European Union by the differential in the minimum wage.

What is very telling is how weak the relationship becomes between the two variables once the CEE countries are eliminated, leaving only the Western European ones (Fig. 8).

It is also worth noticing how the regression line becomes flatter. This means that a move down the productivity axis does not bring with it a much faster move down the wage axis, as in the previous graph when CEE economies were also included. From the point of view of wages, a more favourable productivity-wage relationship exists for Western European economies than for the CEE ones.

Finally, it is worthwhile taking a look at the share of profits and wages within GDP across the EU. While neoclassical economics rarely ever concerns itself with the way GDP is divided up between remuneration of capital and wages, Marxian economics does (Table 2).

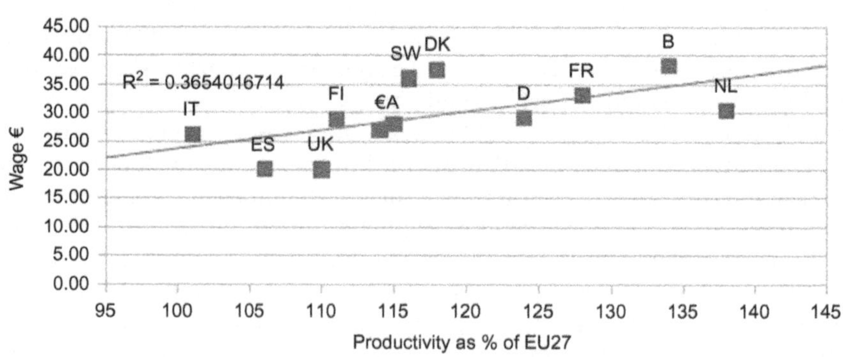

Fig. 8. Linear Regression Trend Line between Productivity as a Percentage of EU27 Average, and Average Wage per Hour in €, Western European Countries, 2010. *Source*: Own calculation based on Eurostat.

Table 2. The Share of Wages in Total GDP in Western and Eastern European Union Member States.

Country	Wage Share in Total GDP, %	
	Average 2004–2007	Average 2008–2009
Austria	60.6	61.3
Belgium	65.2	67.9
Denmark	69.4	74.7
Finland	61.1	65.3
France	66.2	66.5
Germany	65.5	66.2
Netherlands	58.4	59.7
Sweden	69.0	68.7
United Kingdom	66.9	66.6
Czech Republic	49.9	51.2
Estonia	57.4	64.0
Hungary	58.2	58.2
Poland	43.6	45.8
Slovakia	43.6	44.0

Source: ILO.

What is obvious from this table is that the profit-wage share in CEE is considerably less favourable than in Western Europe. A smaller ratio of GDP is spent on wages in this region than in the core economies of Europe. If we add to this the fact that the owners of capital are very often foreign entities in the CEE, this difference also has consequences as far as the outflow of capital from the region is concerned.

NOTES

1. Darvas (2014), Cueresma, Oberhofer, Smits, and Vincellette (2012).
2. See for instance a speech by Lorenzo Bini Smaghi, member of the executive bord of the ECB, available at http://www.ecb.europa.eu/press/key/date/2007/html/sp071001_2.en.html
3. Nölke and Vliegenthart (2009).
4. Hall and Soskice (2001), Pogátsa (2012).
5. OECD – European Commission (2012).
6. TJN (2012).
7. Sraffa (1960).
8. OECD (2013).
9. Dicken (2003, chapter 8).

REFERENCES

Cueresma, J. C., Oberhofer, H., Smits, K., & Vincellette, G. A. (2012). *Drivers of convergence in eleven Eastern European countries*. World Bank Policy Research Working Paper No. 6185. Washington, DC.

Darvas, Z. (2014, May). *Bruegel. From ten years of enlargement anniversary: Waltzing past Vienna*. Retrieved from http://www.bruegel.org/nc/blog/detail/article/1319-10-years-eu-enlargement-anniversary-waltzing-past-vienna/#.U2IGNFcGtbs.twitter

Dicken, P. (2003). *Global shift: Reshaping the global economic map in the 21st century* (4th ed.). London: Sage.

Hall, P., & Soskice, D. (2001). *Varieties of capitalism: The institutional foundations of comparative advantage*. Oxford: Oxford University Press.

Nölke, A., & Vliegenthart, A. (2009). Enlarging the varieties of capitalism: The emergence of dependent market economies in East Central Europe. *World Politics*, *61*(4), 670–702.

OECD. (2013). *OECD skills outlook 2013: First result from the survey of adult skills*. OECD.

OECD – European Commission. (2012). *OECD – Eurostat methodological manual on purchasing power parities*. Luxemburg: Publications Office of the European Union.

Pogátsa, Z. (2012). Slovenia: The only successful case of economic transition. *The Hungarian Review*, *3*(4).

Sraffa, P. (1960). *The production of commodities by means of commodities*. Cambridge: Cambridge University Press.

TJN. (2012). *The price of offshore revisited*. Tax Justice Network.

ABOUT THE EDITORS

Rustam Jamilov is a Fixed Income Analyst at the State Oil Fund of Azerbaijan. He was previously a Research Economist at the Central Bank of Azerbaijan. He has consulted multiple organizations including the World Bank Group, United Nations Development Program, and the Economic Cooperation Organization. Rustam has authored 30+ works in academic journals, newspapers, and edited volumes. His current research interests are in behavioral finance, investment management, and macroeconomic theory. His teaching interests are statistics, econometrics, and monetary economics. Rustam holds a BBA from Central European University, BA from Bocconi University, and MSc from the London School of Economics.

Yusaf H. Akbar joined the CEU Business School as an associate professor of Management and International Business in 2006. He is Founding Editor of the *International Journal of Emerging Markets* and sits on the Editorial Advisory Board of the *European Journal of International Management*. He has published in peer-reviewed journals including *Journal of World Business*, *Business and Politics*, *Global Governance*, *Thunderbird International Business Review*, and *World Competition*. His current research focuses on two related areas: non-market strategies of firms in emerging and transition economies and internationalization strategies of firms into weak institutional contexts. Yusaf has taught for universities and business schools all over the world, including University of Michigan, Stockholm School of Economics, Shanghai Jiaotong University and Queen's University, Canada. He has recently held research fellowships at the Wirtschaftsuniversitaet in Vienna and University of Trieste.

ABOUT THE AUTHORS

Alexandr Akimov is a Senior Lecturer in the Department of Accounting, Finance, and Economics at Griffith University, Australia. He held positions in risk management at the National Bank of Uzbekistan. His current research interests include post-communist economic transition and financial development as well local government and sustainable finance. He has published articles on post-communist Central Asia in journals such as *Problems of Economic Transition, Comparative Economic Studies, Emerging Market Finance and Trade.* He obtained his PhD from University of New England in 2007 and is a Chartered Financial Analyst.

Matei Alexianu is a junior development economist currently working for Adam Smith International, a UK-based development consultancy. He holds a Bachelor's degree in Philosophy, Politics and Economics from the University of Oxford and a Master's degree in Economics from the London School of Economics. His interests include the political economy of Eastern Europe (especially his native Romania) and development economics in general.

Pavol Babos is a junior analyst at the Institute for Forecasting, Slovak Academy of Sciences. Dr. Babos studied at Katholieke Universiteit Leuven and Comenius University, Bratislava, where he currently teaches at the Department of Political Science. Dr. Babos teaches mostly courses on economic policies and quantitative methods. In the past, Dr. Babos has published several journal articles on labor market transitions, political reforms, and generally political economies of Central Eastern Europe. Apart from political economy, Dr. Babos also conducts research on corruption, and voters' behavior.

Jakhongir Kakhkharov is a PhD student at Griffith University in Australia. Mr. Kakhkharov holds a graduate degree from Columbia University in New York and has done postgraduate research in economics at Oxford University. He also holds a diploma with honors from the Institute of Oriental Studies in Tashkent, specializing in International Economic Relations. His past work experience includes a number of consultancy assignments with World Bank, UNDP, GIZ, JICA, ADB and staff positions with US Department of Commerce, ADB, and ABN AMRO Bank. Mr. Kakhkharov has written a number of articles on economic policies in Central Asia.

Martina Lubyova is Director of the Institute for Forecasting of the Slovak Academy of Sciences and Lecturer at the Economics University in Bratislava. She holds PhD in Economics from the University of the State of New York and CERGE-EI in Prague, PhD in Statistics from the Economics University in Bratislava, Doctor of Law and MSc in Biophysics from Comenius University in Bratislava. Prior to taking up her current position, she spent more than 10 years at the service of the International Labour Organisation, where she worked as the Director of ILO Sub-regional Office for Eastern Europe and Central Asia in Moscow, Employment Specialist at the ILO Office in Moscow, and Employment Development Specialist at the ILO Multidisciplinary Team for South Asia in New Delhi. Her other academic stays and international postings include Institute for Higher Studies in Vienna, Tinbergen Institute in Amsterdam, OECD Department for Education, Employment, Labour and Social Affairs in Paris, Czech Academy Sciences and Charles University in Prague. Her research interests are focused mainly on labor and education economics, international migration, forecasting, social affairs, and development. She has been member of OECD Expert group on Migration (SOPEMI) since 1995 and member of editorial boards of several journals focused on social affairs and development.

Paul Marer is Professor of International Business, Economics and Finance at the Business School of Central European University; previously Professor of Business at the Kelley School of Indiana University, Bloomington. Holding a PhD from the University of Pennsylvania, he is the author, co-author, and editor of 20 books and 150 articles and chapters, mainly on the changing economic and business situation in the countries of Central and Eastern Europe, as well as Russia and China.

Rajmund Mirdala is associate professor and head of the Department of Economics at Faculty of Economics, Technical University of Košice, Slovak republic. He is author of four books (Fiscal Policy in the European Converging Economies, Exchange Rates in the Central European Countries, Economic Aspects of Capital Flows Liberalization in the European Transition Economies, Monetary Rules, and Their Importance in the Context of Monetary Union and Economic Crisis). He has published

30+ articles in foreign scientific journals, 10+ articles in domestic scientific and professional journals, 40+ articles in domestic and foreign conferences. He is principal investigator in two projects from national grant schemes, deputy principal investigator in three projects from national grant schemes and researcher in eight domestic and foreign projects. He is a member of 12 editorial boards of foreign scientific journals and reviewer for 13 domestic and foreign scientific journals. His research covers following areas: Macroeconomic and Microeconomic Theory, Monetary Policy, Monetary Integration, International Financial Integration, Exchange Rates, Fiscal Policy, International Capital Flows, Transition Economies, Global Imbalances.

Matthias Nnadi is a lecturer at Cranfield School of Management. Dr. Nnadi's research interests are in financial reporting, emerging markets, and mergers and acquisitions. He is actively involved in accounting training and consultancy, particularly in International Financial Reporting Standards (IFRS) for private firms and International Public Sector Accounting Standards (IPSAS) for government establishments. He is a member of several accounting professional bodies including the Institute of Chartered Institute of Public and Finance Association (CIPFA), British Accounting and Finance Association (BAA), Association of Tax Technicians (ATT), Institute of Financial Accountants (IFA), Federation of Tax Advisers (FTA), and Higher Education Academy (HEA).

Kamil Omoteso is currently the Head, Department of Economics, Finance and Accounting at Coventry University. Dr. Omoteso is an External Examiner at two other UK universities. Dr. Omoteso's research interests cover Accounting and Auditing; Accountability Governance and Ethics; IT and Project Management, and he currently supervises doctoral students within these research areas. Dr. Omoteso is widely published. And he currently serves as an Editorial Board member and a Reviewer for a number of journals. He is the Chair of Centre for African Resources Research and Development (CARRD). One of CARRD's projects, Educational Support Initiative for Africa has been able to donate over 65,000 books and academic journals worth over £1.8m to 21 institutions of higher education across Africa.

Dragiša Otašević works as a Bank Examiner within Banking Supervision at the Deutsche Bundesbank. He previously was employed at the National Bank of Serbia as a Junior Researcher in the Directorate for Economic Research and Statistics where he conducted research on the monetary policy transmission mechanism in Serbia. He holds a MSc in Quantitative Finance from the Faculty of Economics, University of Belgrade. His research interests include banking supervision, macro-finance, policy analysis, and monetary economics.

Zoltán Pogátsa is a Hungarian political economist who teaches at the University of West Hungary, focusing on the economics of European integration. He has published six books and numerous professional and media articles, and is a regular commentator in Hungarian and international media on issues related to European integration and economic development. His book entitled "Heterodox International Political Economics" offers a number of different perspectives on understanding the global economy of the 21st century. In the year 2013, he spent a year on a Greek government research grant in Athens. He summarized his inquiries into the Greek crisis in a book entitled "The Political Economy of the Greek Crisis."

György Simon, Jr. is an independent researcher, Corvinus University of Budapest. He was born in Budapest, Hungary, on September 17, 1964. Between 1984 and 1989, he studied at the Faculty of International Relations of the Moscow State Institute of International Relations (MGIMO), where he received an honors degree of an expert in international relations, summa cum laude. He completed his postgraduate studies at the Chair of World Economics of the same institute in 1993 and became a PhD in economics a year later. His professional experience includes work at the Hungarian Foreign Ministry, the Hungarian Institute of International Affairs (HIIA) and the Hungarian Central Statistical Office (HCSO). Since 2008, he has been a member of the Social Science Research Network (SSRN, Rochester, New York).

İbrahim Ünalmış is an Economist at the Central Bank of Turkey. He has received his BSc degree in Economics from Middle East Technical University, MSc degree in Money, Banking and Finance from Birmingham University, UK, and PhD degree in Economics from University of York, UK. His general research interests are fiscal policy, monetary policy, interactions between fiscal policy and monetary policy, the impact of monetary policy on asset prices and commodity markets especially oil and gold. Specifically, he is interested in developing tools to assess fiscal policy performance of emerging and developing countries, building Dynamic Stochastic General Equilibrium Models to analyze the effects of government spending on external balances of an economy. In addition, he is interested in the effects of monetary policy on the storage behavior of commodity market investors. His articles have been published in IMF Economic Review, Economic Modelling and Finance Research Letters.

Xuan Vinh Vo is currently a lecturer at the School of Banking, University of Economics Ho Chi Minh City (UEH) and Master in Banking and Finance program manager at CFVG Ho Chi Minh City. Dr. Vo used to be a teaching staff at University of Western Sydney and University of New South Wales, Australia. He also has strong industry experience and used to hold different senior management positions including Director of R&D at VNPT Group, Director of Asset Management Company for a commercial bank, and board member of a blue-chip corporation in Vietnam. He obtained the B.Bus from the National Economics University, Hanoi, and B.E. from the University of Technology, Sydney, Master of Applied Finance from the University of Western Sydney as the top graduate and PhD from the University of New South Wales. Dr. Vo has published his research in many international journals including *Research in International Business and Finance*, *Applied Economics*, *Applied Financial Economics*, *Emerging Markets Finance and Trade*, *Global Finance Journal*, and *International Review of Financial Analysis, Contemporary Studies in Economic and Financial Analysis.*

Yi Yu holds a postgraduate degree in Finance and Management from the Cranfield University School of Management. Prior to her postgraduate studies, she worked as an Account Planner with Hitachi Elevator (China) Co Ltd for three years. She had also worked as an Assistant Market Researcher in the China Life Insurance Company.